"With her friendly, hand-holding instructions and photos of exactly what your doughs and fillings should (and shouldn't) look like, Erin Jeanne McDowell has done away with every worry that can vex and intimidate new pie bakers. In the world of *The Book on Pie*, with Erin cheering for you, pie is easy, pie is fun, pie is anything you want it to be."

—**KRISTEN MIGLORE**, creative director of Genius Food52 and author of *Genius Recipes* and *Genius Desserts*

"With this tome, destined to become the pie-baking bible for many generations to come, Erin Jeanne McDowell takes us on the magnificent journey that made her fall in love with pie. Erin adeptly interweaves the love of home baking with the precision of professional pastry, all the while empowering the reader to be a better baker, without a hint of intimidation. By the end of making your first recipe, you won't be able to decide what you love more: your newly acquired pie skills or Erin herself. For me, it's a tie."

—**UMBER AHMAD**, founder of Mah-Ze-Dahr Bakery

THE BOOK ON PIE

THE
BOOK
ON
PIE

Everything You Need
to Know to Bake Perfect Pies

ERIN JEANNE McDOWELL

PHOTOGRAPHS BY MARK WEINBERG

HOUGHTON MIFFLIN HARCOURT
BOSTON · NEW YORK · 2020

For information about permission to reproduce selections from this book,
write to trade.permissions@hmhco.com or to Permissions, Houghton Mifflin Harcourt
Publishing Company, 3 Park Avenue, 19th Floor, New York, New York 10016.

hmhbooks.com

Library of Congress Cataloging-in-Publication Data
Names: McDowell, Erin Jeanne, author. | Weinberg, Mark (Photographer), photographer.
Title: The book on pie : everything you need to know to bake perfect pies / Erin Jeanne McDowell ;
photographs by Mark Weinberg.
Description: Boston ; New York : Houghton Mifflin Harcourt, 2020. | Includes index.
Identifiers: LCCN 2020023318 (print) | LCCN 2020023319 (ebook) | ISBN 9780358229285 (hardback) |
ISBN 9780358229292 (ebook)
Subjects: LCSH: Pies. | Desserts. | LCGFT: Cookbooks.
Classification: LCC TX773 .M19 2020 (print) | LCC TX773 (ebook) | DDC 641.86/52—dc23
LC record available at https://lccn.loc.gov/2020023318
LC ebook record available at https://lccn.loc.gov/2020023319

Book design by Allison Chi and Eugenie S. Delaney

Printed in China
SCP 10 9 8 7 6 5 4 3 2 1

CONTENTS

8   Recipes

12   Acknowledgments

15   Introduction

Chapter One

23   **DOUGHS & CRUSTS**

Chapter Two

79   **DÉCOR & TOPPINGS**

Chapter Three

133   **FRUIT PIES**

Chapter Four

201   **CUSTARD PIES**

Chapter Five

245   **CREAM, CHIFFON & COLD-SET PIES**

Chapter Six

299   **SAVORY PIES**

345   Resources

346   Index

RECILES

RECIPES

Chapter One

DOUGHS & CRUSTS

All-Buttah Pie Dough	48
Chocolate All-Buttah Pie Dough	48
Gluten-Free Pie Dough	49
Rough Puff Pastry	50
Vegan / Dairy-Free Pie Dough	51
Brown Butter Pie Dough	53
Whole Wheat Pie Dough	54
Herby Whole Wheat Pie Dough	54
Graham Flour Pie Dough	54
Cornmeal Pie Dough	55
Pie Doughs Made with Other Flours	55
Caramelized Pie Crust	56
Golden Cheese Pie Dough	57
Saffron Compound Butter Pie Dough	58
Chive, Scallion, or Ramp Pie Dough	58
Roasted Garlic Pie Dough	58
Sun-Dried Tomato Pie Dough	58
Pâte Brisée	59
Hot-Water Crust	60
Roll-Out Cookie Crust	62
Chocolate Roll-Out Cookie Crust	63
Brown Sugar Roll-Out Cookie Crust	63
Citrus Roll-Out Cookie Crust	63
Almond Roll-Out Cookie Crust	63
Spiced Roll-Out Cookie Crust	63
Press-In Cookie Crust	64
Chocolate Press-In Cookie Crust	64
Brown Butter Press-In Cookie Crust	64
Nut Butter Press-In Cookie Crust	64
Chocolate Chip Press-In Cookie Crust	64
Oatmeal Press-In Cookie Crust	64
Coconut Press-In Cookie Crust	64
Olive Oil Press-In Crust	65
Herby Olive Oil Press-In Crust	65
Curry Oil Press-In Crust	65
Smoked Paprika–Olive Oil Press-In Crust	65
Sesame Oil Press-In Crust	65
Truffle Oil Press-In Crust	65
Basic Crumb Crust	66
Mini (Two-Bite) Crumb Crusts	67
Unbaked Crumb Crust	67
Cereal-Treat Crust	69
Peanut Butter Cereal-Treat Crust	69
Coconut Macaroon Crust	70
Haystack Crust	71
Coconut Haystack Crust	71
Meringue Crust	72
Basic Nut Crust	74
Phyllo Dough Crust	76

Chapter Two

DÉCOR & TOPPINGS

Dark Chocolate Black-Bottom Base	110
Milk Chocolate Black-Bottom Base	110
White-Bottom Base	110
Caramelized White-Bottom Base	110
Classic Whipped Cream	111
Mascarpone Whipped Cream	111
Whipped Cream Sauce	112
Extra-Thick and Creamy Whipped Cream	113

Chocolate Whipped Cream 114

Fresh Fruit Whipped Cream 115

    Jammy Whipped Cream 115

    Freeze-Dried Fruity Whipped Cream 115

Nut Butter Whipped Cream 116

Marshmallow Topping 117

    Chocolate Marshmallow Topping 117

    Molasses Marshmallow Topping 117

    Honey Marshmallow Topping 117

Meringue Topping 118

    Fruity Meringue Topping 118

    Chocolate Meringue Topping 118

    Coffee Meringue Topping 118

    Caramel Meringue Topping 118

    Honey Meringue Topping 118

    Peppermint Meringue Topping 118

Streusel for Baking 120

Extra-Clumpy Prebaked Streusel 120

Fruity Poaching Liquid 121

    Non-Fruity Poaching Liquid 121

Thin Fruit Glaze 122

Thick Fruit Coulis 122

Lemon Curd 123

    Lime Curd 123

    Orange Curd 123

    Blood Orange Curd 123

    Grapefruit Curd 123

    Key Lime Curd 123

    Tangerine Curd 123

    Yuzu Curd 123

    Passionfruit Curd 123

Fruity Drippy Glaze 124

Dark Chocolate Drippy Glaze 125

    Milk Chocolate Drippy Glaze 125

    Caramelized White Chocolate Drippy Glaze 125

    White Chocolate Drippy Glaze 125

Salted Caramel Sauce 126

Dark Chocolate Cold-Snap Topping 127

    Milk Chocolate Cold-Snap Topping 127

Caramelized Chocolate Cold-Snap Topping 127

    White Chocolate Cold-Snap Topping 127

    Fruity Cold-Snap Topping 127

Basic Brittle 129

Biscuit Topping (Make It a Cobbler Pie) 130

Jam Twists 131

    Cinnamon Twists 131

Chapter Three

FRUIT PIES

Pure Rhubarb Pie 142

    Strawberry Rhubarb Pie 142

Apple Pie 145

    My Own Personal Favorite Apple Pie 146

    Caramel Apple Pie 146

    Apple Butter Pie 146

Whole-Apple Dumplings 148

    Peach Dumplings 148

    Pear Dumplings 149

    Mini Apple Dumplings 149

    Banana Dumplings 149

Any-Fruit Puff Pastry Tart 150

Roasted Strawberry Pie 153

    Roasted Strawberry Pie (with Frozen Strawberries) 153

Roasted Pineapple Pie 155

Deep-Dish Berry Cobbler Pie 156

Mixed-Berry Hand Pies 159

    Sour Cherry Hand Pies 161

Concord Grape Hand Pies 163

Ginger Cherry Pie 166

    Sour Cherry Pie 168

    Sour Cherry Hand Pie Filling 168

Cranberry-Orange Pie 169

   Gooseberry Vanilla Cream Pie 171

Any-Fruit Tarte Tatin 172

Stone Fruit–Berry Pie 176

Blueberry Lemon Pie 179

Raspberry-Poached Pear
and Almond Pie 182

Candied Clementine Galette 184

Free-Form Honeyed Fig Pie 186

Jam Cookie Tart 189

Any-Fruit Crumb Crostata 190

Rose Peach Pie 193

Cinnamon Plum Pie 194

Easy-Fancy Apple Pie 197

Blood Orange Brûlée Pie 199

Chapter Four

CUSTARD PIES

Classic Custard Pie in Phyllo Crust 206

   Coconut Custard Pie 206

Brown Sugar Chess Pie 208

   Dulce de Leche Chess Pie 208

Blueberry Swamp Pie 210

   Double-Crust Blueberry Swamp Pie 211

Pumpkin Pie 213

   Pumpkin Mascarpone Pie 213

Mascarpone Pie 214

Caramel–Earl Grey Custard Pie
in Gingersnap Crumb Crust 216

   Caramel-Chai Custard Pie in
   Shortbread Crumb Crust 216

Birthday-Cake Pie 219

Fruity Frangipane Pie 221

Cherry Clafoutis Pie 224

   Rhubarb Clafoutis Pie 224

   Raspberry-Lemon Clafoutis Pie 224

   Blueberry Clafoutis Pie 224

   Peach, Plum, or Apricot Clafoutis Pie 224

   Chocolate Clafoutis Pie 224

White Chocolate–Peppermint Pie 226

German Chocolate Pie 229

Carrot Cake Custard Pie 230

Chocolate Sugar Pie 232

   Vanilla Sugar Pie 232

   Citrus Sugar Pie 232

   Spiced Sugar Pie 232

   Maple Sugar Pie 232

   Eggnog Sugar Pie 232

   Pumpkin Sugar Pie 232

Cardamom Crème Brûlée Pie 235

Cheesecake Pie 236

   Jam-Swirled Cheesecake Pie 236

   Chocolate-Swirled Cheesecake Pie 236

   Caramel-Swirled Cheesecake Pie 237

   Pumpkin Cheesecake Pie 237

   Matcha Cheesecake Pie 237

Black-Bottom Pecan Pie 239

Creamy Lemon Custard Pie 240

Tres Leches Slab Pie 242

Chapter Five

CREAM, CHIFFON & COLD-SET PIES

Black Forest Pie 250

Peanut Butter–Banana Cream Pie 252

   Classic Banana Cream Pie 252

   Banulce Pie (the dulce de leche
   version of Banoffee Pie) 253

Orange-Vanilla Panna Cotta Pie 255

Sweet Corn Pie with Blueberry
Whipped Cream 256

Key Lime–Coconut Cream Pie ... 258
  Piña Colada Pie ... 259
  Coconut Cream Pie ... 259
  Classic Key Lime Pie ... 259
Key Lime Pielets ... 260
  Meyer Lemon Pielets ... 260
Peanut Butter Cream Pie with Raspberry Meringue ... 264
Peaches-and-Cream Pie ... 267
Creamy Mango Pie ... 268
  Ginger Mango Pie ... 269
Nectarine Semifreddo Pie ... 270
Triple-Chocolate Caramel Truffle Pie ... 271
Butterscotch Apple Pie ... 274
Breakfast Pie ... 277
Pistachio Cream Pie ... 278
Lemon Meringue Pie ... 280
  Lime/Tangerine/Grapefruit/Yuzu/Passion Fruit Meringue Pie ... 280
  Blueberry Lemon Meringue Pie ... 280
  Rhubarb Meringue Pie ... 280
  Concord Grape Meringue Pie ... 280
  Deep-Dish Berry Meringue Pie ... 280
Eton Mess Pie ... 282
  Citrus Eton Mess Pie ... 282
Striped Citrus Pie ... 284
"Root Beer Float" Baked Alaska Pie ... 287
  Fruity Baked Alaska Pie ... 287
Fresh Watermelon Pie ... 288
Black Raspberry Chiffon Pie ... 290
Chocolate-Covered-Raspberries Pie ... 292
  Chocolate-Covered-Strawberries Pie ... 292

Two-Bite PB&J Pies ... 294
Two-Bite Black-and-White Pies ... 296

Chapter Six

SAVORY PIES

Chicken Pot Slab Pie ... 301
  Extra-Large Chicken Pot Slab Pie ... 303
Green Veggie Quiche ... 304
  Cheese Lover's Quiche ... 304
  BLT Quiche ... 304
Avocado Galette ... 307
Sweet-and-Spicy Kale and Squash Pithiviers ... 308
Smoked Salmon Tart with "Everything" Pie Crust ... 310
Croque Monsieur Pielets ... 312
  Croque Madame Pielets ... 313
Beef and Mushroom Pie ... 314
Roasted Tomato and Gooey Cheese Free-Form Pie ... 317
Red Onion Tarte Tatin ... 318
  Cherry Tomato Tarte Tatin ... 318
Sausage and Caramelized Onion Pie with Soft Pretzel Crust ... 320
Shrimp-Boil Pie ... 323
Peach, Shallot, and Prosciutto Pie ... 325
Ratatouille Galette ... 326
Beet and Herbed Cheese Skillet Pie ... 328
Forager's Mushroom Pie ... 330
Caramel Pork Pie with Chile and Scallions ... 332
Reuben Pie ... 334
Sesame Lamb Pie with Cucumber Salad ... 336
Bacon Jam Mini Pies on Sharp Cheddar Crust ... 339
  Tomato Jam ... 341
  BLT Pies ... 341
  Tomato Jam Pies ... 341
  Tomato Jam Pies on Parmesan Crust ... 341
Frybread Taco Pie ... 342

ACKNOWLEDGMENTS

The book journey starts with my agent, Doe Coover—thank you, always, for your persistent faith that I have something special to put on a page. To Sarah Kwak for being a true partner in this process, I'm so grateful to have worked with you (twice!) and to have your careful eye guiding this project at every step. Thank you to Rux Martin for believing in this project. Thank you to Judith Sutton for lending us your sharp, expert eyes. To Tai Blanche, Allison Chi, and their design team, thank you for incorporating any idea I had and making it better, and for so expertly making this book come to life.

I continue to be thankful to Ben Fink for encouraging me from the start and offering every form of help he could give me. Thank you for telling me to pass it on—I try my hardest to do so. Thank you to my mentor and guidepost, Rose Levy Beranbaum, who is one of the only people in my life who is fluent in every language I speak: baking, writing, and teaching, and loving it all with a meticulous precision I will forever aspire to.

To my husband, Derek, for his support in this process, even when our home was full of far too many people and far too many pies. Thank you for all the times you ate pie for breakfast, lunch, and/or dinner. To Kaitlin Wayne, my girl Friday, who contributed recipes, endless insight, beautiful styling, and so much more to this book—I absolutely couldn't have done it without you. To Jase Kingsland-Shim, for testing recipes, contributing your baking talents, and working so hard during the photo shoot. To my friend Evan Coben, for her constant support, including (but not limited to!) being willing to provide two weeks of priceless assistance for only the cost of a plane ticket—and for giving us all marshmallow heart, then teaching us how to cure it. To my fellow baking Erin, Erin Clarkson, for her friendship, support, and the ability to make me belly laugh even when I'm drowning in lists (and to her husband, Rich, for the amazing stencils, including the Brimley stencil of my dreams). To Shilpa Uskokovic, for recipe testing so beautiful I had to have her hands at the photo shoot too. To Chris Hurte for your support, encouragement, and the emergency cotton candy run.

Thank you to Mark Weinberg, who is as wonderful to work with as his work is beautiful. I'm so grateful that we met photographing pies—it was a sign of all the flaky, delicious things to come! And I'm so grateful for how above and beyond you went for this project; thank you for all your contributions. To Nico Schinco, who snapped behind-the-scenes photos and offered tons of photographic assistance throughout the shoot—I'm thankful for your calming presence and sharp eye for beautiful moments. To Amy Stringer-Mowat of American Heirloom for developing beautiful custom stencils and boards for the photo shoot. To Julia Mitchell and Marine Leman, from my favorite chocolate company, the incredible Valrhona USA, for providing all the chocolate for recipe testing and the photo shoot. Thank you to Lucy Heath, for

shipping her amazing surfaces extra-fast so they arrived in time for the shoot.

To my amazing family for being the inspiration for so much of what I do. I'm forever thankful to my parents for all they've given me, from wisdom to guidance to the freedom to be whatever I wanted to be. Thank you to my brothers, Willie, Jason, and Matt, and my wonderful nieces, Maisy, Joci, and Lucy, and my awesome nephew, Arlo. To my cousins Sarah and Abby, thank you for your friendship and strong, independent-lady vibes. In my first book, my editor teased me for thanking everyone under the sun but leaving out someone very important. So the final thank-you goes to my best friend, Brimley, who can't read this but still deserves to know he's a very good boy.

INTRODUCTION

I have five favorite things about pie: The first is making it—from the moment my hands start cutting cold butter into flour, it just feels indescribably good. The second is baking it: The aroma is better than any scented candle I've ever purchased. The third is, of course, eating it, or even watching others eat a pie that I've made. Pie has a miraculous ability to be simultaneously comforting and special occasion worthy, both homey and fancy. It's delicious for dessert, but also fit for a meal in itself—even for breakfast, my personal ideal time for pie.

My fourth favorite thing about pie is its adaptability. I started baking pies as a teenager, alongside my Grandma Jeanne. We baked pies whenever I visited her, simply because we loved to eat them. I'd show up in the morning, and she'd casually bring out a big bowl of apples and say, "Let's bake a pie," as if she'd just had the idea, rather than admitting she'd been planning it since yesterday's trip to the grocery store. Because of those frequent and delicious baking sessions, pie was one of the first things I knew how to make well. It was one of the first things I learned to bake using my senses. Understanding what a pie should look like, smell like, and feel like at any given stage gave me the flexibility I hadn't had with any other type of baking. Suddenly I didn't even need a recipe—I could just whip up whatever idea came to mind with whatever I had on hand. Ever since, I've been baking fruit pies year-round with whatever is in season. I've dreamt up towering cream pies

that elicit swoons when they are set on the table. I've made hundreds of savory pies, just so I could justify eating pie for dinner. And I've gabbed about pie to anyone who will listen—in classes and demos, on radio and TV, and by answering the questions that roll in on Instagram (my brother nicknamed the week around Thanksgiving when I answer pie questions via the internet the "24-Hour Pie-Sis Hotline").

Which brings me to my fifth and final favorite thing about pie: I love teaching people how to bake it. From helping a friend bake her first cherry pie (until the fruit bubbled through the lattice) in my tiny apartment kitchen to teaching my husband how big the pieces of butter should be when he mixed his crust by hand to standing in front of a couple dozen people taking diligent notes in a kitchen classroom. Helping people bake a perfect pie, whatever that means to them, brings me joy.

While I love pretty much everything about pie, reason five is really why I wrote this book. I wanted to create a true handbook, filled with all the things I've learned. Yes, this book has loads of delicious recipes for every genre of pie, but it also contains everything you need to know to bake your own delicious pies—whatever you can dream up, with whatever you have on hand. I want readers, armed with this book, to learn to use their senses in the kitchen and make their best pies ever.

So, grab an apron and a rolling pin and meet me in your kitchen: *Let's bake a pie!*

EQUIPMENT

Baking a pie doesn't require a ton of special equipment. All you really need is a rolling pin and a vessel to bake it in or on, and you're ready to go. But there are a few other pieces of equipment I also find useful, some of which you may already have in your kitchen. For where to get most of these tools, see Resources (page 345).

SCALE

If you like to bake, you need a scale. It's the most accurate way to measure any ingredient, and once you have one, you'll find yourself using it all the time. (It also helps eliminate some cleanup, because you can measure directly into the bowls you're mixing in.) You can get a decent scale for around $25.

ROLLING PIN

I believe hand tools are a matter of personal preference. I've used every kind of rolling pin, and I've even used a wine bottle as stand-in for a rolling pin when I was in a kitchen without one but couldn't bear to go without pie. I usually opt for wooden pins because I love their sturdiness, but marble rolling pins are good for folks who have trouble keeping things cold (you can chill the pin before you start). I prefer French wooden pins, which have tapered ends. I think they give you a better feel for the dough when rolling it, and you can adjust the pressure easily as you work. Rolling pins with handles work great too, but water can get into the bearings and cause problems over time.

MATS AND ROLLING ACCESSORIES

I like to roll pie dough out directly on a lightly floured work surface (i.e., the countertop) but there are other options that can be helpful. Pastry mats, usually made out of silicone, provide a smooth surface with a nonstick effect that's great for rolling (though you still need to use some flour). Some of these mats also have measures/guides that help you determine when your dough is the right size.

Another useful rolling accessory are bands of varying widths (⅛ to ½ inch / 3 to 13 mm) that can be placed on either end of a rolling pin to aid you in getting the dough to the right thickness. There are also specific rolling pins that roll to these thicknesses, but I like to recommend the bands, since they work with nearly any pin.

BENCH KNIFE
(a.k.a. Bench or Pastry Scraper)

My trusty bench knife is one of the tools I use the most. A bench knife consists of a metal blade attached to a sturdy handle. The blade is usually 4 to 5 inches / 10 to 12 cm wide and sharp enough to cut through dough, but not as sharp as a knife. I use it to portion pastry dough, square off dough at the edges during rolling, and cut dough into strips or pieces. And when I've finished throwing flour all over my kitchen, a few passes of my bench knife can scrape up all that flour and bits of stuck dough and push them right into the trash can.

PASTRY CUTTER

A pastry cutter is a series of thinner metal blades (not particularly sharp) attached to a handle. It's the ideal tool for cutting fat into flour if you're not using your hands (or if you have warm hands). It's also useful in making other recipes, like biscuits and scones.

PIE WEIGHTS

For pie weights to do their job, you need enough to fill the lined pie shell all the way up to the rim of the pie plate. Many bakers are not aware of this, largely because of the way pie weights are sold. The weights I prefer—ceramic pie weights—are sold in such small quantities that I had to purchase four packages to fill a standard 9-inch / 23-cm pie plate. (And pie chains, which are usually made of metal, are nowhere near heavy enough to do the job properly.) Fortunately, since buying so many sets can be cost-prohibitive, dried beans also work well as pie weights (I find it usually takes 2½ to 3 pounds / 1.13 to 1.36 kg); and these can be reused repeatedly (though they will eventually get an "off" odor and need to be discarded).

PIE PLATES

You can bake a pie in any style of pie plate, and I use them all, but I do have certain preferences and recommendations. No matter the style, I recommend pie plates that have at least a ½-inch / 13-mm rim, which will help decorative edges stay in place better.

(CONTINUED)

CERAMIC AND STONEWARE: Ceramic and stoneware pie plates are my favorites for both the way they bake pies and the way they look. Stoneware conducts heat in a way that helps promote uniform browning of the bottom and sides of a pie crust. Some stoneware pie plates can cause sticking, making it more difficult to remove a clean slice, but I have found that those with shiny, polished finishes work best.

METAL: Metal pie plates are the least likely to cause sticking. They are thinner than ceramic or stoneware pie plates, which means they conduct and distribute heat more efficiently. With a high-quality pan, this is a good thing. However, the thinner material also makes them more prone to overbaking or uneven baking, particularly when parbaking or blind-baking a bottom crust. Choose metal pie plates with rims—tins with no edge may lead to shrinking or may not hold crimps/other décor at the edges of the crust. While they are more difficult to find, cast-iron or forged-iron pie pans are a particularly amazing solution in your quest to avoid soggy bottoms!

GLASS: Glass pie plates don't conduct heat as well as metal or stoneware, but they have one major pro: You can see through them! This is especially helpful for beginners, because you can actually see whether or not the crust is golden brown.

DISPOSABLE PIE PLATES: Disposable pie plates are available in both aluminum foil and paper, but I don't love them. In addition to being single use, they are thin, and it can be surprisingly difficult to nail a good bottom crust with them. That said, they are great for pie gifting!

BAKING SHEETS AND OTHER BAKING EQUIPMENT

Who says you need a pie plate to bake a pie? You can bake a pie in or on many types of bakeware. Below are some of my favorite alternatives to pie pans.

BAKING SHEETS: These are my pan of choice for free-form pies, from individual pies to every shape and size of galette. And baking a pie on a baking sheet makes it especially easy to get a nice, crisp bottom crust.

SKILLETS: Skillets, particularly cast-iron skillets, make for awesome pies because they conduct heat well and evenly. They help promote browning on the bottom and sides of crusts, even without a Baking Steel or stone.

CAKE PANS: A regular cake pan is pretty comparable to a metal pie plate, except it has straight instead of slanted sides and no rim for a crimped edge to sit on. I sometimes like using taller cake pans and springform pans in lieu of deep-dish pie plates, especially when making sturdy pies with Hot-Water Crust (page 60).

CASSEROLE DISHES: Casserole dishes are great for potpies, and they can also be used to make larger versions of single- or double-crust pies. Remember, though, that larger pies may require significant adjustments in time and temperature.

RAMEKINS AND INDIVIDUAL BAKING DISHES: Ramekins and individual baking dishes can be used to make wonderful smaller pies, whether potpies or classic single- or double-crust pies.

What Exactly Is a Deep-Dish Pie?

Regular pie plates are 1¼ to 1½ inches / 3 to 4 cm deep; deep-dish pie plates are 1½ to 2½ inches / 4 to 6 cm deep. I have also baked deep-dish pies in springform pans, casserole dishes, and cake pans that are 3 inches / 8 cm deep. Some of the recipes in this book were specifically developed for deep-dish pans, but others can be adjusted to fit them using the guidelines and tips below.

WHAT THIS MEANS FOR YOUR CRUST: My pie crust recipes work for both regular pie plates (with a bit of scrap dough left behind) and deep-dish pie plates (with little or no scrap dough left behind). For the cookie crusts, make 1½ times the crust recipe (refer to the charts for crumb and nut crust recipes for specific guidance on how to adapt those for deep-dish pies). Specialty crusts, like the Cereal-Treat Crust (page 69), usually require a double batch to ensure full, even coverage of a deep-dish pan. For larger or deeper pans, such as springforms, you may need to make a double recipe of your dough.

WHAT THIS MEANS FOR YOUR FILLING: You'll need about 1½ times as much filling for a deep-dish pie pan as you will for a standard pie plate (or up to a double recipe if you want a super-tall, mounded look). It's generally easy to scale up fruit and savory fillings, but it can be more difficult for custard and cream pies. Instead, if you want to turn these into deep-dish pies, I suggest making these into layered pies by adding another layer of filling or a topping to fill the deep-dish pan.

WHAT THIS MEANS FOR BAKE TIME AND TEMPERATURE: Deeper pans mean longer bake times. For parbaking or blind-baking pie shells, this may just mean adding a couple of minutes to achieve the same doneness, but for double-crust pies, it may mean increasing the bake time by 15 to 20 minutes. If you're adjusting a recipe for a fruit or savory pie, you may want to lower the oven temperature by 25 degrees and/or tent the pie with foil partway through baking to help prevent the crust from overbrowning with the longer baking time.

WHAT THIS MEANS FOR YOUR TOPPING(S): Using a deep-dish pan can be a fun way to create layered pies, using different filling and topping combinations; see the Piña Colada Pie (page 259) and the Triple-Chocolate Caramel Truffle Pie (page 271). The deeper pan gives you room for multiple toppings to create impressive mile-high effects!

COOKIE CUTTERS AND PIE STAMPS

Cookie cutters can be used to create decorative effects with pie dough. Pie stamps are small cutters that can create indentations for additional detail. Either one should be dipped lightly in flour every few punches before being pressed firmly into the dough.

PASTRY WHEELS

Pastry wheels are like pizza cutters. They are available in lots of sizes, and some have fluted edges. Pastry wheels can be used to make clean edges on rolled-out dough, and to cut lattice strips or for other decorative effects.

DOUGH DOCKERS

A dough docker is a fabulously handy tool that I recommend if you make a lot of pies—it's comprised of a handle attached to a cylinder topped with multiple pieces that punch small holes in the dough. If you don't have one, though, a fork does a fine job of docking dough.

CRUST TAMPERS

A double-sided wooden tool designed to tamp down any type of press-in crust evenly into a pan. The ends vary in size to help you press the crust evenly into any size pan (one side is larger/wider, the other is smaller), with a handle connecting the two sides. I resisted buying one for a long time, thinking it was unnecessary, but now I can't imagine life without it—it really helps get things even all the way around! You can use a small dry measuring cup to achieve similar results if you don't have a tamper.

BAKING STEELS / BAKING STONES

Baking Steels and baking stones (also known as pizza stones) retain heat, helping ensure proper and even crust browning on the bottom of a pie. Their heat retention also helps keep the oven temperature even and helps the oven come back to temperature faster after the oven door has been opened. I prefer a Baking Steel for pie baking.

STORING, REFRESHING, AND FREEZING PIES

STORING BAKED PIES

Pies should be stored at room temperature or refrigerated. Follow the guidelines in specific recipes, but in general, more stable fillings, like fruit, can be left at room temperature, and creamy fillings, like custards, should be refrigerated. Once a pie is sliced, store it in an airtight container or loosely cover it with plastic wrap or foil.

REFRESHING BAKED PIES

Every recipe in this book provides information on how far in advance it can be made. Pies with baked fillings that are made in advance can often benefit from being refreshed in the oven, whether a whole pie, individual portions, or mini pies. Refreshing can be done briefly, just to recrisp the crust like for custard pies, or for a longer period to also warm the filling through, like for fruit pies. This trick is also handy because many pies need to cool completely to fully set the filling—so, if you want to serve these pies warm, simply refresh them!

WHOLE PIES: To refresh a whole pie, cover the surface of the pie with aluminum foil. Place it on a rack in the lower third of a cold oven, preferably with a Baking Steel or stone on it, turn the oven on to 375°F / 190°C, and allow the oven to preheat, then leave the pie in the hot oven for 10 minutes (to crisp the crust only), 15 minutes (for a warm filling), or 20 minutes (for a hot filling) longer. Then remove the foil and bake for 5 minutes more, or until the crust is noticeably crisp.

Note: To refresh a frozen baked pie, thaw it as directed in following section. Refresh as directed above, covered with foil, for 20 minutes after the oven has preheated, then remove the foil and bake for 7 to 9 minutes longer.

INDIVIDUAL SLICES OR MINI PIES: Wrap the slice(s) or mini pie(s) individually in aluminum foil. Place on a rack in the lower third of the oven, preferably with a Baking Steel or stone, turn the oven on to 375°F / 190°C, and allow the oven to preheat, then remove the foil and continue to bake the slice(s) or mini pie(s) for 5 minutes more, or until the crust is noticeably crisp.

Note: To refresh frozen slices of baked pie or baked mini pies (see Freezing Pies, below), thaw. Refresh as directed above, covered with foil, for 5 minutes after the oven has preheated, then remove the foil and bake for 7 to 9 minutes longer.

FREEZING PIES

Freezing unbaked or baked pies can be tricky, but my tips below will help you make it work!

Freezing Unbaked Pies

I don't love long-term freezing for unbaked pies, but it is possible with some recipes. Consider whether the filling will freeze well, as some ingredients won't. While I normally recommend thawing a whole unbaked pie before baking it, mini pies can often be baked directly from frozen because of their small size. It's best to reduce the baking temperature by 25 degrees and then plan on an additional 12 to 20 minutes of baking time.

Freezing Baked Pies

Freezing baked pies can work surprisingly well. Freezing is most successful with a whole pie, though slices and mini pies can also sometimes be frozen. But some pie fillings freeze well and some don't. Fruit pies, for example, freeze better than custard pies. Some cold-set pies (like ice cream pies, of course) are meant to be frozen, but others, like cream pies, won't retain their texture if frozen and the filling will often leech moisture into the crust when thawed. To freeze a whole baked pie, allow the pie to cool completely, then wrap tightly (still in the pan) in two layers of plastic wrap and one layer of aluminum foil and freeze for up to 1 month. (Slices of baked pie and miniature pies can be frozen the same way, wrapped individually as directed above, frozen until firm, and then transferred to freezer bags.) To serve a frozen baked pie, remove the foil (reserving it) and thaw in the refrigerator for 12 hours for whole pies or 6 to 8 hours for mini pie(s). Remove the plastic wrap, cover the pie(s) loosely in foil, and follow the refreshing instructions above.

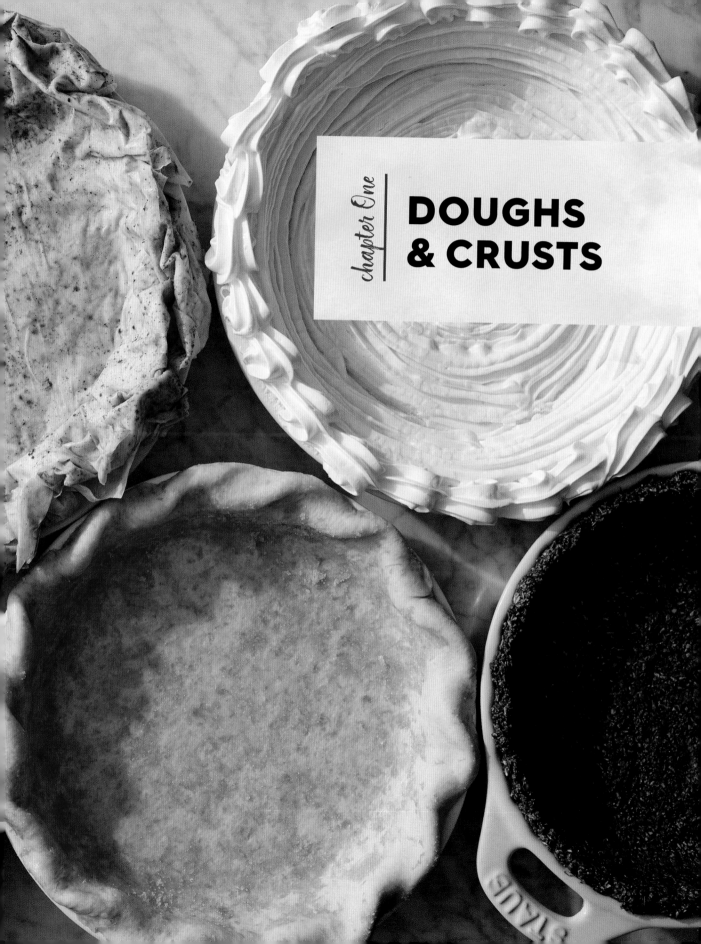

chapter One

DOUGHS & CRUSTS

If you love pie, you no doubt love crust. But you may not love making pie crust, and I'm dead set on changing that. This chapter is chock-full of everything you need to know for making all kinds of crusts, from totally easy press-in cookie crusts to the perfect all-butter crust of your flaky-pie dreams. Can't have gluten? Or dairy? Trying a vegan diet? I've got that covered, too. If you can dream it (or if you crave it)—you can probably make it into a pie. There's a crust here for everyone, plus tons of details and tips to help you totally nail whichever kind you decide to try.

INGREDIENTS

At heart, pie dough is made with four basic ingredients: flour, fat, salt, and water. In the recipes in this book, that fat is almost always butter. Other ingredients, such as spices, cocoa powder, citrus zest, and extracts, can be added for flavor. In general, if an ingredient doesn't contain moisture, it can be made to work in a pie dough. For anything that does contain moisture, some adjustments may need to be made to the basic recipe to ensure proper results.

FLOUR

For a classic pie dough, nothing beats all-purpose flour. Bleached and unbleached both work fine, and I truly don't prefer one over the other. I find any differences to be so subtle that they are nominal, so use what you've got or whichever one is your personal preference.

When it comes to using other flours, the sky is the limit, but, as always in baking, there are some rules to follow. Different flours absorb moisture differently, so some require more water for a properly hydrated dough. Each type also has a different protein content, and this can affect the dough in a variety of ways, particularly the texture of the baked crust. In general, I advise using other flours, like spelt, rye, etc., in conjunction with some all-purpose for the lightest, flakiest result (for more on other flours, see Pie Doughs Made with Other Flours, page 55).

BUTTER

I'm an equal-opportunity butter lover. I've tested the pie dough recipes in this book with different brands, and they all work. Still, there are a few things to consider:

- I always opt for unsalted butter, because it's difficult to determine how much salt there is in any salted butter, and even the flakiest pie dough will feel lacking if it's not properly seasoned. But if you taste your butter and feel like you've got a handle on it, there's no reason you can't use salted butter (but remember to reduce the salt in the recipe).

- Both American and European butters work beautifully in pie dough—it's a matter of understanding how they feel and behave differently when you work with them and your own personal preference. Most major brands of butter in the United States have about 80 percent butterfat, while European butters are closer to 82 percent. That may seem like a small difference, but it means that American butters have a higher moisture content, which makes them firmer. They can be slightly harder to shingle into the flour when well chilled, and the final dough may be a bit tougher to roll out at first. European butters are usually cultured and so boast a bit more flavor, and they are also richer. On the other hand, European butters are more likely to be problematic to work with because of that higher fat content, which can cause them to soften or even melt more readily.

Using Other Fats

Butter is my favorite fat for pie for one reason: It's the most flavorful! But it isn't the only one that works. Here's how to incorporate other fats into any pie dough recipe:

SHORTENING: I do use shortening in my dairy-free/vegan dough recipe, and it works beautifully to make a particularly flaky, tender crust. Because shortening has a higher melting point than butter, it is also easier to work with. I prefer nonhydrogenated shortening (I like Nutiva), but any brand will work. It can be substituted for the butter in any recipe or used half and half in conjunction with another fat.

LARD: Lard is another of my other favorite fats for pie dough. It doesn't have a strong flavor, but it is more flavorful than shortening. Like shortening, it can be substituted for the butter in any recipe or used half and half in conjunction with another fat.

OIL: It is certainly possible to make a pie crust using vegetable oil, but I just don't like the results. The crusts are only "flaky-ish," and that's just not enough! I do like oil for cookie-style crusts (both roll-out and press-in; see page 65).

OTHER RENDERED ANIMAL FATS: Bacon, chicken, and duck fat are all good for pie dough. However, it can be difficult to get them cold enough so they are firm enough to properly cut into the other ingredients. I recommend freezing any of these fats for at least 30 minutes before working with them and to use the fat half and half in conjunction with another firmer fat (e.g., butter or shortening). Plan on achieving a mealier dough, rather than a flaky one (I especially love animal fat for the Hot-Water Crust, page 60).

CREAM CHEESE: Cream cheese makes a wonderful pie dough, adding a subtle tanginess and helping to achieve flakiness too! It is best used half and half in conjunction with another firmer fat (butter or shortening).

NUT BUTTERS: Nut butters add great flavor to pie crust but can be more difficult to work with. Use nut butter half and half in conjunction with the butter (or other fat) in the recipe. Put the measured nut butter onto a piece of parchment paper and spread it into a ½-inch / 13-mm-thick layer. Cover and transfer to the freezer until firm, about 1 hour. Then the frozen butter can be cut into cubes and added along with the other fat (butter or shortening).

Where's the Sugar?

I don't add sugar to my pie doughs because I like pies that aren't too sweet (and that way, I can use the same recipe for savory pies). Instead, I add the sugar for the surface of the dough when appropriate (for more on this, see Finishing Touches for Crusts, page 98). But if you crave a little sweetness, you can whisk up to 12 g / 1 tablespoon of sugar into the flour for each single-crust dough recipe. You'll want to stick to granulated sugar here—steer clear of sugar with larger granules (like raw sugars) or sugars containing moisture (like brown sugar), which can affect the results, even in such small quantities.

SALT

A little bit of salt makes such a difference. I opt for fine sea salt in both my crust and filling recipes—it's easy to dissolve and disperse. Feel free to adjust the salt level in your favorite crust recipes to suit your own taste. And just as sweet pies benefit from a shower of sugar just before baking, savory pies can benefit from a sprinkling of flaky salt or a salty ingredient, like grated Parmesan.

WATER

The only truly important thing concerning your water is that it be cold. If you're capable of working quickly, chilled water is enough, but for most people (or if it is a warm day), it's best to toss a few ice cubes into the water before you start making the recipe, then use the ice water to measure from.

Using Vinegar or Vodka

Many pie crust recipes include a small amount of vinegar or vodka. Both contribute a nominal amount to hydration but primarily help to inhibit the formation of gluten to keep the dough tender. With practice, you can achieve a beautiful, flaky dough without using either of these but they are easy to toss in if you find them helpful.

TO ADD VINEGAR: For a single-crust dough recipe, add 14 g / 1 tablespoon vinegar to the well in the flour before beginning to add the water. I usually opt for white or cider vinegar, but I have even used sherry or malt vinegar when I won't mind a hint of their flavor in the dough.

TO ADD VODKA: For a single-crust dough recipe, add 28 g / 2 tablespoons vodka to the well in the flour before beginning to add the water.

MIXING PIE DOUGH

The basic method for mixing a classic pie dough remains the same regardless of the recipe you're using. However, there are several different tweaks that will produce different results. I'm a firm believer that there isn't one single "right way"— the best way is whatever works best for you, but if you're struggling to find your true pie dough path, the descriptions and tips below will help you find the way. I usually mix the dough by hand, but if you have hot hands, you may opt to use a pastry cutter, or choose the food-processor method (page 30) instead. Using this basic method, you can achieve one of two types of pie dough:

- **FLAKY DOUGH:** In this method, the fat is left in larger pieces (the size of walnut halves) to produce a lighter, flakier dough.
- **MEALY DOUGH:** In this method, the fat is mixed into smaller pieces (the size of peas) to produce a less flaky dough that's denser but still tender.

After mastering these basic methods, there are three other variations that I also love that can be made with only a few adjustments to the original recipe:

- **EXTRA FLAKY PIE DOUGH:** This method enlists the help of two simple folds after mixing to help create a flakier dough.
- **ROUGH PUFF PASTRY:** This method builds on the last, using a total of four folds after mixing to create a super flaky, layered dough.
- **DOUGH FOR DÉCOR:** In this method, the fat is mixed more thoroughly with the flour with the aid of a food processor to produce a less flaky dough that's ideal for detailed décor, like cutouts.

Any of these techniques can be used with any of the pie dough recipes in this chapter.

Dough for Décor · Mealy · Flaky · Rough Puff · Extra Flaky · Pâte Brisée

MIXING PIE DOUGH BY HAND
(The Traditional Method)

My favorite way to make a basic pie dough is to mix it by hand, for reasons half logical and half romantic. On the logical side, mixing by hand allows you to feel the dough and gives you the best chance of getting it right. On the romantic side, mixing the dough by hand makes me feel like I'm *really* baking. There's something about floury hands that makes my kitchen feel nostalgic, happy, and wonderful, all at once.

1. START BY CUTTING YOUR COLD BUTTER (or other fat) into ½-inch / 13-mm cubes. In a large bowl, whisk together the flour and salt. Add the cubes of butter, tossing them through the flour until each piece is well coated. Cut the butter into the flour by pressing the pieces between your fingers, flattening them into big shards. As you work, continue to toss the butter through the flour, recoating the shingled pieces. If you have warm hands, you may want to use a pastry cutter (sometimes I do a few passes with pastry cutter, then toss the mixture with my hands before continuing). Take care to ensure that all the cubes of butter are fully coated in flour as you work.

2. FOR A FLAKY CRUST, continue cutting the butter into the flour just until the pieces of butter are about the size of walnut halves. Or, *for a mealy crust,* work the mixture together until the pieces of butter are about the size of peas or to your desired size.

3. MAKE A WELL IN THE CENTER OF THE FLOUR MIXTURE. Add the amount of ice water listed in the recipe to the well. (Different types, or even brands, of flour hydrate differently, so it is difficult to give a precise amount that will work every time; consider the base amount given as a solid jumping-off point, knowing that you will almost always need to add more.) Using your hands, toss the flour with the water to start to mix the two together (this begins to combine them without creating too much gluten). As the flour begins to hydrate, you can switch to more of a kneading motion—but don't overdo it, or the dough will be tough. Then add more water, about 1 tablespoon / 15 grams at a time, until the dough is properly hydrated. It should be uniformly combined and hold together easily, but it shouldn't look totally smooth. Dough that is too dry may have a sort of "dusty" appearance, or pockets of unhydrated flour; it will not hold together and will look crumbly. Dough that is too wet will feel sticky or tacky to the touch, and it is often smoother and/or lighter in color than a properly hydrated dough. (See What to Do: My Dough Is Too Wet or Too Dry, page 32.)

4. FORM THE DOUGH INTO AN EVEN DISK, ABOUT 1 INCH / 2.5 CM THICK (Or form into another shape if directed by the recipe; or, if you are multiplying the recipe to make multiple crusts, divide the dough as appropriate and shape into disks). Wrap tightly in plastic wrap and refrigerate for at least 30 minutes, or up to 2 days (see Chilling Pie Dough, page 33).

Making Big Batches Using a Stand Mixer

When I need to make a big batch of pie dough, I usually enlist my stand mixer with the paddle attachment. Even with the mixer, I recommend making no more than a quadruple batch of dough at once. Any larger, and it becomes difficult to control the hydration levels. And even when I use the stand mixer for making the dough, I add the water by hand, since I still find it to be the most effective way to nail the hydration.

PIE PEP TALK

"Lightly Floured Surface"

Throughout this book, you'll see the phrase "on a lightly floured surface" often. What I mean is to use no more flour than you need to. Excess flour can make a dough tough or dry, so you want only enough flour to prevent the dough from sticking to your work surface or rolling pin. If your dough feels really sticky, it is likely that it's too wet (in that case, see What to Do: My Dough Is Too Wet or Too Dry, page 32) or that it's too warm and the butter is soft (in this case, chill that dough some mo').

MIXING PIE DOUGH USING A FOOD PROCESSOR

If you have particularly hot hands, you may want to go the food processor route. I find it is still best to add the water by hand, as water likes to hide in the food processor (particularly under and around the blade), but it does a quick, great job of getting the butter portion done. It is also my preferred method for certain doughs such as pâte brisée (page 59) or dough for décor (page 33).

1. Start by cutting the butter (or other fat) into ½-inch / 13-mm cubes. Toss the butter in the flour/salt mixture to coat before adding the whole thing to the food processor. Pulse the mixture in 3-second bursts until the pieces of butter are the desired size. *For a flaky crust,* pulse just until the pieces of butter are about the size of walnut halves. Or, *for a mealy crust,* pulse until the pieces of butter are about the size of peas. I find 10 to 15 pulses usually does the trick.

2. Transfer the mixture to a bowl and add the water as directed on page 28 in step 3 of the instructions for mixing the dough by hand. If it's a particularly hot day, you may want to toss the dough into the refrigerator or freezer for a few minutes before continuing. Continue as directed in step 4 on page 28.

MIXING PIE DOUGH SO IT'S EXTRA FLAKY

This is a technique I learned in pastry school that I've adapted over the years: It combines the classic method of making pie dough with an abbreviated lamination (rolling out the dough and performing a series of folds) to make it extra flaky. I've also found this method to be great for home bakers who have trouble working with dough.

The dough is worked significantly more, but this method produces a light, flaky result rather than making the dough tough. It also makes the dough smoother, which can make it easier to roll out, handle, and crimp.

1. Make the pie dough as for the traditional method (see Mixing Pie Dough by Hand, page 28), making sure the pieces of butter are no smaller than walnut halves—if necessary, err on the side of larger pieces rather than smaller, and chill the dough for at least 30 minutes.

2. On a lightly floured surface, roll out the chilled dough to about ¼ inch / 6 mm thick (the exact size and shape don't matter here, just the thickness). Fold the dough in half, then in half again, into quarters. Refrigerate the dough for 30 minutes, then repeat this folding process once more. Tuck the edges of the dough under to help form the dough into a rounded shape, then wrap it again and chill for at least 30 minutes before using. If you made a larger batch of dough for multiple crusts, you can perform this technique with the full batch (then divide it as necessary) or with each individual portion.

Top row: extra-flaky dough on the first fold. Bottom row: dough after four folds (Rough Puff Pastry, page 50)

What to Do: My Dough Is Too Wet or Too Dry

There will be times where the dough you thought was perfect is too wet (sticky) or too dry (cracking) when you start rolling it out. Here's how to save it.

A slightly **too-wet dough** can often be saved by using extra flour while rolling it out. This may seem counterintuitive, since most recipes say to use as little as possible, but in the case of a too-wet dough, you want to incorporate more flour to soak up some of that excess hydration. Start by generously dusting the surface of the dough disk with flour, and then use a bit more flour on the surface while rolling. Once the dough no longer feels sticky, add as little flour as possible going forward. I usually recommend erring on the side of slightly overhydrating rather than underhydrating a dough, since an overhydrated dough will be easier to fix, but be careful—a very wet crust will be overly crisp and tough.

A **too-dry dough** is harder to fix than a too-wet one, but in most cases, a small amount of additional water is all that's needed. Flatten the dough to about ½ inch / 1 cm thick with your hands. Dip your hand in ice water and flick a few drops of water onto the surface of the dough. Fold the dough over onto itself a few times—try not to knead, as overmixing will make the dough tough. Once the water is incorporated, form the dough into a disk and chill for at least 30 minutes before using. It's worth noting that if your dough has already been rolled out, it may be noticeably tougher by the time you complete this process, even if you salvage the hydration.

Too dry

Perfect

Too wet

YOU CAN MAKE ANY PIE DOUGH AS ROUGH PUFF PASTRY

Want to get even flakier? My rough puff pastry is *the* flakiest dough in this book—but don't let the term "puff pastry" scare you. It starts with larger pieces of butter, then builds on the extra flaky method by rolling out and folding the dough a total of four times. For more, see page 50.

MIXING PIE DOUGH FOR DETAILED DÉCOR

Well-made pie dough is so flaky and tender, it can be difficult to use for décor with particular details, like cutouts, imprints from pie stamps, or sharp edges. So, when making dough for décor, it's best to intentionally make it less flaky. This won't make the décor any less enjoyable to eat, but it will prevent you from tearing your hair out when your carefully placed décor puffs up so much it's uneven or falls off the pie!

Make the dough in the food processor as directed on page 30, mixing until the butter pieces are smaller than the size of peas. You should still see visible pieces of butter in the flour, but they should be very, very small. This works particularly well and quickly in the food processor.

MAKING PIE DOUGH IN ADVANCE

Pie dough can be held for up to 2 days, tightly wrapped in plastic wrap, in the refrigerator. Longer than that, the fat in the dough can oxidize, causing discoloration and textural variances. For longer-term storage, wrap the dough tightly in plastic wrap and then aluminum foil and freeze for up to 3 months; thaw overnight in the refrigerator before using (see page 35).

CHILLING PIE DOUGH

Chilling the dough is important, and many common problems can be avoided by thoroughly chilling the dough. Cold dough is easier to work with, it holds its shape better in the oven, and it bakes up flakier. If you aren't sure if you should give your dough another chill at any point in the dough-making or handling process, it probably means you should: When in doubt, chill it out. There are three main points when you should chill your dough: after mixing, before crimping, and before baking.

CHILLING AFTER MIXING: Chilling the dough properly after mixing is absolutely crucial. If your dough isn't chilled enough at this stage, the fat will be soft and likely to smush into the dough during rolling, resulting in a shorter, crumblier texture rather than the desired tender, flaky effect. Chilling the dough after mixing also helps the dough relax. Chilling allows the natural protein strands (i.e., gluten) that form when flour is hydrated to relax, or to soften the tight strands, making the dough easier to roll out.

Minimum Chill: 30 minutes / **Recommended Chill:** 1 hour / **Max Chill:** 3 days

CHILLING BEFORE CRIMPING: This is the only chilling step that can be considered optional, but it can be super-helpful to the end result. Chilling the dough after rolling it out and transferring it to the pie plate allows it to relax again at this stage. It is especially recommended if you have consistent issues with the crust shrinking, because it allows the dough to relax before you even trim away the excess dough prior to crimping, lessening the possibility of the dough shrinking back. Cover the dough loosely with plastic wrap during this chill, as the surface of the dough can dry out a bit, making it more difficult to crimp later.

Minimum Chill: 5 minutes / **Recommended Chill:** 15 minutes / **Max Chill:** 1 hour

CHILLING BEFORE BAKING: At this stage, chilling is less about relaxing the gluten and more about firming the fat. Cold fat is essential to achieving a flaky crust, and chilling the fat also helps ensure that decorative effects stay sharp and bake up cleanly. How long a pie takes to chill adequately will depend on how long it took you to assemble the pie (for example, a latticed pie might need a longer chill than a simple double crust because it was at room temperature longer during assembly). Cover the pie loosely with plastic wrap to prevent the surface of the dough from drying

out during chilling. But note that you don't want to chill a pie for *too* long at this stage, because that is not always good for the filling (with extended storage times, sugar can continue to macerate, or pull moisture from fruit, and soft or liquid fillings, like custards, can begin to leech into the crust).

Minimum Chill: 15 minutes / **Recommended Chill:** 30 minutes / **Max Chill:** 1 hour

ROLLING OUT PIE DOUGH AND LINING THE PIE PLATE (OR OTHER PAN/BAKEWARE)

There are a few keys to rolling out dough, but, as with most baking, it also just takes a bit of practice. I usually roll out flaky pie doughs directly on a work surface—a chilled marble or stone surface if possible, because the dough will stay cooler—rather than on or between sheets of parchment (for more on this, see page 36).

1. Lightly dust your work surface with flour. I use about a handful of flour to dust the surface and the dough, and I often don't need to use any more during rolling. Use just enough flour to prevent the dough from sticking, as using too much can make the dough tough or dry.

2. Begin to roll out the dough by positioning the rolling pin in the center of the dough, then applying gentle pressure and pushing it away from you. Return the pin to the center and do the same, this time bringing the pin towards you. Although this method may feel a bit awkward at first, it's useful for learning how to apply gentle, even pressure to the dough rather than just pressing

(CONTINUED ON PAGE 36)

When to Use the Freezer

While the freezer is handy for a brief chill or ensuring that decorative features bake up beautifully, freezing can have some adverse effects:

- Freezing rolled-out pie dough can adversely affect the fat. While any pie dough can be frozen in a disk for up to 3 months, once the dough is rolled out, the fat in it is in small, thin layers. Fats with a higher water content (like most American butters) have a tendency to defrost in a funny way if the dough was rolled out too thin, so I do not recommend freezing rolled-out dough.

- Freezing can mess with the way the fat acts in the oven. While you do want dough to be cold, if it is baked from frozen, it may take a while for the butter to soften and thus delay the flaky puff-up effect that occurs when the dough hits the oven heat. This can lead to the butter melting out of the crust, making a greasy and/or smoky mess in your oven and a tough crust.

- Freezing an assembled pie completely can mess with the filling—if even a portion of it hardens in the freezer, it can prevent it from baking properly. The filling may end up too thin, and in fruit pies, you may also be able to taste the thickening agent. This is because the filling was so cold that even by the time the crust is baked, the filling still hasn't come to a "boil," which is necessary for activating the starch and cooking away its noticeable taste.

But the freezer does have its merits. I use the freezer to quickly chill dough at certain stages—e.g., if the dough starts to feel warm while I'm working with it and I need to quickly firm it up a bit. I also freeze disks of pie dough, after wrapping them tightly in plastic wrap and then aluminum foil, for up to 3 months. And for some of the crusts in this chapter, like the Press-In Cookie Crust (page 64), Roll-Out Cookie Crust (page 62), and Hot-Water Crust (page 60), because the fat is more fully incorporated in these recipes, I even recommend freezing as part of the handling.

down while rolling the pin back and forth, which can often make the crust too thin at the edges and thicker in the center.

3. Rotate the dough frequently as you work, or even flip it over. That will help keep the dough from sticking and also allow you to feel the thickness to determine if there are thicker areas you haven't hit evenly with your pin yet. As the dough round (or rectangle) gets bigger, use the pin to help you move it around—roll it up around the pin, then unfurl it in a slightly different spot. Rather than focusing on the diameter of the rolled-out dough, focus on the thickness. When the dough is rolled out evenly to the correct thickness (⅛ to ¼ inch / 3 to 6 mm), it should be the correct size. Of course, you can always use your pie pan as a guide while you roll, placing it lightly on top of the dough to help see when you're getting close.

When your dough is rolled out to the proper thickness, use the rolling pin (or parchment paper, if you used it) to transfer the dough to the pie pan. To use the pin, place it at the end of the dough farthest from you, wrap the edge of the dough up around the pin, and roll the pin toward you, wrapping the dough around the pin. Position the far edge of the dough at the far edge of the pie plate and gently unfurl it into the plate.

FOR A PIE PLATE: Roll out the dough until it's about 1 inch / 3 cm wider than the pie plate. Transfer the dough to the pie plate, then lift up the dough gently at the edges and gently push it into the base of the pie plate.

FOR A DEEP-DISH PIE PLATE/SPRINGFORM PAN: Roll out the dough so it's 2 to 3 inches / 5 to 8 cm wider than your pan. Transfer the dough to the pan, lift the dough gently at the edges, and gently push it into the bottom of the pan.

PIE PEP TALK
How to Roll Out Dough on Parchment

I often recommend rolling out softer/ stickier doughs (like cookie crusts) on parchment paper, which allows you to use only a minimal amount of flour. I place the dough on a piece of parchment and lightly flour the top of the dough and the rolling pin. While some folks like sandwiching the dough between two pieces, I find the top piece often bunches up after a few passes of the rolling pin, leaving dents and marks in the dough. If, however, I want to flip the dough over, I do place a second piece of parchment on top and use the two pieces to help flip the dough over; then I remove the top piece, lightly dust the surface of the dough, and begin again. When you're ready to transfer to a pie plate, lift the edges of the paper to carry the dough to the edge of your pie plate and, once you're hovering over it, flip the dough and gently peel away the parchment paper.

FOR A SQUARE OR RECTANGULAR BAKING PAN/BAKING SHEET: Start with a square or rectangular piece of dough. While you roll out the dough, use a bench knife to help you keep the edges squared off. Doing this several times in the early stages of rolling will really help you maintain that shape. Transfer the dough to the pan and gently press it into the bottom of the pan, gently lifting up the edges as you nudge it in, taking particular care to press it into the corners.

Squaring off Scallion Compound
Butter Pie Dough (see page 58)

Ways to Use Your Dough Scraps

Nearly every pie I ever make has yielded at least a few scraps of leftover dough, so I'm always looking for new ways to use it. If you want to save the scraps for later, even if it's two tiny pieces, just form them into a disk and wrap tightly in plastic wrap; don't press too firmly, though, as that could overwork the dough and/or start to melt the butter. I label the package "Scrap Dough" so I will remember it's already been rolled out and handled once. The leftover dough will keep in the fridge for up to 2 days or in the freezer for up to 3 months. Thaw overnight before using frozen dough.

USING SCRAP DOUGH FOR DÉCOR: Dough that's already been rolled and handled will be less flaky, so it can be great to use for more detailed décor. Scrap dough is handy when you are just making a few cutouts or a single decorative element, like a braid, since they don't require much dough.

MAKING PIE-CRUST COOKIES WITH SCRAP DOUGH: You can make pie-crust cookies in one of two ways. For the first, roll out the dough and cut it into shapes. Transfer to a parchment-lined baking sheet, brush the cutouts with egg wash, and sprinkle generously with sugar (or cinnamon sugar). Bake at 425°F / 220°C until golden brown, 8 to 10 minutes. Or, shape the scrap dough into 1-inch / 2-cm balls (no need for them to be perfect—rustic is the name of the game here). Roll each ball generously in sugar (or cinnamon sugar) and transfer to a parchment-lined baking sheet, leaving at least 1½ inches / 3 cm between the cookies. Bake at 375°F / 190°C until the cookies are golden brown, 15 to 18 minutes.

MAKING PIE CRUST "STREUSEL" (AS A TOPPING OR CRUMBLE) WITH SCRAP DOUGH: Arrange bite-size scraps (plain or coated in sugar) in an even layer on top of a pie before baking. Or, you can bake the streusel separately, as directed in the scrap-dough pastry snacks (at right), and add it to a cooled pie.

**MAKING SCRAP-DOUGH PASTRY
SNACKS:** We used to do this in pastry school. Cut the scraps into bite-size pieces and toss them in egg wash and cinnamon sugar, then place on a parchment-lined baking sheet. Bake at 425°F / 220°C until deeply golden brown, 15 to 18 minutes. Beak apart any pieces and serve as a snack. This technique also works for a savory cracker/bite situation: toss the scraps in finely grated cheese, such as aged cheddar or Parmesan, and bake.

**ANYTHING-ON-PIE-CRUST SNACKS
WITH SCRAP DOUGH:** For this un-recipe, you blind-bake pieces of pie dough, then top them with just about anything (I often do this with fresh scraps after assembling a pie to snack on while the pie bakes). Roll out the scrap dough (don't worry about size or shape—just make sure the dough is about ¼ inch / 6 mm thick) and use the rolling pin to transfer the sheet of dough to a parchment-lined baking sheet. Brush the crust with egg wash and dock it all over with a fork). Bake at 425°F / 220°C until deeply golden and crisp (timing will depend on the size of your dough sheet (15 to 18 minutes for an individually sized portion, or up to 25 minutes for larger pieces). Let the dough cool, then top it with macerated fresh fruit, whipped cream, melted chocolate, or a layer of jam—really anything you enjoy eating on a crust; you can even top squares of crust with sliced or mashed avocado for "avocado toast."

**MAKING SCRAP-DOUGH BABY FRUIT
PIES:** Roll out the scrap dough to ¼ inch / 6 mm thick (this one's worth saving up scraps

for). Cut the dough into rounds using a 3-inch / 8-cm round cutter and transfer to a parchment-lined baking sheet. Brush with egg wash and dock it all over with a fork. Top with thinly sliced fruit and sprinkle with sugar to taste. Or add 1 to 2 tablespoons (7 to 14 grams) cornstarch to ¼ to ½ cup (50 to 99 grams) sugar and toss with the fruit before topping the dough to help thicken any juices. Bake at 425°F / 220°C until deeply golden and crisp; baking time may vary depending on the fruit but start checking at 15 minutes or so. See Mini Pie Pairings (page 262) for more ideas.

AMOUNT OF DOUGH REQUIRED FOR DIFFERENT PANS

The amounts listed are for a single bottom crust; you will need double the amount of dough if you are doing a top crust. The measurements listed are approximate.

PAN SIZE	PIE DOUGH	PUFF PASTRY / ROUGH PUFF	ROLL-OUT COOKIE CRUST	PRESS-IN COOKIE CRUST	HOT-WATER CRUST
9- OR 10-INCH / 23- OR 25-CM STANDARD PIE PLATE	1 recipe: 340 g / 12 ounces	½ recipe: 312 g / 11 ounces	1 recipe: 400 g / 14 ounces	1 recipe: 425 g / 15 ounces	½ recipe: 368 g / 13 ounces
9- OR 10-INCH / 23- OR 25-CM DEEP-DISH PIE PLATE	1 recipe: 340 g / 12 ounces	1 recipe: 625 g / 22 ounces	1 recipe: 400 g / 14 ounces	1 recipe: 425 g / 15 ounces	1 recipe: 735 g / 26 ounces
9-INCH / 23 CM SPRINGFORM PAN	2 recipes: 680 g / 24 ounces	1 recipe: 625 g / 22 ounces	2 recipes: 800 g / 28 ounces	2 recipes: 850 g / 30 ounces	1 recipe: 735 g / 26 ounces
8-BY-8-INCH / 20-BY-20-CM PAN	2 recipes: 680 g / 24 ounces	1 recipe: 625 g / 22 ounces	2 recipes: 800 g / 28 ounces	2 recipes: 850 g / 30 ounces	1½ recipes: 1103 g / 39 ounces
9-BY-9-INCH / 23-BY-23-CM PAN	2 recipes: 680 g / 24 ounces	1 recipe: 625 g / 22 ounces	2 recipes: 800 g / 28 ounces	2 recipes: 850 g / 30 ounces	1½ recipes: 1103 g / 39 ounces
9-BY-13-INCH / 23-BY-33-CM BAKING PAN OR 9½-BY-13-INCH QUARTER SHEET PAN	2 recipes: 680 g / 24 ounces	1½ recipes: 937 g / 33 ounces	2½ recipes: 1000 g / 32 ounces	3 recipes: 1275 g / 45 ounces	2 recipes: 1470 g / 52 ounces
10½-BY-15½-INCH / 27-BY-30-CM BAKING SHEET (A.K.A. JELLY-ROLL PAN)	3 recipes: 1020 g / 35 ounces	2 recipes: 1247 g / 44 ounces	4 recipes: 1600 g / 56 ounces	4 recipes: 1700 g / 60 ounces	2½ recipes: 1837 g / 65 ounces
18-BY-13-INCH / 46-BY-33-CM BAKING SHEET (A.K.A. HALF SHEET PAN)	3 recipes: 1020 g / 35 ounces	2 recipes: 1247 g / 44 ounces	4 recipes: 1600 g / 56 ounces	4 recipes: 1700 g / 60 ounces	2½ recipes: 1837 g / 65 ounces

Galettes and Free-Form Pies

A galette is a classic rustic pie with folded-over edges that is baked on a baking sheet, but there are other kinds of free-form pies as well. My obsession with free-form pies began on a vacation. We were renting a cabin in the woods, and there was a blueberry bush overflowing with fruit in the yard. Although I wanted (no, *needed*) to bake a pie, I didn't have a pie plate. But that wasn't going to stop me! I baked my latticed pie freeform on a baking sheet, and from that day on, I was hooked. The method produces a pie that has an incredibly crisp bottom crust and is really easy to slice.

Almost any pie that you can make in a pie plate can be made free form. The main thing to remember is without the sides of a pie plate to support the crust, the pie will be relatively thin. If a filling is more solid (think chunky pieces of fruit), you can mound it a bit on the crust. But if a filling is more liquid (think custard), you'll probably need to use less filling than for a regular pie because you won't be able have as deep a layer of it. Free-form pies can be single- or double-crusted, and they can have all the same sorts of decorative features as classic pies, including crimped edges, lattice crusts, cutouts, and more!

Free-form pie made with Spelt Crust (page 55) and gooseberry vanilla filling (page 171).

PREPARING THE CRUST EDGES

SINGLE-CRUST PIES: Once you've lined your pie plate with dough, trim away any excess dough, ideally ending up with ½ inch / 1 cm of excess dough all the way around the edges. I like to use scissors for this task—they make it easy to cut cleanly. Then tuck the excess dough under itself so the edges of the crust are flush with the outer rim of the pie plate. Press lightly to seal the dough all around. This technique serves to give you

thicker dough around the edges of the pie, which makes it easier to crimp (and to have the crimp to stay put—see more on crimping on page 80), and this final folded effect at the edges makes the edges of the crust look (and taste!) particularly flaky when you slice the pie.

DOUBLE-CRUST PIES: When I make a double-crust pie, I roll out the first disk of dough and line the pie plate with it, then cover the dough with plastic wrap while I roll out the top crust. Preparing the top crust in advance keeps the dough cool while you assemble the filling. Even if

PIE PEP TALK

Fixing an Error When Lining a Pie Plate

When lining a pie plate, small tears in the dough and dough that is uneven around the edges are two of the most common issues. For either problem, the best thing to do is to patch the error with some extra dough. Use dough from a spot that has excess dough after you line the pie plate. With scissors, cut a piece of dough about the size of your problem spot. If the dough is visibly floury, brush the excess flour away, then dip your finger in cool water and moisten the dough where you're going to attach the scrap. Press firmly to attach and smooth the dough. If the dough isn't super-floury, you can likely just attach it using the warmth of your hand. Chill the pie shell thoroughly again after you've applied any sort of patch.

your filling is already prepared, it's still nice to give the top crust a bit of a chill before assembly: Roll out the second disk of dough, use the rolling pin to transfer it to a parchment-lined baking sheet, and unfurl onto the pan. Cover the dough loosely with plastic wrap and refrigerate while you assemble the filling.

Pour the prepared filling into the pie shell. Use the rolling pin to transfer the top crust to the pie, gently unfurling it over of the filling. Pinch the top and bottom crusts together all around the edges. This both helps them adhere to each other and thins out the place where they touch so it isn't insanely thick. Using scissors, trim away any excess dough, ideally ending up with ½ inch / 1 cm of excess dough all the way around the pie plate (reminder—I like to use scissors for this). Tuck the excess dough under itself so the edges of the crust are flush with the outer rim of the pie plate. Press lightly to seal the dough all around. This technique ensures that the top crust is tucked underneath the bottom crust, creating a solid seal, as well as more dough at the edge for crimping.

PARBAKING

Parbaking refers to partially baking a bottom crust before filling it and continuing to bake it. It is usually done with single-crust pies to ensure that the crust will be fully baked (nice and crisp!) by the time the filling is done. Pie shells can be parbaked up to 24 hours in advance, because they will refresh and recrisp during their second trip to the oven.

For both parbaking and blind-baking (fully baking the bottom crust), the initial preparation is the same: Dock the bottom of your crimped and well-chilled pie crust all over with a fork. For some doughs, particularly cookie-style doughs, docking is enough to prevent the crust from puffing up or sliding down the sides during baking. But for flakier doughs, you'll want to use pie weights. Cut a square of parchment paper that is slightly larger than the pie plate. Place it on top of the pie shell and fill with pie weights (make sure you use enough weights to come up to the inner rim of the pie plate). Your pie crust is now ready to bake. Return it to the refrigerator if you are not ready to bake immediately.

When parbaking or blind-baking a crust, I usually place the pie plate directly on the rack, but you can always bake it on a parchment- or foil-lined baking sheet to catch any rogue butter drips. I also usually skip brushing the edges of parbaked

THE WHYS OF PIES

Why Flaky Doughs Love High Temperatures

Flaky pie and pastry doughs love to be baked at high temperatures (425°F / 220°C). The reason is actually the same reason these doughs like to be nicely chilled when they hit the oven. When the cold fat in the dough hits the heat of the oven, the moisture in the fat evaporates, creating steam. This steam pushes up the dough, creating lightness and flakiness galore. If your pie crusts are not crisp enough, it could be that your oven isn't hot enough. Instead of creating steam, the fat is heating up too slowly, ultimately melting and oozing out of the dough. But if your oven runs hot, you may find you need to start baking at this high temperature until the structure of the crust is set, then reduce the heat for the remainder of baking time to prevent burning. Invest in an oven thermometer (see Resources, page 345) so you can get to know your oven and keep an eye on the temperature as you bake.

or blind-baked crusts with egg wash, because they darken just the right amount with the multiple trips in and out of the oven. That said, if you want a shiny look to your crust, you can brush the edges with beaten egg white before baking. While the method for parbaking and blind-baking classic pie dough is always the same, the recipes in this chapter for other types of crusts provide specific parbaking instructions, because they often require different temperatures and timing.

Preheat the oven to 425°F / 220°C with a rack in the lower third of the oven, and a Baking Steel or stone, if you like to use that. Place your docked/weighted crust (see below for crusts that aren't baked with weights) on the rack and bake for 15 to 17 minutes, until the edges appear set and are just starting to lightly brown. Remove the crust from the oven and use the parchment paper to lift the weights out of the pie shell. Return the crust to the oven and bake until the bottom appears set, 2 to 3 minutes more. Let the crust cool completely.

For a crust that doesn't require pie weights, like cookie or crumb crusts, parbake the crust until it appears set all over and is just beginning to color at the edges (refer to specific recipes for timing info.)

(CONTINUED ON PAGE 46)

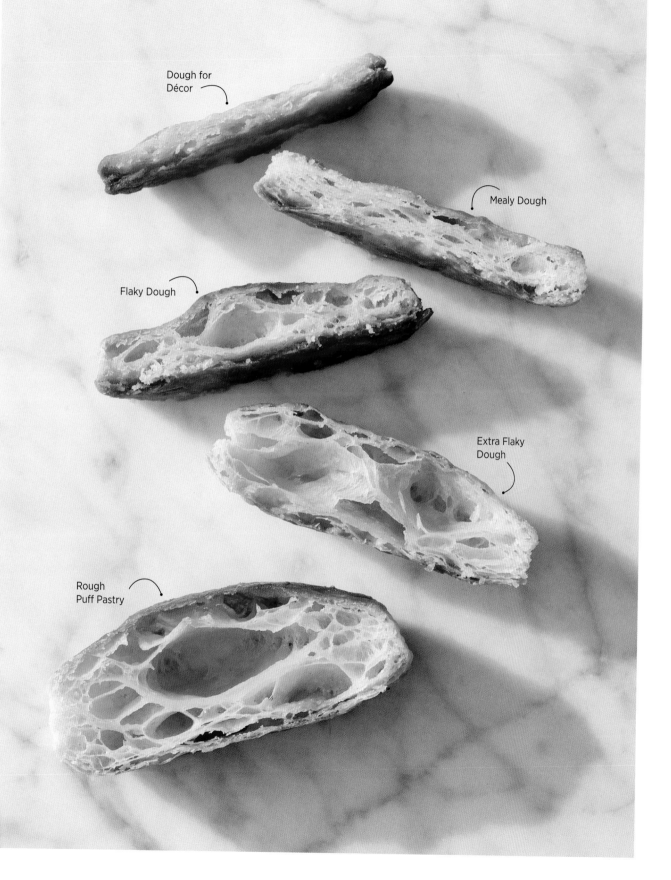

Dough for Décor

Mealy Dough

Flaky Dough

Extra Flaky Dough

Rough Puff Pastry

Parbake: Over-Baked   Parbake: Correct   Parbake: Under-Baked

Blind-Bake: Over-Baked   Blind-Bake: Correct   Blind-Bake: Under-Baked

At this point, you can apply a protective coating to the bottom crust, if desired. A few ideas include:

- A coating of beaten egg white or egg wash, which helps seal the crust.
- A layer of grated firm cheese (like Parmesan), which makes a protective barrier between the crust and the filling.
- The Black-Bottom Base (see page 110), which also adds another layer of flavor.
- Breadcrumbs or fine nut flours, which can soak up some of the excess juices from the filling.

BLIND-BAKING

Blind-baking refers to fully baking a bottom crust before filling it. It is usually done for single-crust pies with a cold-set filling.

Preheat the oven to 425°F / 220°C with a rack in the lower third, preferably with a Baking Steel or stone on it. Place your prepared (docked/weighted) crust in the oven and bake for 15 to 17 minutes, until the edges appear set and are just starting to lightly brown. Remove the crust from the oven and use the parchment paper to lift the pie weights out of the pan. Return the pie to the oven and bake until the crust is evenly golden brown and fully baked, 10 to 12 minutes more. Let the crust cool completely before filling it.

Parbaking Double-Crust Pies

It is possible to parbake the bottom crust of a double-crust pies. It isn't the easiest technique, but it can be helpful when making double-crust deep-dish pies, where there's a lot of filling that can make it trickier to get a crisp bottom crust.

Roll out your dough on a lightly floured surface until it is ⅛ to ¼ inch / 3 to 6 mm thick. Line your pie plate as directed on page 34 but leave about 1 inch / 2.5 cm of excess dough hanging over the edges of the pie plate. This excess will help prevent the dough from shrinking too much. (It may seem like too much dough—don't worry, the unnecessary excess will be removed after parbaking.) Refrigerate the dough again until it's nice and cold (15 to 20 minutes).

Dock the chilled crust and fill with pie weights (if you are making a deep-dish pie, remember that a deeper pan means you'll need more weights!). Bake the bottom crust until it just begins to turn golden at the edges, 15 to 17 minutes. Remove the parchment and pie weights and return the crust to the oven for 2 to 3 more minutes, just to ensure that the crust isn't visibly wet. Let the bottom crust cool for 3 to 5 minutes (don't wait too long, as the crust is easiest to trim while it's still slightly warm). Then use a pair of sharp kitchen scissors to trim the excess crust away from the pan so it is flush with the edge of the pie plate; while you work, use your fingers to gently loosen the edges of the crust from the edge of the pie plate. Let the bottom crust cool completely before continuing.

When the bottom crust is cooled, add your filling. Then roll out your top crust on a lightly floured surface to about ¼ inch / 6 mm thick. Unfurl the dough on top of the pie. Use your handy scissors again to trim the excess dough from the edges, leaving about ½ inch / 1 cm all around. Tuck the excess top crust dough under the parbaked bottom crust. Don't worry if this isn't perfect—just do your best to make sure the two crusts are adhered, and the crimping will take care of the rest! The one drawback to this technique is that it does limit your crimping options. When I have parbaked the bottom crust, I opt for a fork crimp of some sort. It's easy and really ensures that the two crusts are sealed together. (Plus, it's very difficult to do any sort of finger crimp with a partially baked crust underneath that top one.) Another option is to press the crusts together with your finger, then place decorative cutouts around the edges of the pie. Either way, make sure your two crusts are well sealed together before baking.

ALL-BUTTAH PIE DOUGH

MAKES ONE 9-INCH /
23-CM CRUST

DIFFICULTY: MEDIUM

This is my go-to pie dough: all buttah, all the time. Butter can be harder for beginners to work with, because it has a lower melting point than fats such as shortening, but the flavor can't be beat. And once you know how to handle the dough, it's easy. The key? Colder is always better when pie dough is involved. When in doubt, toss everything (the ingredients, the bowl, and maybe even the half-mixed dough) into the fridge before proceeding. The recipe can easily be increased to make up to a quadruple batch of dough (see Making Big Batches Using a Stand Mixer, page 30).

150 g / 1¼ cups all-purpose flour

1 g / ¼ teaspoon fine sea salt

113 g / 4 ounces / 8 tablespoons cold unsalted butter, cut into ½-inch / 13-mm cubes

60 g / ¼ cup ice water, plus more as needed

1. Prepare the dough using your desired mixing method (see page 27).

2. Form the dough into a disk and wrap tightly in plastic wrap. Refrigerate for at least 30 minutes before using. This dough is best baked at 425°F / 220°C. Parbake (see page 43), blind-bake (see page 46), or fill and bake as directed in the recipe of your choice.

VARIATION ///

CHOCOLATE ALL-BUTTAH PIE DOUGH: Replace 30 g / ¼ cup of the all-purpose flour with 28 g / ⅓ cup unsweetened cocoa powder (any kind, but dark or black cocoa powder makes a particularly intense crust; see Resources, page 345). Take care not to overbake the crust—look for a dry, matte appearance all over.

Make Ahead and Storage ━━━━━

The tightly wrapped disk of dough can be refrigerated for up to 3 days. Wrapped in plastic wrap and then in aluminum foil, the dough can be frozen for up to 3 months. Thaw overnight in the fridge before using.

GLUTEN-FREE PIE DOUGH

MAKES ONE 9-INCH /
23-CM CRUST

DIFFICULTY: MEDIUM

Pie is for everyone, even people who can't have regular flour! I prefer the Cup4Cup brand of the commercial gluten-free flours now available, but you could also DIY (see Note). This dough is more prone to getting sticky, so take care not to overhydrate it when adding the water. The result is crisper and slightly less flaky than a crust made with my classic all-buttah dough (opposite). This dough responds especially well to the extra flaky method (page 30) to produce a lighter pastry.

200 g / 1½ cups gluten-free all-purpose or multipurpose flour (I prefer Cup4Cup; see Note)

1 g / ¼ teaspoon fine sea salt

113 g / 4 ounces / 8 tablespoons cold unsalted butter, cut into ½-inch / 13-mm cubes

60 g / ¼ cup ice water, plus more as needed

1. Prepare the dough using your desired mixing method (see page 27).

2. Form the dough into a disk and wrap tightly in plastic wrap. Refrigerate for at least 30 minutes before using. This dough is best baked at 425°F / 220°C. Parbake (see page 43), blind-bake (see page 46), or fill and bake as directed in the recipe of your choice.

Make Ahead and Storage

The tightly wrapped disk of dough can be refrigerated for up to 3 days. Wrapped in plastic wrap and then aluminum foil, the dough can be frozen for up to 3 months. Thaw overnight in the fridge before using.

NOTE ◇◇◇◇◇◇◇◇◇◇◇◇◇◇◇◇◇◇◇◇◇◇◇◇

If you would like to make your own gluten-free flour, whisk together the following ingredients until well combined, then sift before using (makes 217 g / about 1½ cups):

71 g / ½ cup white rice flour

57 g / ½ cup tapioca flour

56 g / ½ cup cornstarch

21 g / ¼ cup nonfat dry milk

19 g / 2 tablespoons potato starch

4 g / 1¾ teaspoons xanthan gum

ROUGH PUFF PASTRY

MAKES TWO 9-INCH /
23-CM CRUSTS

DIFFICULTY: MEDIUM

Rough puff pastry is truthfully, almost as light, flaky, and delicious as traditional puff pastry, but with much less stress and effort. It's incredibly versatile—great for free-form pies and mini pies especially. This makes a quantity similar to about 454 g / 1 pound of frozen puff pastry. Any of the pie dough recipes in this book can be rough-puff-ified by following the method below.

302 g / 2½ cups all-purpose flour

2 g / ½ teaspoon fine sea salt

226 g / 8 ounces cold unsalted butter, cut into
¾-inch / 19-mm cubes

75 g / ⅓ cup ice water, plus more as needed

1. In a medium bowl, stir the flour and salt together to combine. Add the cubes of butter, tossing them through the flour until each individual piece is well coated. Cut the butter into the flour by pressing the pieces between your fingers, flattening them into big shards. As you work, continue to toss the butter through the flour, recoating the shingled pieces. The goal is to flatten each piece of butter only once, leaving the pieces very large (they will get smaller/more dispersed through the process of folding the dough).

2. Make a well in the center of the flour mixture. Add the ice water to the well and, using your hands, toss the flour with the water to start to mix the two together (this begins to combine them without creating too much gluten). As the flour begins to hydrate, you can switch to more of a kneading motion—but don't overdo it, or the dough will be tough. Then add more water, about 1 tablespoon / 15 grams at a time, until the dough is properly hydrated. It should be uniformly combined and hold together easily, but it shouldn't look totally smooth. Divide the dough in half and form each piece into a disk. Wrap tightly in plastic wrap and refrigerate for at least 30 minutes.

3. On a lightly floured surface, working with one piece of dough at a time, roll out the dough to about ½ inch / 1 cm thick (the exact size/shape of the dough doesn't matter here, just the thickness). Brush off any excess flour with a dry pastry brush, then fold the dough in half. Fold the dough in half again into quarters. Wrap the dough tightly in plastic wrap and chill for 15 to 30 minutes, until firm.

4. Repeat step 3 three more times: rolling out the dough, folding it, and chilling it each time before continuing. If you work quickly, you can sometimes do two rounds of folds back to back, but if the dough is soft or sticky, don't rush it.

5. Once the final fold is completed for each piece of dough, tuck the edges of the dough under to help form it into a rounded shape, then wrap again and chill at least 30 minutes before using. This dough is best baked at 400°F / 205°C. Parbake (see page 43), blind-bake (page 46), or fill and bake as directed in the recipe of your choice. Note that the pastry may take longer to parbake or blind-bake because of the lower baking temperature.

Make Ahead and Storage

The tightly wrapped disks of dough can be refrigerated for up to 3 days. Wrapped in plastic wrap and then aluminum foil, the dough can be frozen for up to 3 months. Thaw overnight in the fridge before using.

VEGAN / DAIRY-FREE PIE DOUGH

MAKES ONE 9-INCH / 23-CM CRUST

DIFFICULTY: MEDIUM

Although shortening makes the flakiest dough, I usually avoid it because butter just tastes so dang good. But for those unable to eat dairy, it's a great alternative. I prefer unhydrogenated shortening, which can usually be found in the natural food section of grocery stores. This dough is slightly less flavorful than my classic All-Buttah Pie Dough (page 48), but just as gloriously flaky.

150 g / 1¼ cups all-purpose flour

1 g / ¼ teaspoon fine sea salt

113 g / 4 ounces / 8 tablespoons cold unhydrogenated shortening (I prefer Nutiva brand), cut into ½-inch / 13-mm cubes

60 g / ¼ cup ice water, plus more as needed

1. Prepare the dough using your desired mixing method (see page 27).

2. Form the dough into a disk and wrap tightly in plastic wrap. Refrigerate for at least 30 minutes before using. This dough is best baked at 425°F / 220°C. Parbake (see page 43), blind-bake (see page 46), or fill and bake as directed in your recipe of choice.

Make Ahead and Storage

The tightly wrapped disk of dough can be refrigerated for up to 3 days. Wrapped in plastic wrap and then aluminum foil, the dough can be frozen for up to 3 months. Thaw overnight in the fridge before using.

THE WHYS OF PIES

To Dock or Not to Dock Puff Pastry?

Rough puff pastry can be particularly, well, puffy! It will be light and flaky in any case, but docked dough will be thinner and crisper, while undocked dough will be light and fluffy inside and just lightly crisp outside. For some preparations, such as free-form pies or individual pastries, you want the dough to puff up fully. For others, as when you're using it to line a pan or for a thin-crust presentation (like a flat, crisp crust), it's best to dock the dough (poke it all over with a fork) to keep it flatter. It's also possible to dock only a portion of the dough so that some of it rises higher—for example, when you want an outer wall of pastry around a flatter center for the filling in the recipe (like the puff pastry shells or cases you might buy in the frozen section at a supermarket).

Spiced Pie Doughs

Almost any spice can be added to pie dough to create another level of flavor (and sometimes, a noticeable hint of color). Traditional baking spices are perfect for sweet pies, but your favorite savory spices can make for unique crusts for savory items like potpies and empanadas. Get creative and add your own blend of spices. To make these doughs, whisk the suggested ingredients into the flour.

GINGERBREAD PIE DOUGH: 4 g / 1¼ teaspoons ground ginger, 3 g / 1 teaspoon ground cinnamon, 2 g / ½ teaspoon ground allspice, and 2 g / ½ teaspoon ground cloves

VANILLA BEAN–NUTMEG PIE DOUGH: Seeds scraped from ½ vanilla bean (halved lengthwise) and 2 g / ½ teaspoon freshly grated nutmeg

PUMPKIN SPICE PIE DOUGH: 3 g / 1 teaspoon ground cinnamon, 3 g / 1 teaspoon ground ginger, 1 g / ¼ teaspoon ground cloves, and 1 g / ¼ teaspoon ground allspice

CARDAMOM LEMON PIE DOUGH: 3 g / 1 teaspoon ground cardamom and the grated zest of 1 lemon

SPICY PIE DOUGH: 3 g / 1 teaspoon ground dried chipotle pepper and 1 g / ¼ teaspoon cayenne pepper (or more to taste)

ZA'ATAR PIE DOUGH: 9 g / 1 tablespoon za'atar and 2 g / ½ teaspoon freshly ground black pepper

TURMERIC PIE DOUGH: 9 g / 1 tablespoon turmeric

SESAME, POPPY, CARAWAY, OR NIGELLA SEED PIE DOUGH: 18 g / 2 tablespoons sesame, caraway, or nigella seeds; if desired, gently crush in a mortar and pestle before adding

HERBES DE PROVENCE PIE DOUGH: 9 g / 1 tablespoon herbes de Provence

JERK OR CAJUN PIE DOUGH: 13 g / 1½ tablespoons jerk or Cajun seasoning, ½ teaspoon / 2 g freshly ground black pepper, and 1 g / ¼ teaspoon ground white pepper

CINNAMON PIE DOUGH: 6 g / 2 teaspoons ground cinnamon

GARAM MASALA PIE DOUGH: 6 g / 2 teaspoons garam masala

BROWN BUTTER PIE DOUGH

MAKES ONE 9-INCH / 23-CM CRUST

DIFFICULTY: MEDIUM

Adding the nutty flavor of brown butter to pie dough may seem like a no-brainer, but it does require a few adjustments. Because some of the moisture in the butter is removed during the process of making brown butter, the dough won't be *quite* as flaky as a dough made with regular butter, but the flavor more than compensates.

113 g / 4 ounces / 8 tablespoons unsalted butter
160 g / 1⅓ cups all-purpose flour
1 g / ¼ teaspoon fine sea salt
60 g / ¼ cup ice water, plus more as needed

1. In a medium saucepan, melt the butter over medium heat. Once it has melted, stir it with a small whisk until it begins to foam. Then keep the butter in motion with the whisk so you can keep an eye on the bottom of the pan—you're looking for small brown bits to start to form, 10-12 minutes.

2. Once you see a few brown bits, turn off the heat (if you have an induction or electric stovetop, remove the pan from the burner, as it will stay hot!), and continue to whisk it. The carry-over heat should be enough to finish browning the butter, without any risk of burning it. Transfer the butter to a storage container and refrigerate until thoroughly chilled, at least 2 hours.

3. Cut the brown butter into ½-inch / 1-cm pieces, then prepare the dough using your desired mixing method (see page 27).

4. Form the dough into a disk and wrap tightly in plastic wrap. Refrigerate for at least 30 minutes before using. This dough is best baked at 425°F / 220°C. Parbake (see page 43), blind-bake (see page 46), or fill and bake as directed in the recipe of your choice.

Make Ahead and Storage

The brown butter can be made up to 1 week ahead. The tightly wrapped disk of dough can be refrigerated for up to 3 days. Wrapped in plastic wrap and then aluminum foil, the dough can be frozen for up to 3 months. Thaw overnight in the fridge before using.

WHOLE WHEAT PIE DOUGH

MAKES ONE 9-INCH /
23-CM CRUST

DIFFICULTY: MEDIUM

While it is possible to make a dough 100 percent regular whole wheat flour, it requires significantly more hydration, and I find the resulting crust dense. Using a combination of whole wheat pastry flour and all-purpose flour is the perfect solution. The lower protein content of the pastry flour makes for a softer dough, but the pastry flour is 100 percent whole wheat. If you can't find whole wheat pastry flour, you can substitute 85 g / ¾ cup regular whole wheat flour.

90 g / ¾ cup all-purpose flour

73 g / ¾ cup whole wheat pastry flour
(see headnote)

1 g / ¼ teaspoon fine sea salt

113 g / 4 ounces / 8 tablespoons cold unsalted butter, cut into ½-inch / 13-mm cubes

75 g / ⅓ cup ice water, plus more as needed

1. In a medium bowl, whisk the all-purpose flour, whole wheat pastry flour, and salt together to combine. Prepare the dough using your desired mixing method (see page 27).

2. Form the dough into a disk and wrap tightly in plastic wrap. Refrigerate for at least 30 minutes before using. This dough is best baked at 425°F / 220°C. Parbake (see page 43), blind-bake (see page 46), or fill and bake as directed in the recipe of your choice.

VARIATIONS /////////////////////////////////////

HERBY WHOLE WHEAT PIE DOUGH: Whisk up to 3 tablespoons chopped fresh herbs into the flour mixture. My favorites are thyme, sage, rosemary, and oregano, or a combination.

GRAHAM FLOUR PIE DOUGH: Use 115 g / 1 cup graham flour and 60 g / ½ cup all-purpose flour.

Make Ahead and Storage

The tightly wrapped disk of dough can be refrigerated for up to 3 days. Wrapped in plastic wrap and then aluminum foil, the dough can be frozen for up to 3 months. Thaw overnight in the fridge before using.

CORNMEAL PIE DOUGH

MAKES ONE 9-INCH /
23-CM CRUST

DIFFICULTY: EASY

This golden yellow dough is lovely to work with, and it has a lovely texture once baked. If you're looking for even more texture, try the polenta variation below. This is a naturally mealier dough with a shorter, crumblier texture, which makes it particularly good for décor work.

120 g / 1 cup all-purpose flour

57 g / ½ cup fine yellow cornmeal

1 g / ¼ teaspoon fine sea salt

113 g / 4 ounces / 8 tablespoons cold unsalted butter, cut into ½-inch / 13-mm cubes

75 g / ⅓ cup ice water, plus more as needed

1. In a medium bowl, whisk the flour, cornmeal, and salt together to combine. Prepare the dough using your desired mixing method (see page 27).

2. Form the dough into a disk and wrap tightly in plastic wrap. Refrigerate for at least 30 minutes before using. This dough is best baked at 425°F / 220°C. Parbake (see page 43), blind-bake (see page 46), or fill and bake as directed in the recipe of your choice.

VARIATION

POLENTA PIE DOUGH: Replace the cornmeal with 80 g / ½ cup polenta. The dough may require additional hydration.

Make Ahead and Storage

The tightly wrapped disk of dough can be refrigerated for up to 3 days. Wrapped in plastic wrap and then aluminum foil, the dough can be frozen for up to 3 months. Thaw overnight in the fridge before using.

PIE-DEAS

Pie Doughs Made with Other Flours

These doughs are made with the addition of other flours to the all-purpose to introduce new flavors and textures. They are all insanely delicious and beautiful when baked.

The quantities given below are for a single 9-inch / 23-cm crust. Use the following combinations of flours in place of the full amount of all-purpose flour in the All-Buttah Pie Dough (page 48).

SPELT PIE DOUGH: 100 g / 1 cup spelt flour and 50 g / ½ cup all-purpose flour. Flaky and soft, like the All-Buttah Pie Dough.

SEMOLINA PIE DOUGH: 81 g / 1 cup semolina flour and 120 g / 1 cup all-purpose flour. Mealier and crisp, like the Cornmeal Pie Dough.

RYE PIE DOUGH: 80 g / ¾ cup white or medium rye flour and 90 g / ¾ cup all-purpose flour. Still flaky, but denser than the All-Buttah Pie Dough.

PUMPERNICKEL PIE DOUGH: 70 g / ⅔ cup pumpernickel flour, 90 g / ¾ cup all-purpose flour, and 11 g / 2 tablespoons dark or black cocoa powder (see Resources, page 345). Mealier and denser than the All-Buttah Pie Dough.

BUCKWHEAT PIE DOUGH: 60 g / ½ cup buckwheat flour and 120 g / 1 cup all-purpose flour. Mealier and denser than the All-Buttah Pie Dough.

CARAMELIZED PIE CRUST

MAKES ONE 9-INCH / 23-CM CRUST

DIFFICULTY: MEDIUM

When you make classic French *palmiers,* you roll puff pastry dough in granulated sugar before shaping and baking it, resulting in pastries with a caramelized outer crust. The same technique works with pie dough (and rough puff pastry). Roll the dough in sugar before using it to line the pie plate, and it will caramelize on the outside during baking (see Note). This dough is best used the same day it's made. The high oven temperature ensures the sugar melts, then caramelizes firm on the dough—don't fret about it sticking to the pie plate, but take care not to overbake, as this crust is more prone to burning!

1 recipe pie dough, chilled

50 g / ¼ cup granulated sugar, plus more as needed

1. Roll out the chilled dough on a lightly floured surface to about ½ inch / 1 cm thick. Brush/scrape away any excess flour from the dough and work surface. Sprinkle the top of the dough and the work surface with the sugar and roll the dough out to the desired thickness. Sprinkle more sugar on the work surface and/or dough as needed throughout the remainder of the rolling. Line a pie plate with the dough (see page 34); see Note about chilling the crust.

2. This dough is best baked at 400°F / 205°C. To parbake, dock the crust and bake for 16 to 19 minutes with pie weights, until the crust is beginning to turn pale golden around the edges. Remove the weights and bake for 4 to 6 minutes more, until the crust is lightly golden. To blind-bake the crust, dock the crust, and parbake, baking for 8 to 10 minutes after removing the pie weights, until evenly golden.

VARIATIONS //////////////////////////////

CITRUS-VANILLA CARAMELIZED PIE CRUST: Rub the grated zest of 1 orange, grated zest of 1 lemon, and the seeds scraped from ½ vanilla bean (halved lengthwise) into the sugar. Let the sugar sit for at least 2 hours before using.

SNICKERDOODLE CARAMELIZED PIE CRUST: Stir 1¼ teaspoons ground cinnamon into the sugar before using.

NOTE ◇◇◇◇◇◇◇◇◇◇◇◇◇◇◇◇◇◇◇◇◇◇◇

While pie dough usually benefits from being refrigerated after it's used to line the pie plate and crimped, if the caramelized crust is held in the fridge for too long, the sugar will start to get sticky. It's best to limit refrigeration before baking to 40 minutes maximum.

Make Ahead and Storage

The tightly wrapped disk of dough can be made up to 3 days ahead. Once rolled in sugar, the dough should be used immediately (or after chilling—see Note)

GOLDEN CHEESE PIE DOUGH

MAKES ONE 9-INCH /
23-CM CRUST

DIFFICULTY: MEDIUM

This dough bakes up to a beautiful, totally-even-all-over sort of golden brown—don't be surprised if it's a shade or two darker than traditional pie dough. It's great for savory recipes, of course, but it's also good for sweet pies when you want to add a salty twist (like the Apple Pie, page 145). This dough is particularly yummy made using the mixing method for Rough Puff Pastry (see page 50).

150 g / 1¼ cups all-purpose flour

1 g / ¼ teaspoon fine sea salt

113 g / 4 ounces / 8 tablespoons cold unsalted butter, cut into ½-inch / 1-cm cubes

113 g / 4 ounces shredded firm or semi-firm cheese, such as white cheddar, Gruyère, Manchego, or Parmesan

60 g / ¼ cup ice water, plus more as needed

1. In a medium bowl, whisk together the flour and salt. Mix in the butter as directed in your chosen mixing method (see page 27). Stir in the shredded cheese. Add the water as directed in your mixing method.

2. Form the dough into a disk and wrap tightly in plastic wrap. Refrigerate for at least 30 minutes before using. This dough is best baked at 425°F / 220°C. Parbake (see page 43), blind-bake (see page 46), or fill and bake as directed in the recipe of your choice.

Make Ahead and Storage

The tightly wrapped disk of dough can be refrigerated for up to 2 days. Wrapped in plastic wrap and then aluminum foil, the dough can be frozen for up to 1 month. Thaw overnight in the fridge before using.

SAFFRON COMPOUND BUTTER PIE DOUGH

MAKES TWO 9-INCH /
23 CM-CRUSTS

DIFFICULTY: HARD

This delicious method incorporates flavor into the pie dough by infusing the butter with saffron or blending it with other flavorful ingredients (see variations below). While not strictly required, these doughs benefit from being refrigerated overnight before using. If you don't have time for that, chill the dough for at least 2 hours before using. This dough is classified as "Hard" not because it's difficult to make, but because it can be a little trickier to work with, as the dough can be a little wetter or stickier by nature. Take care when adding the water to ensure you don't overhydrate.

226 g / 8 ounces unsalted butter

Scant 1 g / ½ teaspoon saffron threads

300 g / 2½ cups all-purpose flour

2 g / ½ teaspoon fine sea salt

75 g / ⅓ cup ice water, plus more as needed

1. In a medium saucepan, melt the butter over medium heat. Crumble the saffron threads into the butter, cover the pan, remove from the heat, and let steep for 15 minutes.

2. Transfer the butter to a storage container and refrigerate until thoroughly chilled, at least 2 hours.

3. Cut the chilled butter into ½-inch / 1-cm pieces and make the dough using your desired mixing method (see page 27).

4. Divide the dough in half, form each piece into a disk, and wrap tightly in plastic wrap. Refrigerate for at least 2 hours before using. This dough is best baked at 400°F / 205°C. To parbake this crust, bake for 15 to 17 minutes with pie weights, until the crust is beginning to turn pale golden around the edges, then remove the weights and bake for 4 to 6 minutes longer, until the crust is lightly golden. To blind-bake the crust, parbake, baking for 8 to 10 minutes longer after removing the pie weights, until evenly golden.

VARIATIONS

CHIVE, SCALLION, OR RAMP PIE DOUGH: Use room-temperature butter rather than melting it. In a food processor, blend the soft butter with 130 g / 4½ ounces (about 1 medium bunch) chives, scallions, or ramps, then proceed with the recipe. Increase the flour to 330 g / 2¾ cups.

ROASTED GARLIC PIE DOUGH: Cut the top quarter off a medium head of garlic (about 60 to 70 grams) and place on a piece of foil large enough to enclose it. Drizzle with 10 g / 2 teaspoons extra-virgin olive oil, then wrap in the foil. Roast in a 400°F / 205°C oven for 25 to 30 minutes, until the cloves are deeply caramelized. Let the garlic cool completely, then squeeze the cloves out of their skins into the bowl of a food processor. Use room-temperature butter rather than melting it. Puree the soft butter with the garlic, then proceed with the recipe. Increase the flour to 330 g / 2¾ cups.

SUN-DRIED TOMATO PIE DOUGH: Use room-temperature butter rather than melting it. Puree the softened butter with 83 g / ½ cup roughly chopped sun-dried tomatoes (the oil-packed kind), well drained and patted dry, then proceed with the recipe. Increase the flour to 330 g / 2¾ cups.

Make Ahead and Storage

The tightly wrapped disks of dough can be refrigerated for up to 2 days. Wrapped in plastic wrap and then aluminum foil, the dough can be frozen for up to 2 months. Thaw overnight in the fridge before using.

PÂTE BRISÉE

MAKES ONE 9-INCH /
23-CM CRUST

DIFFICULTY: EASY

Pâte brisée is a French pastry dough that is easy to make and a little less temperamental than my classic All-Buttah Pie Dough (page 48) can be. It's got a tighter structure, because the butter is mixed in more thoroughly and left in very small pieces. Unlike larger pieces of butter, which result in airy flakiness, these small dispersed pieces create a dough that has a sturdiness that's easy to work with. Although its texture is more crumbly than my All-Buttah dough, it is still tender and has a flaky mouthfeel. It is great dough to use for décor. I like to make mine in the food processor, which also makes it especially quick and easy.

150 g / 1¼ cups all-purpose flour

2 g / ½ teaspoon fine sea salt

113 g / 4 ounces / 8 tablespoons cold unsalted butter, cut into ½-inch / 13-mm cubes

45 g / 3 tablespoons ice water, plus more if needed

1. In the bowl of a food processor, pulse the flour and salt to combine. Add the butter and pulse until the mixture resembles coarse meal. Drizzle the water over the flour mixture and pulse to incorporate. If the dough comes together into a ball, immediately stop mixing. If the dough is dry or crumbly, add more water 15 g / 1 tablespoon at a time, pulsing until it comes together.

2. Form the dough into a disk and wrap tightly in plastic wrap. Refrigerate for at least 30 minutes before using. This dough is best baked at 400°F / 205°C. To parbake the crust, bake for 15 to 17 minutes with pie weights, until the crust is beginning to turn pale golden around the edges, then remove the weights and bake for 3 to 5 minutes longer, until the crust is lightly golden. To blind-bake the crust, parbake, baking for 7 to 10 minutes longer after removing the pie weights, until evenly golden.

Make Ahead and Storage

The tightly wrapped disk of dough can be refrigerated for up to 3 days. Wrapped in plastic wrap and then aluminum foil, the dough can be frozen for up to 3 months. Thaw overnight in the fridge before using.

HOT-WATER CRUST

MAKES ONE 9-INCH / 23-CM DEEP-DISH DOUBLE CRUST OR ENOUGH DOUGH FOR UP TO 12 MINI PIES (DEPENDING ON THE SIZE OF THE BAKING PANS)

DIFFICULTY: MEDIUM

A hot-water crust is the traditional pie crust across the pond. It breaks all the rules, as it is made with boiling water and rolled out immediately, with no chilling. My hot-water crust can also be pressed into the pan, rather than rolled out. It's tender and has a tasty butteriness, but its baked texture is crumblier. Because the crust is impressively sturdy, it can be used for double-crust applications or for beautifully tall, impressive deep-dish pies, even with heavy fillings; I particularly love it for savory pies. I use a blend of all-purpose flour and a bit of bread flour, which has a higher protein content and makes the dough even sturdier.

I don't usually parbake or blind-bake hot-water crusts. The crust is baked at a lower temperature for longer than most doughs, which means it doesn't need to be parbaked, even when it will be filled with a heavy or juicy filling.

113 g / 4 ounces / 8 tablespoons cold unsalted butter, cut into ¼-inch / 6-mm cubes

170 g / ¾ cup cold lard or shortening, cut into ¼-inch / 6-mm cubes

76 g / ⅓ cup boiling water, plus more as needed

330 g / 2¾ cups all-purpose flour

40 g / ⅓ cup bread flour

5 g / 1 teaspoon fine sea salt

1. In a medium heatproof bowl, combine the butter and lard or shortening. Pour the boiling water over the fat and use a large fork to stir to combine—some of the fat will melt into the water, but there will still be some larger pieces.

2. Add the flours and salt all at once and stir to combine. Use the fork at first to begin to distribute the water throughout the flour, then switch to a spatula to continue mixing until the dough comes together. If necessary, add additional water 15 g / 1 tablespoon at a time until the dough comes together. Once the dough has formed a ball, let stand until it's cool enough to handle.

3. Knead the dough until uniformly combined. If making a deep-dish pie, divide the dough into 2 pieces: Use two thirds of the dough for the bottom crust, and the remainder of the dough for the top crust. Or, if making mini pies, divide the dough in half.

4. The dough is now ready to be pressed into the pan or rolled out. If you struggle with the dough, wrap it tightly in plastic wrap and refrigerate it for 15 to 20 minutes before proceeding. In any case, if making a deep-dish pie, wrap the portion for the top crust in plastic wrap while you work with the bottom crust.

5. Roll out the dough between two pieces of parchment paper to about ¼ inch / 6 mm thick. Start with a light dusting of flour on both sides of the dough and reapply as needed. As you roll, use the parchment to flip the dough over, peel the parchment away, and replace it before you continue rolling (this helps keep the dough from sticking to the parchment).

6. Use the parchment paper or the rolling pin to transfer the crust to the pie plate. Patch any rips or tears with excess dough. Fill with the filling, then roll out the top crust in the same fashion and transfer to the top of the pie. While specific baking instructions may vary depending on the type of filling, this crust is generally best baked at 350°F to 375°F / 175°C to 190°C.

Make Ahead and Storage ────────

This crust is best used the same day it's made.

THE WHYS OF PIES

How Do You Press in Pie Dough?

I learned this method from Amanda Hesser, cofounder and CEO of Food52, and it makes a beautifully even crust.

To press the dough into a pan, it's easiest to start with the edges of the pan. Place clumps of the dough around the edges of the pan and then press into an even layer, working your way around the pan until the outer portion of the pan is evenly covered. Then crumble the remaining dough into the center of the pan and press into an even layer until the bottom of the pan is completely covered. This is the easiest way to ensure you don't end up with too much dough in the corners of the pan; sometimes I use the bottom of a small dry measuring cup or a dough tamper to help press the dough in evenly, especially in the corners. Then smooth the dough with your finger to even out any thicker spots. If desired, use a paring knife held flush against the rim of the pan to trim away the excess dough, leaving a clean edge.

ROLL-OUT COOKIE CRUST

MAKES ONE 9-INCH /
23-CM CRUST

DIFFICULTY: MEDIUM

This cookie crust is that "just right" combination of lightly crisp at the edges but still soft enough to easily get a fork through. Due to its shorter texture, I do not recommend it for double-crust pies—though it can be used in shallow, more tart-like preparations, like the Jam Cookie Tart (page 189). And because of that texture, it makes a great tart shell for simple fillings like whipped cream and fresh fruit or jam.

Like any roll-out cookie dough, this is made using the creaming method to aerate and combine the fat and sugar before adding the remaining ingredients. Note, though, that it is made with a much lower amount of a chemical leavener (here baking soda) than traditional cookie recipes, as more soda (or baking powder) would cause the crust to puff up more than is desirable. Keep this in mind in case you want to have a go at turning one of your favorite roll-out cookie recipes into a crust!

113 g / 4 ounces / 8 tablespoons unsalted butter, at room temperature
50 g / ¼ cup granulated sugar
35 g / 1 large egg white, lightly whisked
5 g / 1 teaspoon vanilla extract (optional)
180 g / 1½ cups all-purpose flour
2 g / ½ teaspoon fine sea salt
1 g / ¼ teaspoon baking powder

1. In the bowl of a stand mixer fitted with the paddle attachment, cream the butter and sugar on medium-low speed until smooth, 2 to 3 minutes. Add the egg white and vanilla, if using, and mix on medium speed to combine. Scrape the bowl well. Add the flour, salt, and baking powder and mix on low speed until fully incorporated, 45 to 60 seconds.

2. Form the dough into a 1-inch / 2.5-cm-thick disk and wrap tightly in plastic wrap. Refrigerate for at least 30 minutes (or up to 3 days).

3. On a lightly floured surface (or between two pieces of parchment paper; see page 36), roll out the dough to ¼ inch / 6 mm thick. Use the rolling pin to transfer the dough to the pan, unfurling it into the pan, and line the pan as directed on page 34. Use a paring knife held flush against the rim of the pan to trim away the excess dough, leaving a clean edge. Dock the dough all over with a fork, then chill for at least 30 minutes, or freeze until firm, before using.

4. This crust is best baked at 350°F / 175°C. To parbake the crust, bake, without pie weights, for 15 to 18 minutes, until the crust is beginning to turn lightly golden. To blind-bake the crust, bake for 20 to 22 minutes, until evenly golden.

Try rolling out cookie crusts with an engraved or embossed rolling pin, then chill it well—it will leave its impression behind after baking.

VARIATIONS

CHOCOLATE ROLL-OUT COOKIE CRUST: Replace 30 g / ¼ cup of the all-purpose flour with 28 g / ⅓ cup unsweetened cocoa powder.

BROWN SUGAR ROLL-OUT COOKIE CRUST: Replace the granulated sugar with 53 g / ¼ cup packed light or dark brown sugar.

CITRUS ROLL-OUT COOKIE CRUST: Add up to 3 tablespoons / zest of 2 medium citrus fruits (or 1 large) grated citrus zest to the butter and sugar in Step 1.

ALMOND ROLL-OUT COOKIE CRUST: Substitute 48 g / ½ cup almond flour (toasted and cooled, if you like) for 30 g / ¼ cup of the all-purpose flour.

SPICED ROLL-OUT COOKIE CRUST: Add up to 14 g / 1½ tablespoons ground spice (or a mixture of a few) to the flour before adding it to the dough.

Here are a few of my favorite combinations:

- 9 g / 1 tablespoon ground cinnamon, 2 g / ½ teaspoon ground ginger, less than 1 g / ¼ teaspoon ground cloves, less than 1 g / ¼ teaspoon ground nutmeg
- 6 g / 2 teaspoons ground ginger, 2 g / ½ teaspoon ground cloves, and 2 g / ½ teaspoon ground allspice
- 6 g / 2 teaspoons ground cardamom, 6 g / 2 teaspoons ground cinnamon, less than 1 g / ¼ teaspoon ground nutmeg

Make Ahead and Storage

The tightly wrapped disk of dough can be refrigerated for up to 3 days. Wrapped in plastic wrap and then aluminum foil, the dough can be frozen for up to 1 month. Thaw overnight in the fridge before using.

PRESS-IN COOKIE CRUST

MAKES ONE 9-INCH /
23-CM CRUST OR
12 INDIVIDUAL PIE/TART
CRUSTS

DIFFICULTY: EASY

This press-in cookie crust is as easy as cookie dough to make: Just mix the ingredients together, then press into your pie plate—no rolling required. Press-in crust recipes cannot be used to make double-crust pies, but the same dough can often be crumbled over the top as a sort of crumble/streusel topping. See the variations below for different flavor combos, or come up with your own!

113 g / 4 ounces / 8 tablespoons unsalted butter, at room temperature

50 g / ¼ cup granulated sugar

21 g / 1 large egg yolk

5 g / 1 teaspoon vanilla extract (optional)

210 g / 1¾ cups all-purpose flour

2 g / ½ teaspoon fine sea salt

15 g / 1 tablespoon water

1. In the bowl of a stand mixer fitted with the paddle attachment, cream the butter and sugar on medium-low speed until smooth, 2 to 3 minutes. Add the egg yolk and vanilla, if using, and mix on medium speed to combine. Scrape the bowl well. Add the flour and salt and mix on low speed until fully incorporated, 45 seconds to 1 minute. Add the water and mix just until the dough is smooth, about 1 minute more.

2. Turn out the dough and use your fingers to press it into the pan or pans (see sidebar, page 61). Chill for at least 30 minutes, or up to overnight.

3. This crust is best baked at 350°F / 175°C. To parbake the crust, parbake, without pie weights, for 15 to 18 minutes, until the crust is beginning to turn lightly golden. To blind-bake the crust, bake for 20 to 22 minutes, until evenly golden.

VARIATIONS

CHOCOLATE PRESS-IN COOKIE CRUST: Replace 30 g / ¼ cup of the all-purpose flour with 28 g / ⅓ cup unsweetened cocoa powder.

BROWN BUTTER PRESS-IN COOKIE CRUST: Melt the butter in a medium saucepan over medium heat. Reduce the heat to low and cook, stirring occasionally, until the butter begins to simmer and foam, the milk solids turn brown, and the butter smells toasty, 10 to 12 minutes. Cool the butter to room temperature before proceeding with the recipe.

NUT BUTTER PRESS-IN COOKIE CRUST: Replace 43 g / 3 tablespoons of the butter with 68 g / ¼ cup nut butter. Replace the sugar with 53 g / ¼ packed cup light brown sugar. Omit the water.

CHOCOLATE CHIP PRESS-IN COOKIE CRUST: Replace the granulated sugar with 53 g / ¼ cup packed light brown sugar. Replace the water with 15 g / 1 tablespoon milk. After the crust has come together, stir in 113 g / ¾ cup finely chopped chocolate or mini chocolate chips.

OATMEAL PRESS-IN COOKIE CRUST: Replace the granulated sugar with 53 g / ¼ cup packed light brown sugar. Replace 30 g / ¼ cup of the flour with 74 g / ¾ cup rolled oats.

COCONUT PRESS-IN COOKIE CRUST: Replace the granulated sugar with 53 g / ¼ cup packed light brown sugar. Add 50 g / ⅔ cup toasted unsweetened shredded coconut with the flour in step 1.

Make Ahead and Storage

Tightly wrapped in plastic wrap, the dough can be refrigerated for up to 2 days; bring to room temperature before using. Wrapped in plastic wrap and then aluminum foil, the dough can be frozen for up to 3 months. Thaw overnight in the refrigerator before using.

OLIVE OIL PRESS-IN CRUST

MAKES ONE 9-INCH /
23-CM CRUST

DIFFICULTY: EASY

The basic crust recipe works well in both savory and sweet applications, but the variations below using different flavors and types of oils skew more savory.

240 g / 2 cups all-purpose flour
1 g / ¼ teaspoon fine sea salt
60 g / ¼ cup olive oil
75 g / ⅓ cup cold water, plus more as needed

1. In a medium bowl, stir the flour and salt together to combine. Add the olive oil and water and mix until the dough forms a ball. Don't worry if it seems a touch gluey.

2. Turn out the dough and use your fingers to press it into the pan (see sidebar, page 61). Chill for at least 1 hour, or up to overnight.

3. Dock the dough all over with a fork, then fill and bake according to the instructions in your recipe of choice. This crust is best baked at 375°F / 190°C. To parbake the crust, parbake, without pie weights, for 15 to 18 minutes, until the crust is beginning to turn lightly golden. To blind-bake the crust, bake for 25 to 30 minutes, until evenly golden.

VARIATIONS

HERBY OLIVE OIL PRESS-IN CRUST: Stir up to 8 g / 3 tablespoons chopped fresh herbs into the flour in step 1.

CURRY OIL PRESS-IN CRUST: In a small saucepan, heat the oil over low heat for 1 minute. Whisk in 6 g / 1 tablespoon curry powder and heat for 30 seconds. Let the mixture cool to room temperature before using.

SMOKED PAPRIKA–OLIVE OIL PRESS-IN CRUST: Stir 6 g / 2 teaspoons smoked paprika into the flour in step 1.

SESAME OIL PRESS-IN CRUST: Reduce the olive oil to 30 g / 2 tablespoons and add 30 g / 2 tablespoons sesame oil along with the olive oil.

TRUFFLE OIL PRESS-IN CRUST: Reduce the olive oil to 45 g / 3 tablespoons olive oil and add 15 g / 1 tablespoon truffle oil along with the olive oil.

Make Ahead and Storage

The dough can be made up to 1 day ahead and refrigerated. This crust is best used the day it's baked.

BASIC CRUMB CRUST

MAKES ONE 9-INCH / 23-CM CRUST

DIFFICULTY: EASY

Crumb crusts are even easier than press-in cookie crusts. You don't even have to bake them—see the variation at right. The crumbs can be made out of cookies, crackers, cereal, pretzels, even potato chips! Sometimes sugar or other flavorings are added to the crumbs (here the sugar is optional), and then fat (usually melted butter) is added to bind the mixture to form a crust. The crumbs can be coarse, for a crunchier texture, or finer, for a smoother texture. Different base ingredients will behave differently, so the first time I test a crumb crust with a new ingredient, I always have a little extra on hand in case I need more crumbs, or a little extra melted butter, should it be needed.

Crumb crusts don't generally require chilling before baking, but you can refrigerate for up to 1 hour or freeze for 15 minutes, if desired, to firm them up before baking. I'm also including information in a chart on page 40 to help you adapt this easy recipe for any pan size.

210 g / 1¾ cups cookie, cereal, chip, or cracker crumbs

Up to 50 g / ¼ cup granulated sugar (optional)

2 g / ½ teaspoon fine sea salt

85 g / 3 ounces / 6 tablespoons unsalted butter, melted, plus more if needed

1. In a medium bowl, stir the crumbs, sugar, if using, and salt together to combine. Stir in the melted butter and mix to combine. The crust should easily hold together in clumps when you press it together between your fingers (if it doesn't, add a little more melted butter, 14 g / 1 tablespoon at a time, until it does).

2. Press the crust evenly into the bottom and up the sides of an ungreased 9-inch / 23-cm pie plate: First make an even layer in the bottom of the pan, then press the rest of the crumbs up the sides (or halfway up the sides—see page 61). Sometimes I use the bottom of a small dry measuring cup to help press the crust in evenly; this is especially helpful in the corners of the pan.

3. Preheat the oven to 350°F / 175°C (don't use a Baking Steel/stone when baking a crumb crust). To parbake the crust, bake (no docking or pie weights required) for 10 to 12 minutes, until it begins to lightly brown at the edges (or, for darker crumbs, smells lightly toasty). To blind-bake the crust, bake for 15 to 17 minutes, until it is deeply golden brown and/or smells toasty.

MINI (TWO-BITE) CRUMB CRUSTS: Grease the cavities of a mini muffin pan with nonstick spray. Crumble or spoon 15 g / 1 tablespoon of the prepared crust mixture into each of the cavities. Press each portion with your fingers to be flush against the base and up the sides, taking care to press evenly all the way around. Chill the pan in the refrigerator for 15 to 20 minutes, before baking at 350°F / 175°C for 10 to 12 minutes. Cool completely, then use a small offset spatula to unmold the shells before filling. Alternatively, the mini crusts can be frozen for 2 hours after assembling before using a small offset spatula to unmold the pie shells. Keep frozen until ready to fill.

UNBAKED CRUMB CRUST: For cream, chiffon, and cold-set pies, the crust doesn't need to be baked at all! After lining the pan with the crust, freeze it for at least 15 minutes before adding the filling.

Make Ahead and Storage

This crust is best used the day it's made but can be parbaked or blind-baked up to 1 day ahead and stored at room temperature.

PIE PEP TALK

What to Do When a Crumb Crust Shrinks

One of the most common problems I've seen with crumb crusts is that they can shrink or slump down the side of the pie plate when the crust is parbaked. Luckily, this is easily corrected. If you notice that your crust is starting to shrink, remove it from the oven and use a crust tamper (see page 20) or a small metal measuring cup to press the crust that slumped down back up the sides of the pie plate. If this happens consistently when you make crumb crusts, try tamping them down more aggressively and/or refrigerating for 30 minutes before baking.

Scaling Up Crumb Crusts

The basic crumb crust recipe (page 66) makes enough for one 9-inch pie, 35 crusts in mini muffin pans, or 14 crusts in classic muffin pans. Below are yields and amounts for increasing the crust. If you have extra crust, you can freeze it for up to 3 months in a zip-top freezer bag (thaw before reusing).

FOR 1.25 RECIPES: 171 g / 2 cups crumbs, 99 g / 3½ ounces / 7 tablespoons butter, melted

FOR 1.5: 229 g / 2⅔ cups crumbs, 128 g / 4½ ounces / 9 tablespoons butter, melted

FOR 1.75: 258 g / 3 cups crumbs, 142 g / 5 ounces / 10 tablespoons butter, melted

FOR 2: 301 g / 3½ cups crumbs, 170 g / 6 ounces / 12 tablespoons butter, melted

FOR 2.25: 323 g / 3¾ cups crumbs, 185 g / 6½ ounces / 13 tablespoons butter, melted

FOR 2.50: 370 g / 4⅓ cup crumbs, 213 g / 7½ ounces / 15 tablespoons butter, melted

FOR 2.75: 409 g / 4¾ cups crumbs, 226 g / 8 ounces butter, melted

FOR 3.00: 452 g / 5¼ cups crumbs, 255 g / 9 ounces butter, melted

FOR 3.25: 482 g / 5⅔ cups crumbs, 269 g / 9½ ounces butter, melted

Crumb Crust Amounts for Different Pan Sizes

PAN	NUMBER OF RECIPES NEEDED		
	BOTTOM ONLY	BOTTOM AND HALFWAY UP SIDES OF PAN	BOTTOM AND SIDES
MINI MUFFIN PAN (35 CRUSTS) MUFFIN PAN (14 CRUSTS)	—	—	1
9-INCH / 23-CM PIE PLATE	—	1	1
10-INCH / 25-CM PIE PLATE	—	1	1.25
9-INCH / 23-CM DEEP-DISH PIE PLATE	—	1.25	1.5
10-IN / 25-CM DEEP-DISH PIE PLATE	—	1.5	1.75
9-INCH SPRINGFORM PAN	1.25	2.25	3
8-BY-8-INCH BAKING PAN	1.25	1.75	2.25
9-BY-9-INCH BAKING PAN	1.5	2	2.5
9-BY-13-INCH BAKING PAN OR 9½-BY-13-INCH QUARTER SHEET PAN	2.5	2.75	3.25

CEREAL-TREAT CRUST

MAKES ONE 9-INCH /
23-CM CRUST

DIFFICULTY: EASY

In our family, someone always brings a tray of Rice Krispies or other cereal treats to any type of gathering. And even when there are tons of other more impressive desserts, the treats are always the first to go. I've tweaked my standard recipe to fit into a pie plate. It's fun to fill it with anything from ice cream to puddings to whipped cream and fresh fruit!

Up to 85 g / 2½ cups cereal, such as crisped
  rice cereal (exact weight may vary based
  on variety)
28 g / 1 ounce / 2 tablespoons salted butter
99 g / ¾ cup marshmallow creme

1. Lightly grease a 9-inch / 23-cm pie plate with nonstick spray. Place the cereal in a medium bowl.

2. In a small pot, heat the butter and marshmallow creme over medium-low heat, stirring constantly, until fully melted, 2 to 3 minutes. Pour the butter/marshmallow mixture over the cereal and use a silicone spatula to stir until the cereal is well coated.

3. Pour the mixture into the prepared pie plate and use a small metal measuring cup (grease the base lightly with nonstick spray to make it easier) to press the mixture into an even layer in the bottom and up the sides of the pie plate. Press very firmly to tightly pack the crust in place. Let the crust sit for 20 minutes to set before filling it.

VARIATION
PEANUT BUTTER CEREAL-TREAT CRUST: Replace 14 g / 1 tablespoon of the butter with 29 g / 2 tablespoons creamy peanut butter and add a pinch of fine sea salt.

Make Ahead and Storage
The crust can be made up to 2 days ahead and stored at room temperature, tightly covered with plastic wrap.

NOTE ◇◇◇◇◇◇◇◇◇◇◇◇◇◇◇◇◇◇◇◇◇◇◇◇◇◇◇
This recipe can be doubled for a springform pan.

PIE-DEA

Peanut Butter Choco-Schmallow Pie

Try this dreamy, candy-bar-like pie with a Cereal-Treat Crust. Start with a double batch of cereal-treat crust (regular or peanut butter), pressed into a springform pan. Once the crust has cooled, make the Chocolate Filling from the Black Forest Pie on page 250, and strain it into the prepared crust. Cover directly with plastic wrap and refrigerate until completely chilled. Make the Marshmallow Topping on page 117. Remove the plastic wrap from the chocolate filling and pour the marshmallow on top of it. Cool completely, then top with 1 recipe of the Peanut Butter Cream Filling from the Peanut Butter Cream Pie on page 264. Keep chilled until ready to serve.

COCONUT MACAROON CRUST

MAKES ONE 9-INCH / 23-CM CRUST

DIFFICULTY: EASY

I've always loved the combination of fruit with coconut macaroons, which led me to try my hand at making a macaroon crust. The crust gets lightly crisp on the outside but keeps a little bit of chew in the center. This is an awesomely easy and delicious crust I now turn to again and again.

50 g / ¼ cup granulated sugar

35 g / 1 large egg white

14 g / ½ ounce / 1 tablespoon unsalted butter, melted

5 g / 1 teaspoon vanilla extract or 1 g / ¼ teaspoon almond extract (optional)

2 g / ½ teaspoon fine sea salt

170 g / 1½ cups unsweetened shredded coconut

1. Preheat the oven to 325°F / 165°C. Lightly grease a 9-inch / 23-cm pie plate with nonstick spray.

2. In a medium bowl, whisk the sugar, egg white, melted butter, extract, if using, and salt together to combine. Mix only until the mixture is even—don't whisk so much you begin to make the mixture frothy. Switch to a silicone spatula and stir in the coconut.

3. Transfer the mixture to the prepared pie plate and use the spatula to help you press it evenly into the pan. Eventually you'll need to switch to a smaller utensil—or use your hands—to press it evenly into the pan, taking care to press it evenly into the corners of the pan.

4. To parbake the crust, bake (no pie weights needed) for 12 to 14 minutes, until lightly golden at the edges. To blind-bake the crust, bake for 18 to 20 minutes, until deeply golden brown at the edges and starting to brown on the bottom. Cool completely before filling.

Make Ahead and Storage

The crust can be parbaked or blind-baked up to 1 day ahead and stored at room temperature, tightly covered with plastic wrap. The recipe can be doubled for a deep-dish or springform pan.

HAYSTACK CRUST

MAKES ONE 9-INCH /
23-CM CRUST

DIFFICULTY: EASY

Every Christmas, my mom makes huge batches of a no-bake cookie my family loves. We call them haystacks, and I've seen tons of variations over the years. Despite their simplicity, they'd sell out at fundraising bake sales and were always the first items to fly out of our holiday cookie boxes. Adapting this simple no-bake recipe into a pie crust was a no-brainer, for a super-easy sweet, chocolatey crust that comes together in no time.

170 g / 6 ounces chow mein noodles
　　(about 3 cups)
170 g / 6 ounces semisweet chocolate chips,
　　or semisweet chocolate, finely chopped
170 g / 6 ounces butterscotch chips
Pinch of fine sea salt

1. Lightly grease a 9-inch / 23-cm pie plate with nonstick spray (or coat with a thin layer of softened butter). Place the noodles in large zip-top bag, seal the bag, and run a rolling pin over them a few times to break them up into smaller pieces—but not so much that they begin to turn powdery. Transfer to a medium bowl.

2. Melt the chocolate chips and butterscotch chips together with the salt either in a heatproof bowl set over a medium saucepan of simmering water (or use a double boiler) or in the microwave in 20-second bursts, stirring often. The mixture should be totally smooth and lump-free, but be careful not to overheat it, which would cause it to seize and become dry and clumpy—and you'd end up having to start over. Pour the mixture over the crushed noodles and stir until all the noodles are coated.

3. Transfer the mixture to the prepared pie plate and use the spatula to help you press it evenly into the pan. Eventually you'll need to switch to a smaller utensil—or use your hands—to press it evenly into the pan (but this recipe is worth chocolatey fingers). Let the crust sit at room temperature until completely set and firm, at least 30 minutes, before filling it.

VARIATION //
COCONUT HAYSTACK CRUST: Substitute 226 g / 2 cups unsweetened shredded coconut for the chow mein noodles. You don't have to toast the coconut, but the crust will be especially delicious if you do.

Make Ahead and Storage

The crust can be made up to 3 days ahead and stored at room temperature, covered tightly with plastic wrap.

MERINGUE CRUST

MAKES ONE 9-INCH / 23-CM CRUST

DIFFICULTY: HARD

Inspired by my dear friend Rose Levy Beranbaum, this meringue crust is as yummy as it is beautiful—crisp on the outside with a delicious marshmallowy interior. Piping the meringue into the pie plate is the easiest way to ensure it's even all over. If you prefer, though, you can dollop the meringue over the bottom of the pie plate and use a small offset spatula to spread it as evenly as possible over the bottom and up the sides.

Try a free-form round of meringue (either piped or spread) to place on top of your pie for a beautiful finish and a fun textural element (like on the Eton Mess Pie on page 282).

28 g / ¼ cup cornstarch
28 g / ¼ cup powdered sugar
142 g / 4 large egg whites
Scant 1 g / ¼ teaspoon cream of tartar
198 g / 1 cup granulated sugar
5 g / 1 teaspoon vanilla extract (optional)

1. Preheat the oven to 250°F / 120°C.

2. Sift the cornstarch and powdered sugar together into a small bowl. Lightly but thoroughly grease a 9-inch / 23-cm pie plate with nonstick spray, then sift the cornstarch/powdered sugar mixture evenly over it. Be sure the plate is covered—a little bit excess in some spots is preferable to a dry/uncovered spot.

3. In the bowl of a stand mixer fitted with the whip attachment, whip the egg whites with the cream of tartar on medium speed until they begin to look foamy, about 1 minute. Raise the speed to medium-high and whip until the mixture begins to turn white, 30 seconds to 1 minute more. With the mixer running, gradually add the granulated sugar in a slow, steady stream, then continue to whip to medium peaks, 2 to 4 minutes more. Add the vanilla, if using, and mix to combine.

4. The meringue is now ready to be transferred to the prepared pie plate, and the easiest way to do this is to use a piping bag. Cut a ½-inch / 1-cm opening in a disposable pastry bag (or in a bottom corner of a large zip-top bag), or you can use a star tip or other tip to create a beautiful decorative effect. Fill the piping bag with the meringue (you may have to do this in two batches).

5. Pipe the meringue into a tight spiral over the bottom of the pie plate, then pipe a ring around the edge of the base to start to build up the sides. Continue to pipe rings around the sides of the plate until you get to the rim. If desired, you can pipe a decorative final ring to mimic a pie edge or crimp.

6. Gently transfer the pie plate to the oven and immediately lower the temperature to 200°F / 93°C. Bake until the meringue is dry to the touch without any noticeable browning, 2 to 2½ hours. Turn off the oven and let the meringue sit inside for 15 minutes. Then remove the meringue and let it stand at room temperature until completely cool and dry. Once it's cooled, put it somewhere safe and out of the way; if possible, cover it with a large bowl to help protect it from moisture or damage (it's very fragile) until you are ready to fill it.

Make Ahead and Storage

The meringue crust is best used the day it is made.

Meringue Topper

To bake a free-form meringue topper, line a baking sheet
with parchment paper. (If desired, trace an outline or shape
as a guide onto the paper, then flip the paper over.) Pipe
the desired shape directly on the parchment paper, using
the marks as a guide. When using larger piping tips, you may
need to increase the recipe to make more meringue.

BASIC NUT CRUST

MAKES ONE 9-INCH / 23-CM CRUST

DIFFICULTY: EASY

I made my first nut crust as a gluten-free alternative to regular pie crust, but then I fell in love with the toasty flavor, particularly when I made it with pistachios, pecans, walnuts, or pine nuts. The method is also really easy, and it's adaptable for any kind of nut. I find it easiest to chop the nuts for the crust in the food processor to make sure they're fine enough, and uniform.

Nut crusts can be parbaked or blind-baked but note that these crusts aren't super-sturdy until baked. If desired, you can freeze the crust for 20 to 30 minutes before filling and baking to firm it up. Nut crusts are not recommended for double-crust applications.

325 g / 2½ cups finely chopped nuts (see headnote)

Up to 37 g / 3 tablespoons granulated sugar

2 g / ½ teaspoon fine sea salt

56 g / 2 ounces / 4 tablespoons unsalted butter, melted

35 g / 1 large egg white, lightly whisked (see Note)

1. Preheat the oven to 325°F / 165°C. Lightly grease a 9-inch / 23-cm pie plate with nonstick spray.

2. In a medium bowl, stir the nuts, sugar, if using, and salt together to combine. Add the melted butter and egg white and stir until uniformly combined.

3. Press the crust mixture evenly over the bottom and up the sides of the prepared pie plate. To parbake the crust, bake (no docking or weights necessary) for 12 to 15 minutes, until it begins to lightly brown at the edges. To blind-bake the crust, bake for 17 to 20 minutes, until it is deeply brown and smells toasty. Let cool completely before filling.

Make Ahead and Storage

This crust can be assembled up to 1 week ahead and frozen in the pan, wrapped tightly in plastic wrap; thaw overnight in the fridge before baking. The baked crust can be made up to 1 day ahead and stored at room temperature, covered tightly with plastic wrap.

NOTE

For an egg-free version, omit the egg white and add 14 g / 2 tablespoons flax seeds to the nuts. Process them in the food processor with the nuts until the mixture is finely chopped. If necessary, add cool water 4 g / 1 teaspoon at a time until the mixture comes together.

Scaling Up Nut Crusts

Like a crumb crust, this recipe is easily adjusted to fit in other sizes and types of bakeware.

FOR 1.25 RECIPES: 3 cups finely chopped nuts, 2½ ounces / 5 tablespoons melted butter, 1 large egg white

FOR 1.5: 3¾ cups finely chopped nuts, 3 ounces / 6 tablespoons melted butter, 1 large egg white

FOR 1.75: 4¼ cups finely chopped nuts, 3½ ounces / 7 tablespoons melted butter, 1 large egg white

FOR 2: 5 cups finely chopped nuts, 4 ounces / 8 tablespoons melted butter, 2 large egg whites

FOR 2.25: 5½ cups finely chopped nuts, 4½ ounces / 9 tablespoons melted butter, 2 large egg whites

FOR 2.5: 6 cups finely chopped nuts, 5 ounces / 10 tablespoons melted butter, 2 large egg whites

FOR 2.75: 6½ cups finely chopped nuts, 5½ ounces / 11 tablespoons melted butter, 2 large egg whites

FOR 3: 7¼ cups finely chopped nuts, 6 ounces / 12 tablespoons melted butter, 3 large egg whites

FOR 3.25: 7½ cups finely chopped nuts, 6½ ounces / 13 tablespoons melted butter, 3 large egg whites

Nut Crust Amounts for Different Pan Sizes

PAN	BOTTOM ONLY	BOTTOM AND HALFWAY UP SIDES	BOTTOM AND SIDES
9-INCH / 23-CM PIE PLATE	—	1	1
10-INCH / 25-CM PIE PLATE	—	1	1.25
9-INCH / 23-CM DEEP-DISH PIE PLATE	—	1.25	1.5
10-IN / 25-CM DEEP-DISH PIE PLATE	—	1.5	1.75
9-INCH SPRINGFORM PAN	1.25	2.25	3
8-BY-8-INCH BAKING PAN	1.25	1.75	2.25
9-BY-9-INCH BAKING PAN	1.5	2	2.5
9-BY-13 BAKING PAN OR 9½-BY-13-INCH QUARTER SHEET PAN	2.5	2.75	3.25

PHYLLO DOUGH CRUST

MAKES ONE 9-INCH /
23-CM CRUST

DIFFICULTY: MEDIUM

Phyllo dough, deliciously crisp and flaky, is a classic choice for pies in many parts of the world. I love it for both sweet and savory pies. You can add additional flavorings (such as various sweeteners, chopped fresh herbs, or your favorite spices) by sprinkling them between the layers as you stack them. I find that eight layers of phyllo are ideal to mimic the thickness of a more traditional crust.

8 sheets phyllo dough (about 14 by 18 inches / 36 by 46 cm), thawed

OPTIONAL FLAVORINGS
37 g / 3 tablespoons granulated sugar
2 g / ¾ teaspoon ground cinnamon
Pinch of fine sea salt

113 g / 4 ounces / 8 tablespoons unsalted butter, melted

1. Lightly grease a 9-inch / 23-cm pie plate. Unfold the phyllo sheets on your work surface and cover them with a damp towel. If using the optional flavorings, stir the sugar, cinnamon, and salt together in a small bowl.

2. Place one sheet of phyllo on your work surface (keep the remaining sheets covered) and brush it all over with butter. If using, sprinkle an even layer of the sugar mixture over the phyllo. Place another piece of phyllo dough on top, arranging it slightly askew so that the corners of the 2 sheets do not match up. Brush with butter and, if using, sprinkle with more of the sugar mixture. Repeat with the remaining phyllo, butter, and sugar mixture, if using. The assembled crust should look like a sunflower, with multiple corners of the phyllo poking out from all sides.

3. Carefully transfer the phyllo crust to the prepared pie plate. Press gently into the bottom of the pan. Then work around the edges with your fingers, scrunching the layered phyllo together to create a ruffled effect.

4. Phyllo crusts aren't ideal for parbaking or blind-baking—they tend to get crisp enough during the regular bake time. Fill the crust with the filling of your choice and bake as directed in the recipe of your choice.

Make Ahead and Storage
Filled and baked crusts are best the same day they are baked.

Crispy Phyllo Crust Toppers

You can make a beautiful, crispy, phyllo crust topper for any pie. And you can use it for a more traditional double-crust effect or bake it separately to keep it crisp when your filling is more liquid (as in the Classic Custard Pie, page 206). Here are a few ideas to get your creative juices flowing.

- **PHYLLO TOP CRUST:** This works best on a pie with a thicker filling, like a fruit or savory pie. Follow the directions for making the Phyllo Dough Crust through step 2. After you fill the bottom crust, brush the edges of the bottom crust with egg wash. Transfer the top phyllo crust to the top of the pie. You can keep the look neater by trimming the edges flush with the edge of the pie plate, or ruffle the edges to make a fluffy effect. Bake the pie as directed, until the top crust is evenly golden. (Remember, this technique works in recipes that would typically have a top crust, like fruit pies. For custard pies, it's usually best to bake separately (see below).

- **PHYLLO LATTICE:** This also works best on a pie with a thicker filling. Follow the directions for making the Phyllo Dough Crust (page 76) through step 2 (I recommend using the sugar mixture). Cut the dough into 1½-inch / 4-cm-wide strips. Use the strips to weave a tightly woven lattice (see page 92). Bake the pie as directed, until the top crust is evenly golden.

- **PRE-BAKED PHYLLO TOPPER:** The next two toppers can be baked separately, making them a great textural addition to all kinds of pies, even if they wouldn't typically have a top crust, like custard or cold-set pies. Follow the directions for making a Phyllo Dough Crust through step 2 (I recommend using the sugar mixture). Cut the dough into ½-inch / 1-cm-wide strips. Grease an 8-inch / 20-cm cake pan with unsalted butter. Arrange the strips in the pan, allowing them to ruffle naturally and keep a more random, organic shape (see phyllo topper, page 77). If desired, brush the surface with butter. Bake in 375°F / 190°C oven until deeply golden brown, 12 to 15 minutes. Cool completely before gently unmolding and placing on top of a cooled pie.

- **PHYLLO ROSE TOPPER:** Follow the directions for making a Phyllo Dough Crust through step 2 (I recommend using the sugar mixture). Cut the dough into ½-inch / 1-cm-wide strips. Grease an 8-inch / 20-cm cake pan with unsalted butter. Starting in the center, form a spiral shape with the first strip of dough. Continue to build outward, with the strips allowing the layers of the phyllo to fluff up and take up real estate in the pan— don't press it firmly together as you work. If desired, brush the surface with butter. Bake at 375°F / 190°C until deeply golden brown, 12 to 15 minutes, then cool completely before gently unmolding and placing on top of a cooled pie.

chapter two

DÉCOR & TOPPINGS

This chapter is about taking your pies to the next level. I believe that any pie is a beautiful pie, but I have dozens of ways to beautify them even more. From pretty pie crimps to mile-high meringue, this chapter has everything you need to make pies worth boasting about.

CRUST DÉCOR

For me, a pie is all about the crust, so décor techniques that emphasize it are among my favorite ways to gussy up a pie. Some of these effects, like crimps, are done with the dough you use for the pie, while other techniques require extra dough. I save scrap pieces of dough specifically for some of these techniques.

CRIMPING

All of these crimps start with a lined pie plate, made as directed in Preparing the Crust Edges (page 42). Unless otherwise specified, most techniques can be done for single- or double-crust pies.

Utensil Crimps

Forks and other kitchen utensils can be used to make easy and attractive crimps. You can use almost anything you have on hand, the effects are simple to achieve, and the imprints will stay throughout baking. The size and thickness of the utensil, of course, will affect the look of the final crimp—for a finer effect, choose a smaller fork or other utensil.

CLASSIC FORK CRIMP: The thickness and spacing of the tines of the fork will affect the look of the imprints. Dip the tines of a fork into a small amount of flour before you press it firmly into the edges of the crust. Repeat this flouring as necessary—you can usually get away with dipping it every few times. If you want to be extra-precise, start each press by placing the last tine (or first, depending on which way you are working around the pie) in the final imprint of the press you made before. Repeat all around the crust.

CHEVRON FORK CRIMP: My fancified version of the classic fork crimp. Press the floured fork tines into the crust at a 45-degree angle to make a sort of half-triangle shape; the tine on the left will make a longer indentation and the tine on the right will make a shorter one. Then turn the fork and make a second indentation at a 45-degree angle in the opposite direction. The marks should line up at their points to make a chevron shape. Repeat all around the crust.

CRISSCROSSING FORK CRIMP: Press the floured fork tines into the crust all the way around. Then turn the fork 90 degrees to make another indentation, overlapping the first to make a crisscross effect. To be super-precise, line up the tines with the previous indentation before you press again.

SPOON CRIMP: Dip the edge of a spoon lightly into flour and press it gently into the crust to make a sort of half-circle. If desired, you can press the spoon into the crust twice, once toward the outer rim of the pie plate and again closer to the outer edge for a double-crimp look. Repeat all around the crust.

KNIFE CRIMP: This makes a rope-like effect. Start by using your fingers to pinch the prepared pie crust up to give it a bit more height around the edges. Dip a knife into flour, then gently press the back of the knife into the dough on a diagonal to make a divot in the dough. Repeat the process all around, taking care to match the angle of the last press with each new one.

Utensil Crimps

Chevron Fork
Crimp

Crisscrossing
Fork Crimp

Spoon
Crimp

Classic
Fork
Crimp

Knife
Crimp

Épi
Crimp

Tong
Crimp

Pie
Weight
Crimp

TONG CRIMP: Dip the ends of the tongs lightly into flour and press it gently into the crust to make a sort of half-circle. If desired, you can press the tong into the crust twice, once toward the outer rim of the pie plate and again closer to the outer edge for a double-crimp look. Repeat all around.

PIE WEIGHT CRIMP: Dip a ceramic pie weight lightly into flour and press it firmly into the crust, then repeat all around the crust. Leave a small amount of space between the indentations—if you space them too tightly together, the indentations will run into each other.

ÉPI: This technique is named after the unique leaf-shaped baguette, where scissors are used to create the shape in the dough. Start by using your fingers to pinch the pie crust up to give it a bit more height around the edges. Use scissors to snip the dough at a 45-degree angle, entering the dough at a diagonal. Repeat all around the crust, leaving a small amount of space between each snip. You can leave the snipped pieces as is, or gently fan every other piece out in the opposite direction.

Finger Crimps

There are as many ways to crimp a pie crust with your fingers as there are pie bakers. Some people use their knuckles more, while I tend to lean more on my fingertips. There's no one right way—do what feels natural for you. Most crimps require the use of both hands. The wider apart you place your fingers, the more rustic the look will be; the tighter you place them together, the more detailed the final effect will be.

CLASSIC FINGER CRIMP: Form a V-shape with the thumb and forefinger of your dominant hand and place them at the outer edge of the pie crust. Use the index finger of your non-dominant hand (or use your knuckle) to press down lightly and push outward toward the V-shape; press in slightly with the thumb and finger forming the V at the same time. Repeat all the way around the pie.

REVERSE FINGER CRIMP: I call this the reverse method but doing it this way may actually feel more natural to you, and the final results are pretty similar. Form the V-shape with the thumb and forefinger of your non-dominant hand and place them at the inner edge of the pie crust. Use the index finger of your dominant hand (or use your knuckle) to press down lightly and push inward toward the V-shape; press in slightly with the fingers forming the V at the same time. The size of the V will dictate the size of the crimp—repeat all the way around the pie.

ROUNDED CRIMP: This is similar to the classic finger crimp. Form more of a U-shape with the thumb and forefinger of your dominant hand (or use the reverse method for this crimp; see above) and place them at the outer edge of the pie crust. Use the thumb of your non-dominant hand (or use your knuckle) to press down firmly and push outward toward the U-shape; press in slightly with the fingers forming the U at the same time. Repeat all the way around the pie.

SCALLOPED CRIMP: Perform a rounded crimp as above but keep the U-shape small and make the crimps very close together. If desired, after you've completed each crimp, press downward and outward with your thumb again while pushing in with a paring knife to make a sharper scalloped look.

Finger Crimps

Rounded
Crimp

Classic
Finger
Crimp

Combination
Crimp

Rope
Crimp

Scalloped
Crimp

Reverse
Finger
Crimp

Other Finishes

Cutouts

Checkerboard

Braids

Twists

Foldover

Ruffles

ROPE CRIMP: Pinch a bit of the dough at a 45-degree angle between your two forefingers (use the sides of your fingers, not the fingertips) to squeeze the dough upward between them. Repeat all the way around the pie, taking care to match the angle of each new crimp with the last one. Some people find it easier to do this with one hand, using the thumb and forefinger.

COMBINATION CRIMP: Combine crimps in a variety of ways—you can press a fork into the interior of each crimp in either a classic or rounded crimp to create what I like to call the "Fork 'n' Crimp." Or alternate crimp styles around the crust, such as 3 finger crimps, 3 fork crimps, 3 finger crimps, and so forth.

Other Finishes

CHECKERBOARD: The classic edge for chess pie, this technique is especially great for baked single-crust custard or fruit pies. Before trimming away the excess dough, press the edges of the crust firmly down on the rim of the pie plate all the way around (this works best with a pie plate that has a wide rim), then trim away any excess so the dough is flush with the edge of the rim. Use scissors to make cuts through the dough all around the edges; you can use a ruler to measure the distance between each cut if you want this to look really sharp (I like about 1 inch / 2 cm between cuts). Fill the pie, then fold every other flap in over the filling to create a checkerboard effect. (Because this technique will partially cover the filling, it cannot be done for par-baked or blind-baked crusts.)

FOLDOVER: This is an easy technique often used for free-form pies, but it works with a single crust pie too. When you line the pie plate, leave 1 to 1½ inches / 2 to 4 cm of excess dough all around the plate. For a more precise look, you

can trim the rough edges away with scissors; otherwise, simply leave it as is. Add the filling to the pie plate, ideally filling it so it's flush with the rim of the plate. Fold one section of dough over onto the filling, then fold the next portion of dough over, overlapping the first fold. Repeat all the way around the pie. (Because this technique will partially cover the filling, it cannot be done for parbaked or blind-baked pies.)

TWISTS AND BRAIDS: Strips of pie dough can be twisted or braided to create a decorative edge. You'll need to make one extra recipe of dough for this technique (and if your pan is larger, say a 9-by-13-inch / 23-by-33-cm baking pan, you may need to make two extra recipes). Roll out the dough as directed on page 34 to about ¼ in / 6 mm thick (for added effect, use multiple colors of dough, like chocolate and plain, to weave together. Use a pastry wheel, bench knife, or sharp knife to cut the dough into thin strips. The width of the strips can vary depending on your desired look, but you don't want the twist or braid to be significantly wider than the rim of the pie plate. Because twists are made with just 2 strips, you can usually cut them a bit wider (¼ inch / 6 mm) than the strips for braids (⅛ inch / 3 mm), which use 3 strips.

> **TO MAKE TWISTS:** Place 2 strips of dough next to each other on your lightly floured work surface. Starting with the ends farther away from you, begin to twist the strips together; don't squish them together at the top, just press enough that they hold together. You can allow them to twist naturally, or you can adjust them to lie flat as you work. When you get to the other end, pinch the strips of dough gently together (feel free to use a dab of water to secure them). Sometimes I go back to the top after I've finished and retwist the initial portion

Braids and twists also make great top crust effects. Combining crusts like All-Buttah Crust (page 48) with colored crusts like Chocolate All-Buttah Crust (page 48) or Gingerbread Crust (page 52) allows the effects to really pop.

to make sure it is as tight as the rest, before pinching the ends firmly to seal. If you like, you can fill the twists with jam—see Jam Twists, page 131.

TO MAKE BRAIDS: Place 3 strips of dough next to each other on your lightly floured work surface. Starting with the ends farther away from you, begin to braid the dough; you can allow the strips to overlap naturally, or you can encourage them to lie flat as you work. When you get to the other end, pinch the ends of the strips gently together (feel free to use a dab of water to secure them). Sometimes I go back to the top after I've finished and rebraid the initial portion to make sure it is as tight as the rest, before pinching the ends firmly to seal.

The circumference of a standard 9-inch / 23-cm pie plate is 28 inches / 71 cm, so you can either go bold and roll out your rectangle of dough to 29 to 30 inches / 74 to 76 cm long before cutting the strips, allowing you to make one long twist/braid to encircle the pie, or you can roll out two 15- to 16-inch / 58- to 40-cm rectangles, then place the finished twists/braids on the pie so they meet at the ends (use cutouts to cover the seams, if desired). If the dough strips feel too soft at any point during assembly, transfer to the fridge to firm up before continuing. To attach the twists/braids to the crust, brush a little water around the edges of the crust, place the decorative dough on top, and press gently so it adheres. If you opt to use these for a double-crust pie, be sure to first firmly press down the dough at the edges to thin it out before trimming away the excess.

RUFFLES: Strips of pie dough can be arranged to form ruffles at the edges of a pie crust. This is a great way to use up scraps, but you'll need a decent amount for this effect, so you may want to

make an extra recipe of dough. Roll out the dough to ¼ in / 6 mm and use a pastry wheel, bench knife, or sharp knife to cut it into thin strips about the width of the rim of the pie plate. The strips used for the ruffles will be overlapped to create the effect, so you don't need to worry about the length of the strips. Brush a little water around the edges of the pie crust, then place a strip of dough on top and form a little arch with the edge of the strip, making a ruffle, then keep ruffling the dough this way all around the pie; add more strips of dough as needed. If the dough strips feel too soft at any point, transfer to the fridge to firm up before continuing. If you opt to do this for a double-crust pie, be sure to first firmly press down the dough around the edges to thin it out before trimming away the excess.

CUTOUTS FOR DECORATIVE EDGES: Cutouts (for how to make these and more, see Cutouts, page 90) can be used for all kinds of decorative effects, but one of my favorites is to use them as decorative edges. Prepare your cutouts as directed on page 90; be sure to use cutters that are no larger than the rim of the pie plate—if the cutouts hang too far over, they are likely to droop or even fall off when they hit the heat of the oven. The most secure way to use cutouts around the outer edge is to overlap them, attaching each with a bit of water or egg wash. If you opt to do this on a double-crust pie, be sure to first firmly press down the pie dough around the edge to thin it out before trimming away the excess.

TOP-CRUST TECHNIQUES

Crimping isn't the only way to add decorative interest to your pie. A top crust can be a plain covering with a couple of vents cut in it or a serious showstopper.

Marbling Two Doughs for the Top Crust

Mixing two doughs together can create an amazing marbling effect. You can do this with regular pie doughs or cookie-style doughs.

If you want to make a marbled crust using pie dough, the best way to combine the two doughs is using the extra flaky method (see Mixing Pie Dough So It's Extra Flaky, page 30), which involves two sets of folds. Roll out each batch of dough as directed and brush any excess flour off the surface. I prefer to make marbled crusts for double crust pies, so you can see the effect on the top crust—but for single crust, use only half of each of the prepared doughs and save the rest as scrap dough. Tear one of the rolled-out doughs into pieces, scatter them over the other rolled-out dough, and press them gently into the dough. Then gently roll out the dough to attach the two doughs (don't worry if they aren't totally attached). Perform the first fold, which will help combine the doughs. The second folding session will continue to marble the

dough, and after the final roll-out, the dough will have some nice swirls going on.

To make a marbled crust using cookie dough, just break each portion of dough into large clumps and sort of mash them together before you start to roll the dough out (again, for single crusts, use only half of each of the prepared doughs). The more you mix/knead the two together, the more swirled they will become; I prefer cookie doughs mixed together less so that the two colors remain more distinct.

Adding Texture to the Top Crust

There are a variety of textural effects that will create a really cool look on the finished pie. These techniques can be done with a number of different doughs, including classic pie dough such as All-Buttah Pie Dough (page 48), Rough Puff Pastry (page 50), and Roll-Out Cookie Crust (page 62). Remember, the flakier a dough is, the less likely

the effect you choose will have a super-uniform, clean look, but it will still add a lovely result, no matter how pronounced it is.

FORK: One of the easiest ways to add texture to the top crust is to press a fork into the dough. This technique works well on any kind of pie dough or cookie-style crusts. Dip the fork tines into flour occasionally, then press firmly into the dough to leave an imprint (but not so firmly that you press all the way through or tear the dough). You can do this all over, randomly, or in a distinct pattern. You can crisscross the impressions, angle the lines towards each other (à la the Chevron Fork Crimp on page 80), or keep each imprint separate.

TEXTURED ROLLING PIN (OR USING A PLAIN PIN TO ADD TEXTURE): Textured rolling pins, such as those used for roll-out cookies and for some types of pasta, can add beautiful top-crust effects. Roll out the dough, leaving it just slightly thicker than you want it to be ultimately. Brush a textured rolling pin all over with flour and roll it over the dough, pressing firmly. Then use the rolling pin to transfer the dough to the top of the pie.

If you don't have a textured rolling pin, you can make impressions in the dough using a doily, stencil, or other textured item and a regular rolling pin. Roll out the dough, leaving it slightly thicker than you want it to be ultimately. Lightly flour the dough to prevent sticking, place the doily or other item on top, and press firmly with the rolling pin as you move it across the dough. Gently lift the doily or other item off the dough and transfer to the top of the pie.

Techniques like this produce the cleanest results when used with smoother doughs, like roll-out cookie crusts. They can be used with flaky doughs, but the results are likely to be less defined.

SCORING: This cool technique is most effective on Rough Puff Pastry (page 50). Score the top of the dough by lightly cutting designs into the surface with the tip of a paring knife. The design can really be anything—a series of lines or spirals, or whatever you like. When scoring the dough, you want to just barely cut into it, without fully piercing it or making a hole. This effect works particularly well on rough puff pastry because the dough has already formed distinctive layers and you're cutting into the top ones. If you brush the pastry with egg wash before you score it, the score marks will be more vivid, because they'll be lighter than the rest of the golden dough when baked and really stand out. For a more subtle effect, score the pastry, then brush with egg wash.

Decorative scoring on top of a pithiviers

Painting the Top Crust

To paint the top crust, you need a small paintbrush, a small amount of gel food coloring (liquid food coloring isn't concentrated enough to brush on easily and won't leave its color behind as well), and some sort of plain alcohol (I use vodka) to dilute the coloring. Alcohol dissolves food coloring best and evaporates in the oven, leaving the color behind. It's best to paint the top crust of pie dough after you've placed it on the pie, simply so you don't risk messing up the design when you transfer it. Dip your paintbrush directly into gel food coloring (this is *super* concentrated, so a little goes a long way), Then dip it into a tablespoon or two of vodka, and stir to dissolve the color, then start painting! Keep in mind that

most colors are likely to darken slightly in the oven, and that lighter colors may be less likely to show up once the crust begins to brown. I don't use egg wash when I am painting the crust, to keep it blonder overall so the colors stand out more.

Using Cutouts

Cutouts can be used in several different ways for excellent top-crust effects. Dip your cutters into flour between every few cuts, and press down firmly in one smooth motion rather than twisting the cutter as you press. Use a mealier/less flaky dough for cutouts—the flakier the dough, the less crisp and clean-cut the cutout shapes will be. (For how to use cutouts as decorative edges, see page 87.)

CUTOUTS IN THE TOP CRUST: With a careful hand, make cutouts in the rolled-out top crust and remove them. This can be done in just a few places, more or less in lieu of cutting vents in the top crust of the pie, or it can be done all over the crust to allow the filling to peek through. If you want to do cutouts all over the crust, first mark the central portion of the crust by gently pressing the bottom of the pie pan into the crust to give you a circular guideline. You don't want too many of the cutouts to be close to the edges, where you'll be crimping the dough, because that can result in an uneven, messy look. Make cutouts all over the dough, stopping shy of the guideline. Then use the rolling pin to gently transfer the crust to the pie.

CUTOUTS AS THE TOP CRUST: You can also skip a classic top crust and instead layer pie dough cutouts all over the surface of the filling. There's no right or wrong way to layer the cutouts, but I like to overlap them slightly, working in rows or concentric circles. I brush the cutouts with egg wash before I begin to build—this helps ensure more even browning (and less pooling of egg wash in the empty spaces).

Cutouts: Bake Ahead or Directly on Pie?

Sometimes I bake my decorative cutouts separately and then add them to the finished pie by simply arranging them on the top or around the edges. This allows for even browning and also lets me weed out any not-so-good pieces before I arrange them on the pie. This can be done for the decorative pie crust edge (see page 87) by arranging the cutouts around the edges of a single-crust pie. It can also be done when you are using cutouts as a top crust. This guarantees an evenly browned, super-clean look. I brush the cutouts with egg wash (for more help with that browning) and bake them on a baking sheet at 425°F / 220°C until well browned (exact time will vary depending on size of the cutouts). Arrange the cooled cutouts on top of the filling or around the edges of the pie.

LATTICE CRUSTS

There are two main types of lattice crust, woven and unwoven, and either technique can be used for a variety of different styles. An unwoven lattice, made by laying half of the dough strips on a pie in one direction, then layering the remaining strips across them, is the simplest. A woven lattice is made by weaving the strips together. Here are a few tips to help you conquer any lattice technique.

- **ROLL OUT THE DOUGH A BIT THICKER THAN USUAL.** I roll out the dough for a lattice a bit thicker than I would for a regular top crust. This will make the strips easier to handle, even when you're lifting them often.

- **TRANSFER THE ROLLED-OUT DOUGH TO A PARCHMENT-LINED BAKING SHEET.** This is an optional but very useful step. After rolling out the dough, use the rolling pin to transfer and unfurl it onto a parchment-lined baking sheet before cutting your strips. This way, if the dough is getting soft as you work, you can just toss the whole tray into the refrigerator for a chill sesh before continuing.

- **USE A RULER.** Even if you don't care about being super-precise, it's helpful to have a guide to help keep your lattice strips even and straight. I like to use the ruler as a straight edge, even if I end up just eyeballing the width of each strip. You can also carefully cut the first lattice strip to the precise size, then use it as a guide to help you cut the rest.

- **CUT EXTRA STRIPS.** Because every lattice technique is a little different, as is every pie pan, the amount of filling you are using, and your personal preferences in terms of look and style, it can be sometimes difficult to specify exactly how many strips you'll need for a particular lattice crust. So plan on having

a little more extra handy, just in case (it's a great way to use up scrap dough you've been squirreling away in the fridge or freezer).

- **FOLD THE EDGE OF THE DOUGH UP AND OVER INSTEAD OF TUCKING IT UNDER.** For most pie crusts, I recommend folding the excess dough under all around the edge before crimping and finishing the pie. But for lattice, I suggest the opposite: Fold the edges of the bottom crust up and over the edges of

(CONTINUED ON PAGE 94)

the lattice. This helps ensure that the lattice won't come undone during baking, because the bottom crust is helping to hold it in place. To get rid of any visible seams, dip your finger in cool water and press gently to smooth the bottom crust where it meets the lattice.

- **DON'T FRET ABOUT LENGTH.** While it's ideal to have each strip for lattice work be the same length as your pie plate, it's okay that some pieces are shorter. Shorter pieces can be used at the edges of the pie plate or used in woven techniques where their scrappy edges will be hidden under other strips of dough.
- **ROTATE THE PIE PAN AS YOU WORK.** Don't twist your body into crazy positions to form the lattice—rotating the pie plate can make the process easier! In my lattice method, I weave the lattice strips halfway across the pie, starting on the right side (because I'm right-handed). Then, I rotate the pie so that the side I was working on is now on the left and pull the remaining strips halfway across to weave the lattice.
- **CHILL, CHILL, CHILL.** You can never chill your pie too much, and after you've handled all those pieces to make the lattice, it will be ready for some fridge time. Allow at least 30 minutes before baking, because a cold lattice always bakes up best.

HOW TO MAKE A WOVEN LATTICE

1. Roll out the dough on a lightly floured surface and use a rolling pin to gently transfer it to a parchment-lined baking sheet. Use a pastry wheel (fluted or straight) or sharp knife to cut strips from the dough.

2. Lay half of the strips vertically across the pie, spacing them evenly. Rotate the pie 90 degrees so the strips you laid down now run horizontally.

3. Pull every other strip back halfway across the pie, then lay another strip vertically across the pie, slightly off center. Fold the horizontal pieces you pulled back down over this strip.

4. Repeat this process, this time pulling back the strips you did not move the first time, and placing another strip vertically across the pie, spaced evenly from the last one. Fold the horizontal pieces you pulled back over this strip.

5. Repeat with additional vertical strips on this half of the pie, then rotate the pie 180 degrees and continuing on the other side with the remaining strips.

Woven Lattice

6. Trim away the excess dough from the lattice strips, then fold the edges of the bottom crust up and over to encase the ends of the lattice strips. If desired, dip your finger in cool water to smooth out any visible seams. The pie is now ready to be crimped and finished. Chill before baking.

HOW TO MAKE AN UNWOVEN LATTICE

1. Roll out your dough on a lightly floured surface and use a rolling pin to gently transfer it to a parchment-lined baking sheet. Use a pastry wheel (fluted or straight) or sharp knife to cut strips from the dough.

2. Lay half of the strips vertically across the pie, spacing them evenly. Rotate the pie 90 degrees so the strips you laid down now run horizontally.

3. Lay the remaining strips vertically across the pie, spacing them evenly.

4. Trim away the excess dough from the lattice strips, then fold the edges of the bottom crust up and over to encase the ends of the lattice strips. If desired, dip your finger in cool water to smooth out any visible seams. The pie is now ready to be crimped and finished. Chill before baking.

LATTICE STYLES

There's no wrong way to make a lattice crust, and there are dozens of ways to get creative with it.

CLASSIC LATTICE: A classic lattice, woven or unwoven, is made by cutting strips about 1 inch / 2.5 cm wide and leaving at least ½ inch / 1 cm space between them as you place them on the pie.

SKINNY LATTICE: This is similar to a classic lattice, but the strips are much narrower: ⅛ to ¼ inch / 3 to 6 mm wide. This adorable lattice will also test your patience, as thinner pieces take

Unwoven Lattice

longer to weave (or to arrange for an unwoven lattice). Other than that, it's no harder to achieve, but be sure to chill your strips (and/or your pie mid-weave) as you work as necessary to keep things cold. You'll need at least 1½ recipes of dough to make this lattice.

FAT LATTICE (A.K.A. *Fattice*): This is my favorite lattice, and it is especially awesome for lattice beginners. I adore it because it always looks good (woven or unwoven, with space or tightly woven), and the crust always gets nice and crisp because the wider strips have more surface area for browning. Cut strips that are 1½ to 2 inches / 4 to 5 cm wide. This lattice is quick and easy to

Traditional Versus Tightly Woven Lattice

Lattice is most traditionally thought of as a technique where the strips of dough are arranged with space between them, so the filling can peek through the lattice. But I also am a big fan of the tightly woven lattice, where the strips are placed directly next to one another, creating a full top-crust effect rather than leaving spaces between the strips. This technique looks very sleek and it can be done with nearly any style of lattice. There's no need to cut vents, because there is still enough room between strips for steam to escape during baking, but you will need more strips of dough to create the tightly woven look.

Tightly Woven Lattice

prepare, because there are fewer strips and they are less fragile. You'll need at least 1½ recipes of dough to do make this lattice.

DIAGONAL LATTICE: This style is similar to a traditional lattice, but instead of placing the first strips vertically, you lay them across the pie on a diagonal. Then, when you rotate the pie 90 degrees to place the remaining strips, lay them on a diagonal in the opposite direction. This technique results in diamond-shaped spaces between the strips instead of the traditional square shapes.

RANDOM LATTICE: This is the technique for anyone afraid of lattice or anything too fussy. Cut the strips all willy-nilly: all different widths (it doesn't even matter if they are a bit crooked). I use a variety of widths ranging from ⅛ inch / 3 mm to 1½ inches / 4 cm. Arrange the strips in no particular order as you make a classic lattice; I find this techniques looks best as a woven lattice (if it's tightly woven, it has a knitted effect!). There are no concerns about precision or perfection here, but the finished pie has an incredible top texture that's sure to impress. You'll need at least 1½ recipes of dough to make this lattice.

MULTIPLE-STRAND LATTICE: You can make any of the lattice styles described above using multiple strands as you would a single strand. This makes a more complex look that isn't necessarily more difficult to achieve.

STRIPES AND SLATS (A.K.A. *Slattice*): You can also skip the lattice entirely and just lay the strips of dough of any width across the top of the pie. With space between the strips, you'll achieve a sort of striped effect—this is also great using braids or twists of dough. If you overlap the strips, the result is more of a slat effect, like the closed slats of a window blind.

Skinny Lattice

Fat Lattice
(a.k.a. *Fattice*)

Random Lattice

Multiple-Strand
Lattice

Stripes and Slats
(a.k.a. *Slattice*)

RANDOM STRIPS AND SHAPES: Use a pastry wheel or knife, fluted or straight, to cut the dough (on the lined baking sheet) into random strips and shapes. After filling the pie, lay the prepared pie dough strips all over the surface, overlapping them slightly as necessary.

USING TWISTS OR BRAIDS FOR A TOP CRUST

Just as small braids and twists can make beautiful finishes for the edges of pies, they can make beautiful top crusts! Prepare the twists or braids of dough as directed on page 85. Carefully transfer the finished twists or braids to the surface of the pie.

CUTTING VENTS IN THE TOP CRUST

Double-crust pies benefit from having steam vents cut in the top crust, for steam to escape both during and after baking. A vent can be as simple as a small X shape or single line cut in the center of the pie, or more decorative—perhaps several slits cut into the dough or cutouts made with a small cookie cutter. I also like cutting a solid circle (or other shape) out of the center of the pie before transferring it to the top of the pie. If you're cutting slits with a paring knife, be sure to brush the crust with the egg wash and apply any other finishes, like sugar, to the dough before you cut them, because these finishes can actually seal up the vents if applied after cutting.

If you're a fan of pie birds—these are old-fashioned ceramic pieces (usually shaped like a bird) you can use those on lieu of cutting vents. Place the pie bird in the center of the pie before adding the top crust, and cut a small round out of the center of the top crust. Then slide the crust over the pie bird and proceed with trimming the dough and crimping the crust.

FINISHING TOUCHES FOR CRUSTS

Adding a finishing touch to the top crust can make a world of difference. My favorite finish is a simple egg wash and a generous sprinkling of turbinado sugar. The egg wash promotes browning, leaves a subtle shine on the surface of the dough, and helps the sugar adhere. The sugar crystals hold their shape in the oven, caramelizing slightly for an incredible combination of texture and flavor.

> **MY EGG WASH:** 56 g / 1 large egg, whisked well with 15 g / 1 tablespoon cool water

Other Types of Lattices

Who says you need dough to make a latticed pie? Use any of the techniques below to give your pie a classic look with a twist.

PIPED LATTICE: You can pipe an unwoven lattice of stripes of meringue or whipped cream across a cooled, baked pie. Simply pipe stripes across the pie vertically, then again horizontally (this looks great with toasted meringue). For a woven look, use the flat basket-weave tip to create the basket-weave piping technique (a method most commonly used to decorate cakes).

SIFTED LATTICE: This is a great technique to use with the Flavored Sifting Sugars (page 128). Using a stencil or strips of paper as a guide, gently sift powdered sugar stripes over the pie vertically and then horizontally. This technique is most effective when there is a strong color contrast between the pie filling and the sifted ingredient.

STREUSEL LATTICE: Use Extra-Clumpy Prebaked Streusel (page 120) to create a lattice effect on top of a baked and cooled pie. Sprinkle it over in horizontal strips, then rotate the pie 90 degrees and repeat the process to create a lattice look.

BACON LATTICE: Instead of pie dough, weave bacon into a lattice (I love it on any of the quiche recipes, see page 304). A bacon lattice is best baked separately on a parchment-lined baking sheet. Turn a pie plate over onto the parchment and trace a circle around it.

Turn the parchment over, then weave strips of bacon into a lattice, using the traced circle as a guide. (It will be bigger than the surface of the filling at this point, but it will shrink as it bakes.) Use scissors to trim the edges of the bacon strips to make a round lattice. Bake at 375°F / 190°C until very crisp, 25 to 35 minutes. Let cool for 10 minutes on the baking sheet, then use two spatulas to gently remove the lattice from the baking sheet and transfer to the baked pie.

There are a number of other washes to choose from. Milk or cream will contribute a small amount of browning but no shine. Beaten egg yolk will help greatly with browning, but it leaves no shine. Beaten egg white leaves some shine but helps little with browning. That said, sometimes I just want some shine, or just something to help the sugar adhere, and I'll use one of these. The same goes for the sugar—while turbinado is my usual preference, sometimes I opt for regular granulated sugar for its sweetness, or I'll swap turbinado for sanding sugar or pearl sugar for a different look.

I generally do not use egg wash on bottom crusts that are going to be parbaked. I find that with two trips to the oven, they tend to brown enough on their own. If I want to add a little shine to the edges of a crust that's going to be blind-baked, though, I brush them with egg wash before putting the crust back in the oven, after removing the pie weights.

FILLING DÉCOR

Considering the look of the inside of the pie is sometimes what makes it extra-special. Adding a bit of finesse to the filling can make your pie go from "meh" to "WOW."

ARTFUL ARRANGING

Taking a moment to carefully arrange the filling inside the crust can take any pie to the next level. Most of the techniques described below take very little time but create a really impressive end result. Arrange sliced fruit in tight rows in the pie shell or make concentric circles for a spiral-like rose effect. If you're using two kinds of fillings, you might want to arrange them separately to make a dramatic change in color and texture inside the pie (see the Stone Fruit–Berry Pie on page 176).

Or take a moment to arrange the nuts or similar ingredients that will be bound by or suspended inside a filling in a specific pattern before pouring the filling over them.

LAYERING FILLINGS

Layering multiple fillings creates an amazing impact when you slice the pie. One of the easiest ways is to make a black- (or white-) bottom pie by spreading a thin layer of ganache over the bottom of the crust before adding the filling (see Dark Chocolate Black-Bottom Base, page 110). For a more visible result, double the amount of ganache to create a thicker layer. Another way to make a layered pie is to use two (or more) fillings. The base layer should be firm enough to allow you to place another layer on top of it (like the Key Lime–Coconut Cream Pie on page 258. You can also use a variety of cold-set fillings that firm up enough in the refrigerator for another filling to be layered on top (as in the Striped Citrus Pie on page 284 and the Triple-Chocolate Caramel Truffle Pie on page 271.

SWIRLING FILLINGS

For some pies, you can combine the ingredients in a way that results in a visible swirl effect on the surface of the pie. This is especially great for custard pies like the Cheesecake Pie (page 236) or pies with cold-set fillings such as the Eton Mess Pie (page 282). Swirls can be made one of two ways. The first is to gently spoon the second filling randomly over the surface of the first filling, then use a toothpick, skewer, or paring knife to swirl the two together. The second is to use a piping bag. Either way, be gentle and carefully add the second filling from as close as possible to the surface of the pie—if you drop it from too high, it may just sink into the other filling. And don't be

Clockwise from top right: Jam Swirled Cheesecake Pie, Pumpkin Cheesecake Pie, Caramel Swirled Cheesecake Pie, Chocolate Swirled Cheesecake Pie

tempted to swirl *too* much; the effect is generally stronger (particularly after baking) when the fillings are swirled only enough to gently combine, leaving large streaks of both colors. You can also use a spoon or piping bag to help create other effects like spirals, hearts, or feathering.

SPATULA FINISHES

Some cold-set fillings, like puddings, curds, or ganache, are the perfect combination of firm and malleable, allowing you to create decorative effects with a spatula, much as you would when frosting a cake. You can make stripes (see the Breakfast Pie on page 277), swoops (as with the cream on the Sweet Corn Pie on page 256), or spirals (like the Concord Grape Meringue Pie (page 280), among other finishes. I prefer to use a small offset spatula for these effects, since the larger the spatula, the larger the effect will be, and pies tend to be a pretty small canvas.

MOLDED FILLINGS

Some cold-set fillings, particularly those set with gelatin or agar-agar, can be prepared in a mold, and then unmolded into a pie crust with incredible results. My preferred "mold" is a silicone cake pan, but you can also use metal molds or pans, or even just a bowl to create a bombe-like effect. Start by making sure the mold you are using will fit inside the pie plate before beginning. Place the mold on a baking sheet and pour the filling into the mold. Gently transfer the baking sheet and mold to the refrigerator or freezer as directed, and chill until completely set. To release the filling from a silicone mold, use a small offset spatula or the tip of a paring knife to gently loosen the filling from the mold at the edges, then start to peel the mold away, invert the mold, centered, into the pie crust, and gently peel away the mold entirely. If you're using something other than silicone, the most effective way to unmold the filling is to use a little heat, by either soaking a kitchen towel in hot water, wringing it out, and wrapping it around the mold or carefully using a kitchen torch to apply a little heat evenly to the exterior of the mold (don't be overzealous, though, or the filling will start to melt). For an example, see the Orange-Vanilla Panna Cotta Pie (page 255).

TOPPING DÉCOR

Even today, when I think of pie, I think of a diner I used to go to that had a rotating case full of towering whipped cream–topped pies. I like to channel that image anytime I'm applying a topping to a pie—even the simplest pie can become something special with the right topping.

APPLYING TOPPINGS

If a pie recipe calls for whipped cream, meringue, or even macerated fruit, you can certainly just scrape it on and be set. But any of the below techniques will really help your pie pop.

THOUGHTFULLY RUSTIC: When I don't have time for anything fancy, I opt for this technique. I hold a bowl of the topping over the cooled pie and use a small silicone spatula to scrape it out onto the pie. The idea here is you're letting the topping fall where it may, but starting in the center allows it to sort of fall onto itself in a way that creates a beautiful, pillowy effect, and it also keeps the mound higher in the center, without even having to touch it.

SWOOPING: Swoops can be made using a small offset spatula or the back of a small spoon, and the technique is all in the wrist. Apply your topping to the center of the pie, taking care to keep it in the center—you don't want to go all the way out to the edges of the pie yet, because the swooping action will take you there! Then press the spatula or spoon into the topping while sweeping your wrist back and forth in a wave-like motion. The harder you press, the deeper the swoops will be—I like to keep it random to achieve the most swoop-tastic results, with a range of higher peaks and lower valleys. Continue until you like the way it looks—sometimes with this technique, less is more!

SPOONFULS: This is sort of a home baker's version of a classic French *quenelle*—a delicate oblong spoonful of finishes like whipped cream or ice cream used for fancy plated desserts. Sometimes I top pies by simply dolloping spoonfuls of the topping over the surface of the pie, keeping their rounded spooned shape wherever they land. Or use an ice cream scoop to create spherical mounds of topping.

PIPING: When you use a piping tip, you get a certain level of fanciness for very little effort. The comment I hear most often is that folks are afraid to pipe because they are afraid the result will look imperfect or uneven. My answer to that is, embrace it! Use a couple of different tips to create different sizes and shapes and pipe different amounts of topping all over the pie without worrying about uniformity. Alternatively, you can pipe more purposefully—for example, just on the outside edge of the pie.

RANDOM: If you haven't realized it yet, I'm a big fan of random/willy-nilly finishes. Sometimes I combine several of the finishing techniques above to create a beautiful—but imperfect—result. For example, you can start by dolloping spoonfuls of filling all over the top of a pie, then pipe the remaining filling to fill in the gaps. Or start with a swoopy effect and then spread the topping out in

PIE-DEA

Swirling Toppings

Working with more than one topping? In some cases, similar toppings can be swirled together to create a stunning effect. Two different shades of whipped cream, for example, can be gently folded together to create a streaky look before adding to the top of a pie—same for two shades of meringue! Or, when piping a topping, you can use a spatula or spoon to add alternating scoops of the two different colors to the pastry bag so that when you pipe, the finished topping has a swirly look.

some places to create different textures. You can also turn to cake decorating tools to create other effects—like using a cake comb to create ridges in a portion of a pie topping. Random techniques look especially good when you have toppings of more than one color (for example, plain and chocolate whipped cream).

GLAZES

The way to send a pie truly over the top? Finish it with an impressive topping and then add an incredible glaze. Glazes add flavor, color, and another element of glossy beauty to any pie. There are several ways to add a glaze, depending on the desired effect. Keep in mind that some toppings, like meringue, are sensitive to moisture, so you should apply a glaze just before serving.

DRIZZLES: Drizzling can be as simple as dipping a spoon into the glaze and drizzling it back and forth over the pie. Or it can be more effortful—transfer the glaze to a pastry bag and cut a small opening in it for drizzling. Either way, start with a well-chilled pie and a cooled glaze. You know how sometimes less is more? With drizzles, I think more is definitely more.

FULL COATING: To cover the top of a pie with a glaze, you'll want a thin glaze, one that flows easily off the spoon (see, for example, the Chocolate-Covered-Raspberries Pie, page 292). Start with a well-chilled pie and a cooled glaze. Beginning at the center of the pie, spoon the glaze all over it. You may be able to tilt the pie after adding a spoonful of glaze to help distribute it. Work slowly and carefully; some pooling in spots is normal with this method, but you want to aim to get as thin an all-over coating as possible.

DRIPS: If you want to apply a drippy glaze to a pie, it's best to choose one that has a topping with some height (think: mile-high). That ensures there's plenty of distance for the glaze to travel as it drips down the sides of the topping. Start with a well-chilled pie and a cooled thick glaze—one that flows slowly off the spoon. You can use a small spoon to apply the glaze, gently nudging it as you add it to encourage drips to start to fall. But my favorite way is to transfer the glaze to a disposable pastry bag and cut a small opening in the end of the bag, then pipe the glaze where you want it, using the tip of the bag to help encourage the drips to fall.

You can also skip applying the glaze and just serve it in a bowl alongside the pie for guests to add themselves as they dig into their own slices.

GARNISHES

Garnishes, from simple to fancy-pants, are a great way to gussy up any pie, and it's a good way to make a recipe your own. I list a few preferred techniques for garnishing below, followed by some of my favorite garnishes.

TECHNIQUES

CLUSTERS: Arranging a garnish, like chocolate shavings, toasted coconut, or edible flower petals, in a few clusters over the top of the pie allows the filling below to peek through.

ASYMMETRICAL: You can just cover a portion of the pie to create a beautiful garnish that still showcases the filling. I like going in a sort of wonky diagonal across the center of the pie (like the miniature cookies in Ways to Use Your Dough Scraps, page 38), or focusing the garnish to one side or the other, or even embracing a sort of half-moon shape that matches the shape of the pan (as seen on the Blueberry Lemon Meringue Pie, page 280).

ALL OVER AND FULL: This is one of my favorite ways to garnish when you want everyone to get a little of everything in every slice. Arrange the garnishes—fresh fruit, toasted nuts—all over the top of the pie, being very generous. This is as effective with a single garnish (like the chocolate pearls on top of the Triple-Chocolate Caramel Truffle Pie on page 271) as it is with multiple toppings that have different colors and textures (like the fresh blueberries and dollops of whipped cream on the Blueberry Lemon Meringue Pie).

PATTERN: Arrange the garnish in stripes or concentric circles over the top of the pie.

HALF AND HALF: Cover half of the pie with one garnish and the other side with a different one. This looks equally great with garnishes that are the same texture but different colors, such as the Flavored Sifting Sugars on page 128, or that are completely different—think crumbled nut brittle on one half and chocolate shavings on the other.

JUST AROUND THE EDGES: Arrange the garnish just around the edges of the filling. You can start right next to the crust or leave a bit of space between the crust and the garnish.

FAVORITE GARNISHES

FRESH FRUIT: Fresh fruit is one of my favorite garnishes for pies, because it allows you to use the best of the season without fretting about juiciness or any of the other concerns that can plague fruit fillings. Try using multiple kinds of fruit to showcase different colors and textures. In most cases, you'll need to peel, seed, and/or pit the fruit but sometimes I leave cherries whole, because their stems look perky and cute. Slice larger fruits, like peaches or apples, and leave small ones, like berries, whole. Sometimes I stick to one color spectrum (purple plums, blackberries, and black currants, for example), other times I embrace a more random look.

HERBS AND FLOWERS: Herbs and edible flowers are another beautiful garnish for pies. I like to keep the look delicate. It's fun to combine them with another element, like fruit, or to place them on top of a topping like whipped cream or meringue. Scatter them over a fully topped pie or arrange atop the piped border around the edge of a pie.

CHOCOLATE SHAVINGS: Chocolate shavings are simple to make, beautiful, and so yummy! The easiest way to make them is to run a sharp vegetable peeler across a bar or block of chocolate. I rub the chocolate with my hands for a few moments to warm it up and soften it, which will make for curlier curls. Shave the chocolate directly onto the pie, or onto a piece of parchment, which you can then use as a funnel to help you transfer the shavings to the pie. (If you use your hands to transfer them, they are likely to melt.)

CRUST CUTOUTS: Cutouts can be a lovely garnish for a pie, and a great way to use up scraps of dough (see page 91 for how to bake the cutouts). I especially like to use these in a cluster effect with other elements such as nuts, fruit, or small candies.

SIFTED SUGAR: Sifted powdered sugar is a classic finish for many baked goods and can really make a pie pop. Because I can't stop at a simple good thing, I've included a ton of sifting sugar variations on page 128 that will add different flavors and colors to your garnishing arsenal.

NUTS AND CRISPY THINGS: Plain old nuts on their own can be an excellent garnish, toasting them boosts them a bit, and candying them or turning them into a brittle (see Basic Brittle, page 129), takes them up another notch and adds a lovely crunchy texture to the mix. But don't stop there—you can find other crunchy ingredients hiding in your pantry that can make a yummy addition. Think crumbled pretzels, potato chips, graham crackers, or even cereal.

COARSE SUGAR, SPRINKLES, OR SMALL CANDIES: I usually prefer to sprinkle coarse sugar on top of the pie crust before baking, but that doesn't mean it can't come into play when garnishing as well. Ingredients like sanding sugar, colorful sprinkles, pearl sugar (see Resources, page 345), or small candies like chocolate pearls (see Resources) all work here, perhaps paired with other garnishing elements.

SCRAPS FROM OTHER BAKING PROJECTS: When I was growing up, my dad had a strict dining rule: no starch on starch. He meant things like potatoes on pizza, or French fries inside a sandwich, but I think he would support the idea of crumbling leftover brownies, crispy chocolate chip cookies, coconut macaroons, or cake crumbs over the top of a pie. It's a delicious way to recycle.

Pie Scrap Doughnuts

My fabulous assistant and right-hand gal in all things baking, Kaitlin Wayne, casually invented these one day while recipe testing this book (then dropped the mic and left my apartment with the wind in her hair). They're easy to make and so fun and cute—make them with scraps for a snack, or use them to garnish a finished pie.

To make the doughnuts, roll out the dough to about ¼ inch / 3 mm thick. Cut into a doughnut shape using two sizes of round cutters (a large one to cut the main shape, and a small one to cut out the center). Fry them in 2 to 3 inches of hot oil (around 350°F / 175°C) until they're lightly golden all over—they should puff up and become very crisp (exact time will vary depending on the size of your "doughnuts"—1 to 3 minutes per side). Drain the finished "doughnuts" on absorbent paper towels and toss them while they're still warm in cinnamon sugar, powdered sugar, or Flavored Sifting Sugars (page 128) until well coated.

How to Get Neat, Pretty Slices of Pie

Cutting a pie into clean slices isn't always easy, but here are a few tips to help you get the prettiest ones possible.

- **COOL BAKED PIES COMPLETELY OR CHILL COLD-SET PIES THOROUGHLY.**

  Pies slice best when they're fully set. For cold-set pies, this means giving them plenty of time to chill (otherwise, the filling may still be runny or too soft). For baked pies, this means thorough cooling; most fruit fillings will be much softer, or even still liquid, when warm. (If you're someone who loves a warm slice of pie, never fear—just follow the instructions on page 21 for refreshing whole baked pies or slices.)

- **CUT A MINI SACRIFICE SLICE.**

  The hardest part of slicing a pie, in my opinion, is getting the first piece out. So instead of putting that pressure on yourself, just sacrifice a baby slice. Cut a really thin piece and remove it; don't worry if it gets messed up, just slap it on a plate. Once that slice is removed, it's much easier to cut the second slice and to remove it—because there's wiggle room (literally) to help you slide fully under the bottom crust and lift the slice out. Plus, there's always *someone* who says, "I only want a liiiiiiittle piece, please," so the sacrifice probably won't be a sacrifice after all.

- **WIPE THE KNIFE CLEAN BETWEEN CUTS.**

  This is one of those cheffy things I'll never let go of—wiping the knife clean after each cut is a good idea for almost any pie (as well cakes, pastries, bar cookies, and other baked goods). For pies that have a firm topping, such as a chocolate drizzle or the Cold-Snap Topping (page 127), it is helpful to dip the knife briefly into warm water and wipe it dry before each slice.

- **IF ALL ELSE FAILS, ADD SOME WHIPPED CREAM.**

  If your slice slumps over or the crust falls away from the filling, it usually means the crust was either underbaked or has absorbed moisture and become a bit soggy. No problem—just spoon some whipped cream next to or over the problem area, and watch the slice disappear!

DARK CHOCOLATE BLACK-BOTTOM BASE

MAKES 185 G / 1½ CUPS
(ENOUGH FOR ONE
9-INCH / 23-CM PIE)

DIFFICULTY: EASY

Black-bottom bases, which are just a simple ganache, not only add a punch of chocolatey flavor, they also help protect the crust from moisture from a wet filling (like custard or a cream filling). You can make them with any type of chocolate simply by adjusting the ratio of cream to chocolate (see the variations below).

113 g / 4 ounces dark chocolate (I used 72% chocolate), finely chopped (1 cup)

78 g / ⅓ cup heavy cream

1. Place the chocolate in a medium heatproof bowl. In a small saucepan, bring the cream to a boil over medium heat. Pour the hot cream over the chocolate and let sit for 15 seconds undisturbed, then stir gently until the ganache is thick and smooth.

2. To use, pour the ganache into the bottom of a cooled parbaked pie crust and spread into an even layer. Let set for 15 to 20 minutes before adding the filling.

VARIATIONS

MILK CHOCOLATE BLACK-BOTTOM BASE: Substitute an equal amount of milk chocolate for the dark chocolate and reduce the cream to 60 g / ¼ cup.

WHITE-BOTTOM BASE: Substitute an equal amount of white chocolate for the dark chocolate. Place it in a small heatproof bowl, add 30 g / 2 tablespoons heavy cream, set the bowl over a small saucepan of barely simmering water (or use a double boiler), and heat, stirring occasionally, until the chocolate is fully melted.

CARAMELIZED WHITE-BOTTOM BASE: Substitute an equal amount of caramelized white chocolate (see Resources, page 345) for the dark chocolate. Place it into a small heatproof bowl, add 30 g / 2 tablespoons heavy cream, set the bowl over a small saucepan of barely simmering water (or use a double boiler), and heat, stirring occasionally, until the chocolate is fully melted.

Make Ahead and Storage

Although it is possible to make the ganache ahead, this small amount will set up quickly as it stands and can be prone to breaking when reheated. It's so quick to make, I recommend just preparing it when you're ready to use it!

CLASSIC WHIPPED CREAM

MAKES 141, 283, OR 422 G / 1, 3, OR 4 CUPS, DEPENDING ON THE BATCH YOU CHOOSE

DIFFICULTY: EASY

It's never a bad idea to serve pie with plenty of whipped cream. Think your pie is sweet enough? You can leave the sugar out—ain't nothin' wrong with plain ol' whipped cream. For a luxurious twist, try the mascarpone variation below.

HALF BATCH
(for covering only a portion of a 9-inch / 23-cm pie or for a very thin top layer)

118 g / ½ cup heavy cream
25 g / 2 tablespoons granulated sugar
3 g / ½ teaspoon vanilla extract (optional)

FULL BATCH
(for generously covering the whole pie)

235 g / 1 cup heavy cream
50 g / ¼ cup granulated sugar
5 g / 1 teaspoon vanilla extract (optional)

MILE-HIGH BATCH
(for when you're feeling all fancy-pants)

353 g / 1½ cups heavy cream
66 g / ⅓ cup granulated sugar
7 g / 1½ teaspoons vanilla extract (optional)

In the bowl of a stand mixer fitted with the whip attachment, whip the cream on medium-low speed until it begins to thicken, 1 to 2 minutes. Increase the speed to medium and add the sugar in a slow, steady stream, then continue to whip to medium peaks. Add the vanilla, if using, and mix to combine.

VARIATION

MASCARPONE WHIPPED CREAM: Reduce the cream by half. For a half batch, use 75 g / ⅓ cup mascarpone; for a full batch, 113 g / ½ cup; and for a mile-high batch, 170 g / ¾ cup. Place the mascarpone and sugar in the mixer bowl and whip on medium speed until light and fluffy, 2 to 3 minutes. Scrape the bowl well, then reduce the speed to medium-low and add the cream in a slow, steady stream. Raise the speed to medium-high and whip until the mixture is smooth and reaches medium peaks. Add the vanilla, if using, and mix to combine.

Make Ahead and Storage

Plain whipped cream is best made just before it is used, but you can intentionally under-whip the cream (to just under soft peaks), then finish by whipping by hand when you're ready to serve. It will hold this way for up to 4 hours. The mascarpone variation can be made up to 6 hours ahead and held in the refrigerator. Whip a few times gently to refresh before using.

WHIPPED CREAM SAUCE

MAKES 285 G / 1⅓ CUPS

DIFFICULTY: EASY

Known to everyone else in the world as "under-whipped cream," this is my current favorite topping for pie. For years, my favorite topping was just a drizzle of cold heavy cream, and I still love that. But partially whipping the cream gives it the texture of melted ice cream, so it coats each and every bite more evenly. The sweetener and flavoring are optional here, so you do you. (Mama, this one's for you!)

235 g / 1 cup heavy cream
50 g / ¼ cup granulated sugar (optional)
7 g / 1½ teaspoons vanilla extract (optional)

In a medium bowl, whisk the cream and sugar, if using, until the cream begins to thicken. It should be too soft to be whipped cream but aerated enough that it's thick enough to firmly coat a spoon dipped into it. Mix in the vanilla, if using.

Make Ahead and Storage

This can be made up to 24 hours ahead and stored in the refrigerator, but it may lose thickness. If it seems loose after chilling, rewhip it slightly before serving.

PIE-DEAS

Swirled Whipped Cream

Try swirling two shades of whipped cream together by only partially folding them together. This technique works best if you whip the cream to just past soft peaks, then fold the two together with a whisk. Try this with plain + chocolate whipped cream, plain + fruity whipped cream, or fruity whipped cream + chocolate whipped cream (see recipes that follow). You can also add up to 120 g / 1 cup Thick Fruit Coulis (page 122) or up to 160 g / ½ cup Salted Caramel Sauce (page 126) to a full batch of plain whipped cream and fold it in similarly—gently (do not over-mix) to create another flavorful streaked effect.

EXTRA-THICK AND CREAMY WHIPPED CREAM

MAKES 375 TO 646 G / 2½ TO 3½ CUPS, DEPENDING ON THE BATCH YOU CHOOSE

DIFFICULTY: EASY

Using cream cheese in whipped cream adds three kinds of magic. It makes it gloriously thick and extra-creamy. It adds a subtle tanginess that pairs beautifully, especially with fruit pies. And it makes it incredibly stable, up to 24 hours—something plain whipped cream just can't do.

HALF BATCH

(for covering only a portion of a 9-inch / 23-cm pie, or for a very thin top layer)

113 g / 4 ounces cream cheese, at room temperature

38 g / ⅓ cup powdered sugar

235 g / 1 cup heavy cream

10 g / 1 teaspoon vanilla extract (optional)

FULL BATCH

(for generously covering a whole pie)

226 g / 8 ounces cream cheese, at room temperature

76 g / ⅔ cup powdered sugar

470 g / 2 cups heavy cream

5 g / 2 teaspoons vanilla extract (optional)

In the bowl of a stand mixer fitted with the whip attachment, whip the cream cheese and powdered sugar until light and fluffy on medium-low speed, 2 to 3 minutes, stopping to scrape the bowl well halfway through mixing. Raise the speed to medium and add the cream in a slow, steady stream. Try to pour the cream down the side of the bowl to prevent it from being splashed by contact with the whip, then continue to whip to soft peaks. Scrape the bowl well and whip to medium peaks. Add the vanilla, if using, and mix to combine.

Make Ahead and Storage

The cream can be made up to 24 hours ahead—it's best to apply it directly to the pie, but it can also be stored in the refrigerator in an airtight container.

CHOCOLATE WHIPPED CREAM

MAKES 145, 290, OR 435 G / 1, 3, OR 4 CUPS, DEPENDING ON THE BATCH YOU CHOOSE

DIFFICULTY: EASY

A little cocoa powder is a delicious addition to whipped cream. Try using black cocoa powder (see Resources, page 345) for an extra intense chocolate color and flavor.

HALF BATCH
(for covering only a portion of a 9-inch / 23-cm pie, or for a very thin top layer)

118 g / ½ cup heavy cream

25 g / 2 tablespoons granulated sugar

11 g / 2 tablespoons unsweetened cocoa powder

3 g / ½ teaspoon vanilla extract (optional)

FULL BATCH
(for generously covering the whole pie)

235 g / 1 cup heavy cream

50 g / ¼ cup granulated sugar

17 g / 3 tablespoons unsweetened cocoa powder

5 g / 1 teaspoon vanilla extract (optional)

MILE-HIGH BATCH
(for when you're feeling all fancy-pants)

353 g / 1½ cups heavy cream

66 g / ⅓ cup granulated sugar

21 g / ¼ cup unsweetened cocoa powder

7 g / 1½ teaspoons vanilla extract (optional)

1. In the bowl of a stand mixer fitted with the whip attachment, whip the cream until it begins to thicken, 1 to 2 minutes.

2. Whisk the sugar and cocoa powder together in a small bowl. With the mixer running on medium speed, add the sugar mixture in a slow, steady stream, then continue to whip to medium peaks. Add the vanilla, if using, and mix to combine.

Make Ahead and Storage
The whipped cream can be refrigerated in an airtight container for up to 4 hours.

Top to bottom: Chocolate Whipped Cream made with black cocoa, Chocolate Whipped Cream made with regular cocoa, Freeze-Dried Fruity Whipped Cream (dragonfruit), Fresh Fruit Whipped Cream (strawberry), Jammy Whipped Cream (mixed berry), Nut Butter Whipped Cream (peanut butter), Mascarpone Whipped Cream, Classic Whipped Cream

FRESH FRUIT WHIPPED CREAM

MAKES ABOUT 415 G /
2½ CUPS

DIFFICULTY: MEDIUM

Making an easy puree from fresh fruit is the starting point for a super-flavorful whipped cream topping. Looking for something even easier? Check out the variations below, which use items you can find in the grocery store.

340 g / 2 cups prepared fresh fruit (peeled, pitted, chopped, etc., as needed)
50 g / ¼ cup granulated sugar
294 g / 1¼ cups heavy cream

1. In a small pot, combine the fruit and sugar and cook over medium heat until the fruit begins to break down, 3 to 5 minutes. Use a potato masher or large fork to mash the fruit to a coarse puree (if you can't do this easily, cook for 3 to 5 minutes more).

2. Strain the mixture through a fine-mesh sieve set over a bowl, then pour the puree into a liquid measuring cup. You should have about 80 g / ⅓ cup puree. If you have more (it just means your fruit was super-juicy), return it to the pot and simmer to reduce to that amount. Cool completely.

3. In the bowl of a stand mixer fitted with the whip attachment, whip the cream on medium speed to just under soft peaks. Add the cooled puree and continue to whip on medium speed to medium peaks.

VARIATIONS ///

JAMMY WHIPPED CREAM: Replace the fruit and sugar mixture with 113 g / ⅓ cup jam, jelly, or preserves of your choice (skip steps 1 and 2). If the preserves are particularly chunky, you might want to puree them with an immersion blender or in a small food processor before using.

FREEZE-DRIED FRUITY WHIPPED CREAM: Replace the fresh fruit with 43 g / 1½ ounces freeze-dried fruit (skip steps 1 and 2). Pulse it with the sugar in a food processor until it becomes a fine powder, then add to the cream and proceed as directed.

Make Ahead and Storage

The fruit mixture for the basic recipe can be prepped up to 2 days ahead. The whipped cream recipe is best made the same day it will be used (it can be refrigerated for up to 2 hours).

NUT BUTTER WHIPPED CREAM

MAKES 395 G / 1½ CUPS (ENOUGH TO COVER ONE 9-INCH / 23-CM PIE)

DIFFICULTY: EASY

I first created this insanely delicious nutty whipped cream with peanut butter to top a chocolate cream pie, and the result was gush-worthy. Try it with almond butter or chocolate-hazelnut spread too.

135 g / ½ cup smooth nut butter
25 g / 2 tablespoons granulated sugar
173 g / ¾ cup heavy cream
6 g / 1 teaspoon vanilla extract (optional)

In the bowl of a stand mixer fitted with the whip attachment, whip the nut butter and sugar until light and fluffy, 1 to 2 minutes. Scrape the bowl well. With the mixer running on medium speed, add the cream in a slow, steady stream. Try to pour the cream down the side of the bowl to prevent it from being splashed by contact with the whip, then continue to whip to soft peaks. Scrape the bowl well, then whip to medium peaks. Add the vanilla, if using, and mix to combine.

Make Ahead and Storage

This cream can be refrigerated in an airtight container for up to 4 hours.

MARSHMALLOW TOPPING

MAKES ABOUT 425 G / 2½ CUPS (ENOUGH TO COVER ONE 9-INCH / 23-CM PIE)

DIFFICULTY: HARD

Marshmallows are made by whipping cooked sugar until it's fluffy and aerated. Some recipes add egg whites to make the marshmallows more stable, but this version is a true, honest-to-goodness marshmallow. Be sure to use nonstick spray to help with the stickiness factor when handling the marshmallow (and spray your knife with it when you slice the marshmallow-topped pie). Toasting the topping is optional but strongly recommended.

150 g / ⅔ cup cool water
12 g / 1 tablespoon powdered gelatin
198 g / 1 cup granulated sugar
156 g / ½ cup light corn syrup
1 vanilla bean, halved lengthwise, seeds scraped out and reserved, or 10 g / 2 teaspoons vanilla extract

1. Bloom the gelatin: Pour 75 g / ⅓ cup of the water into a small bowl. Sprinkle the gelatin evenly over the surface and let sit while you prepare the sugar mixture.

2. In a medium pot, combine the sugar, corn syrup, the remaining 75 g / ⅓ cup water, and the vanilla bean seeds (if using vanilla extract, you'll add it later). Bring the mixture to a boil over medium heat—you can stir it to help the sugar dissolve until it comes to a boil, but once it begins to bubble, stop stirring. Boil the mixture until it registers 245°F / 118°C on an instant-read thermometer (or attach a candy thermometer to the side of the pot), then remove from the heat and carefully pour the hot syrup into the bowl of a stand mixer fitted with the whip attachment. Add the bloomed gelatin to the hot syrup and whip the mixture until it is white and very fluffy, 4 to 5 minutes. It should be thick enough to hold its shape, not soft or runny. If using vanilla extract, add it now and mix to combine.

3. While the mixture whips, lightly spray any utensils you'll use to transfer the marshmallow to the top of the pie (like a silicone spatula and/or a small offset spatula) with nonstick spray. Have the cooled pie ready for topping.

4. Use the greased spatula to scoop the marshmallow onto the top of the pie. You want to work quickly here—as the marshmallow mixture cools, it will start to set. Use a small offset spatula to spread the marshmallow into an even layer or mound it higher in the middle for a more classic shape. If desired, toast the marshmallow with a kitchen torch.

5. Let sit until the marshmallow is completely cool before slicing the pie (spray the knife with nonstick spray after every few cuts).

VARIATIONS

CHOCOLATE MARSHMALLOW TOPPING: Add 17 g / 3 tablespoons unsweetened cocoa powder (preferably dark or black cocoa; see Resources, page 345) in the last 15 seconds of mixing in step 2.
MOLASSES MARSHMALLOW TOPPING: Reduce the corn syrup to 78 g / ¼ cup and add 113 g / ⅓ cup molasses along with the corn syrup.
HONEY MARSHMALLOW TOPPING: Reduce the corn syrup to 78 g / ¼ cup and add 113 g / ⅓ cup honey along with the corn syrup.

Make Ahead and Storage

The marshmallow topping should be applied to the pie as soon as it's made, but it holds well on the pie for 1 to 2 days.

MERINGUE TOPPING

MAKES 170 TO 340 G /
2½ TO 4½ CUPS
(ENOUGH TO COVER
ONE 9-INCH / 23-CM
PIE)

DIFFICULTY: MEDIUM

Meringue sweetens up and fancies up just about any pie. I like to use it to create all kinds of different finishes, so I offer two versions here, one for a regular pie topping and one for a mile-high application. Meringue looks great just piled on top, all swoopy-like—or you can get fancy with piping (see Lemon Meringue Pie, page 280, for a few ideas).

REGULAR BATCH

71 g / 2 large egg whites
1 g / ¼ teaspoon cream of tartar
99 g / ½ cup granulated sugar
Small pinch of fine sea salt
5 g / 1 teaspoon vanilla extract (optional)

MILE-HIGH BATCH

142 g / 4 large egg whites
2 g / ½ teaspoon cream of tartar
198 g / 1 cup granulated sugar
Large pinch of fine sea salt
10 g / 2 teaspoons vanilla extract (optional)

1. Bring a medium pot filled with about 2 inches / 5 cm of water to a simmer over medium-low heat. Set a medium bowl over the pot, add all the ingredients, and whisk to combine. Then heat, whisking constantly, or beating with a hand mixer, until the mixture reaches 160°F / 71°C on a thermometer.

2. Remove the bowl from the heat and continue to whisk or transfer the heated mixture to the bowl of a stand mixer fitted with the whip attachment. Whip the mixture on medium-high speed until it reaches medium peaks, 2 to 3 minutes for the regular meringue, or 4 to 5 minutes for the mile-high version.

3. Pile the meringue on top of the cooled pie. Spread the meringue out to the edges, but keep it mounded a bit higher in the middle. If desired, toast the meringue with a kitchen torch.

VARIATIONS ///

FRUITY MERINGUE TOPPING: Process 35 g / 1¼ ounces (for the regular batch) or 70 g / 2½ ounces (for the mile-high) freeze-dried fruit with the sugar to form a fine powder before making the meringue.

CHOCOLATE MERINGUE TOPPING: Gently fold 11 g / 2 tablespoons (regular batch) or 22 g / ¼ cup (mile-high) unsweetened cocoa powder (preferably dark or black cocoa; see Resources, page 345) into the finished meringue by hand.

COFFEE MERINGUE TOPPING: Add 7 g / 1 table-spoon (regular batch) or 14 g / 2 tablespoons (mile-high) espresso powder to the mixture when you start whipping it in step 2.

CARAMEL MERINGUE TOPPING: Replace the granulated sugar with 106 g / ½ cup (regular batch) or 212 g / 1 cup (mile-high) packed dark brown sugar.

HONEY MERINGUE TOPPING: Reduce the sugar to 50 g / ¼ cup (regular batch) or 99 g / ½ cup (mile-high) and add 85 g / ¼ cup (regular) or 170 grams / ½ cup (mile-high) honey, preferably wildflower, along with the sugar.

PEPPERMINT MERINGUE TOPPING: Add 2 g / ½ teaspoon (regular batch) or 3 g / ¾ teaspoon (mile-high) peppermint extract along with the salt.

Make Ahead and Storage

Meringue is best used the same day it's made, but it can be stored for up to 1 day (humidity or moisture will shorten its shelf life.)

Caramel Meringue

Fruity Meringue
with blueberry

Honey
Meringue

Fruity Meringue
with raspberry

Fruity Meringue
with pineapple

Chocolate Meringue
with dark cocoa

Chocolate
Meringue with
regular cocoa

Coffee
Meringue

STREUSEL FOR BAKING

MAKES 230 G / 2 CUPS (ENOUGH TO TOP ONE 9-INCH / 23-CM PIE)

DIFFICULTY: EASY

This is a great all-purpose recipe for streusel that will be baked on top of a pie. It makes large clumps that bake up slightly crisp on the outside but soft in the middle. You can flavor the streusel; sometimes I add a splash of vanilla extract or spices like cloves, nutmeg, and/or ginger.

40 g / ½ cup old-fashioned oats

60 g / ½ cup all-purpose flour

15 g / 2 tablespoons whole wheat flour

53 g / ¼ cup packed light brown sugar

1 g / ¼ teaspoon baking powder

2 g / ¼ teaspoon fine sea salt

1 g / ¼ teaspoon ground cinnamon

57 g / 2 ounces / 4 tablespoons cold unsalted butter, cut into ½-inch / 1-cm cubes

1. In a medium bowl, stir the oats, all-purpose flour, whole wheat flour, brown sugar, baking powder, salt, and cinnamon together to combine. Drop in the butter and mix with your hands or a pastry cutter until the mixture forms large clumps.

2. To use, crumble the streusel over the top of a pie before baking. If the streusel is browning too quickly in the oven, tent it with foil.

Make Ahead and Storage

The streusel is best used the same day it is made.

EXTRA-CLUMPY PREBAKED STREUSEL

MAKES 305 G / 2½ CUPS (ENOUGH TO TOP ONE 9-INCH / 23-CM PIE)

DIFFICULTY: EASY

This baked streusel topping forms beautifully large clumps that you can crumble over any kind of pie you like. I like to use it for pies that aren't baked or are too liquid before baking to support the weight of the streusel before baking (like custard pies).

90 g / ¾ cup all-purpose flour

40 g / ½ cup old-fashioned oats

80 g / ⅓ cup packed light brown sugar

1 g / ¼ teaspoon baking powder

1 g / ¼ teaspoon fine sea salt

85 g / 3 ounces / 6 tablespoons cold unsalted butter, cut into ¼-inch / 0.5-cm cubes

1. Preheat the oven to 350°F / 175°C. Line a baking sheet with parchment paper.

2. In a medium bowl, stir the flour, oats, brown sugar, baking powder, and salt together to combine. Add the butter and mix with your hands or a pastry cutter until the mixture forms clumps.

3. Crumble the streusel onto the prepared baking sheet. Bake until evenly golden brown (it will spread a bit and then come together—don't worry!), 15 to 17 minutes. Cool completely, then use your hands to break it up into large crumbles.

Make Ahead and Storage

The streusel can be stored in an airtight container for up to 2 days. If necessary, re-crisp it in a 300°F / 148°C oven for about 5 minutes, then cool completely before using.

FRUITY POACHING LIQUID

MAKES 1495 G /
6½ CUPS

DIFFICULTY: EASY

Poaching fruit before baking it as a pie filling (like the Candied Clementine Galette on page 184) or using it as a topping adds another layer of flavor to it. Poached fruit also makes a delicious topping, too, and is a great way to use underripe fruit. I like to make my basic poaching liquid with fruit, because it adds not only a subtle flavor, but often an impressive color. The fruit that is being poached will gain more color the longer it sits in the poaching liquid, so you can cool it and let the fruit soak for even longer, if desired.

454 g / 1 pound prepared fruit (peeled if desired; chopped if large [like peaches] and pitted if necessary, left whole if small [like raspberries]), thawed if frozen

99 g / ½ cup granulated sugar

226 g / 1 cup water

906 g / 4 cups dry white wine

Whole spices, citrus zest, and/or vanilla bean (optional)

1. In a medium pot, mix the fruit and sugar to combine. Use a potato masher or large fork to coarsely mash the fruit a bit to release some juices. Add the water, bring to a simmer over medium-low heat, and cook until the fruit softens, 8 to 10 minutes. Strain the liquid into a bowl; discard the solids.

2. Return the liquid to the pot, stir in the white wine and any optional spices or flavorings, and bring to a simmer, then add the fruit for poaching. Cook the fruit, turning occasionally to cook evenly and distribute the color, until the fruit begins to soften. If you will be baking the fruit again later, simmer just until the fruit is beginning to become tender; if it will be used as a topping, poach until it's fully tender. Remove the fruit from the poaching liquid, transfer to a bowl, and cool completely. If desired, cool the poaching liquid completely, then pour it over the fruit so it will absorb more color. Drain before using.

VARIATION ///
NON-FRUITY POACHING LIQUID: Omit the fruit for the poaching liquid and increase the water to 454 g / 2 cups. Add the water and sugar directly to the pot in step 2, and bring to a simmer before proceeding.

Make Ahead and Storage ━━━━━
The poaching liquid can be made up to 1 week ahead and stored in an airtight container in the refrigerator.

THIN FRUIT GLAZE

MAKES 325 G / 1¼ CUPS

DIFFICULTY: EASY

This glaze makes an excellent thin, all-over topping, or it can be brushed over fresh fruits to give them a little shine and extra sweetness.

510 g / 3 cups prepared fruit (peeled if desired; chopped if large [like peaches] and pitted if necessary; left whole if small [like raspberries]), thawed if frozen

30 g / 2 tablespoons fresh-squeezed lemon juice

99 g / ½ cup granulated sugar

21 g / 1 tablespoon honey

1. In a medium pot, stir the fruit, lemon juice, and sugar to combine. Cook over medium heat, stirring occasionally, until the fruit breaks down completely and/or is very soft, 10 to 12 minutes.

2. Use a potato masher or large fork to coarsely mash the fruit a bit to release the juices. Strain the glaze through a sieve, transfer to a storage container, and stir in the honey. Cool completely before using.

Make Ahead and Storage

The glaze can be made up to 5 days ahead and stored in an airtight container in the refrigerator.

THICK FRUIT COULIS

MAKES ABOUT 240 G / 1 CUP

DIFFICULTY: EASY

This thick coulis is perfect for fully glazing a pie, but is also beautiful for drizzling, and is even delicious served alongside pie as a sauce. If the fruit is very juicy (like berries), you'll need the higher amount of cornstarch. Less-juicy fruit (like mangoes), will require only the smaller amount.

510 g / 3 cups prepared fruit (peeled if desired; chopped if large [like peaches] and pitted if necessary, left whole if small [like raspberries]), thawed if frozen

28 g / 2 tablespoons fresh lemon juice

99 g / ½ cup granulated sugar, divided

7 to 14 g / 1 to 2 tablespoons cornstarch (see headnote)

1. In a small pot, stir the fruit, lemon juice, and 50 g / ¼ cup of the sugar to combine. Cook over medium heat, stirring occasionally, until the fruit breaks down completely and/or is very soft, 10 to 12 minutes.

2. Use a potato masher or large fork to coarsely mash the fruit a bit to release the juices. Strain the juices through a sieve and discard the solids. Return the strained juice to the pot.

3. In a small bowl, whisk the remaining 50 g / ¼ cup sugar and cornstarch together. Add to the pot and cook over low heat, stirring constantly, until the mixture comes to a simmer and starts to thicken. Reduce the heat to low and cook for 1 minute longer, stirring constantly. Transfer to a storage container and cool completely.

Make Ahead and Storage

The coulis can be made up to 5 days ahead and stored in an airtight container in the refrigerator.

LEMON CURD

MAKES 238 G / 1 CUP

DIFFICULTY: MEDIUM

Mastering a citrus curd is one of those incredibly useful skills you'll turn to again and again. The key to a good curd is to cook it over relatively low heat so that the egg proteins coagulate slowly, creating a silky-smooth end result.

70 g / 2½ ounces / 5 tablespoons unsalted butter
120 g / ½ cup fresh lemon juice
85 g / 4 large egg yolks
66 g / ⅓ cup granulated sugar
Grated zest of ½ lemon
1 g / ¼ teaspoon fine sea salt

1. In a medium saucepan, melt 56 g / 2 ounces / 4 tablespoons of the butter over medium heat. Add the lemon juice, yolks, sugar, lemon zest, and salt and whisk well to combine. Reduce heat to medium-low and cook, stirring constantly with a silicone spatula, until the mixture is thick enough to easily coat the spatula, 4 to 6 minutes (it should hold a clean line on the spatula when you draw your finger through it). Take care to get into the edges of the pot while stirring to keep the mixture cooking evenly.

2. Stir in the remaining 14 g / ½ ounce / 1 tablespoon butter, then strain the curd into a heatproof container. Cover with plastic wrap pressed directly against the surface and refrigerate until fully chilled, at least 2 hours, before using.

Make Ahead and Storage

The curd can be made up to 1 week ahead and stored in an airtight container in the refrigerator.

VARIATIONS

LIME CURD: Replace the lemon juice and zest with lime juice and zest.

ORANGE CURD: Replace the lemon juice and zest with orange juice and zest.

BLOOD ORANGE CURD: Replace the lemon juice and zest with blood orange juice and zest.

GRAPEFRUIT CURD: Replace the lemon juice with grapefruit juice.

KEY LIME CURD: Replace the lemon juice with key lime juice. Eliminate the zest.

TANGERINE CURD: Replace the lemon juice and zest with tangerine juice and zest.

YUZU CURD: Replace the lemon juice with yuzu juice.

PASSIONFRUIT CURD: Replace the lemon juice with passionfruit juice. Eliminate the zest.

FRUITY DRIPPY GLAZE

MAKES 300 G / 1½ CUPS

DIFFICULTY: EASY

This drippy glaze should be thick enough that it drips slowly from a spoon. It's a dreamy finish for pies—the vibrant natural colors of fruit are a perfect accent, spooned or drizzled directly over the pie's surface, or over other toppings like whipped cream.

510 g / 3 cups prepared fruit (peeled if desired; chopped if large [like peaches] and pitted if necessary; left whole if small [like raspberries]), thawed if frozen

50 g / ¼ cup granulated sugar

142 g / 1¼ cups powdered sugar, plus more if needed

15 g / 1 tablespoon heavy cream, plus more if needed

1. In a medium pot, stir the fruit and granulated sugar to combine. Cook over medium heat, stirring occasionally, until the fruit breaks down completely and/or is very soft, 10 to 12 minutes.

2. Use a potato masher or large fork to coarsely mash the fruit a bit to release their juices. Strain the juice through a sieve and discard the solids.

3. Return the strained juice to the saucepan, bring to a simmer over medium heat, and simmer until reduced to about 80 g / ⅓ cup, 4 to 5 minutes. Transfer the juice to a medium bowl and cool to room temperature.

4. Whisk the powdered sugar into the reduced juice. Stir in the heavy cream. If the glaze is too thick, add more cream to thin it; if it is too loose, add more powdered sugar, 7 to 14 g / 1 to 2 tablespoons at a time.

5. Use immediately, or transfer to a storage container and cover with plastic wrap placed directly against the glaze to prevent a skin from forming.

Make Ahead and Storage

The glaze can be made up to 2 days ahead and stored in an airtight container, covered with plastic wrap as directed above.

DARK CHOCOLATE DRIPPY GLAZE

MAKES 420 G / 1¾ CUPS

DIFFICULTY: EASY

This thick glaze is great for drippy effects (see page 105), but it can be used as a topping or sauce for pie. You can swap the dark chocolate for another type if you adjust the cream ratio; see the variations below. The corn syrup will add a little shine and stability to the glaze, but it's fine to skip it, if you prefer.

226 g / 8 ounces dark chocolate (I use 62%), finely chopped

173 g / ¾ cup heavy cream

21 g / 1 tablespoon corn syrup (optional)

1. Place the chocolate in a medium heatproof bowl. In a small saucepan, bring the cream to a boil over medium heat. Pour the hot cream over the chocolate and let sit for 15 seconds undisturbed, then stir, beginning in the center of the bowl with small circular motions and then widening the circles, until the ingredients are uniformly combined and the glaze is smooth. Stir in the corn syrup, if using.

2. Let the glaze cool slightly before using. Or transfer to an airtight container and let cool (gently rewarm the glaze in a heatproof bowl set over a saucepan of simmering water before using).

VARIATIONS /////////////////////////////////

MILK CHOCOLATE DRIPPY GLAZE: Replace the dark chocolate with an equal amount of finely chopped milk chocolate. Reduce the cream to 118 g / ½ cup.

CARAMELIZED WHITE CHOCOLATE DRIPPY GLAZE: Replace the dark chocolate with an equal amount of finely chopped caramelized white chocolate (see Resources, page 345). Reduce the cream to 78 g / ⅓ cup.

WHITE CHOCOLATE DRIPPY GLAZE: Replace the dark chocolate with an equal amount of finely chopped white chocolate. Reduce the cream to 78 g / ⅓ cup.

Make Ahead and Storage

The glaze can be made up to 2 days ahead and stored in an airtight container at room temperature. Reheat gently in a heatproof bowl set over a saucepan of simmering water before using.

SALTED CARAMEL SAUCE

MAKES 420 G / 1¾ CUPS

DIFFICULTY: MEDIUM

My classic salted caramel, enriched with butter and a touch of cream for a thick, smooth sauce, is perfect as a pie topping, or served alongside à la mode slices.

298 g / 1½ cups granulated sugar

81 g / ¼ cup light corn syrup

57 g / ¼ cup water

½ vanilla bean, halved lengthwise, or 7 g / 1½ teaspoons vanilla extract

113 g / 4 ounces / 8 tablespoons unsalted butter, at room temperature

118 g / ½ cup heavy cream

3 g / ¾ teaspoon fine sea salt, or more to taste

1. Combine the sugar, corn syrup, and water in a medium saucepan. If using the vanilla bean, scrape the seeds from it and add the seeds and pod to the pan (if using extract, you will add it later). Bring the mixture to a boil over medium-high heat. You can stir the mixture before it comes to a boil to help dissolve the sugar but stop stirring the moment it starts to boil. Then continue to boil the syrup until it becomes a medium amber color. Once the syrup starts to color, tilt the pan occasionally—it's easier to see the true color of the caramel when you're looking at less of it (otherwise it may seem darker than it really is).

2. As soon as the caramel is close to medium amber, turn off the heat—the caramel will retain heat and continue to cook, so you want to allow for the carry-over cooking. Add the butter and stir gently to combine. Stir in the cream (be careful—the caramel is likely to bubble up and steam a lot; just keep stirring and it will die down). The sauce should be smooth and creamy. If it seized up and you see chunks of caramel, return the pan to low heat and stir occasionally until the sauce is smooth, then remove from the heat.

3. Stir in the salt and the vanilla extract, if using. Let cool to room temperature. The sauce may firm up as it sits. If necessary, rewarm the sauce in 15-second bursts in the microwave to make it more fluid.

Make Ahead and Storage

The sauce can be refrigerated in an airtight container for up to 2 weeks.

DARK CHOCOLATE COLD-SNAP TOPPING

MAKES 250 G / 1⅓ CUPS
DIFFICULTY: EASY

You'll no doubt remember this nostalgic topping from your childhood ice cream dreams, but I've always loved it with other desserts too. Dip the top of a chilled frosted cupcake in it for an all-over finish or spoon it over a cheesecake to add another texture to the creaminess. But my favorite way is spooned atop a chilled pie for a snappy glaze effect.

213 g / 7½ ounces dark chocolate, finely chopped
39 g / ¼ cup coconut oil, melted

1. Melt the chocolate in a medium heatproof bowl set over a medium saucepan of simmering water or in 15-second bursts in the microwave. Stir in the coconut oil.

2. Let the mixture cool for a few minutes before pouring over a chilled pie.

VARIATIONS ///

MILK CHOCOLATE COLD-SNAP TOPPING: Replace the dark chocolate with an equal amount of finely chopped milk chocolate.

CARAMELIZED CHOCOLATE COLD-SNAP TOPPING: Replace the dark chocolate with an equal amount of finely chopped caramelized white chocolate (see Resources, page 345). Reduce the coconut oil to 30 g / 3 tablespoons.

WHITE CHOCOLATE COLD-SNAP TOPPING: Replace the dark chocolate with an equal amount of finely chopped white chocolate. Reduce the coconut oil to 30 g / 3 tablespoons.

FRUITY COLD-SNAP TOPPING: In a spice grinder or a small food processor, or using a mortar and pestle, grind 10 g / ½ cup freeze-dried fruit into a fine powder. Make the white chocolate snap topping and stir in the powdered fruit.

Make Ahead and Storage

The snap topping can be stored in an airtight container at room temperature for up to 2 weeks. If it hardens, microwave it in 15-second bursts until it liquefies again.

Flavored Sifting Sugars

One of my favorite easy ways to fancy up any pie is to give it a sifting of powdered sugar. It's a basic finish that can be as simple as dusting over fresh fruit garnish for contrast and to add a touch of sweetness, or you can bring out a stencil and fancy up a basic custard pie in no time. The recipes below are listed in order of least to most effort required.

All of these will generously garnish a 9-inch / 23-cm pie. Store in an airtight container until ready to use. The plain powdered sugar–based ones will keep indefinitely (like powdered sugar!). The other variations are vulnerable to moisture and humidity, and will keep for at least 3 days and up 1 week.

SPICED SIFTING SUGAR: Whisk 56 g / ½ cup powdered sugar and up to 18 g / 2 tablespoons ground spice (or a mixture of a few) to combine.

CHOCOLATE SIFTING SUGAR: Whisk 38 g / ⅓ cup powdered sugar with 28 g / ⅓ cup unsweetened cocoa powder (preferably dark or black; see Resources, page 345) to combine.

MATCHA SIFTING SUGAR: Whisk 38 g / ⅓ cup powdered sugar with 18 g / 3 tablespoons culinary-grade matcha powder to combine.

COFFEE SIFTING SUGAR: Whisk 56 g / 1 cup powdered sugar with 12 g / 2 tablespoons espresso powder to combine.

MARSHMALLOW SIFTING SUGAR: Place 105 g / 2 cups dehydrated marshmallows (see Resources, page 345) in a food processor with 7 g / 1 tablespoon cornstarch and pulse to a fine powder.

HONEY SIFTING SUGAR: Place 149 g / 1½ cups granulated honey in a food processor with 7 g / 1 tablespoon cornstarch and pulse to a fine powder.

VANILLA SIFTING SUGAR: Place 149 g / ¾ cups granulated sugar in a food processor. Split a vanilla bean in half and scrape the seeds into the sugar, then add the pod to the processor. Add 7 g / 1 tablespoons cornstarch and pulse until the mixture becomes a fine powder.

FRUITY SIFTING SUGAR: Place 66 g / ⅓ cup granulated sugar in a food processor with 28 g / 1 ounce freeze-dried fruit and 7 g / 1 tablespoon cornstarch and pulse to a fine powder.

CARAMEL SIFTING SUGAR: Place 198 g / 1 cup granulated sugar and 42 g / 3 tablespoons water in a small pot and cook over medium heat, stirring, until the sugar begins to melt and the mixture comes to a simmer, then stop stirring. If any sugar granules have clung to the sides of the pot, wash them away with a pastry brush dipped in cool water. Then cook until the caramel becomes a deep amber color. Pour the caramel onto the center of a parchment-lined baking sheet and cool completely. Break the caramel into pieces, transfer to a food processor, add 14 g / 2 tablespoons cornstarch, and pulse to a fine powder. This mixture should be used soon after it is prepared.

BASIC BRITTLE

MAKES 210 G / ABOUT
1½ CUPS BROKEN OR
CRUMBLED BRITTLE

DIFFICULTY: MEDIUM

Brittle, a thin sheet of amber caramel with nuts or seeds, makes a beautiful and tasty finish for pies. Keep it in large shards for a more dramatic look, or finely chop for an all-over crunchy topping. You can add up to 4 g / 1½ teaspoons ground spice (or spices) along with the nuts or seeds for additional flavor.

99 g / ½ cup granulated sugar

59 g / 3 tablespoons corn syrup

85 to 128 g / ½ to ¾ cup unsalted nuts or seeds
   (roasted or raw; I prefer roasted)

3 g / ¾ teaspoon fine sea salt

1. Line a baking sheet with parchment paper and spray lightly with nonstick spray. In a small pot, stir the sugar and corn syrup together and cook over medium heat, stirring constantly, until the sugar begins to dissolve and the mixture comes to a simmer, then stop stirring. If any sugar granules have clung to the sides of the pot, wash them away with a pastry brush dipped in cool water. Then cook until the syrup just barely starts to turn golden brown. Stir in the nuts or seeds and continue to cook until the caramel is uniformly amber, 6 to 8 minutes more. Pour onto the prepared baking sheet (don't spread—just let it flatten itself out into an even layer). Sprinkle the salt over the brittle and cool completely.

2. Break the brittle into pieces or finely chop.

Make Ahead and Storage

The brittle can be made up to 5 days ahead and stored in an airtight container. It will become sticky if exposed to humidity or moisture.

NOTE

For the nuts or seeds, the quantity depends on what you choose; seeds or smaller nuts (such as pine nuts) generally require a smaller quantity than large nuts, like pecans or cashews.

BISCUIT TOPPING (MAKE IT A COBBLER PIE)

MAKES ENOUGH FOR
ONE 9-INCH / 23-CM
PIE

DIFFICULTY: EASY

I make these easy drop-style biscuits all the time, and I also love them as a topping for cobbler. It was only natural to tweak the recipe into a smaller batch to be a pie topping. It's great on top of juicy fruit pies in lieu of a top crust.

120 g / 1 cup all-purpose flour

53 g / ¼ cup packed light brown sugar

3 g / ¾ teaspoon baking powder

1 g / ¼ teaspoon baking soda

2 g / ½ teaspoon fine sea salt

57 g / 2 ounces / 4 tablespoons cold unsalted
   butter, cut into ½-inch / 1-cm cubes

60 g / ¼ cup buttermilk

57 g / 1 large egg

3 g / ½ teaspoon vanilla extract

Turbinado or coarse sugar for sprinkling

1. In a medium bowl, whisk the flour, sugar, baking powder, baking soda, and salt to combine. Add the butter and mix with your hands or a pastry cutter until the mixture resembles coarse meal.

2. In a container with a spout (such as a liquid measuring cup), whisk the buttermilk, egg, and vanilla until well combined. Make a well in the center of the flour mixture and pour the buttermilk mixture into it. Use a silicone spatula to stir the mixture until it comes together into a dough.

3. To use, scoop or spoon over the filling of a fruit pie to cover and sprinkle generously with turbinado or coarse sugar. Bake at 350°F / 175°C until the topping is golden brown and the filling is bubbly, probably 35 to 40 minutes (if the biscuit topping is browning too quickly, tent it with foil). Serve warm. (Note: If the pie recipe says to bake at a higher temperature, that is OK, just know that this lower temperature will lengthen the bake time.)

Make Ahead and Storage

The biscuit topping is best used the same day it is made, but it can be made ahead and held in the refrigerator for up to 2 hours before using.

NOTE

This is a very flexible recipe. You can add 15 to 30 g / 1 to 2 tablespoons more buttermilk for a more batter-like topping. Or use 15 to 30 g / 1 to 2 tablespoons less for a drier, more streusel-like version.

JAM TWISTS

MAKES ABOUT
20 TWISTS

DIFFICULTY: MEDIUM

These little twists are like tiny fruit pies all on their own. This is a great recipe to use up leftover or scraps of dough. The twists make a tasty snack, but I also like to lay them across the top of a pie instead—you can even weave them into a lattice crust before baking (see Notes).

Pie dough for a double crust, chilled (or 454 g / 1 pound dough scraps, formed into 2 disks and chilled)

37 g / 3 tablespoons granulated sugar

3 g / 1 teaspoon ground cinnamon (optional)

103 g / ⅓ cup jam, jelly, or preserves (see Notes)

Egg wash (see page 98)

1. Preheat the oven to 400°F / 205°C. Line a baking sheet with parchment paper.

2. On a lightly floured surface, roll out one disk of dough into a rectangle about ¼ inch / 6 mm thick. Use the rolling pin to transfer the dough to the prepared baking sheet. Refrigerate it while you roll out the second piece. If desired, trim both pieces with a pastry wheel or knife so that all the sides are straight (this will make for neater twists).

3. In a small bowl, stir the sugar with the cinnamon, if using. Spread the jam evenly over the second piece of dough, leaving about ¼ inch / 6 mm uncovered at the edges. Brush the uncovered border of the dough with egg wash, then use the rolling pin to lift up the first piece of dough and unroll it on top of the jam-covered dough (set the lined baking sheet aside). Press firmly at the edges to seal the dough. Brush the top of dough evenly all over with egg wash and sprinkle with the sugar (or cinnamon-sugar).

4. Use a sharp knife or pastry wheel to cut the dough into ½-inch / 13-mm-wide strips. Holding each strip at both ends, twist several times and then transfer to the parchment-lined baking sheet.

5. Bake the twists until they are golden brown and crisp, 10 to 12 minutes. Cool for at least 5 minutes before serving.

VARIATION

CINNAMON TWISTS: Omit the jam and mix 50 g / ¼ cup granulated sugar with 4 g / 1½ teaspoons ground cinnamon. Instead of spreading the dough with jam, sprinkle with the cinnamon sugar and proceed as directed.

NOTES

This works best with a smoother preserve—if your jam is on the chunky side, you may want to blend it using an immersion or regular blender to smooth it before using.

These twists can be used to make top crust effects like lattice, or can be laid in a spiral effect to make a full top crust (see page 144). Bake the pie as directed; if the twists are browning too quickly, tent them with foil. You may only need a portion of the twists—if so, bake the others separately as directed above and enjoy as a snack!

RECOMMENDED CRUSTS
- All-Buttah Pie Dough (page 48)
- Chocolate All-Buttah Pie Dough (page 48)
- Vanilla Bean-Nutmeg Pie Dough (page 52)

chapter three

FRUIT PIES

Fruit pie is probably the most classic kind of pie—and my personal favorite. The most "pie-y" of pies. Tender, juicy fruit, a perfect combination of sweet and tart, all nestled into a buttery, flaky crust. At their core, fruit pies are simple: fruit, sweetener, and a thickening agent, and sometimes other flavorings. But despite the simplicity of fruit pies, every piece of fruit is different, and that can make nailing the ideal pie filling consistency tricky. Tricky, but not impossible!

To make your best fruit pie, you've got to understand the ingredients you're working with. While most fruits can be prepared in a variety of different ways, you can learn to adjust a recipe's method to better match the fruit you're using.

IN-SEASON AND/OR RIPE FRUIT: Fruit that is in season or at peak ripeness is likely to be softer and juicier, and so it may benefit from juiciness-controlling measures such as macerating the fruit and reducing the juices for an uncooked filling. Precooking the filling is likely to yield more consistent results, but the softer the fruit, the more likely it is to break down during precooking (and that's before the bake time). Soft fruit that must be sliced can be cut into larger rather than smaller pieces to help ensure it stays intact.

OUT-OF-SEASON AND/OR UNDERRIPE FRUIT: Fruit that is out of season or underripe is likely to be firmer and less juicy. That makes it ideal for precooked fillings and whole-fruit preparations, as the fruit isn't likely to fall apart even after a lengthy bake time; it also means that you can slice the fruit very thin, if you like. But these fruits may also be less flavorful, and so fillings made with them can benefit from precooking to concentrate flavors (such as roasting) or to add other flavors (such as simmering with a vanilla bean or whole spices).

USING A COMBINATION OF FRUITS: When using several fruits for a pie filling, it can be more difficult to predict the juiciness level. For uncooked fillings, consider macerating the fruits together and reducing their released juices to control the moisture level of the filling. The fruits can also be used for a precooked filling, which allows you to adjust the thickness as needed. If you precook the fruits separately (see Stone Fruit–Berry Pie, page 176), you can even arrange the filling decoratively (see Layering Fillings, page 100).

CHEATER'S GUIDE TO DETERMINING FILLING PREPARATION BY RIPENESS

There's an exception to every rule, but here's how I usually determine what kind of pie to make based on the fruit I have on hand.

RIPENESS	TYPE OF FILLING
OVERRIPE (SOFT)	Precooked fillings, especially smoother/jammy preparations
JUST RIGHT	Uncooked fillings, garnishes, and finishes
UNDERRIPE (FIRM)	Precooked fillings, especially those prepared with flavor-concentrating preparations like grilling or roasting; large whole-fruit preparations

UNDERSTANDING *YOUR* PERFECT SLICE

For me, a perfect fruit pie is *sliceable*—it's okay if there's a little bit of juiciness at the base of each piece, but the filling holds its shape when sliced. A firmer filling also helps ensure that the bottom crust browns and sets well during baking and stays crisp longer after baking. All the same, I'm a big believer that there's no one right way to do things—other people might think this type of filling is too firm for a fruit pie, and that's fine! In fact, you can reduce the thickener in any of the recipes in this chapter by 7 to 21 g / 1 to 3 tablespoons if desired to achieve a juicier result.

USING FROZEN FRUIT

It is A-OK to use frozen fruit for both uncooked and precooked pie fillings, but just be sure to handle the fruit properly before starting the recipe. Begin by fully thawing the fruit in the refrigerator (at least 4 hours, or up to overnight).

FOR UNCOOKED PIE FILLINGS: Drain the thawed fruit in a strainer set over a medium pot; set the fruit aside. Reduce the juices as directed on page 138 before proceeding with the filling recipe.

FOR PRECOOKED PIE FILLINGS: If more than about 80 g / ⅓ cup juices are released during thawing, reduce the juices as directed on page 138 before proceeding with the filling recipe. If less than about 80 g / ⅓ cup juices are released during thawing, you can generally proceed with the recipe as directed, adding the juices along with the fruit when preparing the filling.

How Do I Save Ripe Seasonal Fruit for Later?

The method I use to freeze fruit to bake into pies later is based on a professional technique used to freeze fruit, referred to as "IQF" or "Individually Quick Frozen." Prepare the fruit the way you would like to use it in the pie filling (peeled, sliced, with pits or seeds removed, etc.). Arrange the fruit in a single layer on a baking sheet, without touching one another. Leaving space between the pieces of fruit allows it to freeze more evenly. Transfer the pan to the freezer and freeze the fruit until completely solid, then transfer to zip-top freezer bags or airtight freezer containers. Use within 3 months for best quality, though you can freeze the fruit for up to 6 months.

There are other methods of freezing whereby fruit is frozen with sugar or in syrup, or additives are used to preserve the color and add to storage life. If you are interested in these types of preservation, refer to the *Ball Blue Book Guide to Preserving* for guidelines.

Can I Substitute a Different Fruit in a Recipe?

While I have tried to be thorough, there are many varieties of fruits out there that aren't covered in this book. New varieties and hybrids, like pluots (a delightful mash-up of plums and apricots), are one example. Regional and wild fruits, like huckleberries, are another. But because there's no better use for unique or seasonal fruit that runneth over than a pie, I've included some recommendations below. (Note that I say "treat like" not "tastes like"—these are simply meant to be guidelines for how the fruit is likely to behave in pie preparations.)

- **BOYSENBERRIES**—*Treat like* blackberries, *but remember* they are less sweet and may need more sugar.
- **CHOKECHERRIES**—*Treat like* cherries, *but remember* they are significantly more sour and even have a note of bitterness, so don't skimp on sugar.
- **CRAB APPLES**—*Treat like* apples, *but remember* they are less sweet and may need more sugar for balance, and their smaller size may make them cook faster.
- **DONUT PEACHES**—*Treat like* any ol' peach, *but remember* they are significantly harder to peel.
- **ELDERBERRIES**—*Treat like* currants or cranberries, *but remember* they are best eaten cooked, and that they can be bitter as well as tart and may require extra sugar.
- **GOOSEBERRIES AND/OR GOLDENBERRIES (CAPE GOOSEBERRY)**—*Treat like* currants or cranberries, *but remember* they're a bit higher in moisture and may require additional thickener.
- **HUCKLEBERRIES**—*Treat like* blueberries, *but remember* they are often much smaller, and more prone to breaking down when cooked for extended periods.
- **LINGONBERRIES**—*Treat like* cranberries or rhubarb, *but remember* lingonberries are more intense and tart in flavor; they are great accompanied with something like cream or custard for balance.
- **LOGANBERRIES (SOMETIMES CALLED OLALLIEBERRIES) AND/OR TAYBERRIES**—*Treat like* raspberries and blackberries, *but remember* that as hybrids of these two berries, they can vary in juiciness and seediness.
- **MARIONBERRIES**—*Treat like* blackberries, *but remember* they have an earthier flavor and can sometimes be firmer/less juicy.
- **MULBERRIES**—*Treat like* blackberries, *but remember* they can often be quite seedy, so consider precooked options where the fruit gets strained.
- **MUSCADINES**—*Treat like* slip-skin grapes, such as Concord, *but remember* their seeds must be removed. You can do this by following a similar method to the one for the Concord Grape Hand Pies

(page 163) or cook them until they are soft enough to mash and then strain out the seeds and skins.

- **PAW PAWS**—*Treat like* bananas, *but remember* that their ripeness is judged more as it would be for a peach.
- **PLUOTS**—*Treat like* apricots and plums, *but remember* they are usually juicier than apricots and firmer than plums.
- **PRICKLY PEARS**—*Treat like* berries, *but remember* you must remove the outer skin and chop the fruit to use (it will break down like berries when heated/baked).

- **SALMONBERRIES**—*Treat like* raspberries, *but remember* they are milder in flavor and can often be more tart.
- **SAND PLUMS AND/OR BEACH PLUMS**—*Treat like* plums or apricots, *but remember* the flavor is often more sour and/or perfumey.
- **SASKATOON BERRIES (ALSO KNOWN AS SERVICEBERRIES)**—*Treat like* blueberries, *but remember* they aren't always as juicy.
- **WILD STRAWBERRIES**—*Treat like* regular strawberries, *but remember* they are significantly smaller and sweeter.

TYPES OF FRUIT FILLINGS

Fruit fillings may be uncooked or precooked. Within these two categories, though, there are a variety of different techniques you can enlist, depending on the desired texture, preparation method (raw or cooked fillings), and other flavors you want to incorporate.

UNCOOKED FRUIT FILLINGS

Uncooked fruit fillings are the most common fruit pie fillings: Toss raw fruit (sliced, if necessary) with sugar and a thickener and transfer to a pie crust to bake. But many of the most common pie problems I'm asked about have to do with this method. My filling is too runny. My double-crust pie has a soggy bottom crust. There's a gap between the filling and the top crust. Luckily, there are easy ways to prevent these issues that are adaptable to almost any recipe.

MACERATING THE FRUIT: In a large bowl, toss the fruit with half of the sugar called for in the recipe. If the fruit is prone to browning, add up to 30 g / 2 tablespoons fresh lemon juice (or use the lemon juice called for in the recipe). Let the fruit macerate, tossing occasionally to distribute and dissolve the sugar, for up to 4 hours. Sugar is hygroscopic, meaning it can pull moisture out of things, so it will pull most of the juices out of the fruit, which will accumulate in the bottom of the bowl. If the fruit is very soft or ripe, this process will happen very quickly and will likely yield a lot of juices. If the fruit is firm or out of season, this process may take the full 4 hours and yield less juice.

A Fix for Soggy Fruit Pies

Since it's more difficult to determine the final juiciness of an uncooked fruit filling than a cooked one, it can be helpful to add a protective barrier of sorts between the bottom crust and the filling. A Black-Bottom Base (page 110) is one possibility, or you can add a thin layer of finely ground nuts or nut flour to both absorb some juices and prevent juices from soaking into the bottom crust. You can opt to toast the nut flour for added aroma and flavor; just be sure to cool it completely before adding it.

REDUCING THE JUICES: After macerating the fruit, strain the juices into a medium pot; set the fruit aside in a bowl. Bring the juices to a simmer over medium heat, then reduce the heat to low and simmer until the juices are reduced to 45 g / 3 tablespoons. If you are adding other liquid ingredients to the pie filling, you can also add them here to help the flavors combine as they concentrate. The more you reduce the juices, the thicker they will be—the end result can range from syrupy to sticky caramel-like. Add the reduced juices back to the fruit and toss to combine; the juices will cool quickly when they come in contact with the fruit.

PREPARING THE FILLING: Mix the remaining ingredients into the fruit. I usually start by mixing the remaining sugar and the thickener together (the granules of the sugar help break up the thickener so that it won't clump up when it hits the moisture of the fruit). I add this mixture to the fruit, mix well to incorporate, and then stir in any other ingredients. Once the remaining sugar is added to the filling, it will continue to draw juices out and break the fruit down, so don't combine everything *too* far ahead of when you're ready to assemble/bake the pie.

Determining Doneness in Pies with Uncooked Fruit Fillings

One of the most common mistakes people make with uncooked fruit fillings is underbaking them. Thickeners like cornstarch and flour don't reach their full thickening capacity until the mixture it's in is brought to a boil, which means the pie filling needs to bubble up, and this can take some time. If your crust is browning too quickly, tent it with foil and or lower the oven temperature to ensure that the filling is properly cooked. With single-crust pies, of course, it's easy to see when the filling is bubbling. With double-crust or latticed pies, you have to have a sharper eye: Sometimes the filling will bubble up out of the vents or between the lattice strands, sometimes not. Plentiful steam rising from the vents is another good sign that the filling is cooked enough.

PRECOOKED FRUIT FILLINGS

In my opinion, not enough people make precooked pie fillings. They may say they are old-fashioned, take too much time, or don't allow the fruit to shine because they're "less fresh." But really, none of this is true—except maybe the old-fashioned part. Lots of old recipes for fruit pies recommend

THE WHYS OF PIES

Post-Bake Patience

Fruit fillings are softest/most liquid when hot, and so they are likely to be excessively juicy when the pie is still warm. For the most sliceable results, let the pie cool completely before slicing. If you want to serve a pie warm, see Refreshing Whole Pies (page 21), which will give you the pleasure of a warm slice of pie without the runniness of a still-warm filling.

precooking the filling. Very few of them, though, say *why*, which is that it can be the method with the most consistent and predictable results, particularly for certain kinds of fruit. Precooked fillings don't add much time to the pie-making process, although they do need to be cooled before they can go into a crust. But I mark this in the "pro" column, because it means the fillings lend themselves to being made ahead. And as far as the flavor goes, precooking can actually help prevent watery, unappealing fillings by concentrating the juices, and they can also help achieve delicious, jammy fruit textures.

STOVETOP FRUIT FILLINGS: Most pre-cooked fillings are made in a pot on the stovetop. The overall process is similar to making an uncooked fruit filling, with the additional step of cooking the filling until it thickens and then letting it cool before putting it into the crust. The great advantage here is that you can see the thickness of the filling before you bake the pie, so there's no guesswork as to how it will look in the finished pie.

Partially Precooked Fillings

While I love the consistent results of precooked fillings, sometimes I do want some of the fruit to remain whole or to be extra-juicy in the finished pie. The solution? Make a precooked filling, then stir in some raw fruit at the end. This works especially well for soft fruits, like berries, which tend to break down during even short bake times. For example, the Blueberry Lemon Pie recipe (page 179) starts by cooking a portion of the blueberries and pureeing them to make a jammy filling, and then uncooked berries are added to the filling before baking. The result is the best of both worlds: a flavorful, sliceable pie with just enough juicy punch from the whole berries.

ROASTED FRUIT FILLINGS: One of my favorite, dark-horse ways to make filling is to roast the fruit in the oven, rather than cooking it on the stovetop. This concentrates the flavors, making it a great way to "save" underripe or less-flavorful fruit. It also makes the fruit tender and thickens the juices that come out of the fruit by reducing them in the heat of the oven. This process works so effectively with some fruits (berries and stone fruit, especially) that you don't even need to add additional thickener to obtain a perfectly sliceable but juicy fruit filling—see the Roasted Strawberry Pie on page 153. While roasting can often take longer than cooking a filling on the stovetop, it's relatively hands-off: Toss it in the oven and let it do its thing.

GRILLED FRUIT FILLINGS: "Grilling" is not a word usually associated with pie, but it's a great way to add flavor to fruit fillings (and to keep the oven off for a little longer when making a pie in the summer!). Grilling works best with larger and/or firmer fruits.

Determining Doneness in Pies with Precooked Fruit Fillings

Precooked fillings do not necessarily need to come to the point of boiling during baking. If the filling has been properly reduced or thickened before baking, it may just thicken a bit further in the oven. And in a single-crust pie, instead of becoming glossy and bubbly, it may have a more matte or drier appearance on the surface—but don't worry, it will still be juicy inside! With double-crust or lattice pies, you need a sharper eye—sometimes, it will bubble up out of the vents or between the lattice strands. Other times, plentiful steam rising from the vents is a good sign that the filling is fully heated through.

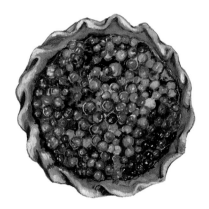

Getting the Texture Right for Fruit Fillings

There are several ways to ensure that fruit fillings have the right consistency. Here's a cheat sheet.

REDUCE THE JUICES: When the juices released by the fruit are reduced down, much of the water content evaporates, leaving a sugary syrup that will get thicker the more it is cooked. Examples: roasting fruit fillings, long-cooking jammy fillings on the stovetop, or macerating the raw fruit and reducing the juices.

KEYS TO SUCCESS: The cooled filling (prebake) will give you a good idea of the texture of the filling after the pie is baked. If it's too soft, continue cooking the juices to reduce them further. If it's too firm, mash additional fresh fruit into the mixture to juice it back up.

ADD A THICKENER: Thickeners like cornstarch or flour can thicken a filling before baking, during baking, or both. Proper cooking of the starch is necessary to achieve maximum thickening capacity, as well as to cook off the flavor of the raw starch.

KEYS TO SUCCESS: In order for the starch in a filling to be fully cooked, it must come to a boil. This can happen when the filling is cooked on the stovetop, during a lengthy bake in the oven, or sometimes both. If the filling hasn't visibly bubbled, the starch may not have cooked fully, and the filling will be runny after cooling.

PUREE OR MASH THE FRUIT: The seeds and skins can help to thicken a fruit filling naturally when it is pureed. This effect isn't usually enough to thicken the filling entirely, but it can be a way to ensure that even really ripe, super-juicy fruit can be used for a filling of the proper consistency.

KEYS TO SUCCESS: Pureeing or mashing the fruit helps to combine the more fibrous portions, as well as aids in distributing natural thickeners like the pectin in currants, apples, and cranberries. If a pureed or mashed filling needs additional thickening, it can be cooked down (reduced!) or thickened with a starch.

PURE RHUBARB PIE

MAKES ONE 9-INCH /
23-CM PIE

DIFFICULTY: MEDIUM

Once when I was out for a slice of pie with my Grandma Jeanne, she looked at the list of pies and sighed, so I asked her what was wrong. "They only have strawberry rhubarb pie," she said. "Not enough people make a plain rhubarb pie—it doesn't need anything!" When the waiter came to take our order, I was surprised when she ordered a slice of strawberry-rhubarb anyway. "Well, it's still *really* good," she said—and of course, she was right. But because of her, this pure rhubarb pie will always be one of my favorites—and for those of you who still want to bring strawberries to the party, see the variation below.

Pie dough for a double crust (see opposite),
    divided in half, shaped into disks, and chilled

640 g / 6 cups thickly sliced rhubarb (about
    3 large or 6 small stalks)

1½ teaspoons vanilla extract

248 g / 1⅓ cups granulated sugar

28 g / ¼ cup cornstarch

½ teaspoon freshly grated nutmeg

Pinch of fine sea salt

Egg wash (see page 98)

Granulated sugar for sprinkling

1. Preheat the oven to 400°F / 205°C with a rack in the lower third (preferably with a Baking Steel or stone on it). Roll out the top and bottom crusts (see page 34). Line the pie plate with the bottom crust as directed on page 36, and chill while you prepare the filling.

2. In a medium bowl, toss the rhubarb with the vanilla. In a small bowl, whisk the sugar, cornstarch, nutmeg, and salt until well combined. Add to the rhubarb and toss well until the fruit is fully coated.

3. Transfer the mixture to the prepared bottom crust and spread into an even layer. Use the rolling pin to gently unfurl the prepared top crust over the filling or, if desired, cut into strips and weave a lattice. Use scissors to trim the dough so there

is only ½-inch / 1-cm excess around the edge of the pie plate. Tuck the excess dough under itself so that it is flush with the edge of the pie plate. Crimp as desired (see page 80), and chill the pie, if necessary.

4. Brush the top crust with egg wash, but don't egg-wash the crimped edges, which tend to brown enough on their own. Sprinkle generously with granulated sugar. Cut a few vents in the top crust.

5. Transfer the pie to the oven and bake until the crust is deeply golden brown, 45 to 55 minutes—ideally, you will see the filling bubble up a bit through the vents. If the crust is browning too quickly, tent the brown portions with foil. Cool the pie completely before slicing and serving.

VARIATION ///

STRAWBERRY RHUBARB PIE: Replace 320 g / 3 cups of the sliced rhubarb with 450 g / 3 cups quartered fresh strawberries. Add an additional 14 g / 2 tablespoons cornstarch in step 2.

Make Ahead and Storage ━━━━━

The pie is best eaten the same day it's made. Store leftovers at room temperature, covered with plastic wrap.

Pure Rhubarb Pie
in Vanilla Bean–
Nutmeg Crust

RECOMMENDED CRUSTS
- Vanilla Bean–Nutmeg Pie Dough (page 52)
- Whole Wheat Pie Dough (page 54)
- Graham Flour Pie Dough (page 54)
- Rough Puff Pastry (page 50)

RECOMMENDED FINISHES
- Skip the top crust and top with Streusel for Baking (page 120), or Biscuit Topping (page 130)
- Serve with Whipped Cream Sauce (page 112)

Strawberry Rhubarb Pie
in All-Buttah Crust

Apple Butter Pie in Rye Crust

Apple Butter Pie in Semolina Crust with Whole Wheat Cutouts

Caramel Apple Pie with Apple Butter Filled Jam Twists

APPLE PIE

MAKES ONE 9-INCH / 23-CM PIE

DIFFICULTY: MEDIUM

If you're looking for a classic apple pie, this is it, with sliced apples that still have a little bite after baking. I precook the filling to ensure it's the perfect consistency—I like a nice, caramel-y sauce around the apples. One of the keys to success for apple pie is to bake it long enough—let the top crust get deeply golden brown to guarantee that the bottom crust is baked through.

1.36 kg / 3 pounds Honeycrisp or other good baking apples (6 large or 8 medium), peeled, cored, and thinly sliced

30 g / 2 tablespoons fresh lemon juice

160 g / ¾ cup packed light brown sugar

50 g / ¼ cup granulated sugar

40 g / ⅓ cup all-purpose flour

4 g / 1½ teaspoons ground cinnamon

2 g / ½ teaspoon ground ginger

Scant 1 g / ¼ teaspoon freshly grated nutmeg

4 g / 1 teaspoon fine sea salt

30 g / 2 tablespoons boiled cider (optional; see Resources, page 345, or DIY instructions on page 197)

28 g / 1 ounce / 2 tablespoons unsalted butter

5 g / 1 teaspoon vanilla extract

Pie dough for a double crust (see below), divided in half, shaped into disks, and chilled

Egg wash (see page 98)

Turbinado sugar for sprinkling

1. In a large pot, toss the apples, lemon juice, and light brown sugar together. Let sit for 30 to 45 minutes, tossing occasionally.

2. In a small bowl, whisk the granulated sugar, flour, cinnamon, ginger, nutmeg, and salt together to combine. Sprinkle this mixture over the apples and stir well to combine. Set the pot over medium heat and cook, stirring constantly, until the apples are lightly softened and the juices have thickened, 6 to 8 minutes.

3. Add the boiled cider, if using, butter, and vanilla to the filling and stir to combine. Transfer the pie filling to a baking sheet or a large casserole dish and spread into an even layer to help it cool faster.

4. Preheat the oven to 400°F / 205°C with a rack in the lower third (preferably with a Baking Steel or stone on it).

5. Roll out the top and bottom crusts (see page 34).

6. Transfer the filling to the prepared bottom crust, packing it in firmly and tightly to eliminate air pockets (this will help prevent the filling from shrinking away from the crust during baking). Use the rolling pin to gently unfurl the prepared top crust over the filling or make cutouts from the top crust. Press all around the edges to seal. Use scissors to trim the dough so there is only ½-inch / 1 cm excess around the edges of the pie plate. Tuck the excess dough under itself so that it is flush with the edge of the pie plate. Crimp as desired (see page 80). Chill the pie in the refrigerator, uncovered, for at least 15 minutes, or up to 30 minutes.

7. Brush the top crust with egg wash, but don't egg-wash the crimped edges, which tend to brown enough on their own. Sprinkle generously with turbinado sugar. Cut a few vents in the top crust.

(CONTINUED)

8. Transfer the pie to a parchment-lined baking sheet and place in the oven. Bake until the crust is deeply golden brown, 55 to 65 minutes—the filling may bubble up a bit through the vents. If the crust is browning too quickly, tent the brown portions with foil. Cool completely before slicing and serving.

VARIATIONS ///

MY OWN PERSONAL FAVORITE APPLE PIE: Yup—there, I said it. Eliminate the filling and replace with the following: In a medium pot, melt 56 g / 4 tablespoons unsalted butter and add 750 g / 6 medium peeled and diced apples. Stir in 212 g / 1 cup dark brown sugar, 30 g / 2 tablespoons lemon juice, 10 g / 2 teaspoons vanilla extract, 6 g / 2 teaspoons cinnamon, and 3 g / ¾ teaspoon fine sea salt. Cook for 3 to 5 minutes, stirring occasionally. In a small bowl, whisk together 66 g / ⅓ cup granulated sugar and 40 g / ¼ cup all-purpose flour. Sprinkle this mixture over the apples and stir well until the mixture thickens, 2 to 3 minutes. Cool completely before assembling the pie.

CARAMEL APPLE PIE: Replace the brown sugar with 160 g / ½ cup Salted Caramel Sauce (page 126), and increase the flour to 60 g / ½ cup—whisk it well into the caramel before adding to the apples.

APPLE BUTTER PIE: Replace the filling above with this one: In a medium bowl, whisk together 1.02 kg / 3 cups prepared apple butter, 66 g / ⅓ cup granulated sugar, 113 g / 2 large eggs, 3 g / 1 teaspoon ground cinnamon, and 5 g / 1 teaspoon vanilla extract until well combined.

Make Ahead and Storage ———

The pie is best eaten the same day it's made. Store leftovers at room temperature, covered with plastic wrap.

RECOMMENDED CRUSTS

- Whole Wheat Pie Dough (page 54)
- Gingerbread Pie Dough (page 52)
- Graham Flour Pie Dough (page 54)
- Cornmeal Pie Dough (page 55)

RECOMMENDED FINISHES

- Salted Caramel Sauce (page 126)
- Classic Whipped Cream (page 111) or vanilla ice cream
- Skip the top crust and finish with Streusel for Baking (page 120)

WHOLE-APPLE DUMPLINGS

MAKES 6 LARGE DUMPLINGS

DIFFICULTY: EASY

A good fruit dumpling is pie at its very simplest: a lightly sweetened piece of fruit wrapped in flaky pie dough and baked until the crust is golden and crisp and the fruit is juicy and soft. There are loads of delicious possibilities (peaches! pears! mini apples!) described in the variations.

About 1350 g / 6 medium-large Honeycrisp or other good baking apples, like Gala, Jonagold, or Granny Smith, peeled

41 g / 3 tablespoons light brown sugar

38 g / 3 tablespoons granulated sugar

1 g / ½ teaspoon ground cinnamon

Scant 1 g / ¼ teaspoon freshly grated nutmeg

Pinch of fine sea salt

1 recipe Rough Puff Pastry (page 50), shaped into a disk and chilled, or a double recipe pie dough (see below), prepared as for Rough Puff Pastry, shaped into a disk and chilled

43 g / 1½ ounces / 3 tablespoons unsalted butter, cut into six 7 g / ½-tablespoon pats

Egg wash (see page 98)

Turbinado sugar for sprinkling

1 recipe Salted Caramel Sauce (page 126) for serving (optional)

1 recipe Classic Whipped Cream (page 111) for serving (optional)

1. Line a baking sheet with parchment paper. Use a paring knife or an apple corer to core the apples. In a small bowl, stir together the brown sugar, sugar, cinnamon, nutmeg, and salt to combine.

2. On a lightly floured surface, roll out the chilled dough to ¼ inch / 3 mm thick. The precise shape doesn't matter, but try to keep it somewhat rectangular. Dock the dough with a fork. Set an apple on the dough and generously cut around it with a pastry wheel to provide enough dough to fully encase the apple, with a little bit of excess that can be pinched together at the top. Then cut 5 more pieces of dough, using the first piece as a guide.

3. Place one piece of dough on the prepared baking sheet and center an apple on top of it. Sprinkle 13 g / 1 tablespoon of the sugar mixture over the outside of the apple and into the cored center. Place one of the pats of butter on top of the apple, or gently press it into the hollow center.

4. Grab one section of dough and gently stretch it outward, then bring it up to the top of the apple. Continue all the way around, letting the dough pleat naturally as you bring it to the top. Hold the pleated dough in place until the fruit is fully wrapped, then pinch it at the top to seal. It doesn't need to be totally closed, but pinching it well will ensure it doesn't come unfurled in the oven. Repeat with the remaining apples and dough. Transfer the dumplings to the refrigerator and chill until the dough is firm, 15 to 30 minutes.

5. Preheat the oven to 400°F / 205°C. Brush the dough all over with egg wash and sprinkle generously with turbinado sugar. Bake until the dough is crisp and golden and the apples are soft on the inside (use a paring knife to check), 35 to 45 minutes.

6. Let cool for about 5 minutes. Serve warm, doused with caramel sauce and whipped cream, if using.

VARIATIONS //////////////////////////////////

PEACH DUMPLINGS: Substitute about 1060 g / 6 large peaches, peeled, for the apples. Use the same technique for coring the apples above to cut around the pit of each peach and remove it. Reduce baking time to 25 to 30 minutes.

PEAR DUMPLINGS: Substitute about 1360 g / 6 large pears, peeled, for the apples. Use a melon baller or spoon to scoop out the core from the bottom of each pear. Reduce the baking time to 25 to 30 minutes if the pears are very ripe or soft.

MINI APPLE DUMPLINGS: Substitute 1120 g / 20 miniature apples for the apples. Reduce baking time to 20 to 25 minutes.

BANANA DUMPLINGS: Substitute 805 g / about 6 medium bananas for the apples. Reduce the baking time to 20 to 25 minutes.

Make Ahead and Storage ──────────

The dumplings are best eaten the day they're made. Store leftovers at room temperature, wrapped tightly in plastic wrap.

RECOMMENDED CRUSTS
- Gingerbread Pie Dough (page 52)
- Chocolate All-Buttah Pie Dough (page 48)
- Caramelized Pie Crust (page 56)

ANY-FRUIT PUFF PASTRY TART

MAKES ONE 12-BY-14-INCH / 30-BY-36-CM TART

DIFFICULTY: MEDIUM

Mastering my rough puff pastry will allow you to make a slew of desserts that are insanely impressive but surprisingly easy. An ultra-flaky puff pastry crust is the ideal base for fresh fruit. It's sturdy enough to use for a free-form tart and to handle some natural juiciness, all the while baking up tender and crisp. Use a single fruit or a combination—just be sure to keep it in an even layer so that the ratio of filling to crust stays just right.

1 recipe Rough Puff Pastry (page 50), chilled, or a double recipe pie dough (see opposite), prepared as for Rough Puff Pastry, shaped into a disk, and chilled

Egg wash (see page 98)

About 1134 g / 2½ pounds fruit, seeds or pits removed as necessary, peeled if desired/appropriate, and sliced if large (e.g., apples or peaches) or left whole if small (cherries or berries) (see Notes)

42 g / 2 tablespoons honey

5 g / 1 tablespoon fresh lemon juice

5 g / 1 teaspoon vanilla extract

66 g / ⅓ cup granulated sugar

14 to 28 g / 2 tablespoons to ¼ cup cornstarch (see Notes)

2 g / ½ teaspoon fine sea salt

Up to 6 g / 1½ teaspoons ground spices (optional)

Turbinado sugar for sprinkling

1. On a lightly floured surface, roll out the dough into a rough rectangle a bit larger than 12 by 14 inches / 30 by 36 cm and about ¼ inch / 3 mm thick. Dock all over with a fork.

2. Use a pastry wheel to cut four 1-inch / 2.5-cm-wide strips from all 4 sides, starting with the 2 longer sides; set aside. Use a rolling pin to transfer the pastry rectangle to a parchment-lined baking sheet. Brush the edges of the rectangle with egg wash and gently lay the strips on top to form a sort of retaining wall. Use the pastry wheel to trim away the excess on the ends of the strips. Dock the edges of the dough with a fork. Transfer to the refrigerator to chill while you prepare the filling.

3. Preheat the oven to 425°F / 218°C with a rack in the lower third (preferably with a Baking Steel/stone on it).

4. In a medium bowl, toss the fruit, honey, lemon juice, and vanilla to combine. In a small bowl, whisk the sugar, cornstarch, and salt together; if using spices, add them here. Add the sugar mixture to the fruit and toss to combine.

5. Arrange the fruit in an even layer on the dough. I like to tightly overlap sliced fruit or tightly arrange whole fruits. Brush the edges of the dough with egg wash and sprinkle generously with turbinado sugar.

6. Transfer to the oven and bake until the pastry is deeply golden brown and the fruit is tender and juicy, 40 to 45 minutes. Cool for at least 15 minutes before slicing and serving.

Make Ahead and Storage

This tart is best eaten the same day it's made. Store leftovers at room temperature, wrapped in plastic wrap.

Right: Raspberries and blackberries in Whole Wheat Rough Puff Pastry
Below: Apples in Rough Puff Pastry

NOTES

The quantity of fruit given is a solid guideline for most fruits—but it is listed as approximate, because you may require slightly more or less, depending on the type of fruit you're using. You may want to plan on an extra piece or two if you're working with larger fruit, or an extra 170 g / 1 cup for smaller fruits to ensure you have enough to cover the surface of your tart.

Use the smaller amount of cornstarch for firmer fruit like apples and the larger amount for juicier fruits like berries.

RECOMMENDED CRUSTS
- Spelt Pie Dough (page 55)
- Gingerbread Pie Dough (page 52)
- Chocolate All-Buttah Pie Dough (page 48)

RECOMMENDED FINISHES
- Whipped Cream Sauce (page 112)
- Salted Caramel Sauce (page 126)

RECOMMENDED CRUSTS
- Vanilla Bean–Nutmeg Pie Dough (page 52)
- Whole Wheat Pie Dough (page 54)
- Graham Flour Pie Dough (page 54)
- Rough Puff Pastry (page 50)

RECOMMENDED FINISHES
- Top with Streusel for Baking (page 120), or Biscuit Topping (page 130) before baking
- Serve with Whipped Cream Sauce (page 112)

Above: Roasted Pineapple
Pie in Spicy Crust
Below: Roasted Strawberry
Pie in Brown Butter Crust

ROASTED STRAWBERRY PIE

MAKES ONE 9-INCH /
23-CM PIE

DIFFICULTY: EASY

Slowly roasting fruit concentrates its flavor by reducing the amount of moisture it contains. For fruit with particularly unpredictable juiciness, like strawberries, using this technique makes for an incredibly pure-flavored filling, with the added bonus of requiring absolutely no thickener.

1500 g / 4½ pounds fresh strawberries (see Note)

149 g / ¾ cup granulated sugar

Grated zest of 1 lemon

1 vanilla bean, halved lengthwise, seeds scraped out and reserved (optional)

2 g / ½ teaspoon fine sea salt

One 9-inch / 23-cm pie crust (see opposite), parbaked and cooled completely (see page 43)

1. Preheat the oven to 275°F / 135°C with racks in the upper and lower thirds.

2. Hull the strawberries and cut them into large pieces—cut large strawberries into quarters, medium strawberries in half, and leave the small guys whole. Transfer to two ungreased baking sheets.

3. In a small bowl, rub the sugar, lemon zest, vanilla bean seeds, if using, and salt together with your fingers to disperse the flavorings. Sprinkle the sugar over the fruit, toss gently to combine, and arrange in a single layer.

4. Roast the strawberries until they are soft but still not falling apart, 3 to 4 hours. Rotate the pans and gently stir the strawberries halfway through roasting. Toward the end of roasting time, the juices will have turned into a syrup, but both the juices and the fruit should still be red, not darkened in color. Transfer the fruit and juices to a medium bowl and cool completely.

5. Raise the oven temperature to 375°F / 190°C; place a Baking Steel or stone on the bottom rack if you have one.

6. Place the cooled crust on a parchment-lined baking sheet. Spoon the roasted strawberries into the cooled pie crust and transfer the pie to the oven. Bake until the crust is deeply golden brown and the strawberry filling has darkened slightly, 22 to 25 minutes. Let the pie cool completely before slicing and serving.

VARIATION ///

ROASTED STRAWBERRY PIE (WITH FROZEN STRAWBERRIES): Replace the fresh strawberries with the same amount of thawed frozen strawberries. Quarter them and arrange in a single layer on a baking sheet, along with any juices they released while thawing. Increase the roasting time to up to 4½ hours.

Make Ahead and Storage

The roasted strawberries can be made up to 3 days ahead and stored in an airtight container in the refrigerator. The pie is best eaten the same day it's made. Store leftovers at room temperature, covered with plastic wrap.

NOTE ◇◇◇◇◇◇◇◇◇◇◇◇◇◇◇◇◇◇◇◇◇◇◇◇◇◇◇◇◇◇◇

Roasted strawberries also make a great topping, especially for cream pies, as well as a delicious refrigerator/freezer preserve.

ROASTED PINEAPPLE PIE

MAKES ONE 9-INCH / 23-CM PIE

DIFFICULTY: MEDIUM

I'd never thought of using pineapple as a baked fruit filling, but the first try had me wondering what took me so long. The filling is juicy and bright, and the pie is nicely sliceable. Roasting the pineapple concentrates the flavor, which is as helpful when it's crazy juicy as it is when you accidentally pick one that's a little underwhelming. (You can parbake the pie crust while the pineapple roasts, if you like.) I also love this pie topped with fresh or macerated fruit, such as strawberries or raspberries.

2 large pineapples (about 1657 g), trimmed, cored, cut into ½-inch / 1-cm rings and then into chunks (about 10 cups)

71 g / ⅓ cup packed brown sugar

113 g / ½ cup fresh lime juice

112 g / ⅓ cup honey

2 g / 1 teaspoon ground cinnamon

1 vanilla bean, halved lengthwise, seeds scraped out and reserved

7 g / 1 tablespoon cornstarch

30 g / 2 tablespoons cool water or pineapple juice

One 9-inch / 23-cm pie crust (see below), parbaked, brushed with egg wash, and cooled completely (see page 43)

1. Preheat the oven to 425°F / 220°C, with racks in the upper and lower third of the oven (preferably with a Baking Steel or stone on the bottom rack).

2. Place the pineapple on a baking sheet. Add the brown sugar and toss with the pineapple until it's well coated. Spread the pineapple out into an even layer and roast on the upper oven rack until it caramelizes to a golden brown, 45 to 50 minutes.

3. While the pineapple roasts, combine the lime juice, honey, cinnamon, and vanilla bean seeds in a medium saucepan and bring the mixture to a simmer over medium-low heat. Stir to melt the honey, then simmer for 1 minute longer.

4. Meanwhile, in a small bowl, whisk the cornstarch and water (or pineapple juice) to form a paste. Whisk the mixture into the lime juice mixture and stir until it thickens. Remove from the heat.

5. Transfer the pineapple to a medium bowl and add the lime juice mixture, tossing well to coat. Reduce the oven temperature to 350°F / 175°C.

6. Place the cooled crust on a parchment-lined baking sheet. Gently transfer the pineapple mixture to the crust. Transfer the pie to the oven and bake on the lower rack (on the steel/stone, if using) until the crust is evenly browned and the pineapple is soft, 25 to 30 minutes. Let the pie cool completely before slicing and serving.

Make Ahead and Storage

This pie is best eaten the day it is prepared. Store leftovers at room temperature, covered with plastic wrap.

RECOMMENDED CRUSTS
- Rough Puff Pastry (page 50)
- Citrus Roll-Out Cookie Crust (page 63)
- Coconut Macaroon Crust (page 70; don't use a Baking Steel/stone)

RECOMMENDED FINISHES
- Salted Caramel Sauce (page 126)
- Classic Whipped Cream (page 111)
- Extra-Clumpy Prebaked Streusel (page 120)

DEEP-DISH BERRY COBBLER PIE

MAKES ONE 9-INCH / 23-CM DEEP-DISH PIE (MAKE SURE YOUR PIE PLATE IS AT LEAST 2½ INCHES / 6 CM DEEP)

DIFFICULTY: MEDIUM

I love cobbler almost as much as I love pie, and no one's about to tell me I can't have both. While I often focus on making my pie fillings thick enough that they can hold a firm slice with just the right amount of juiciness, this one leaves the filling a bit juicier so that the biscuit topping can soak some of it up while it's in the oven.

1010 g / 6 heaping cups (prepared/trimmed) berries—slice strawberries, if using; other berries can be left whole (see Note)

15 g / 1 tablespoon fresh lemon juice

66 g / ⅓ cup granulated sugar

71 g / ⅓ cup packed light brown sugar

40 g / ⅓ cup all-purpose flour

3 g / ¾ teaspoon ground cinnamon

2 g / ½ teaspoon fine sea salt

2 teaspoons vanilla extract, or 1 vanilla bean, halved lengthwise, seeds scraped out and reserved

One 9-inch / 23-cm deep-dish pie crust (see below), parbaked, brushed with egg wash, and cooled completely (see page 43)

1 recipe Biscuit Topping (page 130)

1. In a large bowl, toss the berries with the lemon juice and granulated sugar. Let macerate for at least 1 hour, or up to 3 hours; toss the berries occasionally during the first 15 to 20 minutes to help ensure they're all getting evenly juicy.

2. Place a colander over a medium pot and pour the berries into it. Press down gently on the berries—you don't want to smoosh the fruit too much, but you want to get all of the juices that you can into the pot. Transfer the berries to a bowl.

3. Set the pot over medium heat, bring the juices to a simmer, and simmer until they have reduced to 80 g / ¼ cup. The amount of time this takes will depend on how much juice your berries yielded. Remove from the heat.

4. Meanwhile, preheat the oven to 375°F / 190°C with a rack in the lower third (preferably with a Baking Steel or stone on it).

5. In a small bowl, mix the brown sugar, flour, cinnamon, salt, and vanilla bean seeds, if using (if using extract, you will add it later). Use your fingers to mix the ingredients until they're uniformly combined.

6. Toss the brown sugar mixture with the berries to combine well, then pour the reduced juices over and toss again. If using vanilla extract, add it and toss to combine.

7. Place the cooled crust on a parchment-lined baking sheet. Add the filling to the crust and spread into an even layer. Crumble the biscuit topping evenly over the top of the pie, leaving some of the filling exposed at the edges. Transfer the pie to the oven and bake until the crust is deeply golden brown and the filling is bubbling around the edges and/or a tester inserted into the center of the biscuit topping comes out clean, 35 to 40 minutes. Cool completely before slicing and serving.

(CONTINUED)

Make Ahead and Storage

The pie is best eaten the same day it's made. Store leftovers at room temperature, wrapped in plastic wrap.

NOTE ◇◇◇◇◇◇◇◇◇◇◇◇◇◇◇◇◇◇◇◇◇◇◇◇◇◇◇◇◇◇◇◇

You can use one type of berry or a mix. My favorite combo is 337 g / 2 heaping cups blueberries, 337 g / 2 heaping cups sliced strawberries, and 337 g / 2 heaping cups blackberries or raspberries.

RECOMMENDED CRUSTS
- Cardamom Lemon Pie Dough (page 52)
- Vanilla Bean–Nutmeg Pie Dough (page 52)
- Graham Flour Pie Dough (page 54)

RECOMMENDED FINISHES
- Try the Streusel for Baking (page 120) in place of the Biscuit Topping
- Classic Whipped Cream (page 111)
- Whipped Cream Sauce (page 112)

MIXED-BERRY HAND PIES

MAKES 20 HAND PIES

DIFFICULTY: MEDIUM

Precooking berries for pie filling is a surefire way to ensure the ideal consistency, which is particularly important when making mini pies, when you don't want the filling to ooze out. I like to use a mix of berries, but you can use just a single kind if you like. See the Note for instructions to make these latticed, which truly makes them look like itty, bitty pies.

113 g / 4 ounces raspberries

113 g / 4 ounces strawberries, hulled and chopped

113 g / 4 ounces blueberries

15 g / 1 tablespoon fresh lemon juice

5 g / 1 teaspoon vanilla bean paste or vanilla extract

50 g / ¼ cup granulated sugar

14 g / 2 tablespoons cornstarch

2 g / ½ teaspoon fine sea salt

Pinch of ground cinnamon

Triple recipe pie dough (see below), divided in half, shaped into disks, and chilled

Egg wash (see page 98)

Turbinado or sanding sugar for sprinkling

1. In a medium pot, stir the raspberries, strawberries, blueberries, lemon juice, and vanilla paste or extract to combine. Heat over medium-low heat, stirring occasionally, until the berries start to break down and become juicy, 8 to 10 minutes.

2. Meanwhile, in a small bowl, whisk the sugar, cornstarch, salt, and cinnamon to combine. Sprinkle the mixture over the berries and stir well to combine. Increase the heat to medium and cook, stirring occasionally, until the mixture comes to a simmer. Simmer for 1 minute, stirring constantly. Remove from the heat and cool to room temperature.

3. Line two baking sheets with parchment paper. On a lightly floured surface, roll out one half of the pie dough to about ¼ inch / 6 mm thick. The exact size/shape doesn't matter. Use a 3-inch / 8-cm round cookie cutter to cut out circles from the dough; you should get about 20 rounds. Transfer half of the rounds to one of the prepared baking sheets. Spoon about 26 g / 1 heaping tablespoon of the filling into the center of each round. Brush the edges of each round with egg wash, then place one of the remaining rounds of dough on each. Use a fork to crimp the edges to seal.

4. Repeat with the remaining dough and filling, then refrigerate the assembled hand pies while you preheat the oven.

5. Preheat the oven to 400°F / 205°C with racks in the upper and lower thirds.

6. Brush the hand pies with egg wash (try to avoid brushing too much on the outside edges, which will brown more on their own), and sprinkle generously with turbinado or sanding sugar. Cut a small slash or X in the top of each pie with the tip of a paring knife.

7. Transfer the pies to the oven and bake until deeply golden brown, 20 to 25 minutes. Cool completely before serving.

(CONTINUED)

SOUR CHERRY HAND PIES: Replace the berry filling with Sour Cherry Hand Pie Filling (page 168).

Make Ahead and Storage

The filling can be made up to 3 days ahead—store in the refrigerator in an airtight container. These pies are best eaten fresh, but leftovers will still be delicious 1 to 2 days after baking. You can refresh the pies before eating them; I usually just do this in the toaster or toaster oven for 2 minutes. They can also be frozen after baking: Freeze until solid on a baking sheet, then wrap in plastic wrap and store in a freezer bag for up to 3 months. Refresh the frozen pies from frozen by wrapping individually in aluminum foil and placing them on a baking sheet. Place in the oven and turn the oven on to 375°F / 204°C. Leave the pies in the oven for 5 minutes after it has preheated.

Instead of assembling these as mini double-crust pies, you can make the top crust a lattice! To do this, place all of the rounds you cut from the first piece of dough onto the prepared baking sheets and spoon the filling into the centers. Brush the edges of the rounds with egg wash and refrigerate while you prepare the remaining dough. Roll out the second half of dough on a lightly floured surface to ¼ inch / 3 mm thick. Cut the dough into thin strips ¼- to ½-inch / 3- to 6-mm thick. Cut the strands into smaller lengths—about 1½ inches / 4 cm longer than the diameter of the rounds. Make a woven lattice on top of each round as directed on page 94. Brush the lattice with egg wash, sprinkle with sugar, and bake as directed.

RECOMMENDED CRUSTS
- All-Buttah Pie Dough (page 48)
- Whole Wheat Pie Dough (page 54)
- Rough Puff Pastry (page 50)
- Brown Sugar Roll-Out Cookie Crust (page 63)

Brush the edges of each square with egg wash and place one of the remaining pieces of dough on top of it. Use a fork to crimp the edges to seal.

10. Repeat the process with the remaining dough and jam. Chill the trays of assembled hand pies in the refrigerator for 30 minutes.

11. Preheat the oven to 400°F / 205°C with racks in the upper and lower thirds.

12. Brush the pies with egg wash (try to avoid brushing too much on the edges, which will brown more on their own) and sprinkle generously with turbinado or sanding sugar. Cut a small slash or X in the top of each pie with the tip of a paring knife.

13. Transfer to the oven and bake until deeply golden brown, 20 to 25 minutes. Cool completely before serving.

Make Ahead and Storage

The jam filling can be made through step 5 and refrigerated for up to 3 days or frozen for up to 6 months. These pies are best eaten fresh, but leftovers will still be delicious 1 to 2 days after baking. You can refresh the pies before eating them; I usually just do this in the toaster or toaster oven for 2 minutes. They can also be frozen after baking: Freeze until solid on a baking sheet, then wrap in plastic wrap and store in a freezer bag for up to 3 months. Refresh the frozen pies by wrapping individually in aluminum foil and placing them on a baking sheet. Put the pies in the oven and turn the oven to 375°F / 204°C. Leave the pies in the oven for 5 minutes after the oven has preheated.

RECOMMENDED PIE CRUSTS
- All-Buttah Pie Dough (page 48)
- Whole Wheat Pie Dough (page 54)
- Rough Puff Pastry (page 50)
- Brown Sugar Roll-Out Cookie Crust (page 63)

PIE-DEAS

PB&J Hand Pies

Start with Graham Flour Pie Dough (see page 54). Add 12 g / 2 teaspoons of peanut butter on top of the jam before sealing the hand pies, and proceed as directed.

Pie-ce Cream Sandwiches

Ever wish you could have a hand pie à la mode? Enter: pie-ce cream sandwiches, where two flaky jammy hand pies get filled with ice cream. I like to make blueberry, strawberry, or concord grape hand pies sandwiched with vanilla ice cream, or sub in Nutella for the jam filling in the pies and fill with coffee ice cream.

After baking the hand pies, cool completely. Flip half of the hand pies upside down so their base is facing upward. Have ready 2 pints ice cream—well chilled in the freezer. Use a serrated knife to cut each pint of ice cream into 4 even pieces. Place each slice on top of one of the upside-down hand pies, and top with another cooled hand pie (sugared side up). Freeze the assembled sandwiches immediately, then repeat with the remaining pint of ice cream and hand pies. Keep frozen until ready to serve. *Makes 20 ice cream sandwiches.*

RECOMMENDED FINISHES

- Dip half of the sandwich into Cold Snap Topping (page 127) for a fun twist!

Make Ahead and Storage

The ice cream sandwiches can be made ahead and frozen for up to 3 months. Freeze solid on a baking sheet, then wrap in plastic wrap and store in a freezer bag.

GINGER CHERRY PIE

MAKES ONE 9-INCH / 23-CM PIE

DIFFICULTY: MEDIUM

My husband inspired this pie, which boasts a fairly classic cherry filling spiked with lots of ginger: fresh, ground, and crystallized. And there's even gingerbread pie crust woven into the lattice topping. Sour cherries are best for this pie (and it's OK to use thawed frozen or drained canned cherries), but sweet cherries will also work in a pinch. And for purists, never fear—see the variation for my classic sour cherry filling.

1588 g / 3½ pounds pitted sour cherries (drained if canned, or thawed if frozen)

71 g / ⅓ cup packed light brown sugar

99 g / ½ cup granulated sugar

37 g / ⅓ cup cornstarch

4 g / 1½ teaspoons ground ginger

2 g / ½ teaspoon fine sea salt

One 1-inch / 2-cm piece fresh ginger, peeled and minced

5 g / 1 teaspoon vanilla extract

92 g / ½ cup minced crystallized ginger

Double recipe All-Buttah Pie Dough (page 48), divided in half, shaped into disks, and chilled

1 recipe Gingerbread Pie Dough (page 52), shaped into a disk and chilled

Egg wash (see page 98)

Turbinado sugar for sprinkling

1. In a medium pot, mix the cherries and brown sugar to combine. Cook over medium heat, stirring constantly, until the cherries start to soften and release their liquid, 6 to 8 minutes.

2. Meanwhile, in a small bowl, whisk the granulated sugar, cornstarch, ground ginger, and salt together to combine. Sprinkle this mixture over the cherries and stir well to combine, then stir in the fresh ginger. Cook, stirring occasionally, until the cherries are soft and the liquid has thickened, 7 to 9 minutes. Remove from the heat and stir in the vanilla and crystallized ginger. Pour onto a baking sheet or into a large casserole dish (this will help the filling cool quickly) and cool completely.

3. Preheat the oven to 400°F / 205°C with a rack in the lower third (preferably with a Baking Steel or stone on it).

4. Roll out the top and bottom crusts (see page 34). Line the pie plate with the bottom crust as directed on page 36, and chill. Cut each of the top crust doughs into 10 strips about ½ inch / 1 cm wide. Place on a parchment-lined baking sheet and chill until ready to use.

5. Lay 2 strips of gingerbread dough side by side on your work surface with one strip of plain dough between them. Pinch the top and bottom of this grouped strand together, creating a 1½-inch / 4-cm-wide strip of dough. Repeat this pattern to create another set of strips. Gently twist the two sets of strands together, keeping the strands as flat as possible while you work. Repeat this process with the remaining strips until you have enough twists to cover the top of the pie.

6. Transfer the cooled filling to the prepared bottom crust. Lay the twists evenly across the pie to almost entirely cover the filling. Press all around the edges to seal. Use scissors to trim the dough so there is only ½ inch / 1 cm excess around the edge of the pie plate. Tuck the excess dough under itself so that it is flush with the edge of the pie plate. Crimp as desired (see page 80). Brush

(CONTINUED)

Sour Cherry Pie in Cinnamon Crust (top), and Ginger Cherry Pie in All Buttah and Gingerbread Crust

the top of the pie with egg wash (don't egg-wash the crimped edges, which will brown well on their own), and sprinkle generously with turbinado sugar.

7. Transfer the pie to the oven and bake until the crust is deeply golden brown, 55 to 65 minutes; the filling may bubble up a bit through the spaces between the twists. If the pie is browning too quickly, tent the brown portions with foil. Cool completely before slicing and serving.

VARIATIONS //

SOUR CHERRY PIE: Omit the ground ginger, fresh ginger, and crystallized ginger in the filling. Stir in 2 g / ½ teaspoon almond extract with the vanilla extract. This also makes a great single crust pie—add the filling to a cooled, parbaked crust.

SOUR CHERRY HAND PIE FILLING: Reduce the cherries to 1360 g / 3 pounds, and reduce brown sugar to 53 g / ¼ cup. Omit the ground ginger, fresh ginger, and crystallized ginger in the filling, if desired. Once the filling has thickened in step 2, use an immersion blender to roughly pulse the filling to coarsely puree it, then cool as directed before using.

Make Ahead and Storage ————

The pie is best eaten the same day it's made. Store leftovers at room temperature, wrapped in plastic wrap.

〜〜〜〜〜〜〜〜〜〜〜〜〜〜〜〜

OTHER RECOMMENDED CRUSTS

- Whole Wheat Pie Dough (page 54)
- Caramelized Pie Crust (page 56)
- Spelt Pie Dough (page 55)

RECOMMENDED FINISHES

- Salted Caramel Sauce (page 126)
- Classic Whipped Cream (page 111)
- Ice cream

CRANBERRY-ORANGE PIE

MAKES ONE 9-INCH / 23-CM PIE

DIFFICULTY: MEDIUM

I love sour flavors, so cranberries have a special place in my heart. Because they are high in pectin, they make a naturally thick filling on the stovetop. A thin layer of silky cream cheese filling, spiked with orange zest, helps temper the tartness and round the whole thing out with a little creaminess (the perfect pairing in my book).

CRANBERRY FILLING

906 g / 2 pounds cranberries (fresh or frozen, no need to thaw)

113 g / ½ cup fresh orange juice

99 g / ½ cup granulated sugar

106 g / ½ cup packed light brown sugar

3 g / 1 teaspoon ground cinnamon

2 g / ¾ teaspoon ground ginger

Scant 1 g / ¼ teaspoon ground cloves

2 g / ½ teaspoon fine sea salt

2 g / ½ teaspoon vanilla extract

ORANGE CREAM CHEESE FILLING

226 g / 8 ounces cream cheese, at room temperature

Grated zest of 2 medium oranges

56 g / ½ cup powdered sugar

56 g / 1 large egg, lightly whisked

2 g / ½ teaspoon vanilla extract or Fiori di Sicilia (see Resources, page 345)

1 g / ¼ teaspoon fine sea salt

One 9-inch / 23-cm pie crust (see below), parbaked, brushed with egg wash, and cooled completely (see page 43)

1. Make the cranberry filling: In a medium pot, mix the cranberries (and any juices from thawing), orange juice, granulated sugar, brown sugar, cinnamon, ginger, cloves, and salt to combine. Cook over medium heat until the cranberries begin to soften or break down, 12 to 15 minutes. Reduce the heat to low and continue to cook, stirring frequently, until the mixture has thickened, 6 to 8 minutes; some of the berries will break down and become jammy, some will be whole or in chunky pieces. Stir in the vanilla. Cool completely.

2. Prepare the cream cheese filling: In a medium bowl, using a silicone spatula, stir the cream cheese until smooth. Add the orange zest and mix well, then add the powdered sugar and mix until fully incorporated. Add the egg, extract, and salt and mix to combine.

3. Place the cooled pie crust on a parchment-lined baking sheet. Pour in the cream cheese filling and spread into an even layer. Freeze the pie for 15 minutes.

4. Preheat the oven to 375°F / 190°C with a rack in the lower third (preferably with a Baking Steel or stone on it).

5. Spoon the cooled cranberry filling on top of the chilled cream cheese filling and spread into

(CONTINUED)

an even layer. Transfer the pie to the oven and bake until the crust is deeply golden brown (the filling will have sort of a matte appearance), 35 to 40 minutes. Cool completely before slicing and serving.

VARIATION ////////////////////////////////////

GOOSEBERRY VANILLA CREAM PIE: Replace the cranberries with an equal amount of cleaned gooseberries. Add the brown sugar to the berries in the pot in step 1 and cook as directed. Stir 21 g / 3 tablespoons cornstarch into the granulated sugar and stir into the pot before adding the vanilla at the end of step 1. Stir constantly while cooking over medium heat until the mixture thickens, 1 to 2 minutes. Stir in the vanilla. For the cream cheese filling, omit the orange zest and substitute the seeds of 1 vanilla bean (halved lengthwise and seeds scraped out). This pie is particularly good with streusel topping (page 120) or pie-scrap streusel (page 38).

Make Ahead and Storage ━━━━

The pie is best eaten the same day it's made. Store leftovers at room temperature, wrapped in plastic wrap.

RECOMMENDED CRUSTS

- Gingerbread Pie Dough (page 52)
- Whole Wheat Pie Dough (page 54)

RECOMMENDED FINISHES

- Dress this pie up with a half batch of Mascarpone Whipped Cream (page 111) and garnish with grated orange zest and sugared cranberries (see the sidebar).

PIE-DEAS

Sugared Cranberries

Sugared cranberries are a super-simple, completely beautiful—not to mention festive!—garnish. Many folks make sugared cranberries simply by tossing thawed frozen cranberries in sugar. That works and looks good, but the cranberries are really too tart to actually eat. I briefly cook the cranberries in a sugar syrup, candying them inside before applying sugar to the outside, for a garnish as delicious as it is lovely!

In a medium pot, bring 99 g / ½ cup granulated sugar and 113 g / ½ cup water to a boil over medium heat, stirring to dissolve the sugar. Add 226 g / 8 ounces (about 1¾ cups) cranberries and cook at a very gentle simmer over low heat, stirring occasionally, for 6 to 8 minutes. The cranberries should remain whole, not burst. Drain the cranberries (save the syrup to add to cocktails or other drinks) and toss in 198 g / 1 cup granulated sugar until they're well coated—most of the sugar will adhere to them, but some will be left behind. Store the candied cranberries in an airtight container with the excess sugar until ready to use (they will keep up to 3 days).

ANY-FRUIT TARTE TATIN

MAKES ONE 12-INCH / 30-CM TART

DIFFICULTY: MEDIUM

Just like cake, fruit pies can be prepared upside down. The most common version is the classic French tarte Tatin, which is traditionally made with puff pastry and apples, though it can be made with nearly any fruit (or even with savory ingredients—see the Red Onion Tarte Tatin on page 318). The beauty of a tarte Tatin, a seemingly complicated dessert, is that it is actually one of the more humble (just a few ingredients), and I think, most satisfying, tarts of all. It's terrifically adaptable and can be made in almost any size pan. The crust is baked on top, so it's easy to get it fully baked and golden brown, and then the pie is inverted. Since the fruit is in direct contact with the pan, it softens evenly and becomes beautifully caramelized, with the help of plenty of fat and sugar. See the variations for details on a few of my favorite fruits.

½ recipe Rough Puff Pastry (page 50), chilled, or 1 recipe pie dough (see below), prepared as for Rough Puff Pastry, shaped into a disk, and chilled

43 g / 3 tablespoons unsalted butter

½ vanilla bean, halved lengthwise, seeds scraped out and reserved (optional)

99 g / ½ cup granulated sugar

Pinch of ground cinnamon (optional)

2 g / ½ teaspoon fine sea salt

Enough halved, quartered, or sliced fruit (peeled/pitted/cored etc. as necessary) to tightly cover the bottom of the pan—see the variations

1. Preheat the oven to 400°F / 205°C with a rack in the lower third (preferably with a Baking Steel or stone on it). Line a baking sheet with parchment paper.

2. On a lightly floured surface, roll out the dough into a circle about 13 inches / 33 cm wide. Dock the dough all over with a fork. Use the rolling pin to gently transfer the dough to the baking sheet and unfurl it onto the pan. Refrigerate while you work on the filling.

3. Melt the butter in a 12-inch / 30-cm ovenproof skillet, preferably cast-iron, over medium heat. If using the vanilla bean, rub the seeds into the sugar. Stir the cinnamon, if using, and the salt into the sugar. Sprinkle the sugar mixture evenly over the bottom of the pan and heat for 15 to 30 seconds. Stir to help dissolve the sugar, then continue to cook without stirring until the mixture begins to caramelize, 4 to 5 minutes. You can swirl the pan occasionally to keep the heat distributed and the mixture browning evenly.

4. When the mixture has caramelized, swirl to evenly coat the bottom of the pan. Remove from the heat and carefully arrange the fruit in an even layer in the pan—pack it in as tightly as possible, as it will shrink while it cooks, and you don't want too many gaps after baking.

5. Gently drape the pastry over the fruit, folding it in a little at the edges to encase the fruit. Transfer the pan to the oven and bake until the pastry is deeply golden brown, 25 to 30 minutes. Remove from the oven and cool for 5 minutes.

(CONTINUED)

6. Carefully invert the skillet onto a serving platter or cutting board to unmold the tarte Tatin. If any fruit stays in the pan, use a small offset spatula to gently remove it and replace it on the surface of the tart. Let cool for 5 minutes more before serving.

VARIATIONS //

How much fruit you'll need will depend on the type you're using.

- **APPLES:** 600 to 900 g / 4 to 6 medium baking apples, such as Honeycrisp, Fuji, or Jonagold, peeled, cored, and halved. Place rounded side down (cut side up) in the pan.
- **PEACHES OR NECTARINES:** 740 to 925 g / 4 to 5 medium peaches or nectarines, peeled, pitted, and halved. Place rounded side down (cut side up) in the pan.
- **PINEAPPLE:** 830 g / 1 medium pineapple, peeled, cored, and cut into 1-inch / 2-cm rings, then halved. Overlap the pieces slightly as necessary when you arrange them in the pan.
- **BANANA:** 460 to 575 g / 4 to 5 medium bananas, peeled and halved lengthwise. Place cut side down in the pan.
- **SOUR OR SWEET CHERRIES:** 454 g / 1 pound sour or sweet cherries, pitted. Pack the fruit in as tightly as possible.
- **STRAWBERRIES:** 567 g / 20 ounces strawberries, hulled and halved. Place cut side down in the pan.
- **BLUEBERRIES:** 454 g / 1 pound blueberries. Pack the fruit in as tightly as possible.
- **FIGS:** 567 g / 20 ounces figs, stemmed and halved. Place cut side down in the pan.
- **CRANBERRIES:** 567 g / 20 ounces fresh or thawed frozen cranberries.
- **ORANGES:** 405 to 675 g / 3 to 5 medium oranges. Slice the fruit ¼ inch / 3 mm thick (leaving the peel on), remove any seeds, and layer them in the pan.

Make Ahead and Storage ━━━━━

The tarte Tatin is best eaten the day it's made. Store leftovers at room temperature, wrapped tightly in plastic wrap.

RECOMMENDED CRUSTS
- Vanilla Bean–Nutmeg Pie Dough (page 52)
- Chocolate All-Buttah Pie Dough (page 48)
- Graham Flour Pie Dough (page 54)

RECOMMENDED FINISHES
- Whipped Cream Sauce (page 112) or vanilla ice cream

STONE FRUIT–BERRY PIE

MAKES ONE 9-INCH /
23-CM PIE

DIFFICULTY: MEDIUM

When summer rolls around, I often get requests for pie recipes featuring specific fruits, but of course there are endless possibilities! That's why I love this stone fruit–berry pie, which is made using two precooked fillings (so you get the consistency just right). You can layer the fillings or create designs like stripes, swirls, or spirals; see sidebar, page 178. I usually make it as a single-crust pie to show off those pretty colors, but it also makes a lovely free-form pie or double-crust pie (see Note). If you're still craving it outside the summer season, you can use thawed frozen fruit to make the fillings.

STONE FRUIT FILLING

680 g / 1½ pounds stone fruit, such as peaches, nectarines, apricots, plums, or cherries, peeled if desired, pitted, and roughly chopped

149 g / ¾ cup granulated sugar

1 g / ¼ teaspoon fine sea salt

21 g / 3 tablespoons cornstarch

2 g / ½ teaspoon ground cinnamon

2 g / ½ teaspoon vanilla extract

1 g / ¼ teaspoon almond extract (optional)

14 g / ½ ounce / 1 tablespoon unsalted butter

BERRY FILLING

255 g / 1½ cups fresh berries

99 g / ½ cup granulated sugar

2 g / ½ teaspoon fine sea salt

21 g / 3 tablespoons cornstarch

Scant 1 g / ¼ teaspoon freshly grated nutmeg

3 g / ¾ teaspoon vanilla extract

14 g / ½ ounce / 1 tablespoon unsalted butter

One 9 inch / 23-cm pie crust (see below), parbaked, brushed with egg wash, and cooled completely (see page 43)

2 tablespoons apricot jam or other preserves (optional)

1. Make the stone fruit filling: Place the fruit in a medium pot, add 99 g / ½ cup of the sugar and the salt, and stir until well coated. Cook over medium-low heat, stirring occasionally, until fruit softens but still holds its shape, 10 to 12 minutes. Reduce the heat to medium-low and cook, stirring occasionally, until mixture thickens slightly, 4 to 5 minutes.

2. Meanwhile, in a small bowl, stir the remaining 50 g / ¼ cup sugar with the cornstarch and cinnamon to combine. Whisk this mixture into the pot and cook, whisking constantly, until the mixture thickens. Stir in the vanilla extract, almond extract, if using, and butter, then transfer to a heatproof bowl, cover, and cool completely.

3. Make the berry filling: In a small pot, combine the berries with 50 g / ¼ cup of the sugar and the salt and cook over medium heat just until the berries begin to soften and break down, 6 to 8 minutes.

4. Meanwhile, in a small bowl, whisk the remaining 50 g / ¼ cup sugar with the cornstarch and nutmeg. Sprinkle this mixture over the berries, whisking constantly, then cook over low heat, whisking constantly, until the mixture comes to a

(CONTINUED)

Top to bottom: Plum-Raspberry in Cornmeal Crust, Nectarine-Strawberry in Spelt Crust, Apricot-Blackberry in All-Buttah Crust

simmer and begin to thicken, 1 to 2 minutes. Stir in the vanilla extract and butter. Transfer to a heatproof bowl, cover, and cool completely.

5. Preheat the oven to 400°F / 205°C with a rack in the lower third (preferably with a Baking Steel or stone on it).

6. Place the cooled crust on a parchment-lined baking sheet. Spoon the fillings into the crust (see sidebar, right). Transfer the pie to the oven and bake until the crust is deeply golden brown, 30 to 35 minutes.

7. While the pie is still hot, if using the jam, brush it gently over the filling. Cool completely before slicing and serving.

Make Ahead and Storage

The fillings can be made up to 3 days ahead and refrigerated separately in airtight containers. This pie is best served the day it is prepared.

NOTE

To make this as a double-crust pie, follow the instructions on page 42. Add the fillings to the bottom crust and top with the top crust. Brush the crust with egg wash, sprinkle with turbinado or sanding sugar, and bake for 50 to 60 minutes.

RECOMMENDED CRUSTS
- All-Buttah Pie Dough (page 48)
- Vanilla Bean–Nutmeg Pie Dough (page 52)
- Brown Butter Pie Dough (page 53)

RECOMMENDED FINISHES
- Whipped Cream Sauce (page 112)
- Extra-Thick and Creamy Whipped Cream (page 113)

PIE-DEAS

Design Ideas with Two Fillings

- For a swirled filling, alternate dollops of the two fillings in the crust, then use a small offset spatula to swirl them together and use a silicone spatula to spread the filling into an even layer.

- To make a bull's-eye, spoon the stone fruit filling around the outer edges of the crust, then spoon the berry filling into the center and use a spatula to spread the filling into an even layer.

- For a striped filling, spoon one third of the stone fruit filling across one side of the crust, then spoon half of the berry filling next to it. Repeat, working your way across the crust until it's totally filled, then use a spatula to spread the filling into an even layer.

- To make the filling so it appears striped when sliced, spoon the filling into the crust in concentric circles: three rings of stone fruit and two rings of berry filling.

BLUEBERRY LEMON PIE

MAKES ONE 9-INCH / 23-CM PIE

DIFFICULTY: MEDIUM

Blueberry and lemon is a top-five flavor combination in my book. While most blueberry pies use just a smidge of lemon to complement the flavor of the berries, this recipe gets a huge punch of lemon flavor because it uses a whole half lemon, including the peel, along with the juice from the other half. I also believe that vanilla makes blueberries taste even more deliciously like blueberries, so a whole bean is pureed with it too.

850 g / 5 cups fresh blueberries

About 70 g / ½ medium lemon, sliced, seeds removed, and roughly chopped (skin and all)

About 25 g / juice of ½ medium lemon

1 vanilla bean, halved lengthwise and finely chopped

298 g / 1½ cups granulated sugar

60 g / ½ cup all-purpose flour

1 g / ½ teaspoon ground cinnamon

2 g / ½ teaspoon fine sea salt

28 g / 1 ounce / 2 tablespoons unsalted butter

One 9-inch / 23-cm pie crust (see below), parbaked, brushed with egg wash, and cooled completely (see page 43)

1. In a medium pot, combine 340 g / 2 cups of the blueberries, the chopped lemon (and any juices), the lemon juice, vanilla bean, and 150 g / ¾ cup of the sugar and cook over medium heat until the blueberries begin to soften and break down, 8 to 10 minutes. Remove from the heat.

2. Puree the mixture (including the lemon and vanilla bean) until smooth—I like to do this with an immersion blender right in the pot, but you can also transfer it to a blender or food processor to puree, then return to the pot.

3. Bring the mixture back to a simmer and simmer for 5 minutes over low heat.

(CONTINUED)

4. Meanwhile, in a small bowl, whisk the remaining 149 g / ¾ cup sugar with the flour, cinnamon, and salt. Sprinkle this mixture over the blueberry mixture, whisking constantly, and continue to cook, whisking constantly, until the mixture comes to a simmer again and begin to thicken, 1 to 2 minutes. Stir in the remaining 510 g / 3 cups blueberries and the butter. Transfer to a storage vessel and let cool, covered with plastic wrap placed directly against the surface to prevent a skin from forming (if you're in a hurry, you can pour it onto a baking sheet or into large baking pan to cool). Then refrigerate until ready to use.

5. Preheat the oven to 425°F / 218°C with a rack in the lower third (preferably with a Baking Steel or stone on it).

6. Place the cooled crust on a parchment-lined baking sheet and pour in the blueberry filling. Transfer to the oven and bake until the filling visibly bubbles, 30 to 35 minutes. Cool completely before slicing and serving.

Make Ahead and Storage

The filling can be made up to 1 day ahead and refrigerated in an airtight container. This pie is best served the day it is prepared.

NOTE

You can use frozen blueberries instead—thaw them overnight in the refrigerator. Drain the blueberries, reserving the juices in a medium pot. Before beginning to make the filling, simmer the juices over medium-low heat to reduce to 24 g / 2 tablespoons then proceed as directed.

RECOMMENDED CRUSTS
- Vanilla Bean–Nutmeg Pie Dough (page 52)
- Cornmeal Pie Dough (page 55)
- Citrus Roll-Out Cookie Crust (page 63)

RECOMMENDED FINISHES
- Mascarpone Whipped Cream (page 111)
- Spread a thin layer of Lemon Curd (page 123) on top of the cooled pie
- Try it as a Lemon Meringue Pie (page 280)

RASPBERRY-POACHED PEAR AND ALMOND PIE

MAKES ONE 6-BY-16-INCH / 15-BY-41-CM PIE

DIFFICULTY: HARD

Poaching the pears before making this pie requires some extra effort but produces lovely flavor and a beautiful dip-dyed effect when you slice the fruit. Made with pie dough, the result is crisp and galette-like. With rough puff pastry, it's a bit closer to Danish pastry.

1 recipe Fruity Poaching Liquid (page 121) made with raspberries

907 g / 2 pounds firm-ripe pears (about 4 large), peeled

Pie dough for a double crust (see below), shaped into a disk and chilled, or 1 recipe Rough Puff Pastry (page 50), shaped into a rough rectangular shape and chilled

85 g / 3 ounces / 6 tablespoons unsalted butter, at room temperature

66 g / ⅓ cup granulated sugar

Grated zest of 1 lemon

56 g / 1 large egg, at room temperature

21 g / 1 large egg yolk, at room temperature

5 g / 1 teaspoon vanilla extract

1 g / ¼ teaspoon almond extract

50 g / ½ cup almond flour

30 g / ¼ cup all-purpose flour

2 g / ½ teaspoon fine sea salt

Egg wash (see page 98)

43 g / ½ cup sliced almonds for garnish

1. In a pot large enough to hold the pears in a single layer, bring the poaching liquid to a simmer. Add the pears and simmer, turning the pears occasionally to help them cook and color evenly, until they begin to soften, 10 to 12 minutes. Cool the pears completely in the poaching liquid (see Make Ahead and Storage).

2. Remove the pears from the liquid and cut them in half. Use a melon baller or spoon to scoop the core out of each half. Use a small knife to carefully slice each pear crosswise into ¼-inch / 6-mm-thick slices, holding the slices together as you go to maintain the shape of the pear half.

3. On a lightly floured surface, roll out the dough into a rectangle slightly larger than 8 by 18 inches / 20 by 46 cm and about ¼ inch / 6 mm thick. Trim the dough so the rectangle has clean, sharp edges and is 8 by 18 inches / 20 by 46 cm. Use a rolling pin to transfer the dough to a parchment-lined baking sheet. Cover with plastic wrap and chill while you prepare the filling.

4. In the bowl of a stand mixer fitted with the paddle attachment, mix the butter, sugar, and lemon zest to combine. Add the egg and egg yolk and mix until well combined. Add the extracts and mix well. Add the almond flour, all-purpose flour, and salt and mix to combine.

5. Preheat the oven to 400°F / 205°C with a rack in the lower third (preferably with a Baking Steel or stone on it).

6. Remove the dough from the fridge and spread the filling over it in an even layer, leaving a 1-inch / 2-cm border all the way around. Working with one pear half at a time, gently press on the pear so that the slices fans out slightly. Then use an offset spatula to transfer the fanned pear to the dough: You want to arrange the pears side by side in a row down the length of the rectangle; if desired, you can alternate the directions the pears face to give a different visual look.

7. Gently fold the two longer sides of uncovered dough up and over, encasing the edges of the almond filling. Do the same with the two shorter sides. If necessary, lightly moisten the overlapping dough at the corners with water or egg wash to help the dough adhere to itself.

8. Brush the edges of the crust with egg wash, then sprinkle with the sliced almonds. Bake until the dough is evenly golden brown, 35 to 40 minutes. Cool completely before slicing and serving.

Make Ahead and Storage

The pears can be poached up to 1 day ahead and refrigerated, covered, in the poaching liquid; drain well before using. The pie is best eaten the same day it's made. Store leftovers at room temperature, wrapped in plastic wrap.

RECOMMENDED CRUSTS
- Whole Wheat Pie Dough (page 54)
- Caramelized Pie Crust (page 56)
- Spelt Pie Dough (page 55)

RECOMMENDED FINISHES
- Salted Caramel Sauce (page 126)
- Classic Whipped Cream (page 111) or vanilla ice cream
- Try topping with Streusel for Baking (page 120) before baking the pie

CANDIED CLEMENTINE GALETTE

MAKES ONE 9-INCH / 23-CM GALETTE

DIFFICULTY: HARD

I first saw candied clementines at La Maison du Macaron in New York City. They sat in neat, glittering rows, each one in a ruffly white liner. It was one of those instant moments of awe for me—they were incredible. I had never seen such a beautiful citrus presentation in my life, and then I tasted one: a perfect combination of tart and sweet, with a lovely balance of soft textures and chew. I began to give them as small gifts of appreciation: "Good job," "Congratulations," or "I love you." When I made them for the first time, I used cranberry juice for the syrup, and it tinted the fruit pink. Now I love them baked into a crispy crust, topped with whipped cream.

CANDIED CLEMENTINES

678 g / 3 cups unsweetened cranberry juice (see Notes)

339 g / 1½ cups water

24 g / 2 tablespoons orange blossom water

170 g / ½ cup honey

792 g / 4 cups granulated sugar

1 cinnamon stick

1 vanilla bean, halved lengthwise, seeds scraped out, seeds and bean reserved

About 1395 g / 14 clementines (see Notes), any stems removed

1 recipe Rough Puff Pastry (page 50), shaped into a disk and chilled, or a double recipe pie dough (see below), prepared as for Rough Puff Pastry, shaped into a disk and chilled

Egg wash (see page 98)

Turbinado sugar for sprinkling

Half Batch Mascarpone Whipped Cream (page 111)

Freshly grated nutmeg for garnish

1. Cut a round of parchment paper the size of a medium pot (you can use the pot lid as a guide). Cut a 1-inch / 2-cm circle out of the center. This parchment "lid" will help keep the fruit submerged while it cooks.

2. In the medium pot, combine the cranberry juice, water, orange blossom water, honey, sugar, cinnamon stick, and vanilla bean and seeds and bring to a simmer over medium heat, stirring to dissolve the sugar. Reduce the heat to a gentle simmer.

3. Add the clementines and cover with the parchment circle, pressing it against the surface. Cover the pot and simmer for 1½ hours. Cool the clementines completely in the syrup, then refrigerate, in the syrup, until ready to use.

4. Preheat the oven to 425°F / 218°C with a rack in the lower third (preferably with a Baking Steel or stone on it). Line a baking sheet with parchment.

5. On a lightly floured surface, roll out the dough into a rough rectangle a bit larger than 11 by 15 inches / 28 by 38 cm and about ¼ inch / 3 mm thick. Dock the rectangle all over with a fork.

6. Drain the clementines and arrange on the dough, leaving a 2-inch / 5-cm border all around. (There will be some small spaces between the fruit.) Fold the longer sides of the dough over onto itself several times, rolling it toward the center and stopping when you reach the clementines. Repeat with the shorter sides. Work around the crust with your fingers to pinch the dough well to form the outer edge. Brush the edges of the dough with egg wash and sprinkle with turbinado sugar.

7. Transfer the galette to the oven and bake until the pastry is deeply golden brown, 35 to 40 minutes. Cool completely.

8. When ready to serve, place the whipped cream in a piping bag with a large tip (round or star) and pipe the cream generously all over the pie, filling in any open spaces. Grate nutmeg over the top before serving.

Make Ahead and Storage

The candied clementines can be made up to 1 week ahead and stored, refrigerated, in the syrup. The syrup keeps well for up to 1 month. Th galette is best eaten the same day it's made. Store leftovers at room temperature, wrapped in plastic wrap.

NOTES ◇◇◇◇◇◇◇◇◇◇◇◇◇◇◇◇◇◇◇◇◇◇◇

You'll likely use only 12 clementines for the galette, but I like to cook a few extra, just in case—and if not, you have two beautiful candied clementines to enjoy or gift! You can skip the cranberry juice and just use water. You can also halve or quarter the clementines before placing them on the crust—pack them tightly together, leaving the same uncovered border around the edges. Save the syrup from the candying process—it's great in cocktails or with seltzer. You can also reduce a portion of it down to a thick syrup to drizzle over the finished galette.

RECOMMENDED CRUSTS

- Graham Flour Pie Dough (page 54)
- Gingerbread Pie Dough (page 52)
- Chocolate All-Buttah Pie Dough (page 48)

RECOMMENDED FINISHES

- Dark Chocolate Black-Bottom Base (page 110)
- Salted Caramel Sauce (page 126)
- Thin Fruit Glaze (page 122)

FREE-FORM HONEYED FIG PIE

MAKES ONE 14-INCH /
36-CM PIE

DIFFICULTY: EASY

For me, figs feel fancy all on their own, so I love the idea of keeping a figgy pie filling and shaping freeform. Honey and a touch of apricot jam provide just enough sweetness in this pie, which manages to be simple and effortlessly elegant at the same time.

Pie dough for a double crust (see opposite), shaped into a disk and chilled

Egg wash (see page 98)

680 g / 1½ pounds figs, quartered

84 g / ¼ cup honey

64 / 3 tablespoons apricot jam

½ teaspoon Fiori di Sicilia extract (see Notes, optional—can substitute vanilla or almond extract, if desired)

A hefty pinch of fine sea salt

Turbinado sugar for sprinkling

1. On a lightly floured surface, roll out the dough to a round about 16 inches / 40 cm in diameter. Use a ruler to mark a few scoring guidelines 1 inch / 2.5 cm from the edges of the dough, then use a paring knife or a pastry cutter to cut this outer circle of dough following the score lines, remove the ring of dough and set aside.

2. Use the rolling pin to transfer the round of dough to a parchment-lined baking sheet. Dock the dough all over with a fork. Brush the edges of the dough with egg wash. Gently transfer the 1-inch / 2.5-cm circle of dough to the dough round, placing it on the portion you egg-washed, and trim the ends of the circle as necessary so that you can make one smaller circle that will sit on the edges of the bottom round. Refrigerate while you prepare the filling.

3. Preheat the oven to 425°F / 218°C with a rack in the lower third (preferably with a Baking Steel or stone on it).

4. Place the figs in a medium bowl. In a small saucepan, warm the honey and jam just until the jam becomes more fluid. Pour the mixture over the figs and toss gently to coat. Add the extract and salt and toss gently to combine.

5. Remove the prepared crust from the refrigerator. Pile the figs on the center portion of the crust, either in an even layer or slightly mounded in the center, making sure the figs are relatively snugly packed together

6. Brush the rim of the dough with egg wash and sprinkle generously with turbinado sugar.

7. Bake the pie until the crust is deeply golden brown and the figs have softened, 35 to 40 minutes. Cool for at least 10 minutes before slicing and serving.

Make Ahead and Storage

This pie is best served the day it is made. Store leftovers at room temperature, wrapped in plastic wrap.

NOTES

Fiori di Sicilia is an extract hailing from Italy, where it's often used in panettone, a kind of sweet bread. It has citrus and vanilla flavors and aromas, and I'm obsessed with it (see Resources, page 345).

You can take this pie to a creamier place by spreading 226 g / 8 ounces whole-milk ricotta cheese over the dough before placing the figs on top. Or take it to a savory place by scattering 170 g / 1 cup crumbled Gorgonzola over the figs before baking.

RECOMMENDED CRUSTS
- Whole Wheat Pie Dough (page 54)
- Cardamom Lemon Pie Dough (page 52)
- Golden Cheese Pie Dough (page 57)

RECOMMENDED FINISHES
- Mascarpone Whipped Cream (page 111)
- Salted Caramel Sauce (page 126)
- Whipped Cream Sauce (page 112)

Jam Cookie Tart in Chocolate
Roll-Out Cookie Crust

JAM COOKIE TART

MAKES ONE 9- OR
10-INCH / 23- OR 25-CM
TART

DIFFICULTY: EASY

A classic recipe you should keep in your back pocket. It's simple and adaptable, and you can dress it up or down. It's a great way to use your homemade jam, or that special stuff you picked up at the farm stand. You can make this easy recipe even easier by using a double batch of Press-In Cookie Crust (page 64). Press half of the dough into the pan to line it, then crumble the rest over the surface of the jam once it's filled.

Double recipe Roll-Out Cookie Crust (page 62, see below), divided in half, formed into disks, and chilled
510 g / 1½ cups jam
Powdered sugar for dusting (optional)

1. Place a 9- or 10-inch / 23- or 25-cm tart pan with a removable bottom on a parchment-lined baking sheet.

2. On a lightly floured surface (or between two pieces of parchment paper—see How to Roll Out Dough on Parchment, page 36), roll out half of the dough into a circle slightly larger than the tart pan. Use the rolling pin to gently unfurl the dough over the tart pan, then gently lift the crust up at the edges and nudge downward so it's flush against the bottom and sides of the pan. Use scissors or a paring knife to remove the excess dough, leaving about ¼ inch / 3 mm all around the outside edge. Chill for at least 30 minutes, or up to 1 hour.

3. Preheat the oven to 350°F / 175°C with a rack in the middle (preferably with a Baking Steel or stone on it).

4. Spoon the jam onto the center of the bottom crust and spread into an even layer. Roll out the second half of the dough; You can leave it as a full crust, or do cutouts to reveal the jam below (see page 90), or cut strips and weave a lattice; see page 94). Transfer the top crust to the top of the

tart. Use your fingers to gently pinch the top crust to the excess bottom crust all the way around. Use a paring knife to trim the excess dough from the edges of the pie, holding the blade flush with the edge of the pan as you cut.

5. Transfer the tart to the oven and bake until the dough appears matte and set in the center and is lightly golden around the edges, 40 to 45 minutes.

6. Let the tart cool completely, then, if using, sift powdered sugar over the top before slicing and serving.

Make Ahead and Storage
This tart can be made up to 24 hours ahead and stored, wrapped in plastic wrap at room temperature.

NOTE ◇◇◇◇◇◇◇◇◇◇◇◇◇◇◇◇◇◇◇◇◇◇◇◇
If desired, you can brush the top crust with egg wash (see page 98) or beaten egg white to help it brown evenly and give it a little sheen.

RECOMMENDED CRUSTS
- Almond Roll-Out Cookie Crust (page 63)
- Chocolate Roll-Out Cookie Crust (page 63)
- Citrus Roll-Out Cookie Crust (page 63)
- Press-In Cookie Crust (page 64; see headnote for how to use this crust)

RECOMMENDED FINISHES
- Flavored Sifting Sugars (page 128)
- Whipped Cream Sauce (page 112)

ANY-FRUIT CRUMB CROSTATA

MAKES ONE 9-INCH / 23-CM CROSTATA

DIFFICULTY: EASY

An easy workhorse of a recipe that can carry you through all the seasons. It's great for breakfast, dusted with powdered sugar or packed in a lunchbox for an afternoon snack, or even as an easy dinner party dessert served with whipped cream. I particularly love it with rhubarb, stone fruit, and/or berries.

Triple recipe Streusel for Baking (page 120)

907 g / 2 pounds prepared (seeds or pits removed as needed, peeled if needed/desired) fruit, chopped if large (like peaches)

15 g / 1 tablespoon fresh lemon juice

10 g / 2 teaspoons vanilla extract

99 g / ½ cup granulated sugar

21 g / 3 tablespoons cornstarch

2 g / ½ teaspoon fine sea salt

85 g / ½ cup chopped nuts (optional)

1. Preheat the oven to 375°F / 190°C with a rack in the middle. Lightly grease a 9-inch / 23-cm springform pan.

2. Divide the streusel into two portions: two thirds (about 444 g / 3½ cups) for the crust and the remaining one third (about 222 g / 1¾ cup) for the topping. Press the larger amount of streusel evenly over the bottom and up the sides of the prepared pan—it should be about ¼ inch / 6 mm thick all over.

3. In a large bowl, toss the fruit with the lemon juice and vanilla. In a small bowl, whisk the sugar, cornstarch, and salt together to combine. Add this mixture to the fruit and toss well to combine.

4. Pour the fruit mixture into the crumb crust and press firmly into an even layer. Crumble the remaining streusel evenly over the top. If using, sprinkle the nuts evenly over the streusel.

5. Bake until the crust is deeply golden brown, the fruit is tender, and the juices are bubbling, 45 to 50 minutes. If the top of the crostata starts to darken too quickly, tent it with foil. Let cool completely before slicing and serving.

Make Ahead and Storage

This crostata keeps well for up to 3 days at room temperature, wrapped tightly in plastic wrap.

RECOMMENDED FINISHES
- Flavored Sifting Sugars (page 128)
- Whipped Cream Sauce (page 112)
- Classic Whipped Cream (page 111)

RECOMMENDED CRUSTS
- Caramelized Pie Crust (page 56)
- Almond Roll-Out Cookie Crust (page 63)
- Brown Butter Pie Dough (page 53)

RECOMMENDED FINISHES
- Whipped Cream Sauce (page 112)
- Meringue Topping (page 118)
- Streusel for Baking (page 120)

ROSÉ PEACH PIE

MAKES ONE 9-INCH /
23-CM PIE

DIFFICULTY: MEDIUM

I've long loved my peach pie with a little booze—as in the Bourbon-Rosemary Peach Pie in *The Fearless Baker*. That pie is big and bold, and this is its lovely, delicate cousin. The peaches are macerated to release their juices, and then those juices are combined with rosé wine and cooked down to concentrate the flavors. The result coats the peaches in a beautiful pale pink sauce, and the wine complements the fruit in the most delightful way.

This also makes a delicious double-crust pie. Follow the instructions on page 42. To try the double-crust application pictured, cut the dough into ¼-inch- / 3-mm-thick strips. Roll each strip into a tight spiral, then place over filling, spiral side facing up.

1488 g / 3¼ pounds peaches (about 8 medium), pitted and thickly sliced

15 g / 1 tablespoon fresh lemon juice

149 g / ¾ cup granulated sugar

452 g / 2 cups dry rosé

56 g / 2 ounces / 4 tablespoons unsalted butter

1 g / ¼ teaspoon fine sea salt

28 g / ¼ cup cornstarch

¼ teaspoon almond extract

One 9-inch / 23-cm pie crust (see opposite), parbaked, brushed with egg wash, and cooled completely (see page 43)

1. In a medium bowl, toss the peaches with the lemon juice and 99 g / ½ cup of the sugar until well coated. Let macerate, stirring occasionally, until the peaches release their juices, about 1 hour.

2. Preheat the oven to 400°F / 205°C with a rack in the lower third (preferably with a Baking Steel or stone on it).

3. Drain the peaches, reserving the juices; set the peaches aside. You should have 100 to 150 g / ⅓ to ½ cup juices (if you have more or less, don't worry—you're going to reduce and concentrate these juices). Pour the juices into a medium pot, add the rosé, and bring to a simmer over medium heat. Simmer until the mixture reduces to 132 g / ½ cup. Reduce the heat to low and stir in the butter and salt.

4. Meanwhile, in a small bowl, stir the remaining 50 g / ¼ cup granulated sugar with the cornstarch to combine. Whisk this mixture into the wine mixture and cook, whisking constantly, until the mixture thickens. Stir in the almond extract. Immediately add this mixture to the peaches and stir to combine. The mixture may start to firm up as soon as it hits the peaches—that's OK!

5. Place the cooled pie crust on a parchment-lined baking sheet. Arrange the peach slices in the crust, skin side up, in tight concentric circles (to make a sort of rose shape).

6. Transfer the pie to the oven and bake until the crust is deeply golden brown and the peaches are tender, 40 to 45 minutes. The filling should be visibly bubbling. If the pie starts to darken too quickly, tent it with foil. Let the pie cool completely before slicing and serving.

Make Ahead and Storage

This pie is best served the day it is prepared. Store leftovers at room temperature, covered with plastic wrap.

CINNAMON PLUM PIE

MAKES ONE 9-INCH /
23-CM PIE

DIFFICULTY: EASY

When plums are in season, I find myself eating them constantly. Their juicy loveliness is seriously meant to be a pie filling, and I make them into a precooked filling so I can control the consistency and concentrate the flavors. While it's easy to keep things plain when summer fruit like this is at its peak, I spike the filling with plentiful amount of cinnamon, which gives the filling an incredible warmth. It's finished with plenty of streusel topping and served with a drizzle of cold heavy cream. But if you like, substitute the Meringue Topping (page 118) for the streusel.

1360 g / 3 pounds plums (16 to 20 medium), pitted
    and chopped
297 g / 1½ cups sugar
2 cinnamon sticks
56 g / ½ cup cornstarch
1 g / ¼ teaspoon fine sea salt
3 g / 1½ teaspoons ground cinnamon
10 g / 2 teaspoons vanilla extract
One 9-inch / 23-cm pie crust (see opposite),
    parbaked, brushed with egg wash, and cooled
    completely (see page 43)
1 recipe Streusel for Baking (page 120)

1. Place the plums in a large pot, add 198 g / 1 cup of the sugar, and stir until well coated. Cook over medium-low heat, stirring occasionally, until the fruit completely breaks down, 17 to 20 minutes. Remove from the heat.

2. Puree the plum mixture in the pot using an immersion blender, or transfer to a blender or food processor and puree until relatively smooth (some texture is OK), then return the puree to the pot. Add the cinnamon sticks and cook over medium-low heat, stirring occasionally, until mixture thickens and reduces by about just over half, about 15 minutes. You should end up with about 915 g / 3½ cups.

3. Meanwhile, in a small bowl, stir the remaining 99 g / ½ cup granulated sugar with the cornstarch and salt to combine. Whisk this mixture into the plums and cook, whisking constantly, until the mixture thickens. Stir in the ground cinnamon and vanilla. Remove from the heat and cool completely, then remove the cinnamon sticks.

4. Preheat the oven to 400°F / 205°C with a rack in the lower third (preferably with a Baking Steel or stone on it).

5. Place the cooled crust on a parchment-lined baking sheet. Pour the cooled plum mixture into the crust and spread into an even layer. Sprinkle the streusel evenly over the top.

6. Transfer the pie to the oven and bake until the crust and streusel are deeply golden brown and the jam is bubbly, 40 to 45 minutes. If the pie starts to darken too quickly, tent it with foil. Let cool completely before slicing and serving.

Make Ahead and Storage

The filling can be made up to 3 days ahead and stored in an airtight container in the refrigerator. The pie is best served the day it is prepared.

NOTE ◇◇◇◇◇◇◇◇◇◇◇◇◇◇◇◇◇◇◇◇◇◇◇◇◇◇

Chopped pitted plums (with their juices) freeze well. I freeze them in the quantity needed for this recipe in airtight containers so I can enjoy plum pie through the fall and even into winter (if any survive that long).

RECOMMENDED CRUSTS
- Graham Flour Pie Dough (page 54)
- Rough Puff Pastry (page 50)
- Roll-Out Cookie Crust (page 62)

RECOMMENDED FINISHES
- I like to drizzle cold cream over slices of this pie, but Whipped Cream Sauce (page 112) is a close second

Easy-Fancy
Rhubarb Pie in
Cornmeal Crust

Easy-Fancy Apple Pie
in Whole Wheat Crust

RECOMMENDED CRUSTS
- Pâte Brisée (page 59)
- Gingerbread Pie Dough (page 52)
- Golden Cheese Pie Dough (page 57)

RECOMMENDED FINISHES
- Mascarpone Whipped Cream (page 111)
- Salted Caramel Sauce (page 126)
- Honey Meringue Topping (page 118)

EASY-FANCY APPLE PIE

MAKES ONE 9-INCH /
23-CM PIE

DIFFICULTY: MEDIUM

I've made this apple pie for years. You sub the work you'd usually put into a top crust for arranging the apple slices neatly in a parbaked crust. This special effort ranks this pie as a "Medium," but the result is not at all difficult to achieve, especially considering how impressive it looks. After it's baked, it lands somewhere between the warm comfort of a classic apple pie and the elegance and flavor of a French apple tart. This method for the filling works with other sliceable firm fruits too, like the rhubarb version on the opposite page (see Notes).

907 g / 2 pounds Honeycrisp or other good baking apples, like Jonagold or Gala (4 to 6 medium), peeled if desired, cored, and thinly sliced

28 g / 1 ounce / 2 tablespoons unsalted butter, melted

43 g / 2 tablespoons boiled cider (see Notes)

5 g / 1 teaspoon vanilla extract

50 g / ¼ cup granulated sugar

53 g / ¼ cup packed dark brown sugar

11 g / 1½ tablespoons cornstarch

2 g / 1 teaspoon ground cinnamon

1 g / ½ teaspoon ground ginger

Scant 1 g / ¼ teaspoon ground cloves

Scant 1 g / ¼ teaspoon freshly grated nutmeg

2 g / ½ teaspoon fine sea salt

One 9-inch / 23-cm pie crust (see opposite), parbaked, brushed with egg wash, and cooled completely (see page 43)

1. Preheat the oven to 425°F / 218°C with a rack in the lower third (preferably with a Baking Steel or stone on it).

2. In a large bowl, toss the apples with the melted butter, boiled cider, and vanilla to combine.

3. In a small bowl, whisk the granulated sugar, brown sugar, cornstarch, cinnamon, ginger, cloves, nutmeg, and salt to combine. Add this mixture to the apples and toss well to coat (but be gentle to keep the thin apple pieces whole).

4. Place the cooled pie crust on a parchment-lined baking sheet. Arrange the apples in the crust, overlapping the slices so they fit tightly into the crust: You can do this in a spiral from the outside in, in concentric circles, or in tight rows. Pour any juices from the bottom of the bowl over the apples.

5. Transfer to the oven and bake until the crust is deeply golden brown and the apples are tender and slightly browned, 35 to 40 minutes (if your apple slices are on the thicker side, you may want to bake for up to 45 minutes). Cool for at least 15 minutes before slicing and serving.

Make Ahead and Storage

This pie is best eaten the same day it's made. Store leftovers at room temperature, wrapped in plastic wrap.

NOTES

Boiled cider is one of my most reached-for ingredients in my pantry—see Resources (page 345) for where to find it. Or make your own: Pour 170 g / ¾ cup apple cider into a medium saucepan and boil until it reduces to 43 g / 2 tablespoons. Cool before using.

Other sliceable fruits can be used to make this pie, but the fruits should be on the firmer side and not incredibly juicy. My favorites include rhubarb, pears, and firm/underripe stone fruit.

BLOOD ORANGE BRÛLÉE PIE

MAKES ONE 8-BY-
12-INCH / 20-BY-30-CM
PIE

DIFFICULTY: EASY

This is a truly stunning free-form pie that is totally easy to make. What makes it special is the chocolate pie dough. Not only does that play on the classic flavor combination of chocolate and citrus in a unique way, but it also provides a beautiful dark canvas for the, bright fruit (use dark or black cocoa in the crust for a particularly dramatic effect; see Resources, page 345). The high temperature lightly chars the fruit, giving a sort of brûlée flavor and appearance.

Double recipe Chocolate All-Buttah Pie Dough (page 48), shaped into a disk or square and chilled (this is also great prepared as for Rough Puff Pastry; see page 50)

907 g / 2 pounds blood oranges (6 to 8 medium)

Egg wash (see page 98)

Turbinado sugar for sprinkling

66 g / ⅓ cup granulated sugar

1. Preheat the oven to 425°F / 218°C with a rack in the lower third (preferably with a Baking Steel or stone on it).

2. On a lightly floured surface, roll out the dough into a rectangle a little larger than 8 by 12 inches / 20 by 30 cm. Use the rolling pin to transfer the dough to a parchment-lined baking sheet. Use a pastry wheel to trim the edges straight. Dock the dough all over with a fork and transfer to the refrigerator.

3. Use a knife to slice off the top and bottom of each orange to expose the flesh. Then use the knife to remove the peel and pith from the fruit, following the shape of the fruit all around. Slice each orange about ⅛ inch / 3 mm thick.

4. Remove the crust from the refrigerator. Brush the whole surface with egg wash and sprinkle generously with turbinado sugar.

5. Arrange the blood orange slices on top of the dough, leaving ½-inch / 1-cm border of dough uncovered all around. The fruit can overlap slightly but try to arrange it in a relatively even layer. Sprinkle the granulated sugar evenly over the surface of the fruit.

6. Transfer the pie to the oven and bake until the edges of the crust are deeply golden brown and the fruit appears slightly caramelized, 35 to 40 minutes. Cool for at least 10 minutes before slicing and serving.

Make Ahead and Storage

The pie is best eaten the same day it's made. Store leftovers at room temperature, wrapped in plastic wrap.

OTHER RECOMMENDED CRUSTS
- Cardamom Lemon Pie Dough (page 52)
- Rough Puff Pastry (page 50)
- Vanilla Bean–Nutmeg Pie Dough (page 52)

RECOMMENDED FINISHES
- Salted Caramel Sauce (page 126) and/or Chocolate Whipped Cream (page 114), served on the side

Custard pies are among some of our most popular pies (think pumpkin and pecan) but they are also among the most misunderstood. I've eaten so many sub-par slices over the years: pies with wet, under-baked bottom crusts and/or overbaked fillings that border on chewy. But pie lovers know that done properly, custard pies are the definition of an ideal pie: a crisp but tender crust encasing a creamy filling that's baked to just-set perfection. (Note the word *baked*—every pie in this chapter is made with a filling that requires baking; if you're looking for pies with creamy cold-set fillings, like cream or chiffon pies, skip to Chapter 5.) But their taste is just one reason to love them—their fillings are some of the easiest to whip up, and they're also incredibly versatile. So, abandon any biases and read on to live your best custard pie life.

TYPES OF CUSTARD PIES

The most common type of custard pie is made with a mixture of eggs, dairy, and sugar (you can skip the sugar for a savory custard pie, like quiche; see page 304). But there are several other varieties beyond this—any kind of baked custard qualifies for pie-ifying.

CLASSIC BAKED CUSTARD PIES

After whisking together the custard, the mixture is poured into a parbaked crust. Once it's in the oven, the proteins in the eggs coagulate slowly, causing the custard to set to a sliceable consistency. These pies are baked at a lower temperature than fruit pies (from 325 to 375°F / 165 to 190°C) so the egg proteins will set evenly; at a higher temperature, they're likely to cook unevenly (firm on top, still liquid below) or overbake to a rubbery consistency. Within this category of baked custards, there are a few sub varieties worth noting:

CUSTARD TO BIND INCLUSIONS: This is a fancy way of saying that the custard surrounds another component (or "inclusion")—e.g., the custard poured over pecans to make a pecan pie.

OTHER STYLES: Custards like crème brûlée and *pots de crème* are traditionally baked in cups, but they are equally suited to being wrapped inside a flaky crust. These custards are sometimes made with egg yolks rather than whole eggs and set to a deliciously creamy consistency. Crème brûlée is finished with a layer of sugar that is caramelized into a crackly top layer, a finish that is particularly delicious for pie (see Cardamom Crème Brûlée Pie, page 235).

CHESS PIES

Chess pie, hailing from the South, is another well-known custard pie. It is very similar to a classic custard pie, with the addition of a small amount of a starch-based thickener. Often the thickener is cornmeal, which adds a slight textural interest to the custard, but it may be flour or even cornstarch. Adding a thickener often means fewer eggs can be used as well. Chess pies sometimes also contain an acidic element, such as buttermilk or citrus juice.

SUGAR PIES

Sugar pie (sometimes called "sugar cream pie") is my favorite variety of custard pie. The term is often used to refer to a specific pie, which is popular in Indiana (it's also often known there as "Hoosier pie") and parts of Canada (where it's often made with maple syrup). However, I also use the term to refer to this style of pie, which is made with dairy, sugar, and *flour*. This filling is totally egg-free—it's the starch in the flour that sets the custard in the oven. When I first started sharing recipes based on this technique, I was met with a lot of skeptics who assured me it couldn't be considered custard if it didn't have egg in it. But by definition, custards can be thickened with eggs or starch, or both! The proof is in the pudding— omitting the eggs allows the flavor of the filling ingredients to really shine. And, perhaps best of all, the lack of eggs makes it almost impossible to overbake these sugar pies, meaning they'll always set up perfectly smooth, with no cracks in sight. Sugar pies are generally baked at 350 to 375°F / 175 to 190°C.

FRANGIPANE PIES

While it is not usually considered a custard, I've got to bring frangipane into the mix here, too. Frangipane is a combination of ground nuts, butter, sugar, and eggs, sometimes with a small amount of flour. It is traditionally made with almonds, but most other nuts can also be used (see Fruity Frangipane Pie, page 221). It has a thicker consistency before baking that sets to a sliceable firmness. Because of its consistency and lower moisture content, frangipane can be baked at different temperatures, even up to 400°F / 205°C. It is the filling, for example, of a double-crust pie known as *pithiviers* that is made with puff pastry, a dough that is baked at higher temperatures for maximum flakiness.

PIE-DEAS

The Power of Infusing

One of my favorite ways to add flavor to custard pies is to infuse the milk or other dairy. To do so, bring the liquid to a simmer, then remove from the heat. Add whole spices, fresh herbs, coffee, tea, citrus zest, etc., cover the pot, and allow the mixture to steep for at least 15 minutes, or up to 1 hour. Strain the liquid, and it's ready to use in the recipe. Be sure to just bring the dairy to a simmer, because if it simmers longer, more moisture will evaporate and the milk will reduce, and you may need to add additional dairy to bring it back to the correct amount.

SWAMP PIES

The lesser-known swamp pies—part fruit pie, part custard pie—are a sub-category worthy of attention. First a fruit filling is partially baked in a crust (not a full pie's amount—a little less, to allow room for the swampiness that follows). Then a small amount of custard filling is poured over the fruit, creating something of a hybrid between tart fruit pie and creamy custard goodness. Swamp pies can be made with a single crust or a double crust. The custard partially "soggi-fies" the top crust, but it's set enough during the initial bake to still have a delicious flaky texture. Swamp pies are usually baked at around 375°F / 190°C—the hotter temperature works here because there's a smaller amount of custard.

PREPARING THE CRUST
(AVOIDING THE DREADED SOGGY BOTTOM)

The number one mistake most people make when making a custard pie is not parbaking the crust (see page 43). Parbaking is the only way to ensure that the crust will be baked sufficiently when you make a custard pie, because you're adding a high-moisture filling to it. Beyond that, the fillings are high in protein (from eggs or a starch thickener) and so set to a sliceable consistency in a relatively short baking time (35 to 45 minutes), which isn't enough time for the crust to bake through, especially not when it's drowned under liquid filling! I promise the extra bake time (15 to 17 minutes) is well worth it when the result is a crisp-bottomed, golden-brown-crusted beauty.

Using a Baking Steel or stone (see page 20) can help ensure adequate crust browning and crispness, because it retains heat and drives it to the bottom of the pie plate. It's also advisable to bake on an oven rack in the lowest part of the oven (whether or not you use a steel or stone). And once the crust is parbaked, you can opt to add a protective seal of sorts to help keep it crisp once you add the wet filling (see page 46).

TROUBLESHOOTING CUSTARD PIES

Custard pie fillings are relatively simple to prepare, but there are a few places where they can go awry. Understanding the ingredients and how they work (along with proper baking; see below) is the key to properly set, creamy custards.

HANDLING THE EGGS: It's important not to prepare a custard base (or not to add the eggs to a custard base) until just before ready to pour the filling into the crust and bake it. Sugar is hygroscopic, meaning it will absorb moisture from the surrounding environment. When a mixture of eggs and sugar sits for a long period, the sugar begins to absorb moisture from the eggs, causing

PIE PEP TALK

How to Make a Delicious Faux Edge

OK, you've parbaked the crust for your pie, and you've ensured you'll have no soggy bottom, but your once-perfect crimped edge is a little wonky and worse for the wear. Just follow my favorite tip for any baked good gone awry: Cover up what you don't like! If I'm adding whipped cream or meringue to a baked pie, I usually pipe it around the edge of the filling, but if you aren't happy with your crust, you can pipe an edge on top of it instead! You'll cover up the part of the crust you don't like, add a little sweetness, and make it look like it was supposed to be that way all along!

the eggs to become clumpy and appear almost coagulated. So, mix custards just before using them.

DISTRIBUTING THE STARCH: Starch can be troublesome because it likes to clump up in the presence of liquid. To avoid the problem, whisk the starch with the sugar (or a portion of the sugar). The sugar granules will help break up and distribute the starch, preventing it from clumping up when it's added to the custard base.

STRAINING THE CUSTARD: While many recipes for custard pies don't call for straining, it can sometimes save the day. If the eggs begin to misbehave, or the starch shows signs of clumping, push the custard through a fine-mesh sieve into a bowl, give it a few quick whisks, and it's ready to be added to the crust.

PROPER BAKING: Underbaked custard fillings will be soft and difficult to slice, and over-baked ones may be cracked and rubbery. Remember to allow for some carry-over cooking, and follow the tips for determining doneness in custard pies given below.

DETERMINING DONENESS IN CUSTARD PIES

Every custard pie recipe in this chapter describes the doneness in nearly the same terms. The filling should appear set around the outside edges, but a small portion of the center should still be slightly jiggly (though the filling should *not* appear to be liquid). This is important because of carry-over cooking. Baking the custard until it just barely set allows it to fully set as it cool, without overbaking.

THE WHYS OF PIES

Why You Shouldn't Rush Cooling a Custard Pie

If you try to rush the cooling of a custard pie by refrigerating it, it may cause the filling to weep moisture on the surface of the pie, which can mar the surface or even cause portions of the custard to lose their set with time. For best results, allow custard pies to cool fully at room temperature before refrigerating them.

STORING CUSTARD PIES

Custard pies are among the most flexible pies in terms of storage. They are make-ahead friendly pies, as their filling benefits from slow cooling, and if it's been properly parbaked, the crust will hold up well for up to 24 hours. The crusts can be parbaked up to 24 hours before baking the pie, because they will refresh/recrisp during their second trip to the oven.

Store baked custard pies loosely covered with plastic wrap. I prefer to store them at room temperature (for up to 24 hours), but if that makes you squeamish, you can refrigerate them once they are thoroughly cooled (and they must be refrigerated if they have a topping like whipped cream, of course). Store leftovers in an airtight container in the refrigerator.

CLASSIC CUSTARD PIE IN PHYLLO CRUST

MAKES ONE 9-INCH / 23-CM PIE

DIFFICULTY: EASY

I love a really classic custard filling, like this one—flavored with vanilla and the subtlest touch of warm spices. Nestled in the ultra-crisp layers of a phyllo crust, it's an especially perfect pairing (though it's delicious in nearly any type of crust—pie dough, cookie crusts, and crumb crusts included). While custard pie crusts are generally parbaked, phyllo crusts bake up crisp without it (see page 76), so just pour the custard right into the lined pie plate and bake!

113g / 2 large eggs
43 g / 2 large egg yolks
99 g / ½ cup granulated sugar
283 g / 1¼ cups whole milk
173 g / ¾ cup heavy cream
7 g / 1½ teaspoons vanilla extract
Pinch of ground cinnamon, or more to taste
Pinch of freshly grated nutmeg, or more to taste
Pinch of ground cloves, or more to taste
1 g / ¼ teaspoon fine sea salt
1 Phyllo Dough Crust (page 76)
Ground cinnamon, for finishing (optional)

1. Preheat the oven to 350°F / 175°C with a rack in the center (preferably with a Baking Steel or stone on it).

2. In a medium bowl, whisk the eggs, egg yolks, and sugar until the mixture lightens in color slightly, 1 to 2 minutes. Add the milk, cream, vanilla, cinnamon, nutmeg, cloves, and salt and whisk well to combine.

3. Place the phyllo crust on a parchment-lined baking sheet. Gently pour the custard into the crust. Transfer to the oven and bake until the crust is deeply golden brown and the custard is set around the outside edges but still slightly jiggly in the center, 40 to 45 minutes.

4. Cool completely, then refrigerate until ready to serve.

VARIATION

COCONUT CUSTARD PIE: Stir 113 g / 1⅓ cups sweetened shredded coconut into the custard before pouring it into the pan.

Make Ahead and Storage

The pie can be made up to 24 hours ahead and refrigerated until ready to serve.

OTHER RECOMMENDED CRUSTS
- Cardamom Lemon Pie Dough (page 52)
- Oatmeal Press-In Cookie Crust (page 64)
- Pumpkin Spice Pie Dough (page 52)

RECOMMENDED FINISHES
- Classic Whipped Cream (page 111)
- Freeze-Dried Fruity Whipped Cream (page 115)
- Meringue Topping (page 118)
- Flavored Sifting Sugars (page 128)

Custard Pie in
Phyllo Crust

Coconut Custard Pie
in Cardamom Lemon
Crust

BROWN SUGAR CHESS PIE

MAKES ONE 9-INCH / 23-CM PIE

DIFFICULTY: MEDIUM

Chess pie is a classic Southern pie, with a filling thickened with egg yolks and cornmeal, which gives it a slightly (and delightful) gritty texture amidst the silky-smooth custard. I like to combine this classic with a flavor that they do the very best in the South: caramel-y brown sugar. This pie is delicious on its own, but I love it decked out with lots of toppings—whipped cream, caramel sauce, and some kind of candied nuts.

283 g / 1⅓ cups packed dark brown sugar

30 g / 3 tablespoons fine cornmeal (white or yellow)

113 g / 2 large eggs

85 g / 4 large egg yolks

230 g / 1 cup whole milk

28 g / 1 ounce / 2 tablespoons unsalted butter, melted

7 g / 1½ teaspoons vanilla extract

2 g / ½ teaspoon fine sea salt

One 9-inch / 23-cm pie crust (see below), parbaked, brushed with egg wash, and cooled completely (see page 43)

1. Preheat the oven to 325°F / 165°C with a rack in the lower third (preferably with a Baking Steel or stone on it).

2. In a medium bowl, whisk the brown sugar and cornmeal together to combine. Add the eggs and egg yolks and whisk until the color has lightened noticeably, 1 to 2 minutes. Add the milk, melted butter, vanilla, and salt and whisk until well combined.

3. Place the parbaked pie crust on a parchment-lined baking sheet and pour the filling into the crust. Transfer to the oven and bake until the crust is deeply golden and the custard is set around the outside edges but is still slightly jiggly in the center, 35 to 40 minutes.

4. Cool the pie completely, then chill for at least 1 hour before slicing and serving.

VARIATION

DULCE DE LECHE CHESS PIE: Reduce the dark brown sugar to 71 g / ⅓ packed cup and add 101 g / ⅓ cup dulce de leche along with the egg yolks. Increase the salt to 3 g / ¾ teaspoon. If desired, top the chilled baked pie with a thin layer or drizzle of dulce de leche and/or whipped cream. Try swirling the two together (see page 104).

Make Ahead and Storage

The crust can be parbaked up to 2 days ahead. This pie can be made up to 24 hours ahead and stored in the refrigerator, loosely covered with plastic wrap.

RECOMMENDED CRUSTS
- Oatmeal Press-In Cookie Crust (page 64)
- Cornmeal Pie Dough (55)
- Caramelized Pie Crust (page 56)

RECOMMENDED FINISHES
- Whipped Cream Sauce (page 112)
- Chocolate Whipped Cream (page 114)
- Salted Caramel Sauce (page 126)
- Basic Brittle (page 129)

Left: Dulce de Leche Chess Pie
Right: Brown Sugar Chess Pie

BLUEBERRY SWAMP PIE

MAKES
ONE 9-INCH / 23-CM
PIE

DIFFICULTY: MEDIUM

Swamp pie is a wonderful combination of fruit and custard baked together into one delightful mess. You start by making a double-crusted fruit pie and partially baking it, then you pour a small amount of custard through the vents in the top crust and bake just until it is set. Some of the custard soaks into the fruit to make a delicious creamy-tart combination, and some soaks into the top crust, and the result looks, well, swampy. Although the top crust is traditional (see variation), I like it best with a streusel topping, which stays slightly crisp on the surface even after you swampify everything. For the traditional version, see the variation.

BLUEBERRY FILLING

680 g / 1½ pounds fresh blueberries

Grated zest and juice of 1 lemon

99 g / ½ cup granulated sugar

1 vanilla bean, halved lengthwise, seeds scraped out and reserved, or 10 g / 2 teaspoons vanilla extract

23 g / 3 tablespoons all-purpose flour

2 g / ½ teaspoon fine sea salt

One 9-inch / 23-cm pie crust (see below), parbaked, brushed with egg wash, and cooled completely (see page 43)

1 recipe Streusel for Baking (page 120)

CUSTARD FILLING

176 g / ¾ cup heavy cream

27 g / 2 tablespoons light brown sugar

56 g / 1 large egg

5 g / 1 teaspoon vanilla extract

1. Preheat the oven to 375°F / 190°C with a rack in the lower third (preferably with a Baking Steel or stone on it).

2. Make the blueberry filling: In a medium bowl, toss the blueberries with the lemon zest and juice. If using vanilla extract rather than a vanilla bean, add it now.

3. Place the granulated sugar in a small bowl and, if using, add the vanilla bean seeds and rub the two together with your hands to disperse the vanilla bean seeds. Stir in the flour and salt, then sprinkle this mixture over the blueberries and stir until well combined.

4. Put the parbaked crust on a parchment-lined baking sheet. Pour in the blueberry filling and spread in an even layer. Sprinkle the streusel evenly over the top. Transfer the pie to the oven and bake until the crust is deeply golden and the berries are juicy and bubbly, 35 to 40 minutes.

5. Meanwhile, just before the pie reaches that point, make the custard filling: In a medium bowl, whisk the cream, brown sugar, egg, and vanilla to combine. When the pie reaches the specified doneness, carefully pull out the oven rack and gently pour the cream mixture all over the bubbling filling. If, as you pour, the custard doesn't readily sink in or looks like it might overflow the edges of the crust, make a small well with a paring knife in the center of the blueberry filling and pour the custard into the well so that it can begin to absorb more into the filling.

6. Slide the rack back and bake until the custard is set around the edges but slightly jiggly in the center, 10 to 15 minutes more. Cool the pie completely before slicing and serving.

VARIATION ////////////////////////////////////

DOUBLE-CRUST BLUEBERRY SWAMP PIE: For a traditional swamp pie with a top crust, prepare a double recipe of pie dough; omit the streusel topping. Follow the instructions for preparing double-crust pies on page 42, using the blueberry filling. Bake the pie at 400°F / 205°C for 35 to 40 minutes, until the juices bubble through the vents. Carefully pour the custard filling through the vents in the top of the pie (some will overflow onto the top crust—that's OK). Reduce the oven temperature to 375°F / 190°C and bake for 10 to 15 minutes more, until the custard is just set.

Make Ahead and Storage

This pie is best eaten the day it is prepared. Store leftovers in the refrigerator covered with plastic wrap.

RECOMMENDED CRUSTS
- Graham Flour Pie Dough (page 54)
- Cornmeal Pie Dough (55)
- Vanilla Bean–Nutmeg Pie Dough (page 52)

RECOMMENDED FINISHES
- Whipped Cream Sauce (page 112), to make it even swampier

PUMPKIN PIE

MAKES ONE 9-INCH /
23-CM PIE

DIFFICULTY: MEDIUM

Because pumpkin pie had never been one of my favorites, I set out to make a recipe I truly loved for this book, and I ended up with several contenders! This one is the most classic; see the variation below for a slightly creamier version that is also delicious. I like it best topped with whipped cream, or a pile of fat toasted marshmallows (see Resources, page 345).

170 g / 3 large eggs
106 g / ½ cup packed light brown sugar
99 g / ½ cup granulated sugar
5 g / 1 teaspoon vanilla extract
439 g / 2 cups canned pumpkin puree
6 g / 2 teaspoons ground cinnamon
3 g / 1 teaspoon ground ginger
2 g / ½ teaspoon ground cloves
Scant 1 g / ¼ teaspoon freshly grated nutmeg
2 g / ½ teaspoon fine sea salt
115 g / ½ cup half-and-half
One 9-inch / 23-cm pie crust (see below), parbaked, brushed with egg wash, and cooled completely (see page 43)

1. Preheat the oven to 375°F / 190°C with a rack in the center (preferably with a Baking Steel or stone on it).

2. In a medium bowl, whisk the eggs, brown sugar, granulated sugar, and vanilla together until well combined. Add the pumpkin puree, cinnamon, ginger, cloves, nutmeg, and salt and whisk until well combined. Add the half-and-half and whisk well to combine.

3. Place the parbaked crust on a parchment-lined baking sheet. Pour the filling into the crust. Transfer to the oven and bake until the custard appears set around the edges (it may still be a bit

jiggly in the center—that's OK), 35 to 40 minutes. Cool completely, then refrigerate for at least 2 hours before serving.

4. When ready to serve, spread or pipe the whipped cream onto the surface of the pie. Slice and serve.

VARIATION //
PUMPKIN MASCARPONE PIE: Replace the half-and-half with 226 g / 8 ounces mascarpone cheese; whisk well to combine.

Make Ahead and Storage

The pie can be made up to 24 hours ahead and refrigerated until ready to serve. Add the whipped cream topping just before serving.

RECOMMENDED CRUSTS
- Cardamom Lemon Pie Dough (page 52)
- Oatmeal Press-In Cookie Crust (page 64)
- Pumpkin Spice Pie Dough (page 52)

OTHER RECOMMENDED FINISHES
- Mile-High Batch of Classic Whipped Cream or Mascarpone Whipped Cream (page 111)

OTHER OPTIONS
- Skip the whipped cream and top with Meringue Topping (page 118), or serve with Whipped Cream Sauce (page 112)

MASCARPONE PIE

MAKES ONE 9-INCH / 23-CM PIE

DIFFICULTY: MEDIUM

Thick, creamy mascarpone has become one of my most beloved ingredients. I love the richness of it, especially when it is paired with a subtle hint of spice, as in this recipe. The pie is perfect all on its own, but I love it paired with fruit—try piling it high with sliced seasonal fresh fruit and/or berries or a thin layer of macerated fruit, or drizzle the slices with Thin Fruit Glaze (page 122).

340 g / 12 ounces mascarpone cheese, at room temperature

226 g / 8 ounces cream cheese, at room temperature

1 vanilla bean, halved lengthwise, seeds scraped out and reserved

149 g / ¾ cup granulated sugar

113 g / 2 large eggs

43 g / 2 large egg yolks

Pinch of ground cinnamon

Pinch of ground cardamom

Dash of freshly grated nutmeg

1 g / ¼ teaspoon fine sea salt

One 9-inch / 23-cm pie crust (see below), parbaked, brushed with egg wash, and cooled completely (see page 43)

1. Preheat the oven to 350°F / 175°C with a rack in the center (preferably with a Baking Steel or stone on it).

2. In the bowl of a food processor, pulse the mascarpone and cream cheese until fully combined.

3. In a small bowl, rub the vanilla bean seeds into the sugar. Add the vanilla sugar to the food processor and blend until smooth. Add the eggs, then egg yolks, one at a time, pulsing until the mixture is smooth after each addition. Add the spices and salt and process to combine.

4. Place the parbaked crust on a parchment-lined baking sheet and pour the filling into the crust. Transfer to the oven and bake until the crust is deeply golden brown and the custard is set around the outside edges but is still slightly jiggly in the center, 40 to 45 minutes.

5. Cool completely, then refrigerate for at least 2 hours before slicing and serving.

Make Ahead and Storage

The pie can be made ahead and refrigerated until ready to serve.

RECOMMENDED CRUSTS
- Vanilla Bean–Nutmeg Pie Dough (page 52)
- Citrus Roll-Out Cookie Crust (page 63)
- Brown Butter Press-In Crust (page 64)

RECOMMENDED FINISHES
- Basic Brittle (page 129)
- Freeze-Dried Fruity Whipped Cream (page 115)
- Flavored Sifting Sugars (page 128)

CARAMEL-EARL GREY CUSTARD PIE IN GINGERSNAP CRUMB CRUST

MAKES ONE 9-INCH / 23-CM PIE

DIFFICULTY: MEDIUM

This pie was inspired by my friend Erin Clarkson, a fellow baker who asserts that "if it can be infused, it should be infused with Earl Grey." I took that to heart to create this caramel-spiked pie, infusing the milk and cream with plenty of tea before whisking them into a classic custard filling. And because I adore the combination of chai tea and caramel, there's a variation for that version.

226 g / 1 cup whole milk

78 g / ⅓ cup heavy cream

8 g / ¼ cup loose Earl Grey tea (or 5 Earl Grey tea bags)

212 g / 1 cup packed dark brown sugar

7 g / 1 tablespoon cornstarch

170 g / 3 large eggs

5 g / 1½ teaspoons vanilla extract

2 g / ½ teaspoon fine sea salt

One 9-inch / 23-cm Basic Crumb Crust (page 66) made with gingersnap crumbs, parbaked and cooled completely (see page 43)

1 recipe Salted Caramel Sauce (page 126; optional), well chilled

Full Batch of Classic Whipped Cream (page 111; optional)

1. In medium saucepan, bring the milk and cream to a simmer over medium heat. Remove from the heat, add the tea, and cover the pan. Let steep for 15 to 20 minutes, then strain the liquid into a medium bowl (or just remove the tea bags, if using, and pour into the bowl).

2. Preheat the oven to 350°F / 175°C with a rack in the center (preferably with a Baking Steel or stone on it).

3. In a medium bowl, stir the brown sugar and cornstarch together well to combine. Add this mixture to the milk mixture, along with the eggs, and whisk well to combine. Add the vanilla and salt and whisk until well incorporated.

4. Place the parbaked crust on a parchment-lined baking sheet and pour the custard into it. Transfer to the oven and bake until the crust is deeply golden brown and the custard is set around the outside but still slightly jiggly in the center, 45 to 50 minutes. Cool completely, then refrigerate for at least 2 hours (or up to 24 hours).

5. Pour some or all of the caramel glaze over the top of the pie and spread into an even layer over the surface. A thin layer will set firmer and a thicker layer will be gooier—or you can drizzle it over slices when serving. Refrigerate the pie for at least 1 hour, or until ready to slice and serve.

VARIATION

CARAMEL-CHAI CUSTARD PIE IN SHORTBREAD CRUMB CRUST: Replace the Earl Grey tea with an equal amount of chai tea. Make the crumb crust with shortbread or vanilla cookie crumbs.

Make Ahead and Storage

The pie can be made up to 24 hours ahead and refrigerated until ready to serve.

OTHER RECOMMENDED CRUSTS

- All-Buttah Pie Dough (page 48)
- Brown Butter Press-In Cookie Crust (page 64)
- Phyllo Dough Crust (page 76)

RECOMMENDED FINISHES

- Top the pie with Caramel Meringue Topping (page 118) instead of the caramel glaze, or with Chocolate Whipped Cream (page 114)

Above: Caramel-Chai
Custard Pie
Right: Caramel Earl
Grey Custard Pie

BIRTHDAY-CAKE PIE

MAKES ONE 9-INCH /
23-CM DEEP-DISH PIE

DIFFICULTY: MEDIUM

Just one day after I thought we'd wrapped up recipe testing for this book, my wonderful assistant, Katie, was helping me look through reference images in preparation for the photo shoot. Suddenly she turned to me and whispered, "Birthday cake pie!" As soon as she said it, I knew it needed to happen. Starting with her original idea, we dreamt up a cake batter–like custard filling, speckled with sprinkles and topped with chocolate meringue, inside a flaky crust. I've long believed the best ideas come through collaboration, and this recipe is a shining example of what happens when sweet-minded brains collide (and have access to an entire cabinet of sprinkles).

198 g / 1 cup granulated sugar

40 g / ⅓ cup all-purpose flour

113 g / 2 large eggs, separated

235 g / 1 cup heavy cream

15 g / 4 teaspoons vanilla extract

Scant 1 g / ¼ teaspoon almond extract

2 g / ½ teaspoon fine sea salt

Scant 1 g / ¼ teaspoon cream of tartar

51 g / ⅓ cup round confetti sprinkles (see Note, page 220), plus more for finishing

One 9-inch / 23-cm deep-dish Basic Crumb Crust (page 66) made with vanilla wafers, parbaked and cooled completely (see page 43)

Regular Batch of Chocolate Meringue Topping (page 118)

1. Preheat the oven to 375°F / 190°C with a rack in the lower third (preferably with a Baking Steel or stone on it).

2. In a medium bowl, whisk 99 g / ½ cup of the sugar and the flour to combine. In a small bowl, light whisk the egg yolks. Add the egg yolks, cream, vanilla extract, almond extract, and salt to the sugar mixture and whisk until well combined.

3. Place the egg whites and cream of tartar in the bowl of a stand mixer fitted with the whip attachment and whip on medium-high speed until foamy, 30 seconds to 1 minute. With the mixer running, add the remaining 99 g / ½ cup sugar in a slow, steady stream and then continue to whip to medium peaks, 3 to 5 minutes.

4. Add about one quarter of the meringue to the egg yolk mixture and gently whisk to incorporate (this will help to lighten the mixture and make it easier to incorporate the rest of the meringue). Whisk in the remaining meringue in two or three additions. Gently fold in the sprinkles.

5. Place the parbaked crust on a baking sheet. Pour the custard into the pie crust and gently sprinkle more sprinkles over the top. Bake until the pie appears set, 35 to 40 minutes. Cool to room temperature.

6. Spoon, spread, or pipe the chocolate meringue around the edge of the pie. Garnish with sprinkles.

(CONTINUED)

Make Ahead and Storage

The pie, without the meringue topping, can be made up to 24 hours ahead and stored at room temperature. Store leftovers in an airtight container in the refrigerator.

NOTE

Traditional sprinkles (jimmies) or nonpareils don't work as well in this recipe—they bleed into the mixture more quickly (which can tint it sort of a gray color) and won't stay suspended in the custard.

OTHER RECOMMENDED CRUSTS
- Basic Crumb Crust (page 66)
- Chocolate All-Buttah Pie Dough (page 48)

RECOMMENDED FINISHES
- Dark Chocolate Black-Bottom Base (page 110)
- Flavored Sifting Sugars (page 128)
- Or substitute Chocolate Whipped Cream (page 114) for the meringue

FRUITY FRANGIPANE PIE

MAKES ONE 9-INCH /
23-CM PIE

DIFFICULTY: MEDIUM

A classic nut-based custard, frangipane is delicious paired with fruit. This recipe encourages you to mix it up and use different combinations of fruit and nuts all year round, whatever's in season. If you opt for an almond frangipane, omit the whole nuts and increase the almond flour to 120 g / 1¼ cups—and skip grinding any nuts.

454 g / 1 pound prepared fruit (peeled if desired, seeds or pits removed as necessary), cut into thick slices if large

25 g / 2 tablespoons granulated sugar

15 g / 2 tablespoons all-purpose flour

FRANGIPANE

142 g / 1 cup whole unsalted nuts (any nut will work, but if choosing almonds, see Headnote), toasted and cooled

48 g / ½ cup finely ground almond flour (see Notes)

40 g / ⅓ cup all-purpose flour

2 g / ½ teaspoon fine sea salt

99 g / ½ cup granulated sugar

113 g / 4 ounces / 8 tablespoons unsalted butter, at room temperature

9 g / 1 tablespoon grated orange or lemon zest (optional)

5 g / 1 teaspoon vanilla extract

113 g / 2 large eggs

One 9-inch 23-cm pie crust made with ½ recipe Rough Puff Pastry (page 50) or with any pie dough (see below) prepared as for Rough Puff Pastry, rolled out, fitted into the pan but not trimmed, and chilled (see page 34)

Egg wash (see page 98)

Turbinado sugar for sprinkling

1. Preheat the oven to 400°F / 205°C with a rack in the lower third (preferably with a Baking Steel or stone on it).

2. In a medium bowl, toss the prepared fruit with the sugar, folding gently until the granulated sugar mostly dissolves. Add the flour and gently mix to combine. Set aside.

3. Make the frangipane: In a food processor, pulse the nuts until they form a fine powder. Add the almond flour, all-purpose flour, salt, and granulated sugar and pulse to combine. Add the butter, citrus zest, if using, and vanilla and pulse until the mixture is smooth. Add the egg, processing until incorporated. Scrape the bowl down well, then process once more to ensure everything is evenly combined.

4. Place the chilled pie crust on a parchment-line baking sheet. Pour the frangipane mixture into the crust and spread into an even layer. Add the fruit—don't worry about arranging it in any particular way, this is a rustic pie. Some pieces will be submerged in the frangipane, others will stick out of the top—it's all good.

5. Fold the excess dough over the filling at the edges, sort of as you would for a galette or free-form pie. Brush the exposed crust with egg wash and sprinkle generously with turbinado sugar.

(CONTINUED)

6. Transfer the pie to the oven. Bake until the crust is deeply golden brown, the fruit is tender, and the frangipane appears just set, 45 to 50 minutes.

Make Ahead and Storage

This pie is best served the day it is prepared.

NOTES

To deepen the flavor of the almond flour, toast in a skillet on the stovetop until fragrant.

This also makes a delicious double-crust pie (see page 42), and it could even be referred to as a pithiviers if made with rough puff pastry or pie dough prepared as for rough puff pastry. It's especially beautiful with a scored top (see Scoring, page 89). You'll need a full recipe of Rough Puff Pastry (page 50) or a double recipe of pie dough made as for rough puff pastry. Increase the bake time to 60 to 65 minutes.

RECOMMENDED CRUSTS
- Any pie dough can be made as Rough Puff Pastry
- Whole Wheat Pie Dough (page 54)
- Caramelized Pie Crust (page 56)

RECOMMENDED FINISHES
- Salted Caramel Sauce (page 126)
- Flavored Sifting Sugars (page 128)
- Basic Brittle (page 129)

Clockwise from top left: Honey Roasted Peanut Frangipane with Concord Grapes, Macadamia Frangipane with Mango, Almond Frangipane with Apricots

CHERRY CLAFOUTIS PIE

MAKES ONE 9-INCH / 23-CM PIE

DIFFICULTY: EASY

Clafoutis is a classic French baked custard, usually studded with cherries (but you can use lots of different fruits; see the variations). While a clafoutis doesn't have a crust, I adore this creamy but well-set filling and fruit combo baked in a pie shell for textural contrast.

One 9-inch / 23-cm pie crust (see below), parbaked, brushed with egg wash, and cooled completely (see page 43)

340 g / 12 ounces sweet or sour cherries, pitted

1 vanilla bean, halved lengthwise, seeds scraped out and reserved

99 g / ½ cup granulated sugar

30 g / ¼ cup all-purpose flour

230 g / 1 cup whole milk

78 g / ⅓ cup heavy cream

170 g / 3 large eggs

2 g / ½ teaspoon fine sea salt

Pinch of ground cinnamon

Powdered sugar or Flavored Sifting Sugar (page 128) for dusting (optional)

1. Preheat the oven to 350°F / 175°C with a rack in the lower third (preferably with a Baking Steel or stone on it).

2. Place the parbaked crust on a parchment-lined baking sheet and arrange the cherries in an even layer in it.

3. In a medium bowl, rub the vanilla bean seeds into the sugar. Add the flour and whisk to combine. Add the milk, cream, and eggs and whisk well to combine. Whisk in the salt and cinnamon.

4. Gently pour the custard into the prepared pie crust. Bake until the custard appears set at the edges but is still slightly jiggly in the center, 45 to 55 minutes. Let cool for 15 minutes, then dust with powdered sugar and serve warm; or cool to room temperature and refrigerate until ready to serve, then dust with sugar just before serving, if using.

VARIATIONS

RHUBARB CLAFLOUTIS PIE: Replace the cherries with 226 g / 8 ounces (about 1½ cups) thinly sliced rhubarb.

RASPBERRY-LEMON CLAFOUTIS PIE: Replace the cherries with 283 g / 10 ounces raspberries. Rub the grated zest of 1 lemon into the sugar along with the vanilla bean seeds.

BLUEBERRY CLAFOUTIS PIE: Replace the cherries with 283 g / 10 ounces blueberries.

PEACH, PLUM, OR APRICOT CLAFOUTIS PIE: Replace the cherries with 340 g / 12 ounces chopped peaches, plums, or apricots.

CHOCOLATE CLAFOUTIS PIE: Replace the cherries with 340 g / 12 ounces strawberries (or the amount of fruit listed in any other variation, as desired). Increase the sugar to 132 g / ⅔ cup and the flour to 40 g / ⅓ cup. Whisk 85 g / 3 ounces unsweetened chocolate, melted and cooled, into the custard after you've added the eggs.

Make Ahead and Storage

The pie can be made up to 24 hours ahead and refrigerated until ready to serve.

RECOMMENDED CRUSTS
- Cardamom Lemon Pie Dough (page 52)
- Rough Puff Pastry (page 50)
- Chocolate All-Buttah Pie Dough (page 48)
- Press-In Cookie Crust (page 64)

RECOMMENDED FINISHES
- Dark Chocolate Black-Bottom Base (page 110)
- Whipped Cream Sauce (page 112)

Clockwise from top left: Peach, Chocolate with Strawberry, Blueberry, Cherry, Rhubarb, and Raspberry Lemon Clafoutis Pies.

WHITE CHOCOLATE–PEPPERMINT PIE

MAKES ONE 9-INCH /
23-CM PIE

DIFFICULTY: HARD

Inspired by peppermint bark, this pie features multiple textures (the best part of a good slice of pie): a crisp crust (I especially love this in the Chocolate All-Buttah Pie Dough, page 48), a dense white chocolate filling, and a topping of fluffy peppermint meringue. Then the whole thing is glazed with a swirly "cold snap" topping that gives a little of that firm chocolate bite.

235 g / 1 cup heavy cream

170 g / 6 ounces white chocolate, chopped

99 g / ½ cup granulated sugar

40 g / ⅓ cup all-purpose flour

226 g / 1 cup whole milk

5 g / 1 teaspoon vanilla extract

2 g / ½ teaspoon fine sea salt

One 9-inch / 23-cm pie crust (see below), parbaked, brushed with egg wash, and cooled completely (see page 43)

1 recipe Peppermint Meringue Topping (page 118)

1 recipe White Chocolate Cold-Snap Topping (page 127)

A few drops of liquid red food coloring

Crushed peppermints or candy canes for garnish (optional)

1. Preheat the oven to 375°F / 190°C with a rack in the lower third (preferably with a Baking Steel or stone on it).

2. Bring a medium saucepan of water to a simmer over medium heat. In a medium heatproof bowl, combine the cream and chocolate. Place the bowl over the saucepan of water (the bottom of the bowl should not touch the water) and heat, stirring frequently, until the chocolate is fully melted (take care not to overheat it—white chocolate is prone to burning). Let cool for about 5 minutes, or until no longer warm to the touch, before proceeding.

3. In a medium bowl, whisk the sugar and flour to combine. Whisk in the milk and the white chocolate mixture. Add the vanilla extract and salt and whisk just to combine—too much whisking will lead to lots of air bubbles that can linger on the surface of the custard after you transfer it to the crust.

4. Place the parbaked crust on a baking sheet and pour in the custard. Bake until the filling appears set at the edges but is still jiggly in the center, 30 to 35 minutes. Cool the pie to room temperature, then chill for at least 1 hour (or up to 24 hours) before finishing.

5. Spoon, pipe, or swoop the meringue topping onto pie. Transfer the pie to the refrigerator for 1 hour or to the freezer for 20 to 25 minutes.

6. Transfer the cold-snap topping to a large liquid measuring cup and squeeze a few drops of food coloring into it, letting drops fall in a few difference places on the surface. Gently swirl the measuring cup to barely incorporate the food coloring—do not stir! The idea is to get it lightly swirly (it will continue to swirl when you pour it over the pie).

7. Carefully pour the cold-snap topping over the pie (or, if that makes you nervous, spoon it over with a medium spoon): Start at the top, letting

(CONTINUED)

it run down the sides, then pour (or spoon it) farther down the sides as needed to cover all of the topping. (Some of it will pool on the surface of the pie, but starting from the top minimizes this as much as possible.) Sprinkle the crushed peppermints, if using, over the surface or around the edges of the pie. The cold-snap topping should set quickly at room temperature—if it doesn't, transfer to the refrigerator to firm up before slicing and serving the pie.

Make Ahead and Storage

The pie can be made up to 24 hours ahead and refrigerated until ready to serve.

RECOMMENDED CRUSTS
- Chocolate All-Buttah Pie Dough (page 48)
- Graham Flour Pie Crust (page 54)
- Vanilla Bean–Nutmeg Pie Dough (page 52)

RECOMMENDED FINISHES
- Try this with a Dark Chocolate Black-Bottom Base (or White) (page 110)
- Sub the meringue for Chocolate Whipped Cream (page 114) or Freeze-Dried Fruity Whipped Cream (page 115)

GERMAN CHOCOLATE PIE

MAKES ONE 9-INCH /
23-CM PIE

DIFFICULTY: MEDIUM

The combination of deep, dark chocolate with a delicious caramel-pecan topping can't be beat. Add a buttery, flaky crust, and you'll have one of those crowd-pleasing pies that will be gone in minutes, especially if you serve it à la mode.

CHOCOLATE CUSTARD FILLING

198 g / 1 cup granulated sugar

28 g / ⅓ cup unsweetened cocoa powder

30 g / ¼ cup all-purpose flour

1 g / ¼ teaspoon fine sea salt

113 g / 2 large eggs, at room temperature

57 g / 2 ounces / 4 tablespoons unsalted butter, melted

78 g / ⅓ cup heavy cream

56 g / 2 ounces unsweetened chocolate, melted

10 g / 2 teaspoons vanilla extract

One 9-inch / 23-cm pie crust (see below), parbaked, brushed with egg wash, and cooled completely (see page 43)

COCONUT-PECAN TOPPING

85 g / 4 large egg yolks

227 g / 1 cup evaporated milk

198 g / 1 cup granulated sugar

7 g / 1½ teaspoons vanilla extract

1 g / ¼ teaspoon fine sea salt

191 g / 2¼ cups sweetened shredded coconut

115 g / 1 cup chopped toasted pecans

1. Preheat the oven to 350°F / 175°C with a rack in the center (preferably with a Baking Steel or stone on it).

2. Make the chocolate custard filling: In a medium bowl, whisk the sugar, cocoa powder, flour, and salt to combine. Whisk in the eggs, melted butter, cream, melted chocolate, and vanilla until smooth and well combined.

3. Place the parbaked crust on a baking sheet and pour in the filling. Transfer the baking sheet to the oven and bake until the custard appears set around the edges (it may still be a bit jiggly in the center—that's OK), 30 to 35 minutes. Cool completely, then refrigerate.

4. Make the topping: In a medium pot, whisk the egg yolks, evaporated milk, sugar, vanilla, and salt to combine. Cook over medium-low heat, whisking or stirring, until the mixture begins to thicken, 8 to 10 minutes; I like to use a whisk at the beginning and then switch to a silicone spatula as it thickens to ensure that I can get in the corners of the pot. Stir in the coconut and pecans and transfer the topping to a medium bowl. Cool to room temperature.

5. Spread the coconut-pecan topping evenly over the chilled chocolate filling. Chill the pie for at least 1 hour before slicing and serving.

Make Ahead and Storage

The pie can be made up to 24 hours ahead and refrigerated until ready to serve.

RECOMMENDED CRUSTS
- Chocolate All-Buttah Pie Dough (page 48)
- Graham Flour Pie Dough (page 54)
- Rough Puff Pastry (page 50)

CARROT CAKE CUSTARD PIE

MAKES ONE 9-INCH / 23-CM PIE

DIFFICULTY: EASY

Carrot cake is one of the more controversial desserts in my family. It was my parents' wedding cake, which should indicate how they feel about it. But my two older brothers overindulged on that very same cake, and they have never wanted to go near one since! I've always wanted to pie-ify this classic combination of flavors, and I've found it works best with a carrot custard filling and a topping of my cream cheese whipped cream for a little of that tangy frosting-like finish!

226 g / 4 large eggs

60 g / ¼ cup heavy cream

57 g / 2 ounces / 4 tablespoons unsalted butter, melted

212 g / 1 cup packed light brown sugar

85 g / ¼ cup honey

15 g / 1 tablespoon vanilla extract

2 g / ½ teaspoon ground cinnamon

1 g / ¼ teaspoon fine sea salt

223 g / 2¼ loosely packed cups grated peeled carrots (about 4 medium)

30 g / ¼ cup all-purpose flour

86 g / ¾ cup chopped toasted pecans or walnuts

One 9-inch / 23-cm pie crust (see below), parbaked, brushed with egg wash, and cooled completely (see page 43)

Full Batch of Extra-Thick and Creamy Whipped Cream (page 113)

Micro or baby carrots, for finishing (optional; see Resources, page 345)

1. Preheat the oven to 375°F / 190°C with a rack in the center (preferably with a Baking Steel or stone on it).

2. In a medium bowl, whisk the eggs, cream, melted butter, brown sugar, honey, vanilla, cinnamon, and salt until well combined. In another medium bowl, toss the carrots with the flour until well combined, then toss in the nuts. Fold this mixture into the custard with a silicone spatula.

3. Place the parbaked crust on a baking sheet and pour in the custard. Transfer the baking sheet to the oven and bake until the custard appears set around the edges (it may still be a bit jiggly in the center—that's OK), 30 to 35 minutes. Cool completely, then refrigerate for at least 2 hours.

4. Spread or pipe the whipped cream into an even layer on the surface of the chilled pie, top with mini carrots, if using, then slice and serve.

Make Ahead and Storage

The pie can be made up to 24 hours ahead and refrigerated until ready to serve.

RECOMMENDED CRUSTS

- Cardamom Lemon Pie Dough (page 52)
- Oatmeal Press-In Cookie Crust (page 64)
- Citrus Roll-Out Cookie Crust (page 63)

Top: German Chocolate Pie
Bottom: Carrot Cake Custard Pie

CHOCOLATE SUGAR PIE

MAKES ONE 9-INCH / 23-CM PIE

DIFFICULTY: EASY

Sugar pie is one of my favorite types of custard pie, partly because of the simple fact that it's virtually impossible to mess up! The custard filling is thickened with flour, rather than eggs, which means that the surface sets beautifully smooth without risk of cracking (for more on sugar pies, see page 202). I include a bunch of variations here, since it's become one of my go-to pies. It's also a great base for creating your own layered pie; see Layering Fillings, page 100.

99 g / ½ cup granulated sugar

60 g / ½ cup all-purpose flour

28 g / ⅓ cup cocoa powder (dark or black cocoa works especially well here; see Resources, page 345)

106 g / ½ cup packed light brown sugar

403 g / 1¾ cups whole milk

235 g / 1 cup heavy cream

7 g / 1½ teaspoons vanilla extract

2 g / ½ teaspoon fine sea salt

One 9-inch / 23-cm pie crust (see opposite), parbaked, brushed with egg wash, and cooled completely (see page 43)

1. Preheat the oven to 375°F / 190°C with a rack in the lower third (preferably with a Baking Steel or stone on it).

2. In a medium bowl, whisk the sugar, flour, and cocoa powder to combine. Add the brown sugar and mix to combine. Whisk in the milk, cream, vanilla extract, and salt and mix just to combine—too much whisking will lead to lots of air bubbles that can linger on the surface of the custard after you transfer it to the crust.

3. Place the parbaked crust on a parchment-lined baking sheet and pour in the custard. Bake until the filling appears set at the edges but is still jiggly in the center, 28 to 32 minutes. Cool to room temperature, then chill for at least 2 hours, or until ready to slice and serve.

VARIATIONS

VANILLA SUGAR PIE: Omit the cocoa powder and increase the vanilla extract to 15 g / 1 tablespoon, or substitute seeds scraped from 1 vanilla bean (halved lengthwise).

CITRUS SUGAR PIE: Omit the cocoa powder and add the grated zest of 1 large or 2 small citrus fruits to the custard.

SPICED SUGAR PIE: Omit the cocoa powder and add up to 1½ tablespoons ground spices along with the salt.

MAPLE SUGAR PIE: Omit the cocoa powder and replace the brown sugar with 78 g / ½ cup maple sugar.

EGGNOG SUGAR PIE: Omit the cocoa powder. Replace the cream with 230 g / 1 cup eggnog and add 2 g / ½ teaspoon freshly grated nutmeg along with the salt.

PUMPKIN SUGAR PIE: Omit the cocoa powder. Replace the light brown sugar with dark brown sugar. Reduce the milk to 230 g / 1 cup and the cream to 153 g / ¾ cup. Whisk in 212 g / 1 cup pumpkin puree and 6 g / 2 teaspoons pumpkin pie spice at the end.

Make Ahead and Storage

The crust can be parbaked up to 2 days ahead. The finished pie can be made up to 24 hours ahead and refrigerated until ready to serve.

Clockwise from top left:
Chocolate Sugar Pie,
Spiced Sugar Pie,
Citrus Sugar Pie,
Vanilla Sugar Pie,
Pumpkin Sugar Pie,
Maple Sugar Pie

RECOMMENDED CRUSTS
- Chocolate All-Buttah Pie Dough (page 48)
- Graham Flour Pie Crust (page 54)
- Vanilla Bean–Nutmeg Pie Dough (page 52)

RECOMMENDED FINISHES
- Dark Chocolate Black-Bottom Base (page 110)
- Chocolate Whipped Cream (page 114)
- Flavored Sifting Sugars (page 128)
- Basic Brittle (page 129)

CARDAMOM CRÈME BRÛLÉE PIE

MAKES ONE 9-INCH /
23-CM PIE

DIFFICULTY: MEDIUM

I love fire, and I love any excuse to break out my kitchen torch. Enter this beautifully spiced crème brûlée pie, flavored with cardamom and vanilla and topped with a sugar crust you can torch to caramelized perfection. When you slice into it, the shards of caramel combine with the creamy custard and the crisp crust, and it's heavenly.

392 g / 1⅔ cups heavy cream

8 whole cardamom pods, gently cracked

½ vanilla bean, halved lengthwise, seeds scraped out, seeds and pod reserved

132 g / ⅔ cup granulated sugar

128 g / 6 large egg yolks

2 g / ½ teaspoon fine sea salt

One 9-inch / 23-cm pie crust (see below), parbaked, brushed with egg wash, and cooled completely (see page 43)

Superfine sugar for finishing

1. In a small pot, bring the cream, cardamom, vanilla pod, and vanilla bean seeds to a simmer over medium heat. Remove the pot from the heat, cover, and let the cream steep for 15 to 20 minutes.

2. Preheat the oven to 350°F / 175°C with a rack in the center (preferably with a Baking Steel or stone on it).

3. Strain the steeped cream into a medium bowl; discard the cardamom pods and vanilla bean. Add the granulated sugar, egg yolks, and salt and whisk well to combine.

4. Place the parbaked crust on a parchment-lined baking sheet and pour in the custard. Transfer the baking sheet to the oven and bake until the custard appears set around the edges (it may still be a bit jiggly in the center—that's OK), 35 to 40 minutes. Cool completely, then refrigerate for at least 2 hours.

5. When ready to serve, sprinkle an even layer of superfine sugar over the surface of the pie. Brûlée the sugar with a kitchen torch until evenly melted and caramelized. Let the pie sit for 5 minutes before slicing and serving.

Make Ahead and Storage

The pie can be made through step 4 up to 1 day ahead and refrigerated.

RECOMMENDED CRUSTS

- Caramelized Pie Crust (page 56)
- Cardamom Lemon Pie Dough (page 52)
- Vanilla Bean–Nutmeg Pie Dough (page 52)

CHEESECAKE PIE

MAKES ONE 9-INCH /
23-CM DEEP-DISH PIE

DIFFICULTY: MEDIUM

The filling for cheesecake is a custard, just like any of the recipes in this chapter, and since it's baked in a crust, I would argue it is more *pie* than *cake* to begin with. At least that's what I tell my husband, who requests cheesecake for nearly every special occasion. To further pie-ify it, I sometimes opt to skip the classic crumb crust and make it with a dough crust, either a cookie crust or flaky pie dough. Take this to another level with flavorful and beautiful swirls; see the variations below.

454 g / 1 pound cream cheese, at room temperature

198 g / 1 cup granulated sugar

Grated zest of 1 lemon

15 g / 1 tablespoon fresh lemon juice

226 g / 4 large eggs

10 g / 2 teaspoons vanilla extract

60 g / ¼ cup heavy cream

2 g / ½ teaspoon fine sea salt

One 9-inch / 23-cm deep-dish crust (see below), parbaked, brushed with egg wash, and cooled completely (see page 43)

1. Preheat the oven to 325°F / 165°C with a rack in the center (preferably with a Baking Steel or stone on it).

2. In the bowl of a food processor, pulse the cream cheese, sugar, lemon zest, and lemon juice until well combined. Add the eggs one at a time, pulsing to combine and scraping the bowl well after each addition. Add the vanilla, cream, and salt and process to combine, then scrape the bowl well and pulse again—the custard should be totally smooth.

3. Place the parbaked crust on a parchment-lined baking sheet and pour the custard into the crust. Transfer to the oven and bake until the crust is deeply golden brown and the custard is set around the outside edges but still slightly jiggly in the center, 60 to 70 minutes. Turn the oven off, prop the oven door open, and let the pie cool in the oven for 2 hours.

4. Remove the pie from the oven and cool completely, then refrigerate for at least 6 hours before slicing and serving.

VARIATIONS

JAM-SWIRLED CHEESECAKE PIE: After making the cheesecake filling, transfer 121 g / ½ cup of it to a medium bowl. In a small saucepan, whisk 156 g / ½ cup jam or jelly over medium heat until it becomes liquid, about 1 minute (if it has big chunks, you may want to blend it to make it smoother before proceeding). Whisk the jam into the reserved filling to combine, 15 to 30 seconds. Pour the remaining filling into the crust. Drizzle or pipe the jam mixture over the surface and use a toothpick or skewer to swirl it into the filling. Bake as directed.

CHOCOLATE-SWIRLED CHEESECAKE PIE: Omit the lemon zest. After making the cheesecake filling, transfer 182 g / ¾ cup of it to a medium bowl. Whisk in 28 g / ⅓ cup unsweetened cocoa powder (preferably dark or black cocoa; see Resources, page 345). Pour the remaining filling into the crust. Drizzle or pour the chocolate batter over the surface, then use a toothpick or skewer to swirl it into the custard. Bake as directed.

CARAMEL-SWIRLED CHEESECAKE PIE: Omit the lemon zest. After making the cheesecake filling, transfer 121 g / ½ cup of it to a medium bowl. Whisk in 80 g / ⅓ cup prepared caramel sauce or 85 g / ⅓ cup dulce de leche. Pour the remaining filling into the crust. Drizzle or pour the caramel mixture over the surface and use a toothpick or skewer to swirl into the filling. Bake as directed.

PUMPKIN CHEESECAKE PIE: Omit the lemon zest and heavy cream. After making the cheesecake filling, transfer 182 g / ¾ cup of it to a medium bowl. Add 213 g / 1 cup canned pumpkin puree to the remaining filling and blend well. Pour the pumpkin custard into the prepared crust, then drizzle or pour the plain filling over the surface and use a toothpick or skewer to swirl it into the custard. Bake as directed.

MATCHA CHEESECAKE PIE: After making the cheesecake filling, transfer 182 g / ¾ cup of it to a medium bowl. Add 12 g / 2 tablespoons culinary grade matcha to the remaining filling and blend well. Pour the matcha filling into the prepared crust, then drizzle or pour the plain filling over the surface and use a toothpick or skewer to swirl the two to combine. Bake as directed.

Make Ahead and Storage

The pie can be made up to 24 hours ahead and refrigerated until ready to serve.

RECOMMENDED CRUSTS
- All-Buttah Pie Dough (page 48)
- Citrus Roll-Out Cookie Crust (page 63)
- Brown Butter Press-In Cookie Crust (page 64)

RECOMMENDED FINISHES
- Classic Whipped Cream (page 111)
- Fresh Fruit Whipped Cream (page 115)
- Flavored Sifting Sugars (page 128)

BLACK-BOTTOM PECAN PIE

MAKES ONE 9-INCH /
23-CM PIE

DIFFICULTY: EASY

Imagine the caramel-y flavors of traditional pecan pie paired with a melty layer of deep, dark chocolate. It's best to err on the side of underbaking this pie to keep the filling at that just-right level of delightfully gooey.

One 9-inch / 23-cm pie crust (see below), parbaked and cooled completely (see page 43)

1 recipe Dark Chocolate Black-Bottom Base (page 110)

319 g / 2½ cups pecan halves

71 g / 2½ ounces / 5 tablespoons unsalted butter, melted

212 g / 1 cup packed dark brown sugar

191 g / ½ cup maple syrup

170 g / 3 large eggs

21 g / 1 large egg yolk

45 g / 3 tablespoons heavy cream

10 g / 2 teaspoons vanilla extract

Scant 1 g / ¼ teaspoon almond extract

2 g / ½ teaspoon fine sea salt

2 g / ½ teaspoon ground cinnamon

1. Preheat the oven to 375°F / 190°C with a rack in the bottom third (preferably with a Baking Steel or stone on it).

2. Line a baking sheet with parchment paper and place the cooled crust on it. Pour the black bottom base into the pie shell and spread into an even layer. Arrange the pecans in an even layer on top of the chocolate. Set aside while you prepare the custard.

3. In a medium bowl, whisk the melted butter, brown sugar, maple syrup, eggs, egg yolk, cream, extracts, salt, and cinnamon until well combined. Gently pour the custard over the pecans.

4. Transfer the baking sheet to the oven and bake until the crust is golden brown and the custard appears set on the outside but is still slightly jiggly in the center, 35 to 40 minutes. Cool completely before slicing and serving.

Make Ahead and Storage

The pie can be made up to 1 day ahead and stored at room temperature. Store leftovers at room temperature, wrapped tightly in plastic wrap.

RECOMMENDED CRUSTS

- Vanilla Bean–Nutmeg Pie Dough (page 52)
- Whole Wheat Pie Dough (page 54)
- Chocolate All-Buttah Pie Dough (page 48)

RECOMMENDED FINISHES

- Classic Whipped Cream (page 111)
- Chocolate Whipped Cream (page 114)
- Dark Chocolate Drippy Glaze (page 125)

CREAMY LEMON CUSTARD PIE

MAKES ONE 9-INCH / 23-CM PIE

DIFFICULTY: MEDIUM

Lemon is a classic flavor, but it's one I often wrote off until I married my husband. He obviously has a lot of baked goods in his life, but lemon is the surefire way to his heart. This pie combines the tartness he loves with the creaminess of a dairy-based custard pie that I love.

99 g / ½ cup granulated sugar

Grated zest of 1 lemon

14 g / 2 tablespoons cornstarch

339 g / 1½ cups whole milk

113 g / ½ cup buttermilk

113 g / 2 large eggs

64 g / 3 large egg yolks

60 g / ¼ cup fresh lemon juice

2 g / ½ teaspoon lemon oil or lemon extract

2 g / ½ teaspoon vanilla extract

2 g / ½ teaspoon fine sea salt

One 9-inch / 23-cm pie crust (see below), parbaked, brushed with egg wash, and cooled completely (see page 43)

160 g / ⅔ cup Lemon Curd (page 123)

Edible flowers, for finishing (optional; see Resources, page 345)

1. Preheat the oven to 350°F / 175°C with a rack in the lower third (preferably with a Baking Steel or stone on it).

2. In a medium bowl, rub the sugar and lemon zest together. Add the cornstarch and whisk to combine. Add the milk, buttermilk, eggs, and egg yolks and whisk well to combine. Add the lemon juice, lemon oil or extract, vanilla, and salt and whisk to combine.

3. Place the parbaked crust on a parchment-lined baking sheet and gently pour the custard into the crust. Bake until the custard appears set at the edges but is still slightly jiggly in the center, 45 to 50 minutes. Cool completely, then refrigerate for at least 2 hours.

4. Once the pie is fully chilled, spread the lemon curd on top of it in an even layer. Refrigerate until ready to serve. If using, top with edible flowers.

Make Ahead and Storage

The pie can be made up to 24 hours ahead and refrigerated until ready to serve.

RECOMMENDED CRUSTS
- Cardamom Lemon Pie Dough (page 52)
- Caramelized Pie Crust (page 56)
- Roll-Out Cookie Crust (page 62)
- Press-In Cookie Crust (page 64)

RECOMMENDED FINISHES
- Flavored Sifting Sugars (page 128)
- Substitute Meringue Topping (page 118) for the lemon curd, or swap the curd for Thin Fruit Glaze (page 122)

TRES LECHES SLAB PIE

MAKES ONE 9-BY-13-INCH / 23-BY-33-CM PIE

DIFFICULTY: MEDIUM

This slab pie features creamy custard in a flaky crust, topped with a thin layer of dulce de leche and plenty of whipped cream. For a brighter twist, top the whipped cream with fresh fruit instead of the dulce de leche.

Double recipe pie dough (see below), shaped into a disk and chilled

1 recipe White-Bottom Base (page 110)

120 g / 1 cup all-purpose flour

60 g / ½ cup nonfat dry milk

2 g / ½ teaspoon fine sea salt

1 g / ½ teaspoon ground cinnamon

396 g / One 14-ounce can sweetened condensed milk

340 g / One 12-ounce can evaporated milk

230 g / 1 cup whole milk

176 g / ¾ cup heavy cream

7 g / 1½ teaspoons vanilla extract

1 g / ¼ teaspoon almond extract

383 g / 1½ cups dulce de leche

Full Batch of Classic Whipped Cream (page 111)

Ground cinnamon for sprinkling

1. On a lightly floured surface, roll out the pie dough to a rectangle about 15 by 18 inches / 38 by 46 cm. Dock all over with a fork. Use the rolling pin to gently transfer the dough to a 9-by-13-inch / 23-by-33-cm pan, unfurling it over the pan. Working around the sides of the pan, gently lift up the edges of the dough and press it into the bottom of the pan, taking care to press it flush against the sides as well, making full contact in each of the corners. There will be a generous overhang all the way around; trim it to 1½ inches / 4 cm. Refrigerate for 30 minutes.

2. Preheat the oven to 425°F / 220°C (unless the crust recipe specifies a lower bake temperature) with a rack in the lower third (preferably with a Baking Steel or stone on it).

3. Place a piece of parchment on the prepared crust and fill with pie weights. Transfer the pan to the oven and parbake for 17 to 20 minutes, until the edges start to turn golden, then remove the parchment and pie weights and bake for 5 to 6 minutes more, until the bottom appears fully baked and set. Cool completely. Lower the oven temperature to 350°F / 175°C.

4. Use a pastry brush to brush the white base all over the bottom and sides of the crust. (If you have any holes or cracks, just fill them in with white chocolate.)

5. In a medium bowl, whisk the flour, dry milk, salt, and cinnamon to combine. Add the sweetened condensed milk, evaporated milk, whole milk cream, vanilla, and almond extract and whisk well to combine. Don't whip too much, or you will incorporate air bubbles that will stay trapped in the custard.

6. Pour the custard into the prepared crust (it will only come about halfway up the sides of the crust) and gently transfer to the oven. Bake until the custard appears just barely set when you jiggle the pan (it should still have a little bit of Jell-O-like movement), 30 to 35 minutes. Cool completely, then transfer to the refrigerator, covered loosely in plastic wrap, and chill for at least 1 hour.

7. When the pie is chilled, dollop or pipe the dulce de leche all over the pie and spread into a thin even layer (if the dulce de leche is too thick or stiff to work with, warm it up in 10-second bursts in the microwave until it's thin enough to be easily spreadable). Pipe or spoon the whipped cream on top. Sprinkle or sift the cinnamon over the whipped cream. (If using fresh fruit instead of dulce de leche, arrange it on top of the whipped cream just before serving, and skip the cinnamon.) Refrigerate until ready to slice and serve.

Make Ahead and Storage
The crust can be parbaked up to 2 days ahead. The finished pie can be made up to 24 hours ahead and refrigerated until ready to serve.

RECOMMENDED CRUSTS
- All-Buttah Pie Dough (page 48)
- Brown Butter Press-In Cookie Crust (page 64)
- Caramelized Pie Crust (page 56)

RECOMMENDED FINISHES
- Swap the plain whipped cream for a fruity whipped cream (see page 115)
- Decorate the surface with fresh fruit
- Skip the whipped cream and go for the Meringue Topping (page 118), Fruity Meringue Topping (page 118), or Flavored Sifting Sugars (page 128)

chapter five

CREAM, CHIFFON & COLD-SET PIES

Welcome to the most colorful, fun, and, above all, *creamy* chapter of this book. Here you'll find the stuff of fairy-tale pie dreams. These aren't rustic fruit pies, or sturdy and reliable custard pies, these are pies mounded high with happiness, and often topped with way too much (read: just the right amount of) whipped cream. These are the pies I make when I really want to impress, because everyone loves them: the way they taste and the way they look, not to mention how fun they are to make. While fruit pies may be the most classic "cooling on the windowsill" sort of pie, these are the towering beauties that spin in diner display cases and perch atop bakery shelves, garnering the love of anyone who passes by. Tuck in—this one's gonna be good!

TYPES OF COLD-SET PIE FILLINGS

The pies that fall into this category are called by a lot of different names, though most of them can be used interchangeably. What they have in common is no oven time except for the crust—the fillings are prepared on the stovetop or not cooked at all. But they do require refrigerator (or freezer) time to chill and become sliceably set.

STOVETOP CUSTARD FILLINGS

A lot of cold-set pies are filled with stovetop custards or are made with fillings that start with stovetop custards and then are lightened with cream or meringue (see below). These stovetop custards include, most notably, puddings, creams, and curds.

PUDDINGS: Puddings are dairy-based custards that can be thickened with starch or eggs, or both. They can be flavored in lots of ways—with the addition of chocolate, extracts, nuts/nut butter, and/or liquor, or by infusing the liquid (see page 203).

CREAMS: This is a general term that can cover any number of stovetop custards, such as pastry cream, crème anglaise, and more. Like puddings, creams can be thickened with starch or eggs, or both.

CURDS: Curds are thickened juice-based fillings. The most well-known curd is citrus, but these can actually be made from lots of different juices. Curds generally contain a high proportion of butter. They are usually thickened with egg yolks, but some curd fillings for pies also add a starch to aid in making them more sliceable.

WHIPPED CREAM–BASED FILLINGS

The fillings for pies most commonly referred to as cream pies are made with a flavorful base that is lightened with whipped cream. The whipped cream lightens the texture of the filling because of all the air beaten into the cream and, in turn, it thickens the mixture as it chills and those air bubbles contract slightly. It also makes the filling incredibly rich, creamy, and delicious, because whipped cream makes everything better. The bases for whipped cream fillings can be fruit purees, nut butters, melted chocolate, stovetop custards, or curds—the possibilities are endless. In some cases, the cream is not thoroughly folded in to create a swirly/striated effect.

MERINGUE-BASED FILLINGS

Pies with meringue-based fillings are most often referred to as chiffon pies. The filling consists of a flavorful base that is lightened with meringue. Like whipped cream, the meringue serves as an aerator to lighten the texture of the filling, along with providing some structure and sweetening the filling. The bases for the fillings are typically the same sorts of bases used for whipped cream pies (above), although some recipes use both whipped cream and meringue (such as mousse, for example).

GELATIN-SET FILLINGS

Some cold-set fillings are set with gelatin. These are some of the easiest pie fillings to make, because so little cooking is involved. For some gelatin-set fillings, whipped cream or meringue is also folded in. Gelatin-set fillings can be poured directly into cooled blind-baked pie crusts, or they can be molded using molds, cake pans, or bowls to create impressive effects (see Molded Fillings, page 103).

My recipes call for powdered gelatin, which is available in most grocery stores. You can substitute leaf/sheet gelatin in equal quantity by weight. Bloom leaf gelatin by briefly soaking it in cool water.

Substituting Agar-Agar for Gelatin

The best, and easiest to use, vegetarian/vegan-friendly alternative to gelatin I've found is agar-agar, a thickener derived from seaweed. Powdered agar-agar can be substituted in equal quantity for gelatin by volume (1 tablespoon powdered agar-agar is about 3 grams). Unlike gelatin, agar-agar doesn't need to be bloomed, but it does need to be fully dissolved in the liquid, so it's best to stir it into any liquid before it is heated to ensure it completely dissolves. Even when fully dissolved, it may result in a slightly grainier texture than gelatin-set fillings, but it sets to a beautiful firmness without having to make many adjustments in recipes when substituting it. Agar-agar has a slightly salty flavor, so I do recommend reducing the salt in any recipe by half.

PREPARING THE CRUST FOR COLD-SET PIES

Because cold-set fillings don't get baked, any crust for a cold-set pie must be fully prepared; this usually means blind-baking the crust. Although crusts can be blind-baked up to 24 hours ahead, remember that unlike a parbaked crust for, say, a custard pie, the crust won't be "refreshed" with a second trip to the oven. A fully baked crust should be at the final level of browning and crispness that you want when you take it out of the oven. Once the crust is blind-baked, you can add a protective "seal" of sorts to help keep it crisp even after you add a wet filling (see page 46).

Cold-set pies also allow for a shortcut here—crumb crusts can be made and frozen (no baking required) before being filled; see Unbaked Crumb Crust (page 67).

TROUBLESHOOTING COLD-SET PIES

Cold-set pies have some of the same ingredient concerns as custard pies, but they also come with their own unique set of tricks that can be helpful in getting creamy, just-set-enough fillings.

What to Do if Your Cold-Set Pie Doesn't Set

Sometimes your best pie intentions don't work out and the filling is goopy instead of set to a sliceable consistency. If you notice this problem before you put the filling into the crust (or even afterward, if you can spoon the filling out of the crust without going crazy), there is a simple remedy: Whip 230 to 460 g / 1 to 2 cups heavy cream to medium peaks and fold it into the loose base to help firm it up (and make it into a true *cream pie*). If you only notice this after the pie is assembled and you can't remove the filling, you can turn to the freezer. While the freezer won't solve the problem of runniness, it will firm up the filling, definitely enough to make it easier to slice, serve, and eat. Plus, most pies in this chapter are delicious served extra-cold (think ice cream or frozen custard).

UNDERSTANDING TEMPERING

The word "tempering" is used to describe the technique of combining two mixtures gradually so that they ultimately combine more effectively.

In a recipe that uses whipped cream or meringue, tempering usually means adding a small amount (about one quarter) of the aerated mixture to the base and mixing fairly vigorously to combine. This first addition lightens the base, making it easier to very gently fold in the remaining amount in a few additions. Done properly, this ensures that the aerated mixture deflates as little as possible, so it retains its optimal level of fluffiness.

For puddings, curds, and other stovetop fillings, tempering refers to pouring a small amount of the heated liquid into the other ingredients (often including eggs or egg yolks) and whisking well to combine before returning the entire mixture to the pot and cooking until thickened. Tempering prevents the eggs from heating too quickly, which could result in coagulation or a "scrambled egg" effect instead of a smooth, silky custard.

UNDERSTANDING "FIRST BOIL"

When a cold-set recipe uses just eggs as the thickener, you generally don't want the custard to come to a boil, because the eggs are likely to scramble at such a high temperature. Instead, gentle cooking over lower heat will slowly coagulate the egg protein so that the mixture thickens smoothly. But when a recipe uses just a starch as the thickener, you need to cook the custard until it thickens properly, which usually means bringing it to a boil or heating until it is bubbling gently.

When both eggs and starch are used in a recipe, you have to handle things a bit differently. Eggs contain an enzyme that consumes starch. Bringing a custard to a boil activates the starch to thicken it but it also ensures that this enzyme is killed. The term I was taught for this in pastry school was *first boil*—which means allowing a few fat bubbles to break the surface from the center of the pot, rather than seeing lots of small bubbles

Garnishes— Why to Wait

Cold-set pies are great pies to make ahead, because the fillings really benefit from the fridge time. However, most garnishes and decorative finishes won't. Finishes like sauces, whipped cream, and meringue don't hold as well on the top of a pie for an extended period (4 to 6 hours). So, when I make a cold-set pie ahead of time, I go just up to the point of pouring the filling into the crust, covering it, and chilling. I add the toppings closer to serving to make sure the pie looks its best!

around the edges of the pot. This indicates that the mixture has been heated enough to nix that enzyme and activate the starch to create a filling that's become thick in the pot and will become even thicker after chilling.

COVERING THE SURFACE

Cold-set fillings like puddings, creams, and curds are best covered *directly* with plastic wrap, so that the plastic is in contact with the surface. This helps prevent a skin from forming. Then, when the filled pie is thoroughly chilled, simply peel the plastic wrap away. But if the filling is delicate and you don't want to risk messing it up, the pie can be refrigerated uncovered for up 8 hours.

BLACK FOREST PIE

MAKES ONE 9-INCH /
23-CM DEEP DISH PIE

DIFFICULTY: MEDIUM

It's impossible not to love this pie: a thick layer of super-creamy chocolate pudding topped with a thin layer of juicy cherries and plenty of whipped cream. Use black cocoa (see Resources, page 345) in a chocolate crust (see below) for an especially beautiful result.

1 recipe Dark or Milk Chocolate Black-Bottom Base (page 110), still warm

One 9-inch / 23-inch pie crust (see below), blind-baked and cooled completely (see page 46)

FILLING

228 g / 1 cup whole milk

118 g / ½ cup heavy cream

85 g / 3 ounces bittersweet chocolate, finely chopped

57 g / 2 ounces unsweetened chocolate, finely chopped

99 g / ½ cup granulated sugar

21 g / 3 tablespoons cornstarch

2 g / ½ teaspoon fine sea salt

64 g / 3 large egg yolks

14 g / ½ ounce / 1 tablespoon unsalted butter, at room temperature

5 g / 1 teaspoon vanilla extract

TOPPING

567 g / 1¼ pounds cherries, pitted and halved

15 g / 1 tablespoon fresh lemon juice

66 g / ⅓ cup granulated sugar

14 g / 2 tablespoons cornstarch

5 g / 1 teaspoon vanilla extract

2 g / ¼ teaspoon almond extract

Full Batch of Classic Whipped Cream (page 111)

Whole or halved pitted cherries for garnish

1. Pour the warm black-bottom base into the cooled pie crust and spread into an even layer over the bottom.

2. Make the filling: In a medium pot, heat the milk and cream over medium-low heat until the mixture begins to simmer. Turn off the heat, add both chocolates, and stir until fully combined. Turn the heat back on to medium-low and heat, stirring constantly, until the chocolate is fully melted. Keep warm over low heat.

3. In a medium bowl, whisk the sugar, cornstarch, and salt together to combine. Add the egg yolks and whisk until well combined. Pour about one quarter of the hot chocolate mixture into the bowl to temper the yolk mixture, whisking constantly. Return this mixture to the pot, whisking, and cook over medium-low heat, stirring constantly with a silicone spatula, until the mixture is very thick and large bubbles break the surface, 2 to 3 minutes.

4. Remove the pot from the heat and stir in the butter and vanilla extract. Strain the pudding into the prepared pie crust and spread into an even layer. Place a piece of plastic wrap directly against the surface and chill until set, 35 to 45 minutes.

5. While the pie sets, make the topping: In a medium pot, toss the cherries and lemon juice to combine. In a small bowl, stir the sugar and cornstarch together to combine. Add this mixture to the cherries and cook over medium heat, stirring constantly, until the cherries are softened but not broken down and the mixture has thickened, about 5 minutes. Stir in the vanilla and almond extracts. Transfer the topping to a shallow baking dish (or baking sheet) to help it cool quickly to room temperature.

6. Once the topping is cool, remove the plastic wrap from the chocolate filling and spoon the cherry mixture over it in an even layer. Return the pie to the refrigerator until ready to serve.

7. When ready to serve, spread or pipe the whipped cream evenly over the pie and garnish with cherries.

Make Ahead and Storage

This pie can be made up to 24 hours ahead and refrigerated, but it is best to add the whipped cream topping just before serving. Store leftovers covered with plastic wrap in the refrigerator.

RECOMMENDED CRUSTS
- Chocolate All-Buttah Pie Dough (page 48)
- Chocolate Press-In Cookie Crust (page 64)
- Brown Butter Pie Dough (page 53)

RECOMMENDED FINISHES
- Thick Fruit Coulis, made with cherries (page 122)
- Flavored Sifting Sugars (page 128)
- Basic Brittle (page 129)

PEANUT BUTTER–BANANA CREAM PIE

MAKES ONE 9-INCH / 23-CM PIE

DIFFICULTY: MEDIUM

I thought long and hard about how to bring banana cream pies into this book. The pie that reigned supreme was this one, which boasts peanut butter pudding topped with plenty of sliced bananas and whipped cream (and, if you're feeling fancy, topped with shards of honey-roasted peanut brittle). But I can't deny the allure of the classic combination of banana and toffee (i.e., banoffee pie), so you can find my version, made with dulce de leche, below, along with instructions for plain ol' Banana Cream Pie.

FILLING

452 g / 2 cups whole milk

118 g / ½ cup heavy cream

192 g / ¾ cup creamy peanut butter (not natural)

106 g / ½ cup packed light or dark brown sugar

50 g / ¼ cup granulated sugar

37 g / ⅓ cup cornstarch

3 g / ¾ teaspoon fine sea salt

56 g / 2 large eggs

64 g / 3 large egg yolks

28 g / 1 ounce / 2 tablespoons unsalted butter

10 g / 2 teaspoons vanilla extract

One 9-inch / 23-cm pie crust (see below), blind-baked, brushed with egg wash, and cooled completely (see page 43)

450 g / 3 or 4 medium bananas, peeled and thickly sliced

Full Batch of Nut Butter Whipped Cream (page 116) made with peanut butter, or Classic Whipped Cream (page 111)

1 recipe Basic Brittle (page 129) made with peanuts (optional)

1. Make the filling: In a medium pot, bring the milk, heavy cream, and peanut butter to a simmer over medium heat, stirring occasionally to help the peanut butter melt.

2. Meanwhile, in a medium bowl, whisk the brown sugar, granulated sugar, cornstarch, and salt to combine. Add the eggs and yolks and whisk well to combine.

3. When the milk mixture comes to a simmer, pour about one quarter of it into the eggs, whisking constantly to temper them. Pour this mixture back into the pot, whisking constantly. Reduce the heat to medium-low, switch to a silicone spatula, and cook, stirring constantly, until the mixture thickens and large bubbles break the surface. Remove from the heat and stir in the butter until it's melted and the pudding is smooth. Stir in the vanilla.

4. Strain the pudding into the cooled pie crust and spread into an even layer. Cover the filling with plastic wrap placed directly against the surface and refrigerate until fully cooled and set, at least 2 hours (or up to 24 hours).

5. When ready to serve, remove the plastic wrap and arrange the bananas in an even layer on top of the pie, overlapping the slices so they are well packed together. Spread, spoon, or pipe the whipped cream topping on top.

6. Just before serving, crumble the brittle, or break it into large shards, and sprinkle over the whipped cream, if using.

VARIATIONS ///

CLASSIC BANANA CREAM PIE: Omit the peanut butter and brown sugar. Increase the granulated sugar to 149 g / ¾ cup. Use Classic Whipped Cream to top the pie and omit the brittle.

BANULCE PIE (THE DULCE DE LECHE VERSION OF BANOFFEE PIE): Omit the peanut butter and brown sugar in the filling and increase the granulated sugar to 149 g / ¾ cup. Spread 272 g / 1 cup dulce de leche over the bottom of the cooled pie crust. Arrange half of the banana slices in an even layer on top of the dulce de leche. Strain the pudding onto the bananas and chill as directed in step 4. Top the pie with the remaining bananas and the whipped cream. If desired, drizzle additional dulce de leche over the pie. Omit the brittle.

Make Ahead and Storage

The crust can be blind-baked up to 24 hours head. The pie can be prepared through step 4 up to 24 hours ahead and kept refrigerated. Store leftovers in the refrigerator in an airtight container.

RECOMMENDED CRUSTS

- All-Buttah Pie Dough (page 48)
- Chocolate All-Buttah Pie Dough (page 48)
- Peanut Butter Cereal-Treat Crust (page 69)
- Basic Crumb Crust (page 66)

RECOMMENDED FINISHES

- Swap out the peanut butter whipped cream for Chocolate Whipped Cream (page 114) and decorate the pie with chocolate shavings (see page 107)

ORANGE-VANILLA PANNA COTTA PIE

MAKES ONE 9-INCH / 23-CM PIE

DIFFICULTY: HARD

Panna cotta makes a beautiful pie filling because it sets firm, smooth, and oh-so creamy. It's often molded into different shapes, so why not do the same when using it for a pie filling? A silicone cake pan, particularly a Bundt shape, makes for a stunning end result. The dreamy Creamsicle flavor and the sweet cookie crust are the perfect flavor pairing.

113 g / ½ cup cool water

25 g / 2½ tablespoons powdered gelatin

198 g / 1 cup granulated sugar

1 vanilla bean, halved lengthwise, seeds scraped out and reserved

Grated zest of 2 oranges

3 g / ¾ teaspoon fine sea salt

340 g / 1½ cups whole milk

392 g / 1⅔ cups heavy cream

151 g / ⅔ cup strained fresh orange juice

1 recipe Orange Curd (page 123) or 340 g / 1 cup orange marmalade

One 9-inch / 23-cm cookie crust (either Press-In Cookie Crust, page 64, or Roll-Out Cookie Crust, page 62), blind-baked and cooled completely (see Note)

1. Have ready a 9-inch / 23-cm-wide nonstick or silicone Bundt or gelatin mold. Place the cool water in a small bowl, sprinkle the gelatin over it, and let bloom for 5 minutes.

2. Rub the sugar, vanilla bean, orange zest, and salt together to help distribute the seeds and zest. Transfer the sugar mixture to a medium pot, add the milk, and bring to a simmer, stirring to dissolve the sugar.

3. When the sugar is dissolved, add the bloomed gelatin and stir over low heat until fully melted. Transfer the mixture to a large container with a pour spout. Stir in the cream and orange juice. Pour the mixture into the prepared mold and transfer to the refrigerator to chill until completely set, at least 2 hours (or up to 24 hours).

4. When the panna cotta is set, spread the orange curd or marmalade evenly over the bottom of the cooled crust. Run the tip of a paring knife around the edges of the panna cotta to start to loosen it, then carefully stick the knife farther into the mold at one point, and lift it away from the sides of the pan. Once it starts to release from the mold, it should be easy, but if necessary, continue to use the tip of a knife or a small offset spatula to help nudge it away from the mold.

5. When the panna cotta is nearly completely released from the mold, gently invert it onto the center of curd/marmalade layer. Transfer to the refrigerator to chill for at least 30 minutes (or up to 12 hours). Keep chilled until ready to slice and serve.

Make Ahead and Storage

The crust can be blind-baked up to 24 hours ahead. The panna cotta can be prepared through step 3 up to 24 hours ahead. The pie can be prepared up to 12 hours ahead. Store leftovers in the refrigerator in an airtight container.

NOTE

This pie looks best made in a shallow pie plate (or a tart pan). In the photo, an embossed rolling pin was used to create the textured crust (see page 63).

RECOMMENDED CRUSTS
- Brown Sugar Roll-Out Cookie Crust (page 63)
- Oatmeal Press-In Cookie Crust (page 64)
- Brown Butter Press-In Cookie Crust (page 64)

SWEET CORN PIE WITH BLUEBERRY WHIPPED CREAM

MAKES ONE 9-INCH / 23-CM PIE

DIFFICULTY: MEDIUM

I first made this pie with my funky, wonderful hometown of Lawrence, Kansas, in mind. I've long loved good summer corn as an ingredient in desserts. This creamy stovetop pudding lets it shine in all its sweet, golden glory. Topped with a pile of blueberry whipped cream, this pie is the stuff of sweet, summery dreams.

330 g / 1½ cups fresh or frozen corn kernels (thawed if frozen)

170 g / ¾ cup whole milk

1 vanilla bean, halved lengthwise, seeds scraped out and reserved

118 g / ½ cup heavy cream

149 g / ¾ cup granulated sugar

37 g / ⅓ cup cornstarch

Scant 1 g / ¼ teaspoon freshly grated nutmeg

Pinch of ground cinnamon

2 g / ½ teaspoon fine sea salt

64 g / 3 large egg yolks

28 g / 1 ounce / 2 tablespoons unsalted butter, at room temperature

One 9-inch / 23-cm pie crust (see below), blind-baked, brushed with egg wash, and cooled completely (see page 43)

1 recipe Fresh Fruit Whipped Cream (page 115) made with blueberries

1. Make the filling: In a medium pot, combine 163 g / ¾ cup of the corn, the milk, and vanilla bean seeds and blend with an immersion blender until relatively smooth (or do this in a regular blender or food processor and transfer to the pot). Whisk in the heavy cream.

2. In a small bowl, whisk the sugar, cornstarch, nutmeg, cinnamon, and salt to combine. Whisk this into the milk mixture and bring to a simmer over medium-low heat, whisking constantly.

3. Meanwhile, whisk the egg yolks in a small bowl. When the milk mixture is simmering, pour about one quarter of it into the egg yolks, whisking constantly, to temper them. Pour this mixture back into the pot, whisking constantly, reduce the heat to medium-low, and cook, stirring constantly with a silicone spatula, until the mixture thickens and comes a boil (you're looking for fat bubbles coming from the center of the pot). Remove the pot from the heat and stir in the butter until it's melted.

4. Fold the remaining 163 g / ¾ cup corn kernels into the pudding. Pour into the cooled pie crust and spread into an even layer. Cover the filling with plastic wrap placed directly against the surface and refrigerate until completely cooled and set, at least 2 hours (or up to 24 hours).

5. When the pie is chilled, spread or pipe the whipped cream topping on top. Keep refrigerated until ready to slice and serve.

Make Ahead and Storage

This pie can be made through step 4 up to 24 hours ahead, but it is best to add the whipped cream topping shortly before serving. Store leftovers in the refrigerator in an airtight container.

RECOMMENDED CRUSTS
- Cornmeal Pie Dough (page 55)
- Press-In Cookie Crust (page 64)
- Cinnamon Pie Dough (page 52)

KEY LIME–COCONUT CREAM PIE

MAKES ONE 9-INCH / 23-CM PIE

DIFFICULTY: MEDIUM

Can't decide between two of your favorite pie flavor? Make a pie that's *both*. That's how this pairing of tart Key lime filling with a hefty layer of my favorite coconut cream filling on top was born. (Classic coconut cream lovers and fans of classic Key lime pie, check the variations below.)

KEY LIME FILLING

43 g / 2 large egg yolks

283 g / 1¼ cups sweetened condensed milk

113 g / ½ cup Key lime juice (bottled is fine—or substitute fresh lime juice)

Grated zest of 1 lime, plus more to garnish

1 g / ¼ teaspoon fine sea salt

One 9-inch / 23-cm pie crust (see below), parbaked, brushed with egg wash, and cooled completely (see page 43; be sure to use a pie plate at least 2 inches / 5 cm deep)

COCONUT CREAM FILLING

182 g / ¾ cup canned coconut milk

113 g / ½ cup whole milk

58 g / ¼ cup heavy cream

66 g / ⅓ cup granulated sugar

21 g / 3 tablespoons cornstarch

56 g / 1 large egg

21 g / 1 large egg yolk

14 g / ½ ounce / 1 tablespoon unsalted butter

2 g / ½ teaspoon vanilla extract

48 g / ¾ cup toasted unsweetened shredded coconut

Full Batch of Classic Whipped Cream (page 111)

1. Preheat the oven to 350°F / 175°C with a rack in the center (preferably with a Baking Steel or stone on it).

2. Make the Key lime filling: In a medium bowl, whisk the egg yolks until thick and pale yellow. Whisking constantly, gradually pour in the sweetened condensed milk, then whisk constantly for another 30 seconds. Whisk in the lime juice, lime zest, and salt until well combined.

3. Place the parbaked pie crust on a parchment-lined baking sheet. Pour the filling into the pie crust, allowing it to settle into an even layer. Bake the pie until the custard appears set, 10 to 13 minutes. Cool to room temperature, then chill while you make the coconut cream filling.

4. Make the coconut cream filling: In a medium pot, bring the coconut milk, milk, and heavy cream to a simmer over medium heat.

5. Meanwhile, in a medium bowl, whisk the sugar with the cornstarch to combine. Add the egg and yolk and whisk well to combine.

6. When the milk mixture comes to a simmer, pour about one quarter of it into the egg yolks, whisking constantly, to temper the yolks. Pour this mixture back into the pot, whisking constantly. Reduce the heat to medium-low, switch to a silicone spatula, and cook, stirring constantly, until the mixture thickens and comes a boil. Remove the pot from the heat and stir in the butter and vanilla.

7. Strain the mixture into a medium heatproof bowl, then fold in two thirds (36 g / ½ cup) of the coconut (reserve the remaining coconut for garnish). Transfer to the pie crust and spread into an even layer. Cover with plastic wrap placed directly against the surface and refrigerate until set, at least 2 hours (or up to 24 hours).

8. When the pie is chilled, spread, spoon, or pipe the whipped cream on top. Garnish with the reserved coconut and additional lime zest. Refrigerate until ready to slice and serve.

VARIATIONS

PIÑA COLADA PIE: Omit the Key lime filling and blind-baked crust. Make the Roasted Pineapple Pie (page 155) in a deep-dish pie plate. Pile the coconut filling on top, mounding it in the center. Reduce the whipped cream to a half batch and spoon or pipe it around the edges of the pie.

COCONUT CREAM PIE: Use a deep dish pie plate. Omit the Key lime filling and double the coconut filling.

CLASSIC KEY LIME PIE: Omit the coconut filling. For the Key lime filling, use 86 g / 4 large egg yolks, 397 g / one 14-ounce can sweetened condensed milk, 170 g / ¾ cup Key lime juice, grated zest of 1 lime, and 2 g / ½ teaspoon fine sea salt. Garnish the pie with the whipped cream and lime zest.

Make Ahead and Storage

The pie can be made through step 7 up to 24 hours ahead and kept refrigerated. Store leftovers in the refrigerator in an airtight container.

RECOMMENDED CRUSTS
- All-Buttah Pie Dough (page 48)
- Chocolate All-Buttah Pie Dough (page 48)
- Roll-Out Cookie Crust (page 62)
- Basic Crumb Crust (page 66)

RECOMMENDED FINISHES
- Dark Chocolate Black-Bottom Base (page 110)
- Chocolate Whipped Cream (page 114)

Left to right: Piña Colada Pie in Brown Butter Crust, Classic Key Lime Pie in Basic Crumb Crust, Coconut Cream Pie in All-Buttah Crust, Key Lime-Coconut Cream Pie in Spiced Roll-Out Cookie Crust

KEY LIME PIELETS

MAKES 12 MINI PIES
DIFFICULTY: EASY

These tiny pies are filled with a magical custard that is set using only citrus juice, which gently sets the cream to silky-smooth perfection as the custard chills. I bake these in a muffin pan, making them adorably mini and easy to pick up and enjoy. If you have any extra custard, pour it into a ramekin or small bowl and let it set in the fridge for a baker's treat!

1 recipe Press-In Cookie Crust (page 64)

99 g / ½ cup granulated sugar

Grated zest of 1 lime

288 g / 1¼ cups heavy cream

60 g / ¼ cup Key lime juice (bottled is fine—or substitute fresh lime juice)

2 g / ½ teaspoon vanilla extract

1 g / ¼ teaspoon fine sea salt

1. Preheat the oven to 350°F / 175°C with a rack in the center. Grease the cavities of a muffin pan with nonstick spray.

2. Divide the dough into 12 even pieces. Crumble one portion of dough into each cavity of the prepared pan. Then use your fingers to press the dough evenly over the bottom and up the sides of each cavity. Use a small fork or the tip of a paring knife to dock the dough all over. Chill in the refrigerator for 15 to 20 minutes.

3. Bake the crusts until they are lightly golden at the edges and appear set all over, 14 to 18 minutes. If the dough puffs up during baking, prick it with a fork when you remove the crusts from the oven so it lies flat again. Cool completely, then use an offset spatula to gently unmold the cooled crusts onto a baking sheet (they should release easily).

4. In a small pot, rub the sugar and lime zest together to combine. Add the cream and heat over medium-low heat, whisking, to dissolve the sugar—do not let the cream come to a boil. Transfer the mixture to a large container with a pour spout and whisk in the lime juice, vanilla, and salt.

5. Carefully pour the custard into the cooled crusts, filling each one just over three-quarter full. Cover loosely with plastic wrap and refrigerate until the filling it set, at least 2 hours (or up to 24 hours). Keep refrigerated until ready to slice and serve.

VARIATION

MEYER LEMON PIELETS: Replace the lime zest and juice with Meyer lemon zest and juice.

Make Ahead and Storage

The pielets can be made up to 24 hours ahead and kept refrigerated in an airtight container.

RECOMMENDED CRUSTS
- Coconut Press-In Cookie Crust (page 64)
- Oatmeal Press-In Cookie Crust (page 64)
- Brown Butter Press-In Cookie Crust (page 64)

RECOMMENDED FINISHES
- Meringue Topping (page 118)
- Classic Whipped Cream (page 111)
- Flavored Sifting Sugars (page 128)

Meet the Easiest Mini Pie Crust of All Time

Mini pies have a reputation for being tedious because you're dealing with so many more pieces, but that doesn't have to be true! In fact, one of my quickest, easiest crust recipes works best for miniature pies, and all you need are 6-inch / 15-cm flour tortillas, melted butter, and cinnamon sugar.

Preheat the oven to 350°F / 175°C. Grease a muffin pan (or jumbo muffin pan) with nonstick spray. Heat a large skillet over medium heat. Lightly heat one tortilla in the pan, turning once, until it's malleable, and then, working quickly, brush both sides of the tortilla generously with melted butter, sprinkle generously with cinnamon sugar, and press into one of the cavities of the prepared muffin pan (it won't sit perfectly flat against the sides and is likely to have a ruffled effect). Repeat with the remaining tortillas, then bake until crisp, 7 to 9 minutes. Let cool completely, unmold, and fill as desired. My favorite fillings include whipped cream and berries or ice cream!

Mini Pie Pairings

Miniature pies can be simple, quick, and easy to assemble. The "equations" below give you jumping-off points, then let your imagination run wild with tiny pie possibilities!

CUT SHAPES OF DOUGH + PREPARED FRUIT + SPRINKLING OF SUGAR

Roll out scrap dough to ¼ inch / 6 mm thick (this one's worth saving up scraps for). Cut the dough into rounds using a 3-inch / 8-cm round cutter and transfer to a parchment-lined baking sheet. Brush with egg wash and dock it all over with a fork. Top with a handful of prepared fruit (peeled if necessary/desired, pits or seeds removed, chopped if large). Sprinkle each with granulated sugar and bake at 425°F / 220°C until deeply golden and crisp; baking time may vary depending on the fruit, but start checking at 15 minutes or so.

BLIND-BAKED PRESS-IN COOKIE CRUST + WHIPPED CREAM + FRESH FRUIT

Bake pie shells as directed for the Key Lime Pielets on page 260. Spoon a Full Batch of Classic Whipped Cream (page 111) into each of the crusts, and top each with a small handful of fresh fruit.

CUT SHAPES OF DOUGH + SPOONFULS OF JAM, PRESERVES, OR CURD + CHOPPED NUTS SPRINKLED AROUND THE EDGES

Roll out the dough scraps and cut into portions as directed above in Cut Shapes of Dough. Spoon 15 g / 1 heaping tablespoon jam, preserves, or curd into each center, leaving

the outside 1 inch / 2 cm of dough uncovered all the way around. Sprinkle about 170 g / 1 cup coarsely chopped nuts generously around the outside edge of each pie, fully covering each piece of dough. Bake at 425°F / 220°C until deeply golden and crisp.

BLIND-BAKED PRESS-IN COOKIE CRUST + TOASTED NUTS + MERINGUE

Bake pie shells as directed for the Key Lime Pielets on page 260. Fold 255 g / 1½ cups coarsely chopped toasted nuts (cool completely before chopping) into a Full Batch of Meringue Topping (page 118). Spoon into the crusts and torch to toast, if desired.

BLIND-BAKED CUT SHAPES OF PIE DOUGH + CHILLED FRESH OR MACERATED FRUIT + COLD-SNAP TOPPING

Prepare the blind-baked cut shapes of pie dough as directed in the Anything-on-Pie-Crust instructions on page 39 and cool completely. Serve alongside a bowl of chilled fresh fruit (macerate it with a bit of sugar, to taste, if desired), and the Dark Chocolate Cold-Snap Topping (page 127). To eat, spoon a bit of fruit and topping onto each piece of dough and eat—building each portion as you eat, like pie party food.

FROZEN PRESS-IN CRUMB CRUST + ICE CREAM + SPRINKLES

Prepare the crusts as directed in the two-bite pies on page 67, baking and cooling completely. Use a small offset spatula to gently unmold from the pan, then freeze for 30 minutes, or until firm. Add a generous scoop of ice cream to each frozen shell, and top with sprinkles. Freeze until ready to serve.

TORTILLA CRUST + WHIPPED CREAM + DRIPPY CHOCOLATE GLAZE + SALTED CARAMEL SAUCE

Prepare the tortilla crusts as directed on page 261. Spoon a Mile High Batch of Classic Whipped Cream (page 111) into each of the crusts, and drizzle with Dark Chocolate Drippy Glaze (page 125) and Salted Caramel Sauce (page 126).

PEANUT BUTTER CREAM PIE WITH RASPBERRY MERINGUE

MAKES ONE 9-INCH / 23-CM PIE

DIFFICULTY: MEDIUM

This is the pie for when you're ready to break out of "Easy" recipes and into "Medium." The peanut butter filling is easy to make, and then the meringue feels like an incredible triumph to swoop over the top. The pie looks straight out of a fairy tale, and the nostalgic flavor combo of PB&J is the icing on the cake (the meringue should turn pale pink naturally, but you can always add a drop or two of food coloring if you want to amp up the color).

235 g / 1 cup heavy cream

56 g / ½ cup powdered sugar

170 g / ¾ cup creamy peanut butter

226 g / 8 ounces cream cheese, at room temperature

99 g / ½ cup granulated sugar

10 g / 2 teaspoons vanilla extract

2 g / ½ teaspoon fine sea salt

One 9-inch / 23-cm pie crust (see below), blind-baked, brushed with egg wash, and cooled completely (see page 43)

Mile-High Batch of Fruity Meringue Topping (page 118) made with raspberries

1. In the bowl of a stand mixer fitted with the whip attachment, whip the cream and powdered sugar to medium peaks. Transfer to a medium bowl and refrigerate.

2. Wipe out the mixer bowl and return it to the mixer stand; switch to the paddle attachment. Add the peanut butter, cream cheese, and granulated sugar to the bowl and cream until light and fluffy, 4 to 5 minutes. Add the vanilla and salt and mix to combine.

3. Add about one quarter of the whipped cream to the peanut butter mixture and mix vigorously to combine (this first addition will temper the mixture by lightening it). Remove the bowl from the mixer stand and gently fold in the remaining whipped cream in two or three additions.

4. Pour the filling into the cooled pie crust and spread into an even layer. Chill for at least 1 hour (or up to 24 hours).

5. Just before serving, spread or pipe the meringue on top of the chilled pie. If desired, toast the meringue with a kitchen torch.

Make Ahead and Storage

This pie can be made through step 4 up to 24 hours ahead and kept refrigerated; it is best to add the meringue topping as close to serving as possible.

RECOMMENDED CRUSTS
- Graham Flour Pie Dough (page 54)
- Chocolate All-Buttah Pie Dough (page 48)
- Nut Butter Press-In Crust (page 64)

RECOMMENDED FINISHES
- Swap the meringue for Freeze-Dried Fruity Whipped Cream (page 115)
- Nut Butter Whipped Cream (page 116)
- Chocolate Whipped Cream (page 114)
- Finish with Fruity Drippy Glaze (page 124)

From top:
Peaches-and-
Cream Pie in
Press-In Cookie
Crust; Nectarine
Semifreddo Pie in
Brown Butter Press-In
Crust

PEACHES-AND-CREAM PIE

MAKES ONE 9-INCH /
23-CM PIE

DIFFICULTY: EASY

It's a classic flavor combination for a reason—there's no better pairing than sweet, juicy peaches and rich cream. This easy-to-throw-together pie is perfect for summer, but since the filling uses peach jam, and the topping can be made with frozen peaches out of season, you can also make it for a little taste of summer even when peaches are long gone from the market.

FILLING

313 g / 1⅓ cups heavy cream

226 g / 8 ounces mascarpone cheese

113 g / ⅓ cup peach jam

56 g / ½ cup powdered sugar

5 g / 1 teaspoon vanilla extract

1 g / ¼ teaspoon almond extract

1 g / ¼ teaspoon fine sea salt

Pinch of ground cinnamon

One 9-inch / 23-cm pie crust (see below), blind-baked, brushed with egg wash, and cooled completely (see page 43) or Basic Crumb Crust, frozen (see page 66)

TOPPING

340 g / 12 ounces peaches (about 2 medium), pitted and thickly sliced (or substitute thawed frozen peaches; see headnote)

15 g / 1 tablespoon fresh lemon juice

43 g / 2 tablespoons honey

1. Make the filling: In the bowl of a stand mixer fitted with the whip attachment, whip the cream to soft peaks. Add the mascarpone and whip to medium peaks. Add the jam, powdered sugar, vanilla extract, almond extract, salt, and cinnamon and whip until well combined and the mixture is very thick.

2. Pour the filling into the cooled pie crust and spread into an even layer. Cover with plastic wrap placed directly against the surface and refrigerate for at least 8 hours (or up to 24 hours).

3. When you're ready to serve, make the topping: Toss the peaches, lemon juice, and honey together in a medium bowl until well combined. Arrange the peaches in a pile on top of the pie, then slice and serve.

Make Ahead and Storage

The pie can be made up to 24 hours ahead and kept refrigerated; add the topping just before serving. Store leftovers in the refrigerator in an airtight container.

RECOMMENDED CRUSTS
- Caramelized Pie Crust (page 56)
- Brown Butter Press-In Cookie Crust (page 64)
- Basic Crumb Crust, fresh or frozen (page 66)
- Basic Nut Crust (page 74)

RECOMMENDED FINISHES
- Try topping the pie with Flavored Sifting Sugars (page 128)
- Substitute Thick Fruit Coulis (page 122) made with peaches for the topping in the recipe

CREAMY MANGO PIE

MAKES ONE 9-INCH /
23-CM PIE

DIFFICULTY: MEDIUM

My first big-city apartment was around the corner from a row of little food carts. My two favorites: a tiny older man who sold chopped mangoes, and a cooler cart full of ice cream cups. On summer days, I'd walk Brimley down the street after snagging some of both. I'd stir the mango into the melty cup of ice cream—the combination of juicy mango flavor and creamy ice cream ultimately inspired this pie (try the ginger variation below to spice things up a little).

FILLING

75 g / ⅓ cup cool water

9 g / 1 tablespoon powdered gelatin

235 g / 1 cup heavy cream

106 g / 3 large egg whites

99 g / ½ cup granulated sugar

340 g / 1⅔ cups mango puree (see Note)

One 9-inch / 23-cm pie crust (see below), blind-baked, brushed with egg wash, and cooled completely (see page 43)

OPTIONAL TOPPING

Half Batch of Classic Whipped Cream (page 111)

120 g / ½ cup Thick Fruit Coulis (page 122), made with mango

1. Make the filling: Place the water in a small bowl and sprinkle the gelatin over it. Let bloom for 5 minutes.

2. In the bowl of a stand mixer fitted with the whip attachment, whip the cream to medium peaks. Transfer to a medium bowl and refrigerate. Clean and dry the mixer bowl and whip attachment.

3. In the clean mixer bowl, whisk together the egg whites and sugar until well combined. Set the bowl over a medium pot of barely simmering water and continue to whisk until the mixture reaches 160°F / 71°C on a thermometer. Transfer the mixture to the mixer stand and, using the whip attachment, whip the meringue to stiff peaks.

4. Melt the gelatin in the microwave, 15 to 20 seconds (or melt over the pot of simmering water). Place the mango puree in a large bowl and stir in the melted gelatin.

5. Add about one third of the whipped cream to the mango mixture and mix well to combine (this first addition helps to lighten the puree and make it easier to mix in the rest of the cream). Add the remaining cream in two additions, folding gently with a silicone spatula to combine. Add the meringue in the same way, first adding a small portion to lighten, then adding the remaining meringue in two additions, folding just until incorporated.

6. Pour the filling into the cooled pie crust and spread into an even layer. Cover with plastic wrap and refrigerate until set, at least 4 hours (or up to 24 hours).

7. If using the optional topping, prepare it just before serving: Place the whipped cream in a medium bowl, drizzle the mango coulis over it, and gently fold the two together to partially combine (the idea is to streak/swirl the whipped cream with the fruit mixture). Spoon, swoop, or pipe the cream onto the center or around the edges of the pie.

Ginger Mango Pie in Gingersnap Crumb Crust (left) and Mango Pie in Chocolate Crumb Crust (right) and Coarse Sugar Sprinkles (see Resources, page 345)

VARIATION

GINGER MANGO PIE: Stir 10 g / 1 tablespoon grated peeled fresh ginger and 3 g / 1 teaspoon ground ginger into the mango puree in step 4. If desired, garnish with diced candied ginger.

Make Ahead and Storage

The pie can be made up to 24 hours ahead and kept refrigerated; add the optional topping just before serving. Store leftovers in the refrigerator in an airtight container.

NOTE

Mango puree (also called mango pulp) is often sold canned or frozen in Indian and Middle Eastern grocery stores (See Resources, page 345). To make your own, puree 397 g / 14 ounces (about 2 heaping cups) peeled and chopped mango. In a food processor or blender, blend the mango puree with 15 g / 1 tablespoon fresh lemon juice and 66 g / ⅓ cup granulated sugar until smooth. This should make about 378 g / 1¾ cups of puree, which can be substituted for the amount in the recipe. If the puree appears fibrous, you may want to strain it before using.

RECOMMENDED CRUSTS

- Chocolate All-Buttah Pie Dough (page 48)
- Oatmeal Press-In Cookie Crust (page 64)
- All-Buttah Pie Dough (page 48)
- Basic Crumb Crust (page 66)
- Basic Nut Crust (page 74)

RECOMMENDED FINISH

- Instead of making the swirly whipped cream topping, you can spread the mango coulis evenly over the surface of the chilled pie (keep the whipped cream or nix it)

NECTARINE SEMIFREDDO PIE

MAKES ONE 9-INCH /
23-CM DEEP-DISH PIE

DIFFICULTY: MEDIUM

Semifreddo is an easy-to-make no-churn frozen dessert that makes a great pie filling. Freeze the pie solid, but allow it to stand for 10 to 15 minutes before serving to soften slightly. This recipe works with other stone fruit as well.

NECTARINE PUREE

- 510 g / 18 ounces ripe nectarines (about 3), peeled if desired (I don't!), pitted, and roughly chopped
- 30 g / 2 tablespoons fresh lemon juice
- 99 g / ½ cup granulated sugar

SEMIFREDDO BASE

- 352 g / 1½ cups heavy cream
- 43 g / 2 tablespoons honey
- 2 g / ½ teaspoon fine sea salt
- 15 g / 1½ teaspoons vanilla extract
- 128 g / 6 large egg yolks
- 99 g / ½ cup granulated sugar

One 9-inch / 23-cm deep-dish pie crust (see below), blind-baked, brushed with egg wash, and cooled completely (see page 43)

TOPPING

- 340 g / 12 ounces ripe nectarines (about 2), pitted and thinly sliced
- 13 g / 1 tablespoon light brown sugar
- 21 g / 1 tablespoon honey

1. Make the puree: In a large bowl, toss the nectarines with the lemon juice and granulated sugar until well coated. Let macerate at room temperature for 30 minutes to 1 hour.

2. Transfer the nectarines, with their juices, to a blender or food processor and puree until totally smooth. Strain the mixture through a fine-mesh sieve into a bowl and set aside.

3. Make the semifreddo base: In the bowl of a stand mixer fitted with the whip attachment, whip the cream, honey, and salt to medium peaks.

Add the vanilla and mix to combine. Transfer to a medium bowl and refrigerate.

4. Bring a medium saucepan of filled with about 2 inches / 5 cm of water to a simmer over medium heat. In a medium heatproof bowl, whisk the egg yolks and granulated sugar to combine, then set the bowl over the pan of simmering water (the bottom of the bowl should not touch the water). Heat the mixture over medium-low heat, whisking constantly, until it reads 160°F / 71°C on a thermometer; the mixture will lighten to a pale yellow color.

5. Remove the bowl from the heat and whisk the nectarine puree into the egg yolk mixture until well combined. Gently fold in the whipped cream until fully incorporated.

6. Pour the mixture into the cooled pie crust. Cover the filling with plastic wrap place directly against the surface and freeze for at least 6 hours (or up to 5 days).

7. When ready to serve, let the pie stand at room temperature while you prepare the topping: Toss the nectarines, brown sugar, and honey together and let macerate for 10 to 15 minutes.

8. Spoon the nectarines over the whole pie, or serve alongside the slices.

Make Ahead and Storage

This pie can be made up to 5 days ahead and kept frozen, wrapped tightly in plastic wrap.

TRIPLE-CHOCOLATE CARAMEL TRUFFLE PIE

MAKES ONE 9-INCH /
23-CM DEEP DISH PIE

DIFFICULTY: HARD

My most candy-bar–esque pie, this beauty boasts white, milk, and dark chocolate layers separated by gooey layers of caramel. To achieve a chewy texture that's just firm enough, I cheat and use store-bought caramels, which melt beautifully but then firm up again just as well. If you like, finish the pie with a pile of crunchy Valrhona chocolate pearls in white, milk, and dark chocolate to take it truly over the top.

DARK CHOCOLATE GANACHE

226 g / 8 ounces dark chocolate, finely chopped

118 g / ½ cup heavy cream

One 9-inch / 23-cm pie crust (see below), blind-baked, brushed with egg wash, and cooled completely (see page 43)

340 g / 12 ounces store-bought caramel candies, unwrapped

60 g / ¼ cup heavy cream

MILK CHOCOLATE GANACHE

226 g / 8 ounces milk chocolate, finely chopped

78 g / ⅓ cup heavy cream

WHITE CHOCOLATE GANACHE

238 g / 10 ounces white chocolate, finely chopped

106 g / ⅓ cup plus 2 tablespoons heavy cream

White, milk, and dark chocolate pearls, for finishing (optional; see Resources, page 345)

1. Make the dark chocolate ganache: Place the chocolate in a medium heatproof bowl. In a small saucepan, bring the heavy cream to a simmer over medium heat (be careful to watch it—cream can boil over quickly). Pour the hot cream over the chocolate and let sit for 15 seconds.

2. Using a silicone spatula, start mixing in the center of the bowl, stirring in small concentric circles. As the ganache starts to come together, make the circles wider and wider until the ganache is fully combined and smooth (if it's not smooth, place the bowl over a medium saucepan of simmering water and heat, stirring frequently,

until melted). Pour the ganache into the cooled pie crust and spread into an even layer. Transfer to the refrigerator and let set until firm, 15 to 20 minutes.

3. When the dark chocolate layer is set, combine the caramels and cream in a microwave-safe container. Microwave in 15-second bursts, stirring in between each, until the mixture is smooth (see Notes). Pour half of the caramel (about 170 g / 6 ounces) on top of the ganache, and quickly spread into an even layer (the caramel will start to firm up as soon as it comes in contact with the chilled ganache). Set aside.

4. Make the milk chocolate ganache: Follow steps 1 to 2 above, using the milk chocolate and cream. Pour the ganache over the caramel and spread into an even layer. Transfer to the refrigerator and let set until firm, 15 to 20 minutes.

5. If necessary, reheat the remaining caramel mixture in the microwave in 10-second bursts, stirring after each, until fluid. Pour on top of the milk chocolate ganache and quickly spread into an even layer (it will set up quickly). Set aside.

6. Make the white chocolate ganache: Follow steps 1 to 2 again, using the white chocolate and cream. Pour the ganache over the caramel and spread into an even layer.

(CONTINUED)

7. Let the pie sit at room temperature for at least 2 hours (or up to 24 hours), until the white chocolate ganache is firm (this also allows the remaining filling to come to room temperature, which is ideal for serving). If using, top generously with chocolate pearls.

Make Ahead and Storage

The pie can be made up to 24 hours ahead and kept refrigerated until ready to serve. Store leftovers in the refrigerator in an airtight container.

NOTES

Sometimes, ganache can "break" and look separated or grainy. Agitating the ganache vigorously will help bring it back together. You can also try warming it in a heatproof bowl over a saucepan of simmering water for 20 seconds, then stirring vigorously to try to bring together. Even easier is to use an immersion blender—just submerge it in the ganache and blend until it becomes shiny again.

You can also melt the caramel and cream in a medium heat-safe bowl set over a medium-size pot of barely simmering water. Stir frequently to encourage the mixture to melt and combine.

RECOMMENDED CRUSTS
- Pâte Brisée (page 59)
- Chocolate Roll-Out Cookie Crust (page 63)
- Chocolate All-Buttah Pie Dough (page 48)
- Basic Nut Crust (page 74)

RECOMMENDED FINISHES
- Flavored Sifting Sugars (page 128)
- Salted Caramel Sauce (page 126)
- Dark Chocolate Drippy Glaze (page 125)

BUTTERSCOTCH APPLE PIE

MAKES ONE 9-INCH / 23-CM PIE

DIFFICULTY: MEDIUM

Another two-fer pie, with a sweet spiced apple pie filling that's baked to bubbly perfection, cooled, and then topped with a layer of creamy butterscotch pudding. I love the combination of creamy with a fairly traditional apple pie filling—it's sort of like eating an à la mode pie but without any ice cream at all.

APPLE FILLING

28 g / 1 ounce / 2 tablespoons unsalted butter

397 g / 14 ounces peeled and diced apples such as Honeycrisp, Jonagold, or Gala (about 3 medium)

5 g / 1 teaspoon vanilla extract

107 g / ½ cup packed dark brown sugar

5 g / 1½ teaspoons ground cinnamon

2 g / ½ teaspoon freshly grated nutmeg

2 g / ½ teaspoon fine sea salt

37 g / 3 tablespoons granulated sugar

15 g / 2 tablespoons all-purpose flour

One 9-inch / 23-cm pie crust (see below), parbaked, brushed with egg wash, and cooled completely (see page 43)

BUTTERSCOTCH PUDDING FILLING

340 g / 1½ cups whole milk

118 g / ½ cup heavy cream

106 g / ½ cup packed dark brown sugar

2 g / ½ teaspoon fine sea salt

28 g / ¼ cup cornstarch

43 g / 2 large egg yolks

14 g / ½ ounce / 1 tablespoon unsalted butter

10 g / 2 teaspoons vanilla extract

Full Batch of Classic Whipped Cream (page 111)
Ground cinnamon for sprinkling

1. Make the apple filling: In a medium pot, melt the butter over medium heat. Add the apples, tossing to coat with the butter. Add the vanilla, brown sugar, cinnamon, nutmeg, and salt, stir to combine, and cook, stirring occasionally, until the sugar dissolves and the apples start to soften, 3 to 4 minutes.

2. In a small bowl, whisk the granulated sugar and flour to combine. Stir into the apple mixture and cook, stirring constantly, until the mixture thickens, 2 to 3 minutes. Remove from the heat and let the filling cool completely (you can speed up this process by spreading it into an even layer on a baking sheet).

3. Preheat the oven to 400°F / 205°C with a rack in the lower third (preferably with a Baking Steel or stone on it).

4. Place the parbaked pie crust on a parchment-lined baking sheet. Pour in the cooled apple filling and spread into an even layer. Bake until the crust is golden brown and the filling is bubbly, 35 to 40 minutes. Cool completely.

5. When the pie is cool, make the pudding: In a medium pot, bring the milk and cream to a simmer over medium heat.

6. Meanwhile, in a medium heatproof bowl, whisk the brown sugar, salt, and cornstarch together to combine.

7. When the milk mixture is simmering, whisk the egg yolks into the sugar mixture and whisk well to combine. Pour in about one quarter of the hot milk

(CONTINUED)

mixture to temper the yolks, whisking constantly. Return this mixture to the pot and cook over medium-low heat, stirring constantly with a silicone spatula, until it is very thick and large bubbles break the surface, 3 to 4 minutes. Remove from the heat and stir in the butter and vanilla.

8. Strain the pudding through a fine-mesh sieve onto the cooled apple filling and spread into an even layer. Cover with plastic wrap placed directly against the surface and refrigerate until set, at least 1 hour (or up to 24 hours).

9. When ready to serve, spread, spoon, or pipe the whipped cream on top of the pie. Garnish with a sprinkle of cinnamon.

Make Ahead and Storage

The pie can be made up to 24 hours ahead and kept refrigerated, covered tightly with plastic wrap. Add the whipped cream topping just before serving. Store leftovers in an airtight container in the refrigerator.

RECOMMENDED CRUSTS

- Vanilla Bean–Nutmeg Pie Dough (page 52)
- Chocolate All-Buttah Pie Dough (page 48)
- Basic Nut Crust (page 74)

RECOMMENDED FINISHES

- Salted Caramel Sauce (page 126) or Caramelized White Chocolate Drippy Glaze (page 125) for drizzling

Breakfast Pie

BREAKFAST PIE

MAKES ONE 9-INCH / 23-CM PIE

DIFFICULTY: EASY

When people ask me what my favorite kind of pie is, I usually say "breakfast pie"—i.e., any pie I'm eating for breakfast. And while I love leftover fruit pie at breakfast-time, the term got me thinking about a pie that was made with the most important meal of the day in mind: a crisp crumb crust made with granola and a super-easy yogurt filling that comes together in minutes. The tangy filling thickens overnight—a lovely make-ahead breakfast item, topped with your favorite fresh fruit.

206 g / ⅔ cup jam, marmalade, or preserves

One 9-inch / 23-cm Basic Crumb Crust (page 66) made with granola (use one not too full of large nut pieces or dried fruit), blind-baked and cooled completely (see page 46)

340 g / 12 ounces cream cheese, at room temperature

71 g / ⅓ cup packed light brown sugar

454 g / 2 cups plain Greek yogurt (fruit or vanilla-flavored is fine too, but the filling will be a bit sweeter)

15 g / 1 tablespoon fresh lemon juice

5 g / 1 teaspoon vanilla extract

2 g / ½ teaspoon fine sea salt

About 340 g / 2 cups berries or sliced fresh fruit of choice

Honey for drizzling (optional)

1. Spoon the jam into the bottom of the cooled crumb crust and spread into an even layer. Chill while you make the filling.

2. In the bowl of a stand mixer fitted with the paddle attachment, cream the cream cheese and brown sugar until light and fluffy, 4 to 5 minutes. Add the yogurt, lemon juice, vanilla, and salt and mix well to combine.

3. Pour the filling into the chilled pie crust and spread into an even layer. Refrigerate for at least 8 hours (or up to 24 hours; cover loosely with plastic wrap if refrigerating for longer than 8 hours).

4. When ready to serve, arrange the fruit on top of the pie. If desired, drizzle honey over the fruit. Slice and serve.

Make Ahead and Storage

The pie can be prepared up to 24 hours ahead and kept refrigerated. Store leftovers in the refrigerator in an airtight container.

OTHER RECOMMENDED CRUSTS
- Oatmeal Press-In Cookie Crust (page 64)
- Basic Crumb Crust (page 66) made with a different cereal

RECOMMENDED FINISHES
- Flavored Sifting Sugars (page 128)
- Thick Fruit Coulis (page 122)
- Half batch of Fresh Fruit Whipped Cream (page 115)

PISTACHIO CREAM PIE

MAKES ONE 9-INCH / 23-CM PIE

DIFFICULTY: MEDIUM

The homemade answer to the instant-pudding pistachio cream pies of my youth, this recipe starts with a from-scratch pistachio cream and then turns it into a creamy pudding filling. The filling is fabulous in a classic flaky pie crust, but I particularly love it in the Basic Nut Crust (page 74) made with pistachios. You can use a smaller amount of whipped cream just around the edges or cover the entire pie for an even creamier result.

FILLING

- 160 g / 1⅓ cups unsalted raw pistachios, preferably blanched
- 198 g / 1 cup granulated sugar
- 173 g / ¾ cup heavy cream
- 565 g / 2½ cups whole milk
- 28 g / ¼ cup cornstarch
- 56 g / 2 large eggs
- 64 g / 3 large egg yolks
- 4 g / 1 teaspoon fine sea salt
- 28 g / 1 ounce / 2 tablespoons unsalted butter
- 7 g / 1½ teaspoons vanilla extract
- 1 g / ¼ teaspoon almond extract

One 9-inch / 23-cm pie crust (see opposite), blind-baked, brushed with egg wash, and cooled completely (see page 46)

TOPPING

- Half or Full Batch of Classic Whipped Cream (page 111)
- 47 g / ⅓ cup finely chopped unsalted raw pistachios
- Large pearl sprinkles, for finishing (optional; see Resources, page 345)

1. Make the filling: In a blender or food processor, blend the pistachios with 99 g / ½ cup of the sugar until relatively finely ground (it's OK if it's still a bit coarse). With the blender or food processor running, add the cream and puree into a smooth paste.

2. Transfer the pistachio cream to a medium pot and whisk in the milk to combine. Bring to a simmer over medium heat, stirring constantly.

3. Meanwhile, in a medium bowl, whisk the remaining 99 g / ½ cup sugar and the cornstarch to combine. Add the eggs, egg yolks, and salt and whisk well to combine.

4. When the milk mixture comes to a simmer, pour about one quarter of it into the eggs, whisking constantly, to temper the eggs. Pour this mixture back into the pot, whisking constantly, reduce the heat to medium-low, and switch to a silicone spatula. Cook, stirring constantly, until the mixture thickens and comes a boil (you're looking for fat bubbles coming from the center of the pot). Remove the pot from the heat and stir in the butter, vanilla, and almond extract, mixing until the butter is melted and the pudding is smooth.

5. Strain the filling into the cooled pie crust and spread into an even layer. Cover the filling with plastic wrap placed directly against the surface and refrigerate until chilled and set, at least 2 hours (or up to 24 hours).

6. When the pie is chilled, spoon or pipe the whipped cream onto the pie. Sprinkle the chopped pistachios over the whipped cream. Keep refrigerated until ready to slice and serve.

Make Ahead and Storage

The pie can be made through step 5 up to 24 hours ahead. Store leftovers in the refrigerator in an airtight container.

RECOMMENDED CRUSTS
- Chocolate All-Buttah Pie Dough (page 48)
- All-Buttah Pie Dough (page 48)
- Basic Crumb Crust (page 66)
- Basic Nut Crust (page 74)

RECOMMENDED FINISHES
- White-Bottom Base (page 110)
- Basic Brittle (page 129)
- Or replace the plain whipped cream with Chocolate Whipped Cream (page 114)

LEMON MERINGUE PIE

MAKES ONE 9-INCH /
23-CM PIE

DIFFICULTY: MEDIUM

A bright, silky, tart citrus filling and sweet, fluffy meringue is one of the most perfect pie pairings there is. The recipe below is for a classic lemon, but you'll find many equally delicious variations below with other kinds of citrus, as well as with totally different tart fruits like rhubarb and passion fruit.

198 g / 1 cup granulated sugar

28 g / ¼ cup cornstarch

113 g / 4 ounces / 8 tablespoons unsalted butter

302 g / 1¼ cups fresh lemon juice (from about 7 lemons)

213 g / 10 large egg yolks

2 g / ½ teaspoon fine sea salt

One 9-inch / 23-cm pie crust (see below), blind-baked, brushed with egg wash, and cooled completely (see page 46)

Mile-High Batch of Meringue Topping (page 118)

1. In a small bowl, whisk the sugar and cornstarch to combine. In a medium pot, melt the butter over medium heat. Reduce the heat to medium-low, add the sugar mixture, along with the lemon juice, egg yolks, and salt, and cook, whisking constantly, until the mixture begins to thicken, 1 to 2 minutes.

2. Continue to cook, stirring constantly with a silicone spatula, scraping along the edges until the curd thickens and comes to a boil (look for fat bubbles in the center), 2 to 3 minutes more.

3. Strain the curd into the cooled pie crust and spread into an even layer. Cover with plastic wrap placed directly against the surface of the filling and transfer to the refrigerator to chill for at least 2 hours (or up to 24 hours).

4. Just before serving, add the meringue topping: Dollop the meringue onto the center of the chilled pie and use a small offset spatula to push the meringue out toward the edges, but leave a mound in the middle. If desired, use a kitchen torch to toast the meringue.

VARIATIONS ///

LIME/TANGERINE/GRAPEFRUIT/YUZU/PASSION FRUIT MERINGUE PIE: Replace the lemon juice with 242 g / 1 cup juice from any of these fruits. Combine with 61 g / ¼ cup fresh lemon juice and proceed as directed.

BLUEBERRY LEMON MERINGUE PIE: Top the baked Blueberry Lemon Pie (page 179) with the meringue.

RHUBARB MERINGUE PIE: Omit the top crust for the Pure Rhubarb Pie (page 142) and top the baked pie with the meringue.

CONCORD GRAPE MERINGUE PIE: Use a parbaked crust and the filling for the Concord Grape Hand Pies (page 163) and top the cooled baked pie with the meringue.

DEEP-DISH BERRY MERINGUE PIE: Omit the biscuit topping for the Deep-Dish Berry Cobbler Pie (page 156) and top the baked pie with the meringue.

Make Ahead and Storage ━━━

The pie can be made, without the meringue topping, up to 24 hours ahead; add the meringue just before serving. Store leftovers in the refrigerator in an airtight container.

RECOMMENDED CRUSTS
- All-Buttah Pie Dough (page 48)
- Rough Puff Pastry (page 50)
- Citrus Roll-Out Cookie Crust (page 63)

Left row, top to bottom: Lemon Meringue in All-Buttah Crust, Passion Fruit Meringue in Gluten-Free Crust, Tangerine Meringue in Vegan Pie Crust, and Deep-Dish Berry Meringue Pie in Chocolate All-Buttah Crust
Right row, top to bottom: Concord Grape Meringue in Whole Wheat Crust, Rhubarb Meringue in Rye Crust, Yuzu Meringue in All-Buttah Crust, and Grapefruit Meringue in Polenta Crust

ETON MESS PIE

MAKES ONE 9-INCH /
23-CM PIE

DIFFICULTY: MEDIUM

This is not your average pie, since it boasts meringue as the crust rather than the topping (though you can finish it with a meringue topper if desired). This is the pie version of its namesake dessert, an irresistibly delicious "messy" pile of meringue, jam, and whipped cream. While this pie looks super-impressive, it won't slice perfectly—it's more of a slice-and-scoop-into-serving-bowls situation. It is, after all, a mess, but a delicious one.

FILLING

400 g / 2½ cups prepared fruit (peeled if desired, pitted if necessary, chopped if large [such as peaches or plums], left whole if small [such as berries or cherries])

30 g / 2 tablespoons fresh lemon juice

99 g / ½ cup granulated sugar

14 g / 2 tablespoons cornstarch

1 vanilla bean, halved lengthwise, seeds scraped out, seeds and bean reserved (optional)

Full Batch of Mascarpone Whipped Cream (page 111)

1 Meringue Crust (page 72), unmolded and cooled completely

TOPPING

300 g / 1¾ cups prepared fruit (see above)

37 g / 3 tablespoons granulated sugar

1 Meringue Topper (page 73; optional)

1. Make the filling: In a medium pot, stir the fruit and lemon juice to combine. In a small bowl, stir the sugar, cornstarch, and vanilla bean seeds and bean, if using, to combine. Sprinkle the mixture over the fruit and stir to combine, then cook over medium-low heat, stirring occasionally, until the fruit begins to soften and the mixture thickens and comes to a simmer.

2. Pour the mixture onto a baking sheet or into a large casserole dish and spread into an even layer (this will help it cool faster). Remove and discard the vanilla bean if you used it.

3. Spoon the whipped cream into a large bowl and drizzle the cooled fruit mixture over the top. Using a silicone spatula, gently fold the two together—the idea is to mix only a few times so the whipped cream is streaked with the fruit mixture.

4. Spoon the filling into the cooled meringue crust and spread into an even layer. Transfer to the refrigerator to chill while you make the topping, no more than 1 hour.

5. Make the topping: In a small bowl, toss the fruit and sugar together. Let macerate for 5 to 10 minutes, then spoon it on top of the chilled pie filling. If using, place the meringue topper (piped side up) on top of the fruit. Serve immediately, or refrigerate for no longer than 3 hours before slicing and serving.

VARIATION ///

CITRUS ETON MESS PIE: Omit the fruit filling. Fold 1 recipe Lemon Curd or other citrus curd (page 123) into the Mascarpone Whipped Cream as directed in step 3, so the cream is streaked with the citrus curd. Proceed as directed.

Make Ahead and Storage ━━━━

This recipe is best prepared the same day it is served and served within 2 hours of assembly. However, it is possible to make it up 12 hours ahead and store in the refrigerator, but be aware that the meringue crust (and topper, if using) will continue to soften, absorbing moisture as it sits. Store leftovers in the refrigerator in an airtight container.

RECOMMENDED CRUSTS

- Substitute a Roll-Out Cookie Crust (page 62), Press-In Cookie Crust (page 64), or Crumb Crust (page 66) for the meringue crust—the meringue topper is still optional.

RECOMMENDED FINISHES

- Flavored Sifting Sugars (page 128) or a drizzle/glaze of Fruity Cold-Snap Topping (page 127)

STRIPED CITRUS PIE

MAKES ONE 9-INCH /
23-CM PIE

DIFFICULTY: MEDIUM

I crave the tart flavors and adore the beautiful variety of colors of citrus fruits. In the depth and dark of winter, they're such a welcome source of freshness and juicy goodness, a sign of the light and brightness that's around the corner come springtime. This pie is an ode to my three favorite types of citrus: tangerine, grapefruit, and blood orange. To intensify the colors, you can add a couple drops of red food coloring to the blood orange curd and/or pink food color to the grapefruit curd.

BLOOD ORANGE CURD

99 g / ½ cup granulated sugar

21 g / 3 tablespoons cornstarch

56 g / 2 ounces / 4 tablespoons unsalted butter

226 g / 1 cup fresh blood orange juice

64 g / 3 large egg yolks

Pinch of fine sea salt

One 9-inch 23-cm pie crust (see below), blind-baked, brushed with egg wash, and cooled completely (see page 46)

GRAPEFRUIT CURD

99 g / ½ cup granulated sugar

21 g / 3 tablespoons cornstarch

56 g / 2 ounces / 4 tablespoons unsalted butter

226 g / 1 cup fresh grapefruit juice (preferably Ruby Red)

64 g / 3 large egg yolks

Pinch of fine sea salt

TANGERINE (OR ORANGE) CURD

99 g / ½ cup granulated sugar

21 g / 3 tablespoons cornstarch

56 g / 2 ounces / 4 tablespoons unsalted butter

226 g / 1 cup fresh tangerine (or orange) juice

64 g / 3 large egg yolks

Pinch of fine sea salt

Half Batch of Mascarpone Whipped Cream (page 111)

1. Make the blood orange curd: In a small bowl, whisk the sugar and cornstarch to combine. In a small pot, melt the butter over medium heat. Reduce the heat to medium-low, add the sugar mixture, along with the blood orange juice and egg yolks, and cook, whisking constantly, until the mixture begins to thicken, 1 to 2 minutes.

2. Switch to a silicone spatula and continue to cook, stirring constantly (be sure to get into the edges of the pot), until the curd thickens and comes to a boil (you're looking for fat bubbles coming from the center of the pot), 2 to 3 minutes more.

3. Strain the curd into the cooled pie crust and spread into an even layer. Press a piece of plastic wrap directly against the surface of the filling and transfer to the refrigerator to cool for 30 to 45 minutes. Wash out the pot and strainer; you'll use them again.

4. Make the grapefruit curd following the instructions above, then strain the curd on top of the chilled blood orange curd (remove the plastic wrap first, of course!) and spread into an even layer. Press another piece of plastic wrap directly against the surface of the filling and transfer to the refrigerator to cool for 30 to 45 minutes. Wash out the pot and strainer again.

5. Make the tangerine curd following the instructions above, then strain the tangerine curd on top of the chilled grapefruit curd and spread into an even layer. Press another piece of plastic wrap directly against the surface of the filling and transfer to the refrigerator to cool for at least 2 hours (or up to 24 hours).

6. When the pie is well chilled, spoon, spread, or pipe the whipped cream on top. Keep refrigerated until ready to slice and serve.

Make Ahead and Storage

The pie can be made up to 24 hours ahead and kept refrigerated. Store leftovers in the refrigerator in an airtight container.

NOTE ◇◇◇◇◇◇◇◇◇◇◇◇◇◇◇◇◇◇◇◇◇◇◇◇◇◇◇◇
You can substitute other citrus juices in any of the layers here or have the layers go in any order—just note that some flavors won't have a strong color difference (e.g., lemon and lime). But you can always add a drop or two of food coloring (see the headnote) to help distinguish between them.

RECOMMENDED CRUSTS
- Citrus Roll-Out Cookie Crust (page 63)
- All-Buttah Pie Dough (page 48)
- Citrus-Vanilla Caramelized Pie Crust (page 56)

OTHER RECOMMENDED FINISHES
- Mile-High Meringue Topping (page 118)
- Classic Whipped Cream (page 111)

"ROOT BEER FLOAT" BAKED ALASKA PIE

MAKES ONE 9-INCH / 23-CM PIE

DIFFICULTY: HARD

Reducing root beer on the stovetop turns it into a thick, caramel-like syrup that you can fold into softened ice cream to make beautiful ribbons. In this recipe, that mixture is piled into a pie crust and frozen, and in the freezer, the root beer syrup softens in the ice cream, resulting in an incredible float-like texture. Just before serving, top the pie with mounds of fluffy meringue for a stunning contribution to the "float" effect.

1361 g / 6 cups root beer (four 12-ounce bottles/cans)

1 vanilla bean, halved lengthwise, seeds scraped out, seeds and bean reserved (optional)

1360 g / 1½ quarts vanilla ice cream, softened to a thickly spreadable consistency

One 9-inch / 23-cm pie crust, blind-baked and cooled completely (see page 46)

Mile-High Batch of Meringue Topping (page 118)

1. Make the root beer syrup: In a medium pot, combine the root beer and vanilla bean seeds and bean, if using, bring to a simmer over medium heat, and simmer until the root beer reduces to about 165 g / ½ cup. The timing will vary based on the size of your pot, but it may take 30 to 40 minutes. (Don't feel you need to watch it closely in the initial stages; once it gets to about 334 g / 1 cup, though, it will start to reduce much faster.) Remove the vanilla bean if you used it and cool the syrup for 5 minutes.

2. Place about half of the softened ice cream in a large bowl and drizzle half of the cooled root beer syrup over it. Scoop the remaining ice cream on top, then drizzle with the remaining syrup. Working quickly, gently fold the mixture together just to begin to combine—mix only a few times, so the ice cream is ribboned with the syrup.

3. Scoop the filling into the cooled crust and use a small offset spatula to spread it out toward the edges, leaving it mounded in the center. Transfer to the freezer for at least 6 hours (or up to 12 hours).

4. When ready to serve, add the meringue topping to the pie, covering it completely and again trying to maintain the mounded shape. Use a kitchen torch to evenly toast the meringue, then slice and serve immediately.

VARIATION //

FRUITY BAKED ALASKA PIE: Replace the root beer with an equal amount of fruit juice and proceed as directed.

Make Ahead and Storage

This pie can be made through step 3 up to 2 days ahead and kept in the freezer, wrapped tightly in plastic wrap. Add the meringue topping just before serving. Store leftovers in the freezer in an airtight container.

RECOMMENDED CRUSTS
- Brown Butter Press-In Cookie Crust (page 64)
- Basic Crumb Crust, fresh or frozen (page 66)
- Chocolate Roll-Out Cookie Crust (page 63)

RECOMMENDED FINISHES
- Salted Caramel Sauce (page 126) or White Chocolate Drippy Glaze (page 125) for drizzling

FRESH WATERMELON PIE

MAKES ONE 9-INCH /
23-CM PIE

DIFFICULTY: MEDIUM

My parents are avid gardeners, and we feast on their home-grown hauls each summer. Among their best crops, in my opinion, are the melons they grow in a small patch in front of the house. Once indifferent to melon, I changed my mind forever when my parents started growing them and harvesting them at peak ripeness. The sweet, juicy fruit is undeniably summery, crisp, and refreshing—a combination I desperately wanted to capture in a pie. The idea of watermelon pie made me think of the Jell-O pies in my vintage cookbooks, and so this gelatin-set filling was born, but made with fresh watermelon juice, it's bursting with all that refreshing crisp summer-ness. (For a vegan/vegetarian version, see the Note below.)

950 g / 5 cups cubed watermelon

75 g / ⅓ cup fresh lemon or lime juice

99 g / ½ cup granulated sugar

3 g / ¾ teaspoon fine sea salt

75 g / ⅓ cup cool water

25 g / 2½ tablespoons powdered gelatin

One 9-inch / 23-cm pie crust (see below), blind-baked, brushed with egg wash, and cooled completely (see page 46)

Full Batch of Classic Whipped Cream (page 111)

Chocolate shavings (see page 107) for garnish (optional)

1. In a blender or food processor, puree the watermelon with the citrus juice until fully broken down and relatively smooth.

2. Strain the mixture into a medium saucepan (you should end up with about 800 g / 4 cups), add the sugar and salt, and bring the mixture to a simmer over medium heat.

3. While the mixture heats, place the water in a shallow bowl and sprinkle the gelatin over it. Let bloom for 5 minutes.

4. Add the bloomed gelatin to the watermelon mixture and stir over low heat until it fully melts. Pour the mixture into the cooled crust. Gently transfer to the refrigerator and chill until fully set, at least 3 hours (or up to 24 hours).

5. Just before serving, top the pie with the whipped cream and chocolate shavings, if using.

Make Ahead and Storage

The pie can be prepared up to 24 hours ahead and kept refrigerated; add the whipped cream (and optional chocolate shavings) just before serving. Store leftovers in the refrigerator in an airtight container.

NOTE ◇◇◇◇◇◇◇◇◇◇◇◇◇◇◇◇◇◇◇◇◇◇◇◇◇◇◇◇◇◇

To make a gelatin-free version of the filling, substitute 5 g / 2½ tablespoons powdered agar-agar for the gelatin, stirring it into the warm liquid at the end of step 2. Reduce the salt to 1 g / ¼ teaspoon.

RECOMMENDED CRUSTS
- Basic Crumb Crust, fresh or frozen (page 66)
- Chocolate All-Buttah Pie Dough (page 48)
- Roll-Out Cookie Crust (page 62)

RECOMMENDED FINISHES
- Swap the plain whipped cream for Fresh Fruit Whipped Cream (page 115) or a Flavored Sifting Sugar (page 128)

BLACK RASPBERRY CHIFFON PIE

MAKES ONE 9-INCH / 23-CM PIE

DIFFICULTY: MEDIUM

One of my closest friends loves all things black raspberry. Before I met her, I never really understood the true glory of this fruit. The flavor rides the line between sweet and sour, and the color is the stuff of dreams. It's a fruit made for pie, and this is my ode to it: first a sweet jammy layer and then a fluffy, fruity black raspberry chiffon topping. You can rub the sugar for the filling with the scraped seeds of 1 vanilla bean or zest from 1 medium piece of citrus before preparing the filling to add another layer of flavor. Don't skimp on the whipped cream, and prepare for oohs and ahhs.

JAMMY FILLING

567 g / 20 ounces black raspberries (about 5 cups; see Note), thawed if frozen

132 g / ⅔ cup granulated sugar (vanilla or citrus sugar is especially delicious here)

28 g / ¼ cup cornstarch

Scant 1 g / ¼ teaspoon freshly grated nutmeg

One 9-inch / 23-cm pie crust (see below), parbaked, brushed with egg wash, and cooled completely (see page 43)

CHIFFON FILLING

454 g / 16 ounces black raspberries (about 4 cups), thawed if frozen

99 g / ½ cup granulated sugar

1 g / ¼ teaspoon fine sea salt

5 g / 1 teaspoon vanilla extract

56 g / ¼ cup cool water

4 g / 1½ teaspoons powdered gelatin

106 g / 3 large egg whites

Scant 1 g / ¼ teaspoon cream of tartar

Half Batch of Extra-Thick and Creamy Whipped Cream (page 113)

1. Make the jammy filling: In a medium pot, stir the black raspberries and ⅓ cup (66 g) sugar to combine, then cook over medium-low heat, stirring occasionally, until the berries begin to break down, 8 to 10 minutes. Mash with a potato masher or large fork until the mixture resembles a coarse puree.

2. Strain the mixture to remove the seeds—press and scrape firmly to get all the juices. Return the strained puree to the pot.

3. In a small bowl, whisk the remaining ⅓ cup sugar and the cornstarch to combine. Add to the pot and cook over medium heat, stirring constantly, until the mixture thickens to the consistency of jam, 1 to 2 minutes. Whisk in the nutmeg and cool completely.

4. Preheat the oven to 350°F / 175°C with a rack in the center.

5. Place the cooled pie crust on a parchment-lined baking sheet and pour the cooled filling into the crust. Transfer to the oven and bake until the crust is deeply golden brown and the filling is bubbly, 20 to 25 minutes. Cool completely.

6. Make the chiffon filling: In a medium pot, stir the black raspberries and ¼ cup (50 g) sugar to combine, then cook over medium-low heat, stirring occasionally, until the berries break down, 8 to 10 minutes. Mash with a potato masher or large fork until the mixture resembles a coarse puree.

7. Strain the mixture to remove the seeds—press and scrape firmly to get all the juices. You should have about 144 g / ½ cup puree. If you have less, your puree is too thick; add water 14 g / 1 tablespoon at a time until you have the correct amount. If you have more, your puree is too thin. Return it to the pot and cook over medium-low heat, stirring constantly, until the it thickens to the appropriate consistency. Transfer the puree to a medium bowl to cool to room temperature (if you make it ahead and chill it, bring it to room temperature before proceeding).

8. Place the cool water in a small bowl and sprinkle the gelatin over it. Let bloom for 5 minutes.

9. Melt the gelatin in the microwave in 15-second bursts, then stir into the cooled black raspberry puree.

10. In the bowl of a stand mixer fitted with the whip attachment, whip the egg whites with the cream of tartar on medium speed until they begin to become foamy, 1 to 2 minutes. With the mixer running, add the remaining ¼ cup sugar in a slow, steady stream and continue to whip to medium peaks. Add the salt and vanilla and mix to combine.

11. Whisk about one quarter of the meringue into the black raspberry puree, mixing well to combine. Using a silicone spatula, gently fold in the remaining meringue in two or three additions until thoroughly incorporated. Pour the chiffon filling over the cooled jammy filling—use a small offset spatula to spread in an even layer. Cover with plastic wrap placed directly against the surface and chill for at least 1 hour (or up to 24 hours).

12. When ready to serve, spread or pipe the whipped cream into an even layer around the outer edges of the pie. Keep refrigerated until ready to serve.

Make Ahead and Storage

The puree for the chiffon filling can be made up to 3 days ahead—refrigerate in an airtight container. The pie can be made up to 24 hours ahead and kept refrigerated until ready to serve. Add the whipped cream topping just before serving. Store leftovers in an airtight container in the refrigerator.

NOTE

You can substitute raspberries or blackberries, or a mixture of the two, for the black raspberries.

RECOMMENDED CRUSTS
- Chocolate All-Buttah Pie Dough (page 48)
- Roll-Out Cookie Crust (page 62)
- Oatmeal Press-In Cookie Crust (page 64)

RECOMMENDED FINISHES
- Dark Chocolate Black-Bottom Base (page 110)
- Replace the whipped cream with Chocolate Whipped Cream (page 114)

CHOCOLATE-COVERED-RASPBERRIES PIE

MAKES ONE 9-INCH /
23-CM PIE

DIFFICULTY: MEDIUM

A beautifully fluffy chocolate mousse enrobes whole raspberries to make this stunner of a pie. It reveals its beauty when you slice into it, exposing cross-sections of the fruit. The chocolate-berry combination makes it a perfect Valentine's Day pie (try it with strawberries, too—below!).

FILLING

- 226 g / 8 ounces cream cheese, at room temperature
- 85 g / ¾ cup powdered sugar
- 10 g / 2 teaspoons vanilla extract
- 3 g / ¾ teaspoon fine sea salt
- 283 g / 10 ounces bittersweet chocolate, melted and still fluid
- 705 g / 3 cups cold heavy cream
- 340 g / 12 ounces fresh raspberries

One 9-inch / 23-cm pie crust (see opposite), blind-baked, brushed with egg wash, and cooled completely (see page 46)

Half Batch of Chocolate Whipped Cream (page 114; optional)

120 g / ½ cup Thick Fruit Coulis (page 122) made with raspberries (optional)

1. Make the filling: In the bowl of a stand mixer fitted with the whip attachment, whip the cream cheese and powdered sugar until light and fluffy, 3 to 4 minutes. Add the vanilla and salt and mix to combine. Scrape the bowl well. With the mixer running, add the warm chocolate and whip on low speed until just combined.

2. With the mixer running on medium-low speed, add about one third of the cream in a slow, steady stream, then whip until the mixture begins to thicken; scrape the bowl well. With the mixer on medium speed, add the remaining cream in a slow, steady stream, and then whip on medium-high speed to medium-stiff peaks.

3. Pour about one quarter of the filling into the cooled pie crust and spread into an even layer. Arrange the raspberries (rounded side up) in a single layer in the filling, pressing them gently into the filling but not fully submerging them.

4. Pour the remaining filling over the raspberries and spread into an even layer. Gently tap the pie on the work surface to help the filling settle around the berries. The filling will be higher than the edge of the crust; use a small offset spatula to mound it higher in the center than at the edges. Cover the filling directly with plastic wrap and refrigerate until set, at least 4 hours (or up to 24 hours).

5. When ready to serve, spoon, spread, or pipe the whipped cream, if using, around the outside edges of the pie. Spoon the coulis, if using, into the center and gently spread into an even layer. Keep refrigerated until ready to slice and serve.

VARIATION

CHOCOLATE-COVERED-STRAWBERRIES PIE:
Replace the raspberries with small hulled strawberries. Place them hulled side down in the filling in step 3. It's important to use smaller strawberries to ensure they'll be fully covered—if you can only find large ones, trim the stem ends to shorten them (save the trimmings to make the coulis).

Make Ahead and Storage

The pie can be made through step 4 up to 24 hours ahead. Store leftovers in the refrigerator in an airtight container.

RECOMMENDED CRUSTS
- Chocolate All-Buttah Pie Dough (page 48)
- Chocolate Roll-Out Cookie Crust (page 63)
- Pâte Brisée (page 59)
- Basic Crumb Crust (page 66)

RECOMMENDED FINISHES
- Swap out the coulis for an equal amount of Dark Chocolate Drippy Glaze (page 125)
- Or swap out the plain whipped cream for the Fresh Fruit Whipped Cream (page 115) made with raspberries

TWO-BITE PB&J PIES

MAKES 24 BITE-SIZE PIES

DIFFICULTY: MEDIUM

When I was growing up, my mom would pack me prank lunches on April Fool's Day. One year, I bit into my usual pb&j to discover it was actually peanut butter, marshmallows, and chocolate chips—and, yes, my mom was the coolest in the eyes of the lunchroom that day.

These were created out of a desire to make a perfect pie for nestling inside a lunchbox the way my mom would sneak perfect treats in for me. They have since become a crazy-popular recipe among my regular taste testers because of their adorable two-bite size and their delightfully nostalgic flavor.

1 recipe Press-In Cookie Crust (page 64; see below for suggestions)

91 g / ⅔ cup creamy peanut butter

113 g / 4 ounces cream cheese, at room temperature

50 g / ¼ cup granulated sugar

5 g / 1 teaspoon vanilla extract

1 g / ¼ teaspoon fine sea salt

115 g / ½ cup heavy cream

28 g / ¼ cup powdered sugar

234 g / ¾ cup jelly (I like strawberry or grape)

1. Preheat the oven to 350°F / 175°C with a rack in the center.

2. Grease the cavities of a mini muffin pan with nonstick spray. Crumble or spoon 15 g / 1 tablespoon of the dough into each cavity. Press each portion of dough with your fingers flush against the bottom and up the sides of each cavity, taking care to press evenly all the way around. Use a small fork or the tip of a paring knife to dock the dough all over. Refrigerate for 15 to 20 minutes.

3. Bake the crusts until they are lightly golden at the edges and appear set all over, 10 to 12 minutes. Cool completely, then use an offset spatula to gently unmold the cooled crusts onto a serving platter.

4. In the bowl of a stand mixer fitted with the whip attachment, whip the peanut butter, cream cheese, and granulated sugar until light and fluffy, 4 to 5 minutes. Add the vanilla and salt and mix to combine.

5. With the mixer running on low speed, add the cream in a slow, steady stream. Once it's incorporated, raise the speed to medium-high and whip to soft peaks. Scrape the bowl well, add the powdered sugar, then continue to whip to medium peaks.

6. Transfer the filling to a disposable pastry bag and cut a ½-inch / 1-cm opening in the end (or fit with a ½-inch / 1-cm round or star tip). Pipe the filling into the cooled crusts, filling them just over three-quarters full.

7. In a small saucepan, heat the jelly over medium-low heat until it's liquid. Cool for 3 to 5 minutes, then spoon 10 g / 1½ teaspoons jelly over the top of each pie. (Alternatively, transfer the cooled jelly to a disposable pastry bag, cut a ¼-inch / 6 mm opening in the tip, and pipe jelly on top of each pie, covering the filling completely.)

8. Refrigerate the pies for at least 30 minutes (or up to 24 hours) before serving.

Two-Bite PB&J Pies
and Two-Bite Black-
and-White Pies

Make Ahead and Storage

The pies can be made up to 24 hours ahead and
kept refrigerated in an airtight container.

RECOMMENDED CRUSTS
- Chocolate Press-In Cookie Crust (page 64)
- Nut Butter Press-In Cookie Crust (page 64)
- Oatmeal Press-In Cookie Crust (page 64)

TWO-BITE BLACK-AND-WHITE PIES

MAKES 24 BITE-SIZE PIES

DIFFICULTY: MEDIUM

For these tiny pies, a tender cookie crust forms the base for the creamy chocolate and vanilla fillings. Use black cocoa (see Resources, page 345) if possible for the darkest chocolate filling. But these sweet bite-size wonders will wow regardless—a true crowd-pleaser in tiny pies that are easy to serve and eat.

CHOCOLATE CREAM FILLING

113 g / ½ cup whole milk

29 g / 2 tablespoons heavy cream

113 g / 4 ounces bittersweet chocolate, finely chopped

50 g / ¼ cup granulated sugar

5 g / 1 tablespoon cocoa powder (preferably black cocoa)

21 g / 3 tablespoons cornstarch

Pinch of fine sea salt

21 g / 1 large egg yolk

14 g / ½ ounce / 1 tablespoon unsalted butter

3 g / ½ teaspoon vanilla extract

VANILLA CREAM FILLING

113 g / ½ cup whole milk

29 g / 2 tablespoons heavy cream

50 g / ¼ cup granulated sugar

14 g / 2 tablespoons cornstarch

Pinch of fine sea salt

21 g / 1 large egg yolk

14 g / ½ ounce / 1 tablespoon unsalted butter

5 g / 1 teaspoon vanilla extract

1 recipe Press-In Cookie Crust (page 64; see below for recommendations)

1. Make the chocolate cream filling: In a small pot, heat the milk, cream, and chocolate over medium-low heat just to a bare simmer.

2. Meanwhile, in a small bowl, whisk the sugar, cocoa powder, cornstarch, and salt to combine. When the milk mixture is hot, add the egg yolk to the sugar mixture and whisk to combine.

3. When the milk mixture has come to a bare simmer, pour about half of it into the egg yolk mixture in a slow, steady stream, whisking constantly. Then pour the mixture back into the saucepan and cook over low heat, stirring constantly with a silicone spatula, until it thickens and just comes to a boil (you are looking for a few large bubbles coming from the center of the pot). Stir in the butter and vanilla until well combined.

4. Strain the filling into a small bowl, cover with plastic wrap pressed directly against the surface, and refrigerate until thoroughly chilled, at least 2 hours (or up to 24 hours).

5. Make the vanilla cream filling: In a small pot, heat the milk and cream over medium-low heat just to a bare simmer.

6. In a small bowl, whisk the sugar, cornstarch, and salt to combine. When the milk mixture is hot, add the egg yolk to the sugar mixture and whisk to combine.

7. When the milk mixture has come to a bare simmer, pour about half of it into the egg yolk mixture in a slow, steady stream, whisking constantly. Then pour the mixture back into the saucepan and cook over low heat, stirring constantly with a silicone spatula, until it thickens and just comes to a boil (you are looking for a few large bubbles coming from the center of the pot). Stir in the butter and vanilla until well combined.

8. Strain the filling into a bowl, cover with plastic wrap placed directly against the surface, and refrigerate until thoroughly chilled, at least 2 hours (or up to 24 hours).

9. Preheat the oven to 350°F / 175°C with a rack in the center.

10. Grease the cavities of a mini muffin pan with nonstick spray. Spoon or crumble 15 g / 1 tablespoon of the dough into each cavity. Press each portion of dough with your fingers flush against the bottom and up the sides of the cavity, taking care to press evenly all the way around. Use a small fork or the tip of a paring knife to dock the dough all over. Refrigerate for 15 to 20 minutes.

11. Bake the crusts until they are lightly golden at the edges and appear set all over, 10 to 12 minutes. Cool completely, then use an offset spatula to gently unmold the cooled crusts onto a serving platter.

12. Use a whisk or electric hand mixer to whip the vanilla cream filling to lighten it. Transfer it to a disposable pastry bag and cut a ¼-inch / 6-mm opening in the end (or fit with a pastry tip of about the same size). Do the same to lighten the chocolate cream filling, then transfer it to a pastry bag with the same opening/tip.

13. Pipe vanilla cream filling into one half of each crust, going all the way up to the top of the crust. Move the pastry bag back and forth as you pipe to create a squiggly effect with the filling. Pipe chocolate cream filling into the other side. Keep refrigerated until ready to serve.

Make Ahead and Storage

The fillings and crusts can be made up to 24 hours ahead and held separately. One assembled, the pies can be held up to 24 hours ahead and refrigerated in an airtight container.

RECOMMENDED CRUSTS
- Chocolate Press-In Cookie Crust (page 64)
- Oatmeal Press-In Cookie Crust (page 64)
- Coconut Press-In Cookie Crust (page 64)

RECOMMENDED TOPPINGS
- Add a little extra black and white flair by piping a little Classic Whipped Cream (page 111) on the vanilla side and a little Chocolate Whipped Cream (page 114) on the chocolate side of each mini pie.

Buckle up for this chapter, because it's full of some of the most delicious savory pies I've ever dreamed up. One of the things that I love about savory pies is they allow for a bit more flexibility than dessert pies—like cooking as opposed to baking. (And, let's be real, making them is one of the ways I repurpose dinner leftovers; see Leftover Pie, page 327.) Once you're familiar with the basics of savory pies, you can wing it a lot more than you can with traditional pie fillings—think stews, curries, hot dips, and more!

DOUGH FOR SAVORY PIES

Here are a few things you might want to consider for savory pies, dough-wise.

BUILDING FLAVOR: You don't need to rely only on your filling to give a savory pie a punch of flavor. Adding herbs or spices to the dough, or even using a compound butter (see page 58), are great ways to add more flavor to your pie starting from the get-go!

WHEN TO PARBAKE: Just like sweet pies, just about any single-crust savory pie will benefit from parbaking the crust. For more on this, see the section on parbaking (page 43).

ABOUT DEEP-DISH PIES: Lots of savory pie recipes opt for a deep-dish pie plate, because you want plenty of filling when the pie is the main course. If you want to convert a recipe intended to be made in a regular pie pan, you may need to increase the filling if you want to make it in a deep-dish pan. For more on this, see page 19.

SAVORY FILLINGS

The main thing to consider when you want to free-style a savory pie is how the filling will work inside a crust. Think about the style of pie you'll be baking (classic? free-form? deep-dish?) and its overall baking time. Will the ingredients you're using cook sufficiently in that amount of time, or will they require precooking? Moisture is one of the biggest concerns when choosing a filling, and precooking ingredients like meat, mushrooms, onions, and tomatoes, among others, allows you to cook off excess moisture and/or concentrate flavors. You can also think about whether the filling will have large pieces of ingredients or will be soft and smoother.

PRECOOKING INGREDIENTS FOR SAVORY FILLINGS

Just as with the unpredictably juicy fruits for a sweet pie filling, savory ingredients can benefit from being cooked ahead. The main reason to cook something ahead is to ensure a tender final product. An ingredient like butternut squash or carrots, for example, may not cook sufficiently in the amount of time it takes for a crust to brown. But precooking ingredients also helps to release their excess moisture and allows you to accommodate for any shrinkage that occurs with ingredients like meat or mushrooms. This is also why I love to use leftovers to make pies—the ingredients are already cooked!

CHICKEN POT SLAB PIE

MAKES ONE 9-BY-13-INCH / 23-BY-33-CM PIE

DIFFICULTY: MEDIUM

While I love the *concept* of potpies, I'm a tried-and-true crust lover, and I want crust on the bottom as well as on top. Enter this slab pie: plenty of filling, but plenty of crust too. I like to use rough puff pastry for an ultra-tender but shattery crust. A tightly woven lattice keeps the filling nicely packed inside (and it also allows for the option to score some of the strands for a dynamic look; see Scoring, page 89).

85 g / 3 ounces / 6 tablespoons unsalted butter

440 g / 2 medium sweet onions, such as Vidalia, diced

200 g / 4 large stalks celery, diced

220 g / 4 medium carrots, peeled and diced

15 g / 3 cloves garlic, minced

4 g / ¾ teaspoon kosher salt, or more to taste

3 g / ¾ teaspoon freshly ground black pepper

60 g / ½ cup all-purpose flour

907 g / 4 cups chicken broth

1 bay leaf

4 sprigs fresh rosemary

4 sprigs fresh thyme

77 g / ⅓ cup heavy cream

575 g / 4 cups chopped cooked chicken

190 g / 1⅓ cups fresh or frozen peas

Double recipe Rough Puff Pastry (page 50), shaped into two rectangles and chilled, or a quadruple recipe pie crust (see below), prepared as for Rough Puff Pastry, shaped into 2 rectangles, and chilled

Egg wash (see page 98)

1. In a large pot, melt 28 g / 1 ounce / 2 tablespoons of the butter over medium heat. Add the onions, celery, and carrots and cook until the onions are translucent, 5 to 6 minutes. Add the garlic and sauté until fragrant, about 1 minute. Season with salt and pepper.

2. Add the remaining 56 g / 2 ounces / 4 tablespoons butter. Once it has melted, whisk in the flour and cook, stirring constantly, until the mixture is just starting to turn golden brown,

2 to 3 minutes. Gradually whisk in the chicken broth, then bring to a simmer. Add the bay leaf, rosemary, and thyme and simmer for 15 minutes.

3. Stir in the cream, chicken, and peas, return to a simmer, and simmer for 4 to 5 minutes more. Remove the filling from the heat and cool completely. Remove and discard the bay leaf and herb stems.

(CONTINUED)

4. While the filling is cooling, prepare the pie crust: On a lightly floured surface, roll out half of the dough to a rectangle about 15 by 18 inches / 38 by 46 cm. Dock all over with a fork. Use a rolling pin to gently transfer the dough to a 9-by-13-inch / 23-by-33-cm baking pan, unfurling it over the pan. Working around the edges of the pan, gently lift the dough up and press it into the bottom and up against the sides of the pan, ensuring it makes full contact with the pan, even in the corners. There will be a generous overhang all the way around—trim it to 1½ inches / 4 cm. Refrigerate for 30 minutes.

5. Preheat the oven to 425°F / 220°C with a rack in the lower third (preferably with a Baking Steel or stone on it). Place a piece of parchment over the prepared crust and fill with pie weights. Bake for 17 to 20 minutes, until the edges of the dough start to turn golden. Remove the parchment and pie weights and bake for 5 to 6 minutes more, until the bottom appears baked and set.

6. While the crust is still hot, use kitchen scissors to trim the dough so that it's just over the edges of the pan all the way around. Cool the parbaked crust completely.

7. On a lightly floured surface, roll out the remaining disk of dough ¼ inch / 6 mm thick. Use the rolling pin to transfer it to a parchment-lined baking sheet; leave in one piece for a traditional double crust, or score it (see Scoring, page 89), or cut into strips for a tightly woven lattice (see page 96).

8. Pour the filling into the cooled pie crust. Brush the edges of the crust with egg wash. Place the top crust on top of the pie, or weave a lattice (page 94), and trim the excess dough even with the edges of the bottom crust. If desired, cut a few steam vents (see page 98). Use a fork to press the top crust to the bottom to seal. If the dough feels soft after assembly, refrigerate the pie before proceeding.

9. Brush the top of the pie with egg wash and bake until the crust is deeply golden brown (the filling may bubble up through the top crust a bit), 40 to 50 minutes. Cool for at least 15 minutes before slicing and serving.

VARIATION ///

EXTRA-LARGE CHICKEN POT SLAB PIE: You can use this recipe to create a big party-friendly chicken potpie in a half sheet pan (13 by 18 inches / 23 by 46 cm). Use a triple recipe of Rough Puff Pastry or 6 times a pie crust recipe (made as for rough puff pastry). Divide in half and shape into 2 rectangles. Roll out half of the dough for the bottom crust to a 17-by-22-inch / 38-by-56-cm rectangle. Gently transfer to the pan, carefully pressing into the base. Dock the crust all over, then bake the crust for 17 to 20 minutes with pie weights, and then 5 to 6 minutes without. Roll out the second half of dough to a similar size as the base to create the top crust. There may not be quite enough dough to do a tightly woven lattice top, but plenty to do a classic lattice, if desired. Bake the pie for 40 to 50 minutes. Cool for at least 15 minutes before serving.

Make Ahead and Storage

The filling can be made up to 3 days ahead and refrigerated, covered. The bottom crust can be parbaked up to 24 hours ahead and stored at room temperature, covered. This pie is best eaten the same day it's made. Store leftovers in the refrigerator, wrapped in plastic wrap.

RECOMMENDED CRUSTS
- Any pie dough recipe can be made as rough puff pastry: Golden Cheese Pie Dough (page 57), Saffron Compound Butter Pie Dough (page 58)

GREEN VEGGIE QUICHE

MAKES ONE 9-INCH / 23-CM QUICHE

DIFFICULTY: MEDIUM

I have three requirements for quiche: a very crisp crust, a very custardy filling, and lots of flavorful ingredients suspended inside it. This green veggie quiche is my absolute fave, but when I'm feeling decadent, I make the Cheese Lover's or BLT variations below.

One 9-inch / 23-cm pie crust (see below), parbaked and cooled completely (see page 43)

112 g / 1 cup finely grated Parmesan cheese

28 g / 1 ounce / 2 tablespoons unsalted butter

170 g / ½ bunch asparagus, ends trimmed, stalks cut into 1-inch / 2.5-cm pieces

150 g / 1 large leek, halved lengthwise and thinly sliced

130 g / 4 scallions, thinly sliced

58 g / 2 packed cups spinach

75 g / ½ cup fresh or frozen peas

340 g / 6 large eggs

77 g / ⅓ cup whole milk

60 g / ¼ cup heavy cream

2 g / ½ teaspoon kosher salt

2 g / ½ teaspoon freshly ground black pepper

40 g / ½ cup shredded Gruyère or white cheddar cheese

1. Place the cooled pie crust on a parchment-lined baking sheet. Spread 56 g / ½ cup of the grated Parmesan over the bottom of the crust in an even layer.

2. In a large sauté pan, melt the butter over medium heat. Add the asparagus and cook for 3 to 4 minutes. Add the leek and scallions and cook until wilted, 1 to 2 minutes. Stir in the spinach in batches, waiting until each addition is wilted before adding more. Add the peas and stir to combine. Remove from the heat and cool completely.

3. Preheat the oven to 375°F / 190°C with a rack in the lower third (preferably with a Baking Steel or stone on it).

4. Transfer the cooled vegetables to the prepared pie crust—don't pack them down firmly, sort of fluff the mixture up a bit as you add it.

5. In a medium bowl, whisk the eggs, milk, cream, salt, and pepper until well combined. Gently pour the custard over the vegetables. Sprinkle the remaining 56 g / ½ cup Parmesan and the Gruyère or cheddar evenly over the top.

6. Transfer the quiche to the oven and bake until the custard appears set around the edge but is still slightly jiggly in the center, 30 to 35 minutes. If desired, turn on the broiler and broil for 1 to 3 minutes to give the top more of a crust. Cool for at least 15 minutes before slicing and serving warm, or cool completely before serving.

VARIATIONS ///

CHEESE LOVER'S QUICHE: Omit the butter and veggies. Dollop 226 g / 8 ounces ricotta cheese in small spoonfuls on top of the Parmesan on the bottom crust. Whisk 60 g / ¾ cup grated Monterey Jack cheese and 160 g / 2 large shallots, finely chopped, into the custard before pouring it into the crust. Top with the Parmesan and Gruyère or cheddar and baked.

BLT QUICHE: Omit the butter and veggies. Heat a large skillet over medium heat, add 340 g / 12 ounces thick-cut bacon, chopped, and cook until the bacon is very crisp. Remove from the

Back to front: Green Veggie Quiche in Whole Wheat Crust, BLT Quiche in Spelt Crust, Cheese Lover's Quiche in Cheese Cracker Crumb Crust

pan and drain off all but 15 g / 1 tablespoon of the bacon fat. Add 100 g / ½ medium red onion, thinly sliced, and 290 g / 2 cups cherry tomatoes to the pan and sauté over medium-low heat until the onions are translucent and the tomatoes have burst, 5 to 6 minutes. Add 56 g / 2 cups arugula in batches, waiting until each batch is wilted before adding more. Cool the filling completely, then transfer to the prepared crust. Pour the custard over the filling, top with the Parmesan and Gruyère or cheddar, and bake.

Make Ahead and Storage

The crust can be parbaked up to 24 hours ahead. The quiche is best eaten the same day it's made. Store leftovers in the refrigerator, wrapped in plastic wrap.

RECOMMENDED CRUSTS

- All-Buttah Pie Dough (page 48)
- Saffron Compound Butter Pie Dough (or other Compound Butter variations—page 58)
- Golden Cheese Pie Dough (page 57)

AVOCADO GALETTE

MAKES ONE 12-BY-16-INCH / 30-BY-41-CM GALETTE

DIFFICULTY: MEDIUM

My pie-ified riff on avocado toast—lemony avocado slices arranged on top of a crisp blind-baked rectangle of puff pastry or pie dough. It's a truly luscious combination, and a flakier take on this typical breakfast, lunch, or snack.

1 recipe Rough Puff Pastry (page 50), shaped into one disk and chilled, or a double recipe pie dough (see below), prepared as for Rough Puff Pastry, shaped into one disk, and chilled

Egg wash (see page 98)

22 g / 3 tablespoons sesame seeds

648 g / 5 medium avocados, halved, pitted, peeled, and very thinly sliced

30 g / 2 tablespoons fresh lemon juice

Olive oil for drizzling

Flaky salt and freshly ground black pepper

Red pepper flakes

1. On a lightly floured surface, roll out the puff pastry into a rough rectangle a bit larger than 12 by 16 inches / 30 by 41 cm and about ¼ inch / 3 mm thick. Use the rolling pin to transfer the dough to a parchment-lined baking sheet. Use a pastry wheel or paring knife to trim the dough on all sides to make the edges straight. Brush the dough with egg wash, then dock all over with a fork. Sprinkle the sesame seeds evenly over the dough. Transfer to the refrigerator to chill while you preheat the oven.

2. Preheat the oven to 425°F / 220°C with a rack in the lower third (preferably with a Baking Steel/stone on it).

3. Bake the dough until it's evenly golden brown, 30 to 40 minutes. (Note: Here we made it with pumpernickel dough, which creates a very dark crust.) Cool completely.

4. When ready to serve, arrange the avocado slices evenly over the cooled crust, leaving about a 1½-inch / 4-cm border uncovered all around. Brush the lemon juice over the avocados, taking care to cover all the exposed surfaces. Drizzle olive oil over the avocado and sprinkle with flaky salt, pepper, and red pepper flakes. Serve immediately.

Make Ahead and Storage

This galette is best eaten the same day it's made. Store leftovers at room temperature, wrapped in plastic wrap.

NOTE

I regularly use pie dough scraps to make individual portions of this galette. They make a perfect snack or breakfast, topped with an egg. Roll out the dough ¼ inch / 3 mm thick (size/shape doesn't matter, though you can trim it into a specific shape or use a cutter). Brush with egg wash, dock, top with some sesame seeds, and bake until crisp. Top with ½ to 1 whole avocado, sliced, and with the remaining ingredients to taste.

OTHER RECOMMENDED CRUSTS
- You can make any pie crust in the book as rough puff! Try it with: Spelt Pie Dough (page 55), Whole Wheat Pie Dough (page 54), and Pumpernickel Pie Dough (pictured; page 55).

SWEET-AND-SPICY KALE AND SQUASH PITHIVIERS

MAKES ONE 12-INCH / 30-CM PIE

DIFFICULTY: MEDIUM

This hearty pie is the perfect way to ring in autumn, but I serve it well into winter. The filling is roasted on a baking sheet, then encased in a double-crust puff pastry pie (or pithiviers). What makes this filling so good is the sweet and briny Peppadew peppers that bring all the flavors together.

60 g / 1 head garlic

45 g / 3 tablespoons extra-virgin olive oil

567 g / 20 ounces butternut or honeynut squash, peeled, seeded, and diced (about 431 g / 3 cups, from 1 small squash)

390 g / 1 large sweet onion, diced

Kosher salt and freshly ground black pepper

145 g / 1 large bunch lacinato kale, stems removed, and torn into bite-size pieces

220 g / 1 cup finely chopped Peppadew peppers

22 g / 1 tablespoon honey

4 g / 1 teaspoon red pepper flakes

1 recipe Rough Puff Pastry (page 50), shaped into disks and chilled, or a double recipe pie dough (see below), prepared as for Rough Puff Pastry, shaped into 2 disks, and chilled

Egg wash (see page 98)

1. Preheat the oven to 375°F / 190°C with a rack in the lower third.

2. Cut off the top third of the head of garlic and set the garlic on a piece of foil large enough to enclose it. Drizzle 15 g / 1 tablespoon of the olive oil over the top of the garlic and wrap it in the foil. Toss the squash and onion together on a large baking sheet. Add the remaining 30 g / 2 tablespoons olive oil and toss well to coat, then spread out the vegetables in an even layer. Season the squash and onion with salt and pepper. Add the garlic to the baking sheet.

3. Transfer to the oven and roast until the squash and onion are tender and starting to brown, about 30 minutes. Add the kale to the squash/onion

mixture and toss well to combine. Return to the oven and roast for 10 to 15 minutes. Remove from the oven, and remove the garlic from the pan.

4. Add the peppers to the vegetable mixture, drizzle with the honey, sprinkle with the pepper flakes, and stir to combine. After the garlic has cooled a bit, squeeze out the cloves and stir into the veggie mixture, mashing the garlic up as you stir. Cool the filling completely.

5. While the filling is cooling, prepare the dough: On a lightly floured surface, roll out one half of the dough to a round about 12 inches / 30 cm across. Trim the edges with a pastry wheel and dock generously all over with a fork. Use a rolling pin to gently transfer the dough to a parchment-lined baking sheet, unfurling it over the pan. Place another piece of parchment on top and refrigerate.

6. Preheat the oven to 425°F / 220°C with a rack in the lower third (preferably with a Baking Steel or stone on it).

7. Gently spoon the cooled filling into the center of the dough and spread into an even layer, leaving a 1-inch / 2.5-cm border uncovered all the way around. Brush the border with egg wash.

8. On a lightly floured surface, roll out the remaining dough to a round about 13 inches / 33 cm across and ¼ inch / 6 mm thick. Use the rolling pin to transfer it to the pie, unfurling it

so it lines up with the bottom crust. Crimp (see page 80) the edges all the way around to seal. If the dough feels soft after assembly, refrigerate the pie.

9. If desired, score the top crust (see Scoring, page 89); brush it with egg wash before or after scoring, depending on the desired look. Bake until the crust is deeply golden brown (the filling may visibly bubble through the top crust a bit), 40 to 50 minutes. Cool for at least 15 minutes before slicing and serving.

Make Ahead and Storage

The filling can be made up to 3 days ahead and refrigerated in an airtight container. This pie is best eaten the same day it's made. Store leftovers at room temperature, wrapped in plastic wrap.

RECOMMENDED CRUSTS

- Any pie dough recipe can be made as rough puff pastry: Golden Cheese Pie Dough (page 57), Saffron Compound Butter Pie Dough (or other Compound Butter Pie Doughs—page 58).

SMOKED SALMON TART WITH "EVERYTHING" PIE CRUST

MAKES ONE 12-INCH /
30-CM TART

DIFFICULTY: MEDIUM

I'm not saying I love puff pastry so much that it could ever truly replace a bagel, but I am saying that I love me some smoked salmon and cream cheese with all the fixins so much that I decided to try it in tart form. My assistant and fellow bagel lover, Katie, had the brilliant idea to cut a hole in the center of the crust so this delicious breakfast or brunch tart (or breakfast-for-dinner pie) even looks like a big bagel.

1 recipe Rough Puff Pastry (page 50), shaped into a disk and chilled, or a double recipe of pie dough (see below), prepared as for Rough Puff Pastry, shaped into a disk, and chilled

Egg wash (see page 98)

30 g / 3 tablespoons everything bagel topping (see Note)

WHIPPED CREAM CHEESE

283 g / 10 ounces cream cheese, at room temperature

52 g / ¼ cup drained capers, roughly chopped

Grated zest of 1 lemon

1 g / ½ teaspoon freshly ground black pepper

365 g / 2 medium tomatoes, cores removed and thinly sliced

340 g / 12 ounces thinly sliced smoked salmon

43 g / ⅓ cup minced red onion

26 g / ⅓ cup thinly sliced scallions

Small sprig fresh dill for garnish

1. On a lightly floured surface, roll out the dough into a circle a bit larger than 12 inches / 30 cm across and about ¼ inch / 3 mm thick. Use the rolling pin to transfer the dough to a parchment-lined baking sheet. Using a cake pan, a plate, or a round of parchment paper as a guide, trim the dough into a 12-inch / 30-cm-wide round. Use a 4-inch / 10-cm guide (or cookie or biscuit cutter) to cut a round of dough from the center and remove it (save it with your dough scraps). Brush the dough with egg wash, then dock all over with a fork. Sprinkle the everything topping evenly over the dough.

2. Transfer the dough to the refrigerator to chill while you preheat the oven.

3. Preheat the oven to 425°F / 220°C with a rack in the lower third (preferably with a Baking Steel or stone on it).

4. Bake the dough until it's evenly golden brown, 25 to 30 minutes. Cool completely.

5. Meanwhile, make the whipped cream cheese: In the bowl of a stand mixer fitted with the whip attachment, whip the cream cheese, capers, lemon zest, and pepper until light, fluffy, and well combined. Refrigerate, covered, until ready to use.

6. When ready to serve, transfer the cream cheese to a disposable pastry bag (or a large zip-top bag) and cut a ½-inch / 1-cm opening in the tip (or a bottom corner of the bag). Pipe the mixture in a back-and-forth motion over the crust, aiming to make a ring in the center of the dough round, and covering most of it. Arrange the tomato slices on top of the cream cheese in an even layer, mostly covering the cream cheese. Arrange the smoked salmon on top of the tomatoes so it appears a bit ruffle-y; don't just lay the slices flat. Scatter the red onion, scallions, and dill on top. Serve immediately.

Make Ahead and Storage

This tart is best eaten just after assembly. Store leftovers in the refrigerator, wrapped in plastic wrap.

NOTE ⬦⬦⬦⬦⬦⬦⬦⬦⬦⬦⬦⬦⬦⬦⬦⬦⬦⬦⬦⬦⬦⬦

If you're unable to purchase everything topping, you can make your own: In a small bowl, whisk 15 g / 2 tablespoons white sesame seeds, 15 g / 2 tablespoons black sesame seeds, 12 g / 2 tablespoons poppy seeds, 20 g / 2 tablespoons dried garlic flakes, 20 g / 2 tablespoons dried minced onion, and 10 g / 2 teaspoons kosher salt together (this will make more than you need for this recipe).

RECOMMENDED CRUSTS

- You can make any pie crust in the book as rough puff pastry: Pumpernickel Pie Dough (page 55), Whole Wheat Pie Dough (page 54), Rye Pie Dough (page 55)

CROQUE MONSIEUR PIELETS

MAKES 8 PIELETS

DIFFICULTY: MEDIUM

Croque monsieur—a French ham and cheese sandwich drowned in béchamel—is already perfect in every way. But, it turns out, it pie-ifies pretty perfectly too. For these individual pastries, a base of rough puff pastry is topped with ham, cheese, and a thick béchamel sauce, which melts over everything in the oven to encase it in a beautiful golden-brown crust. Definitely consider topping each with a runny fried egg to croque madame it up.

BÉCHAMEL

43 g / 1½ ounces / 3 tablespoons unsalted butter

100 g / 2 shallots, minced

15 g / 2 tablespoons all-purpose flour

170 g / ¾ cup whole milk

12 g / 1 tablespoon Dijon mustard

Pinch of fine sea salt

1 g / ½ teaspoon white pepper

Scant 1 g / ¼ teaspoon freshly grated nutmeg

1 recipe Rough Puff Pastry (page 50), chilled, or a double recipe pie dough (see below), prepared as for Rough Puff Pastry, shaped into disks, and chilled

Egg wash (see page 98)

226 g / 8 ounces prosciutto, serrano ham, or thinly sliced high-quality ham

226 g / 8 ounces Gruyère cheese, shredded

Chopped fresh chives for garnish

1. Make the béchamel: In a small pot, melt the butter over medium heat. Add the shallots and cook until tender and translucent, 4 to 5 minutes. Sprinkle the flour over the shallots, stir well to combine, and cook over medium-low heat for 30 seconds to 1 minute. Gradually add the milk and bring to a simmer, whisking constantly. Continue to simmer until the sauce thickens, 2 to 3 minutes. Whisk in the mustard, salt, pepper, and nutmeg, then transfer to a medium bowl to cool completely.

2. Line two baking sheets with parchment. On a lightly floured surface, roll out half of the dough into a large rectangle about 6 by 16 inches / 15 by 41 cm and slightly thicker than ¼ inch / 6 mm. Use a pastry wheel, bench knife, or sharp knife to cut the dough into 4 equal pieces (each about 3 by 8 inches / 8 by 20 cm) and transfer to one of the prepared baking sheets; stagger them, but they can be pretty close together. Refrigerate while you repeat with the second half of the dough, placing the pieces on the second baking sheet (if necessary, you can place a piece of parchment on top of the first sheet of pastry and stack the other tray on top).

3. Preheat the oven to 425°F / 220°C with a rack in the lower third (preferably with a Baking Steel or stone on it).

4. Brush each piece of dough with egg wash, then dock all over with a fork. Arrange 28 g / 1 ounce of ham in the center of each rectangle and top with 21 g / ¾ ounce of the shredded cheese. Spoon 30 g / 1 heaping tablespoon béchamel in a line down the center of each pastry over the cheese.

5. Transfer the pan to the oven and bake until the crusts are deeply golden brown and the béchamel and cheese have formed a golden brown crust, 30 to 35 minutes. Serve hot, garnished with chives.

Croque Monsieur and Madame Pielets on Golden Cheese Crust (left), and Smoked Salmon Tart on "Everything" Crust (right)

VARIATION ///////////////////////////////////////

CROQUE MADAME PIELETS: Top each pielet with a fried egg before garnishing with chives.

Make Ahead and Storage

Leftover pielets reheat beautifully. Store, wrapped tightly in plastic wrap, in the refrigerator for up to 2 days. To reheat, unwrap the pastries and place on a parchment-lined baking sheet. Turn the oven to 400°F / 205°C with a rack in the middle and place the baking sheet on it. Leave the pielets in the oven for 5 minutes after it has preheated, and they will be crisp and heated through.

RECOMMENDED CRUSTS

- Golden Cheese Pie Dough (page 57)
- Chive Compound Butter Pie Dough (page 58)
- Herby Whole Wheat Pie Dough (page 54)

BEEF AND MUSHROOM PIE

MAKES ONE 9-INCH /
23-CM DEEP-DISH PIE

DIFFICULTY: MEDIUM

Here's my version of those classic, towering savory pies from the U.K., filled with a tender beef and mushroom stew. I like to bake this style of pie in a springform pan, and depending on how deep the pan is, it can be tricky to line it without small tears in the dough. Luckily, my hot-water crust is super-patchable—in fact, you can even forgo rolling out the bottom crust altogether and press it in. Just take care to make it even over the bottom and up the sides of the pan.

BEEF-AND MUSHROOM FILLING

30 g / 2 tablespoons vegetable oil

906 g / 2 pounds beef stew meat, cut into 1-inch /
   2-cm cubes

Kosher salt and freshly ground black pepper

283 g / 10 ounces cremini or button mushrooms,
   quartered

226 g / 8 ounces thick-cut bacon, diced

230 g / 1 medium sweet onion, diced

200 g / 2 stalks celery, diced

225g / 3 medium carrots, peeled and diced

40 g / ⅓ cup all-purpose flour

301 g / 1⅓ cups stout beer (or other dark beer)

454 g / 2 cups beef broth

1 bay leaf

4 g / 2 tablespoons chopped fresh thyme

1 recipe Hot-Water Crust (page 60)
Egg wash (see page 98)

1. Make the filling: In a large pot, heat the oil over medium heat. Season the beef with salt and pepper. Add the beef to the pot, working in batches to avoid crowding the pot, and sear, turning occasionally, until well browned on all sides, 1 to 2 minutes per side. Transfer the beef to a large plate as it is browned.

2. Add the mushrooms to the pot and cook until they are tender and beginning to brown, 5 to 7 minutes. Using a slotted spoon, remove from the pot and add to the plate with the beef.

3. Drain off any oil remaining in the pot. Add the bacon and cook until well browned and crisp. Using a slotted spoon, remove the bacon from the pot and set aside with the beef/mushrooms, leaving the bacon fat in the pot.

4. Add the onion, celery, and carrots to the pot and cook until just starting to soften, 4 to 5 minutes. Sprinkle with the flour and stir well to combine. Add the beer and stir well to combine and to release any browned bits from the bottom of the pot. Add the beef broth and bay leaf and bring to a simmer.

5. Add the beef, mushrooms, and bacon to the pot, stirring to combine, and return to a simmer. Continue to simmer, uncovered, until the beef is tender, 40 to 50 minutes. Stir in 3 g / ½ teaspoon salt, 3 g / ¾ teaspoon pepper, and the thyme. Remove from the heat and cool completely.

6. While the filling is cooling, prepare the pie crust. Divide dough into 2 pieces—you'll use about two thirds of the dough to line the bottom and sides of the pan and about one third of it for the top. Wrap the portion for the top dough in plastic wrap while you prepare the bottom crust.

7. Using parchment paper (see page 36), roll out the larger piece of dough to a round ¼ inch / 3 mm thick and line a 9-inch / 23-cm springform pan with it: Gently lift up the dough at the edges of the pan and press it into the base—you want it to be flush against the bottom and sides of the pan—allowing the excess dough to hang over the edges of the pan. If the dough rips or tears, simply patch it with a scrap of dough.

8. Preheat the oven to 375°F / 190°C with a rack in the lower third (preferably with a Baking Steel or stone on the bottom rack).

9. Spoon the cooled filling into the prepared bottom crust and spread into an even layer. Roll out the remaining dough, again using parchment paper, and gently transfer it to the top of the pie. Gently press the edges of the top crust and bottom crust together to seal, and crimp as desired (see page 80).

10. Brush the crust with egg wash, avoiding the edges, which tend to brown enough on their own. Cut a few vents in the top crust. Transfer the pie to the oven and bake until the crust is deeply golden brown (the filling may bubble up through the top crust a bit), 50 minutes to 1 hour. Cool for at least 15 minutes before slicing and serving.

Make Ahead and Storage

The filling can be made up to 3 days ahead and refrigerated in an airtight container. This pie is best eaten the same day it's made. Store leftovers in the refrigerator in an airtight container.

OTHER RECOMMENDED CRUSTS
- This filling is also delicious in a pie dough or Rough Puff Pastry crust—use the recipe for the Chicken Pot Slab Pie (page 301) for guidance.

RECOMMENDED CRUSTS
- Rye Pie Dough (page 55)
- Golden Cheese Pie Dough (page 57)
- Chive, Scallion, or Ramp Pie Dough (page 58)

ROASTED TOMATO AND GOOEY CHEESE FREE-FORM PIE

MAKES ONE 13-BY-13-INCH / 33-BY-33-CM PIE

DIFFICULTY: MEDIUM

I first made this pie for a small dinner party for my friend Liliana and her family when my own family was in town visiting. It was late summer, so I made a free-form pie with lots of cherry tomatoes and covered them with a soft cheese. The cheese melts into the tomatoes, the two melding into one incredible flavor. We crunched away at flaky slices under twinkly lights and this pie earned a special place in my heart and memory.

907 g / 2 pounds cherry tomatoes

30 g / 6 large cloves garlic, unpeeled, smashed with the side of a knife

45 g / 3 tablespoons extra-virgin olive oil

3 g / 1 tablespoon chopped fresh rosemary, plus a few sprigs for garnish

3 g / 1 tablespoon chopped fresh thyme, plus a few sprigs for garnish

4 g / ¾ teaspoon kosher salt

2 g / ½ teaspoon freshly ground black pepper

1 recipe Rough Puff Pastry (page 50), chilled, or a double recipe pie dough (see opposite), prepared as for rough puff pastry, shaped into a disk, and chilled

50 g / ½ cup grated Parmesan cheese, plus more for finishing

340 g / 12 ounces Brie, Camembert, or other soft-rind creamy cheese, cut into 1-inch / 2.5-cm thick slices

Egg wash (see page 98)

1. Preheat the oven to 400°F / 205°C.

2. Spread the tomatoes and garlic out on an unlined baking sheet. Drizzle the olive oil over the tomatoes and toss well to coat. Sprinkle the rosemary and thyme evenly over the tomatoes, then season with salt and pepper. Transfer the baking sheet to the oven and roast until the tomatoes are blistered and collapsed, 25 to 30 minutes. Let the tomatoes cool completely. Raise the oven temperature to 425°F / 220°C.

3. While the tomatoes cool, on a lightly floured surface, roll out the dough to a square a little large than 15 by 15 inches / 38 by 38 cm and about ¼ inch / 3 mm thick. Transfer to a parchment-lined baking sheet (don't worry if it hangs over the edges of the pan for now—you will be folding the edges over) and dock it all over with a fork.

4. Squeeze the roasted garlic out of its skin into a small bowl and use a fork to mash it with the Parmesan. Spread the mixture onto the dough, leaving at least 2 inches / 5 cm uncovered around the edges. Arrange the tomatoes in a single layer on the dough, again leaving the edges uncovered. Scatter the cheese evenly over the tomatoes. Fold the uncovered edges of the dough up over the tomatoes, encasing the perimeter of the filling.

5. Brush egg wash over the edges of the dough and sprinkle a little more Parmesan on top.

6. Transfer the baking sheet to the oven and bake the pie until the crust is evenly golden brown and very crisp, 30 to 35 minutes. Allow the galette to cool for 15 minutes before serving, garnished with the rosemary and thyme sprigs.

Make Ahead and Storage

This pie is best eaten the day it's made. Store leftovers at room temperature, wrapped tightly in plastic wrap.

RED ONION TARTE TATIN

MAKES ONE 12-INCH /
30-CM PIE

DIFFICULTY: MEDIUM

The upside-down tarte Tatin method works great with vegetables as well as with fruits, although some will require a few extra steps of cooking because of their higher moisture content. The sherry and balsamic vinegar cook down to help deeply caramelize the onions without the sugar used in a dessert pie. In the peak of summer tomato season, try the cherry tomato variation below.

½ recipe Rough Puff Pastry (page 50), chilled, 1 recipe pie dough (see below), prepared as for Rough Puff Pastry, shaped into a disk, and chilled

56 g / 2 ounces / 4 tablespoons unsalted butter

About 1200 g / 5 to 7 small red onions, peeled, stem ends left intact, and cut in half from root to tip

Kosher salt and freshly ground black pepper

60 g / ¼ cup sherry

15 g / 1 tablespoon balsamic vinegar

4 sprigs fresh thyme

2 sprigs fresh rosemary

Grated Parmesan cheese for finishing (optional)

1. Preheat the oven to 400°F / 205°C with a rack in the lower third (preferably with a Baking Steel or stone on it). Line a baking sheet with parchment paper.

2. On a lightly floured surface, roll out the dough into a circle about 13 inches / 33 cm wide. Dock the dough all over with a fork. Use the rolling pin to gently transfer the dough to the prepared baking sheet, unfurling it onto the pan. Chill while you work on the onions.

3. In a 12-inch / 30-cm ovenproof skillet, preferably cast iron, melt the butter over medium heat. Add the onions, rounded halves down, packing them as tightly as possible into the pan (they will shrink as they cook). Cook, undisturbed, until the onions have softened slightly and begun to brown, 12 to 15 minutes.

4. Gently flip each of the onions and season with salt and pepper, then flip again so the browned side is down again. Add the sherry and balsamic vinegar, bring to a simmer, and cook until reduced slightly, 1 to 2 minutes. Arrange the herb sprigs in between the onions.

5. Transfer the skillet to the oven and roast until the onions are golden and tender, 15 to 20 minutes.

6. Remove the skillet from the oven and use a fork or pair of tongs to push the onions to pack them tightly together—this should be easier now that they've softened. Gently drape the pastry over the onions, folding it in a little at the edges to encase them.

7. Return the pan to the oven and bake until the pastry is very golden brown, 20 to 25 minutes. Remove from the oven and cool for 5 minutes.

8. Carefully invert the tarte Tatin onto a cutting board and lift off the pan. Let cool for 5 minutes more. If using, finish with a generous grating of Parmesan cheese.

VARIATION //

CHERRY TOMATO TARTE TATIN: Replace the onions with 907 g / 2 pounds cherry tomatoes. In step 3, cook the tomatoes for 15 to 20 minutes, until the juices they release have reduced. Season the tomatoes without flipping them in step 4, then proceed as directed. If desired, replace the rosemary sprigs with 3 sprigs fresh oregano.

Make Ahead and Storage

This pie is best eaten the day it's made. Store leftovers at room temperature, wrapped tightly in plastic wrap.

RECOMMENDED CRUSTS

- Spelt Pie Dough (page 55)
- Golden Cheese Pie Dough (page 57)
- Saffron Compound Butter Pie Dough (page 58)

SAUSAGE AND CARAMELIZED ONION PIE WITH SOFT PRETZEL CRUST

MAKES ONE 12-INCH / 30-CM PIE

DIFFICULTY: HARD

In pastry school, I used to work bread-baking shifts around campus. One of the things we often made were called "stuffed pretzels," rounds of soft pretzel dough with a mound of filling in the center. I always loved them, and I dreamt of making a giant, sliceable, sharable version. Hence this "pie," which boasts a soft and chewy soft pretzel crust and a filling made with lots of caramelized onions, sausage, and soft cheese.

PRETZEL CRUST

422 g / 3½ cups bread flour

25 g / 2 tablespoons granulated sugar

4 g / 1 teaspoon instant yeast

4 g / 1 teaspoon fine sea salt

170 g / ¾ cup warm water (about 95°F / 35°C)

28 g / 1 ounce / 2 tablespoons unsalted butter, at room temperature

Coarse or flaky salt for sprinkling

FILLING

340 g / 4 links garlic or Italian sausage

15 g / 1 tablespoon extra-virgin olive oil

14 g / ½ ounce / 1 tablespoon unsalted butter

450 g / 2 large sweet onions, thinly sliced

Kosher salt and freshly ground black pepper

15 g / 1 tablespoon balsamic vinegar (use the good stuff)

142 g / 5 ounces soft herb cheese, such as Boursin, or goat cheese

5 g / 1 tablespoon chopped fresh sage

4 g / 2 teaspoons chopped fresh oregano

2 g / 1 teaspoon chopped fresh rosemary

LYE SOLUTION
(see Notes for a replacement if this whole lye thing is freaking you out)

7 g / 0.25 ounce food-grade lye (see Notes)

170 g / ¾ cup boiling water

113 g / ½ cup cold water

1. Make the dough: In the bowl of a stand mixer fitted with the dough hook, mix the flour, sugar, yeast, salt, water, and butter on low speed for 3 minutes. Raise the speed to medium and mix for 4 minutes more. Transfer the dough to a lightly greased bowl. Cover with plastic wrap and let rise in a warm place for 1 hour, or until it's doubled in size.

2. While the dough rises, make the filling: Preheat the oven to 375°F / 190°C. Line a baking sheet with aluminum foil.

3. Place the sausages on the foil-lined baking sheet. Pierce each a few times with the tip of a paring knife. Transfer the sausages to the oven and bake until cooked through, 12 to 15 minutes. Set aside to cool.

4. In a large sauté pan, heat the olive oil and butter over medium heat. Add the onions and cook until they become translucent, 4 to 5 minutes. Reduce heat to low and cook, stirring occasionally, until the onions are deeply golden brown and caramelized, 35 to 40 minutes. Season with salt and pepper.

5. Add the balsamic vinegar to the onions and stir well (if any brown bits have collected at the bottom of the pan, it will help release them). Remove from the heat.

(CONTINUED)

6. When the dough has risen, roll it out on a lightly floured surface into a circle about 12 inches / 30 cm wide. Gently transfer it to a parchment-lined baking sheet. If in the process it shrinks to less than 12 inch / 30 cm, use your fingers to gently press and/or stretch it to make it a bit bigger. Cover with greased plastic wrap or a clean kitchen towel and let rise for 20 minutes.

7. While the dough rises, make the lye solution (see Note for important safety instructions). Wear protective eyewear (such as goggles or other glasses) and latex gloves when working with lye. Carefully pour the lye into a medium metal bowl.

8. Pour the boiling water over the lye and stir with a metal spoon until the lye is dissolved. Stir in the cold water and set aside. Be sure to label the mixture so it isn't mistaken for water in your kitchen.

9. Toward the end of the rise time, preheat the oven to 425°F / 220°C.

10. Wearing gloves, brush the dough all over 3 or 4 times with the lye solution. Sprinkle the edges of the dough with coarse or flaky salt. Dollop the cooled onions evenly over the dough and gently spread into an even layer, leaving a 1-inch / 2.5-cm border of dough all the way around. Cut the sausages into ½-inch / 1-cm-thick slices (I like to cut them on a sharp bias for a more interesting shape) and arrange evenly over the onions. Sprinkle the cheese, sage, oregano, and rosemary over the top.

11. Transfer to the oven and bake until the pretzel dough is deeply golden brown and the sausage is browned and beginning to crisp, 25 to 30 minutes. Cool for at least 10 minutes before serving, or cool completely and serve at room temperature.

Make Ahead and Storage

The pie is best eaten the same day it's made, but leftovers can be refreshed. Wrap leftover slices in aluminum foil and refresh as described on page 21.

NOTES ◇◇◇◇◇◇◇◇◇◇◇◇◇◇◇◇◇◇◇◇◇◇◇◇◇◇◇◇

Lye guarantees the best pretzel results—it makes the crust really brown and the pretzels super-chewy. But it is also a powerful chemical that can give you a chemical burn if not handled carefully. When preparing the lye solution, it's important to protect your eyes (sunglasses work in a pinch, but goggles are best). Never touch powdered lye with your hands. Pour it into the bowl or use a spoon. When using the solution, it's important to cover any exposed skin (wear gloves). Wash your hands when you're finished with the lye, and wear gloves while you wash the bowl and any utensils that were in contact with the lye solution.

If you prefer, you can replace the lye solution with more common ingredients. Place 42 g / 3 tablespoons baking soda in a medium bowl and pour 1 cup boiling water over it, stirring until dissolved. Use as directed in Step 10.

SHRIMP-BOIL PIE

MAKES ONE 10-BY-16-INCH / 25-BY-41-CM PIE

DIFFICULTY: EASY

My first true "boil" dinner was at my friend Rob's house in the Hudson Valley early one fall. Rob set up a long table covered with newspaper between rows of apple trees. It was one of the first crisp days of the year, and we drank hard cider while Brimley dashed through the leaves and our feast bubbled away. I was in awe when Rob poured the whole thing out into the center of the paper-lined table. I relive a little of that magic when I make this shrimp-boil pie, which is best served with a side of friends, and maybe a little hot sauce.

1 recipe Rough Puff Pastry (page 50), shaped into a 1-inch / 2-cm rectangle and chilled

Egg wash (see page 98)

43 g / 1½ ounces / 3 tablespoons unsalted butter

30 g / 3 cloves garlic, minced

10 g / 1 tablespoon Old Bay seasoning

283 g / 10 ounces baby red or gold potatoes, halved (quartered if larger than bite-size)

225 g / 1½ cups corn kernels (preferably cut fresh from the cob; see Note)

340 g / 12 ounces smoked andouille sausage, sliced ½ inch / 1 cm thick on the bias

454 g / 1 pound medium (36–40) shrimp, peeled

113 g / 1 medium lemon, cut into wedges

10 g / ¼ cup chopped fresh parsley

Hot sauce for serving (optional)

1. Preheat the oven to 400°F / 205°C with a rack in the lower third (preferably with a Baking Steel or stone on it).

2. On a lightly floured surface, roll out the dough into a rectangle a little larger than 10 by 16 inches / 25 by 41 cm and about ¼ inch / 3 mm thick. Use the rolling pin to transfer it to the prepared baking sheet. Brush the dough all over with egg wash, then dock all over with a fork. If desired, use a pastry wheel or paring knife to trim the edges to make them straight. Refrigerate while you prepare the filling.

3. In a small pot, melt the butter over medium heat. Add the garlic and cook until fragrant, about 1 minute. Remove from the heat and stir in the Old Bay.

4. In a large bowl, toss the potatoes, corn, and sausage together. Add the seasoned butter and toss until everything is evenly coated.

5. Remove the dough from the refrigerator and arrange the filling evenly over it (if there's butter left in the bottom of the bowl, leave it there). Add the shrimp to the bowl and toss with the remaining butter to coat; set aside.

6. Transfer the pie to the oven (shrimp comes later!) and bake until the crust is lightly golden brown and the potatoes are tender, about 30 minutes.

7. Arrange the shrimp evenly over the surface of the dough, return to the oven, and bake until the shrimp are fully cooked and the dough is deeply golden brown, 12 to 15 minutes. Let the pie cool for 10 minutes.

8. Squeeze the lemon juice over the pie and finish with the parsley. Serve immediately, with hot sauce, if desired.

(CONTINUED)

Make Ahead and Storage

This pie is best eaten the same day it's made. Store leftovers in the refrigerator in an airtight container. Leftovers can be refreshed as described in Refreshing Whole Pies on page 21.

NOTE

To give this a more classic look, when you cut the corn off the cob, try to get some portions of kernels that stay stuck together (this happens more readily with very fresh corn). Carefully set these portions aside, then arrange them on top of the filling after assembling the pie (step 5).

OTHER RECOMMENDED CRUSTS
- Whole Wheat Pie Dough (page 54)
- Spelt Pie Dough (page 55)
- Cornmeal Pie Dough (page 55)

Top: Shrimp Boil Pie
Below: Peach, Shallot, and Prosciutto Pie

PEACH, SHALLOT, AND PROSCIUTTO PIE

MAKES EIGHT 4-BY-4-INCH / 10-BY-10-CM INDIVIDUAL PIES

DIFFICULTY: MEDIUM

I love the combination of salty prosciutto with sweet summer peaches. This rectangular pie is scored into squares before baking and then cut into individual portions to serve. Don't skimp on the Parmesan at the end—you want a full, fluffy layer of cheese on each piece.

Double recipe Golden Cheese Pie Dough (page 57), prepared as for Rough Puff Pastry (page 50), shaped into a rectangle, and chilled

Egg wash (see page 98)

75 g / 3 medium shallots, thinly sliced

About 740 g / 1 pound 10 ounces peaches (4 medium), halved and pitted

85 g / ¼ cup honey

10 g / 2 tablespoons chopped fresh rosemary

Aleppo pepper or red pepper flakes

56 g / 2 ounces thinly sliced prosciutto

85 g / 3 ounces Parmesan cheese, finely grated, to finish

1. Preheat the oven to 425°F / 220°C with a rack in the lower third (preferably with a Baking Steel or stone on it). Line a baking sheet with parchment paper.

2. On a lightly floured surface, roll out the dough to a rectangle slightly larger than 8 by 16 inches / 20 by 41 cm and a bit thicker than ¼ inch / 3 mm. Use the rolling pin to gently transfer the dough to the prepared baking sheet, unfurling it onto the pan. Use a pastry wheel to trim the dough to 8 by 16 inches / 20 by 41 cm. Brush the entire surface with egg wash and dock generously all over with a fork.

3. Use a paring knife to score the dough (do not cut all the way through, just mark it) lengthwise in half to make two 4-by-16-inch / 10-by-41-cm rectangles. Then score each rectangle crosswise at 4-inch / 10-cm intervals so you have 8 marked squares.

4. Divide the shallot slices evenly among the 8 squares. Place a peach half in the center of each square. Drizzle 11 g / 1½ teaspoons honey on top of each peach, then sprinkle with the rosemary and red pepper.

5. Transfer to the oven and bake until the crust is deeply golden brown and the peaches and shallots are tender, 35 to 40 minutes. Cool for at least 10 minutes.

6. Arrange one eighth (7 g / ¼ ounce) of the prosciutto on top of each square. Garnish the whole thing generously with grated Parmesan cheese and use a knife to cut the pie into the 8 marked squares.

Make Ahead and Storage

This pie is best eaten the same day it's made. Store leftovers in the refrigerator, wrapped in plastic wrap.

OTHER RECOMMENDED CRUSTS
- Rough Puff Pastry (page 50) or another dough made as for Rough Puff Pastry, such as Saffron Compound Butter Pie Dough (or other Compound Butter Pie Doughs—page 58)

RATATOUILLE GALETTE

MAKES ONE 12-INCH /
30-CM GALETTE

DIFFICULTY: MEDIUM

The end-of-summer harvest is always so bountiful that I often find myself making a few pots of ratatouille to use up all the produce I haul home from the market. I add a creamy layer of ricotta to the bottom of this galette, which soaks up some of the juices from the vegetables as they cook.

1 recipe Rough Puff Pastry (page 50), shaped into a single disk and chilled, or a double recipe pie dough (see below), prepared as for Rough Puff Pastry, shaped into a disk, and chilled

283 g / 10 ounces whole-milk ricotta cheese (about 1 heaping cup)

33 g / ⅓ cup grated Parmesan cheese, plus more for finishing

100 g / 2 small shallots, minced

10 g / 3 cloves garlic, minced

56 g / 1 large egg, lightly whisked

5 g / 1 tablespoon chopped fresh oregano

1 g / 2 teaspoons chopped fresh thyme

2 g / ½ teaspoon fine sea salt, plus more to taste

2 g / ½ teaspoon freshly ground black pepper, plus more to taste

227 g / 8 ounces red bell pepper (1 large), quartered, stem, seeds, and ribs removed

227 g / 8 ounces yellow bell pepper (1 large), quartered, stem, seeds, and ribs removed

227 g / 8 ounces zucchini (1 medium), thinly sliced

227 g / 8 ounces summer squash (1 medium), thinly sliced

300 g / 10½ ounces Italian eggplant (1 medium), thinly sliced

227 g / 8 ounces tomatoes (2 medium), thinly sliced

30 g / 2 tablespoons extra-virgin olive oil

Egg wash (see page 98)

Chopped, torn, or small whole fresh basil leaves for garnish

Chopped, torn, or small whole fresh parsley leaves for garnish

1. Line a baking sheet with parchment paper. On a lightly floured surface, roll out the dough into a round 15 to 16 inches / 38 to 41 cm wide and ¼ inch / 6 mm thick. Use the rolling pin to transfer the dough to the prepared baking sheet, unfurling it onto the pan—the edges may hang over the pan at this point, but you'll fold them over later. Cover with plastic wrap and refrigerate while you prepare the filling.

2. In a medium bowl, stir the ricotta, Parmesan, shallots, garlic, egg, oregano, thyme, salt, and pepper until well combined. Set aside.

3. Cut the bell peppers into pieces about the same width as the zucchini and squash slices.

4. Preheat the oven to 425°F / 220°C with a rack in the lower third (preferably with a Baking Steel or stone on it).

5. When the oven is hot, remove the crust from the fridge and uncover it. Spoon the ricotta mixture into the center of the dough and spread into an even layer, leaving a 1½-inch / 4-cm border uncovered all around. Arrange the vegetables in concentric circles over the ricotta mixture, overlapping the slices tightly and alternating types of vegetables as you work. Drizzle the olive oil evenly over the vegetables and season with more salt and pepper.

6. Fold the excess dough up over to encase the filling, pleating it as needed. Brush the exposed dough with egg wash and sprinkle grated Parmesan generously over it.

7. Bake the galette until the crust is deeply golden brown and the vegetables are tender, 45 to 50 minutes. Cool for at least 20 minutes before slicing and serving warm, or cool completely and serve at room temperature. Garnish with basil and parsley just before serving.

Make Ahead and Storage

The pie is best eaten the same day it's made, but leftovers can be refreshed as described on page 21.

RECOMMENDED CRUSTS
- Try this with Spelt Pie Dough (page 55), Saffron Compound Butter Pie Dough (or other Compound Butter Pie Dough—page 58), or Golden Cheese Pie Dough (page 57).

Leftover Pie: It's What's for Dinner

- Step One: Go to your fridge.
- Step Two: Find leftover roasted veggies, stir-fry, beef stew, or casserole *du jour*.
- Step Three: Toss those ingredients into a parbaked pie crust, and you're already halfway to dinner!

BEET AND HERBED CHEESE SKILLET PIE

MAKES ONE 12-INCH / 30-CM PIE

DIFFICULTY: MEDIUM

One summer in Kansas, I helped my mom harvest some fresh beets from the garden. I sliced them thin and arranged them tightly in a skillet, then roasted them until the tops were lightly crisp and the centers were soft. That dish inspired this pie, which is made even better with a base of a tangy, chive-y cheese mixture and my Golden Cheese Pie Dough.

1245 g / 2¾ pounds medium red beets (see Note), peeled

1245 g / 2¾ pounds medium yellow beets, peeled

1 recipe Golden Cheese Pie Dough (page 57), shaped into a disk and chilled

226 g / 8 ounces goat cheese, crumbled

226 g / 8 ounces mascarpone cheese

56 g / 1 large egg, lightly whisked

25 g / ½ cup minced fresh chives, plus more for garnish

5 g / 1 tablespoon minced fresh rosemary

2 g / ½ teaspoon fine sea salt

2 g / ½ teaspoon freshly ground black pepper, plus more to taste

28 g / 1 ounce / 2 tablespoons unsalted butter, melted

Flaky salt

Egg wash (see page 98)

1. Preheat the oven to 375°F / 190°C with a rack in the lower third.

2. Wrap each beet in aluminum foil and place on a baking sheet. Roast until just barely fork-tender, 35 to 40 minutes. Cool completely. Remove the beets from the foil and pat dry. Slice the beets ⅛ inch / 3 mm thick. Set aside.

3. On a lightly floured surface, roll out the dough into a round about 15 inches / 38 cm wide and ¼ inch / 6 mm thick. Use the rolling pin to transfer the dough to a 12-inch / 30-cm ovenproof skillet, preferably cast iron, unfurling it into the pan. Gently lift up the edges of the dough and nudge it into the bottom of the pan. Cover with plastic wrap and refrigerate.

4. In a medium bowl, stir the goat cheese, mascarpone, egg, chives, rosemary, salt, and pepper to combine. If necessary, preheat your oven again to 375°F / 190°C, with a rack in the lower third (preferably with a Baking Steel/stone on it).

5. Remove the crust from the fridge and unwrap it. Spoon the goat cheese mixture into the center of the dough and spread into an even layer. Arrange the beets in tight bundles or concentric circles on the goat cheese. Brush the beets with the melted butter and sprinkle with flaky salt and more pepper.

6. Fold the excess dough up around the edges to encase the filling, pleating the dough as necessary. Brush the dough evenly with egg wash.

7. Bake the pie until the crust is deeply golden brown and the vegetables are tender, 45 to 50 minutes. Cool for at least 20 minutes before slicing and serving warm, or cool completely and serve at room temperature. Garnish with more chives just before serving.

Make Ahead and Storage

The pie is best eaten the same day it's made, but leftovers can be refreshed as described on page 21.

NOTE ◇◇◇◇◇◇◇◇◇◇◇◇◇◇◇◇◇◇◇◇◇◇◇◇

You can substitute any kind of beets, or use just one color. It's best if the beets are close to the same size.

OTHER RECOMMENDED CRUSTS

- Try this with Herby Whole Wheat Dough (page 54), Rye Pie Dough (page 55).

FORAGER'S MUSHROOM PIE

MAKES ONE 10-BY-16-INCH / 25-BY-41-CM PIE

DIFFICULTY: MEDIUM

When I lived in the Hudson Valley, I would occasionally forage for wild ingredients like ramps or mushrooms. I would arrange my find, whole or in large pieces, on dough, creating a freeform pie, where both their flavor and beauty could shine. While I rarely get the chance to roam the woods anymore, this free-form pie is my ode to those wild ingredients. The base is a sauce of creamy melted leeks, which is topped with roasted mushrooms. Splurge on a few different kinds of mushrooms for this so you can enjoy the different textures and flavors.

850 g / 30 ounces assorted mushrooms, such as oyster, chanterelle, morels, trumpet, and/or cremini, cleaned well

45 g / 3 tablespoons extra-virgin olive oil, plus more for drizzling

Kosher salt and freshly ground black pepper

28 g / 1 ounce / 2 tablespoons unsalted butter

170 g / 2 packed cups (halved and thinly sliced leeks (about 2 medium leeks)

118 g / ½ cup heavy cream

Scant 1 g / ¼ teaspoon freshly grated nutmeg

Double recipe pie dough (see opposite), using extra flaky method (see page 30), shaped into a 1-inch / 2-cm rectangle, and chilled

Egg wash (see page 98)

Small sprigs fresh rosemary for garnish

Small sprigs fresh thyme, for garnish

1. Preheat the oven to 425°F / 220°C.

2. Prepare the mushrooms: Use a paring knife to trim the mushrooms into medium-large pieces, leaving clusters of whole mushrooms whenever possible.

3. Transfer the mushrooms to a baking sheet, toss with the olive oil, and season with salt and pepper. Spread the mushrooms out in an even layer and transfer to the oven. Roast until the mushrooms are tender (they will shrink a lot, but may not brown much), 25 to 30 minutes. Set aside to cool.

4. In a medium sauté pan, melt the butter over medium heat. Add the leeks and season with salt and pepper. Cook the leeks over medium-low heat until they are very soft, almost melted, 8 to 10 minutes.

5. Add the cream and nutmeg, bring to a simmer, and simmer until the cream reduces and the mixture thickens, 3 to 4 minutes. Set aside to cool while you prepare the dough.

6. Set your oven rack towards the base of the oven (preferably with a Baking Steel or stone on it). Line a baking sheet with parchment paper.

7. On a lightly floured surface, roll out the dough into a rectangle a little larger than 10 by 16 inches / 25 by 41 cm and ¼ inch / 3 mm thick. Use the rolling pin to transfer it to the prepared baking sheet. Brush the dough all over with egg wash, then dock all over with a fork. If desired, use a pastry wheel or paring knife to trim the edges to make them straight.

8. Spoon the cooled leek mixture onto the center of the dough and spread into an even layer, leaving a 1-inch / 2-cm border uncovered all the way. Arrange the mushrooms on top of the leek mixture, overlapping them as needed them but keeping them in a relatively even layer. Drizzle a little olive oil over the mushrooms.

9. Transfer the pan to the oven and bake until the crust is deeply golden brown and the mushrooms are crisp, 40 to 45 minutes. Garnish the pie with the herbs as soon as it comes out of the oven. Cool for 5 to 10 minutes before serving warm, or cool completely and serve at room temperature.

Make Ahead and Storage

This pie is best eaten the same day it's made. Store leftovers in the refrigerator in an airtight container. Leftovers can be refreshed as suggested in Refreshing a Whole Pie, on page 21.

RECOMMENDED CRUSTS
- Whole Wheat Pie Dough (page 54)
- Spelt Pie Dough (page 55)
- Golden Cheese Pie Dough (page 57)

CARAMEL PORK PIE WITH CHILE AND SCALLIONS

MAKES ONE 9-INCH /
23-CM PIE

DIFFICULTY: MEDIUM

The filling for this pie was inspired by Vietnamese caramel pork. Nestled in a rough puff pastry crust and then finished with tons of scallions, herbs, and fresh chiles when it comes out of the oven, this is the ultimate dinner pie. You can customize the toppings to suit your tastes—pickled onions and carrots or a drizzle of spicy mayo would be delightful additions.

CARAMEL PORK FILLING

159 g / ¾ cup packed light brown sugar

45 g / 3 tablespoons water

1.13 kg / 2½ pounds boneless pork shoulder, cut into 1-inch / 2.5-cm cubes

345 g / 1½ cups coconut water, plus more if needed

30 g / 2 tablespoons fish sauce

30 g / 2 tablespoons soy sauce

30 g / 2 tablespoons seasoned rice vinegar

100 g / 4 shallots, minced

15 g / 3 cloves garlic, minced

Freshly ground black pepper

½ recipe Rough Puff Pastry (page 50), chilled

Egg wash (see page 98)

TOPPINGS

50 g / 5 scallions

6 g / 2 tablespoons chopped fresh basil

6 g / 2 tablespoons chopped fresh mint

6 g / 2 tablespoons chopped fresh cilantro

Thinly sliced red chiles, such as Thai bird or Fresno

1. Make the pork filling: In a large Dutch oven, combine the brown sugar and water and stir over medium-low heat just until the brown sugar melts and the mixture begins to bubble; once it bubbles, immediately stop stirring and cook until the caramel darkens slightly in color, 2 to 3 minutes.

2. Pat the pork dry and add to the pot, stirring well to coat the pork. If the caramel seizes or hardens, continue to stir until it melts and becomes liquid again. Then add the coconut water, fish sauce, soy sauce, rice vinegar, shallots, garlic, and lots of black pepper and stir well to combine. Bring the mixture to a simmer over medium heat, then reduce the heat to low and simmer, uncovered, until the pork is tender and the sauce is thickened (liquid has evaporated), 1 to 1½ hours. If the pork is not tender after 1½ hours, add an additional 115 g / ½ cup coconut water (or tap water), bring to a simmer, and continue to simmer until the pork is tender and the liquid has evaporated. Cool to room temperature.

3. While the filling cools, roll out the dough on a lightly floured surface into a round about 12 inch / 38 cm across and ¼ inch / 6 mm thick. Use the rolling pin to transfer the dough to a 9-inch / 30-cm ovenproof skillet, preferably cast iron, unfurling it into the pan. Gently lift up the edges of the dough and nudge it into the bottom of the pan. Cover with plastic wrap and transfer to the refrigerator while you preheat the oven.

4. Preheat the oven to 400°F / 205°C with a rack in the lower third (preferably with a Baking Steel or stone on it).

5. Place the skillet with the crust on a parchment-lined baking sheet. Spoon the filling into the crust, then fold the edges of the dough over to encase the filling, pleating the dough as necessary. Brush the dough all over with egg wash.

6. Transfer the pan to the oven and bake until the dough is deeply golden brown, 40 to 45 minutes. Cool for at least 15 minutes.

7. Meanwhile, trim the ends off the scallions on a strong bias and discard. Use a sharp knife to slice the scallions very thin on the bias. Fill a medium bowl with ice water, add the scallions to it, and let sit in the water for 10 to 15 minutes, then drain well and pat dry.

8. Sprinkle the herbs evenly over the top of the pie. Scatter the chiles over and pile the scallions on top. Serve immediately.

Make Ahead and Storage

The caramel pork can be made up to 12 hours ahead and refrigerated in an airtight container. This pie is best eaten the same day it's made. Store leftovers in the refrigerator, wrapped in plastic wrap.

OTHER RECOMMENDED CRUSTS
- Spelt Pie Dough (page 55) or Golden Cheese Pie Dough (page 57), prepared as for Rough Puff Pastry (page 50)

REUBEN PIE

MAKES ONE 14-BY-14-INCH / 36-BY-36-CM PIE

DIFFICULTY: MEDIUM

My husband isn't into birthdays, but I'm essentially a five-year-old when it comes to them. During our first year of dating, I may have gone a little overboard on his birthday, but I had learned my lesson by year two, when I simply had his favorite sandwich, a Reuben, delivered to his office from his favorite deli, along with a slice of his favorite NYC cheesecake. The tradition has continued—I even brought him a Reuben the day we signed our marriage license! This pie is his favorite sandwich done my way: pie-ified. The concept for the Russian dressing plus Swiss cheese topping is taken from classic Southern tomato pies, where a mixture of mayonnaise and cheese is spread over the filling before baking. The mayonnaise sort of melts in the oven, coating the filling, and the cheese makes a delicious top crust of sorts.

TOPPING

174 g / ¾ cup mayonnaise

79 g / ¼ cup chili sauce or ketchup

40 g / ½ cup finely minced onion

17 g / 1 tablespoon prepared horseradish

10 g / 2 teaspoons hot sauce (optional)

5 g / 1 teaspoon Worcestershire sauce

2 g / ½ teaspoon paprika

2 g / ½ teaspoon fine sea salt, or more to taste

2 g / ½ teaspoon freshly ground black pepper, or more to taste

171 g / 1½ cups grated Swiss cheese

Double recipe Rye or Pumpernickel Pie Dough (page 55), shaped into a disk and chilled

60 g / ¼ cup whole-grain mustard

145 g / 1 cup well-drained sauerkraut

906 g / 2 pounds thickly sliced pastrami

Egg wash (see page 98)

Caraway seeds for sprinkling

Flaky sea salt for sprinkling

1. Preheat the oven to 425°F / 220°C with a rack in the lower third (preferably with a Baking Steel or stone on it).

2. Make the topping: In a medium bowl, whisk the mayonnaise, chili sauce or ketchup, onion, horseradish, hot sauce, if using, Worcestershire, and paprika to combine. Season with the salt and pepper. Stir in the cheese.

3. On a lightly floured surface, roll out the dough into a rectangle about 16 by 16 inches / 41 by 41 cm and slightly thicker than ¼ inch / 6 mm thick; no need to trim the dough if it's uneven. Use the rolling pin to transfer it to a parchment-lined baking sheet and unfurl it onto the sheet (some of the dough will hang over the edges, but you'll be folding it in later). If the dough feels soft at this point, transfer to the refrigerator to chill before continuing.

4. Dollop the mustard over the center portion of the dough, then spread it into an even layer (it will be very thin), leaving a 2-inch / 5-cm border uncovered all the way around. Arrange the sauerkraut in an even layer on top of the mustard. Layer the pastrami on top, slightly overlapping the slices to form an even layer. (Since pastrami is likely to be cut differently, the method of presentation doesn't really matter here—just make an even layer.) Spoon the topping over the pastrami and use the back of the spoon to help

nudge it into an even layer on the surface of the pie, again leaving the border uncovered.

5. Fold two opposite sides of the dough over to partially encase the filling, then do the same to the other two sides—this will give the pie a neat squared look. Brush the exposed crust with egg wash and sprinkle generously with caraway seeds and everything bagel seasoning.

6. Transfer the pie to the oven and bake until the crust is deeply golden brown, 40 to 45 minutes. Cool for at least 5 minutes before serving warm.

Make Ahead and Storage

This pie is best eaten the same day it is made, but leftover slices can be refreshed fairly successfully. Wrap the slices in aluminum foil. Preheat the oven 400°F / 205°C with a rack in the middle. Place the wrapped slices in the oven and reheat for 10 minutes, then unwrap to expose the top and reheat for another 5 minutes to help crisp it up.

RECOMMENDED FINISHES
- Serve with a side of coleslaw or—if it won't carb you to death—potato salad. Sour pickles also highly recommended.

SESAME LAMB PIE WITH CUCUMBER SALAD

MAKES ONE 9-INCH / 23-CM DEEP-DISH PIE

DIFFICULTY: MEDIUM

This is a shining example of what I like to call "dinner pie"—an all-in-one dish that you can serve for supper (always alongside a big green salad). Dinner pie can often be made ahead, as the flavors of the filling will intensify if it sits overnight. You can also make a double batch of this lamb filling to serve with rice one night, then bake the leftovers into a dinner pie. If I say "dinner pie" enough, will it catch on? Stay tuned.

SESAME LAMB FILLING

1135 g / 2½ pounds boneless lamb shoulder, cut into bite-size pieces

8 g / 1½ teaspoons kosher salt

3 g / 1 teaspoon freshly ground black pepper

15 g / 1 tablespoon neutral oil (such as vegetable or peanut)

10 g / 2 teaspoons Asian sesame oil

460 g / 2 medium red onions, diced

100 g / 10 scallions, sliced into ½-inch / 1-cm-wide pieces

A 1½-inch / 4-cm piece fresh ginger, peeled and minced

20 g / 4 cloves garlic, minced

22 g / 3 tablespoons sesame seeds (white or black, or a mixture)

25 g / 1½ tablespoons sambal oelek, or more to taste

43 g / 3 tablespoons soy sauce

57 g / ¼ cup rice vinegar

460 g / 2 cups beef broth

One 9-inch / 23-cm deep-dish pie crust (see page 338), parbaked, brushed with egg wash (see page 98), and cooled completely

CUCUMBER SALAD

454 g / 1 pound English (seedless) cucumber, halved lengthwise and seeds scooped out

30 g / 2 tablespoons rice vinegar

7 g / 1½ teaspoons Asian sesame oil

5 g / 1 teaspoon soy sauce

19 g / 1 tablespoon honey

3 g / ½ teaspoon kosher salt, or more to taste

Pinch of red pepper flakes

9 g / 3 tablespoons chopped fresh cilantro, plus whole leaves for garnish

6 g / 2 tablespoons chopped fresh mint, plus whole leaves for garnish

30 g / ¼ cup toasted sesame seeds

1. Make the sesame lamb filling: Pat the lamb dry and season with the salt and pepper. In a large Dutch oven, heat the neutral oil over medium heat. When the oil is hot, working in batches to avoid crowding the pot, add the lamb and cook until well seared on all sides, 1 to 2 minutes per side. Transfer the meat to a plate and reserve.

2. Wipe out the Dutch oven to remove excess oil. Add the sesame oil and turn the heat down to low. Add the onions and cook for 4 to 5 minutes, until they start to become translucent and soft. Add the scallions, ginger, and garlic and cook for 2 minutes, stirring frequently.

3. Add the sesame seeds and sambal oelek and cook for 30 seconds, stirring constantly. Return the lamb to the pot and toss well to combine. Add the soy sauce, rice vinegar, and beef broth and bring to a simmer over medium heat. Reduce the heat to low and cook, uncovered, until the lamb is tender, 1 to 1½ hours (it will cook more in the oven later, but it should be nicely tender at this time). Remove the pot from the heat and cool to room temperature.

(CONTINUED)

4. Preheat the oven to 375°F / 190°C with a rack in the lower third (preferably with a Baking Steel or stone on it). Place the parbaked crust on a parchment-lined baking sheet.

5. While the oven preheats, make the cucumber salad: Cut the cucumber halves into ½-inch / 1-cm slices. Working with a few at a time, place them cut side down and use the side of a knife to smash the cucumbers firmly, then transfer them to a colander placed in a medium bowl. Add 2 large pinches of salt to the cucumbers and toss well. Let them drain while the pie bakes, tossing them occasionally.

6. When the oven is preheated, spoon the cooled filling into the crust and spread into an even layer. Transfer to the oven and bake until the filling is bubbly and the crust is deeply golden, 40 to 45 minutes. Let the pie cool for 20 minutes.

7. While the pie cools, pat the cucumbers dry. In a medium bowl, whisk the rice vinegar, sesame oil, soy sauce, honey, salt, and red pepper flakes until the salt is dissolved. Add the cucumbers and toss to combine. Stir in the chopped herbs.

8. To serve, use a slotted spoon to remove the cucumbers from the juices and transfer to the top of the pie (alternatively, you can serve them alongside). Sprinkle the pie with the sesame seeds, cilantro, and mint leaves. Serve immediately.

Make Ahead and Storage

The sesame lamb can be made up to 2 days ahead and refrigerated in an airtight container. The cucumber salad can be made up to 24 hours ahead and refrigerated in an airtight container. This pie is best eaten the same day it's made. Store leftovers in the refrigerator, wrapped in plastic wrap.

RECOMMENDED CRUSTS

- All-Buttah Pie Dough (page 48)
- Za'atar Pie Dough (page 52)
- Saffron Compound Butter Pie Dough (or other Compound Butter Pie Dough—page 58)
- Also insanely delicious inside the Frybread Crust (page 342)

PIE-DEA

Falafel Pie

In the bowl of a food processor, pulse 130 g / 4 green onions, 10 g / 2 peeled cloves garlic, 85 g / 3 ounces (1 large bunch) fresh Italian parsley, 70 g / 2½ ounces (½ large bunch) fresh cilantro, and 43 g / 1½ ounces (½ large bunch) fresh mint, and 385 g / 2½ cups drained cooked chickpeas until the mixture is combined and coarsely chopped. Add 60 g / ¼ cup extra virgin olive oil, 56 g / 1 large egg, and season with 5 g / 1 teaspoon kosher salt and 2 g / ½ teaspoon freshly ground black pepper. Puree until smooth.

Prepare a Phyllo Crust (page 76) and place it on a baking sheet. Spread 65 g / ¼ cup chile garlic paste (such as Sambal Oelek) in the base of the crust. Pour the filling into the crust and spread into an even layer. Bake in a 375°F / 190°C oven until the crust is deeply golden brown and the filling is set, 30–35 minutes. Garnish with labneh, feta, chopped cucumbers, and/or chopped tomatoes, and serve with lemon wedges

BACON JAM MINI PIES ON SHARP CHEDDAR CRUST

MAKES SIXTEEN 4-BY-4-INCH / 10-BY-10-CM PIES

DIFFICULTY: EASY

Bacon jam is everything: sweet, salty, tangy, and black peppery. I love it as a simple pie filling for these small pies with my deeply golden and crisp cheese crust. It's also good with tomato jam on my Parmesan crust, or try the BLT version; both variations are below.

BACON JAM

454 g / 1 pound bacon, finely chopped

325 g / 1 large sweet onion, minced

15 g / 3 cloves garlic, minced

141 g / ⅔ cup packed light brown sugar

113 g / ½ cup apple cider

75 g / ⅓ cup apple cider vinegar

2 g / ½ teaspoon Korean chili powder (or other chile powder; optional)

Freshly ground black pepper

Triple recipe Golden Cheese Pie Dough (page 57) made with sharp cheddar, shaped into one 1-inch / 2.5-cm-thick rectangle, and chilled

Egg wash (see page 98)

1. Make the bacon jam: Heat a large pot over medium-high heat. Add the bacon and cook, stirring occasionally, until the fat renders out and the bacon is crisp, 7 to 9 minutes. Use a slotted spoon to transfer the bacon to a paper towel–lined plate to drain.

2. Drain off all but 15 g / 1 tablespoon of the bacon fat from the pot (reserve for another use, if desired). Add the onion and cook until very tender, 7 to 9 minutes. Add the brown sugar and cook, stirring frequently, until fully dissolved. Add the apple cider and cider vinegar and bring the mixture to a simmer. Reduce the heat to low and simmer, uncovered, stirring occasionally, until the liquid reduces almost entirely and the onions are very tender, 8 to 10 minutes. Stir in the garlic.

3. Season the mixture with the chili powder and lots of black pepper and stir until well combined. Return the bacon to the pot and stir until well combined. Use an immersion blender to puree the mixture until thicker and slightly smoother (or do this in a food processor). Cool completely.

4. Preheat the oven to 425°F / 220°C with racks in the upper and lower thirds. Line two baking sheets with parchment paper.

5. On a lightly floured surface, roll out the dough to a square slightly larger than 16 by 16 inches / 61 by 61 cm and ¼ inch / 6 mm thick. Trim the edges of the dough with a paring knife or pastry wheel so they are straight.

6. Cut the dough into 16 equal pieces: First, cut the dough into horizontally into 4 strips, then each strip crosswise into 4 pieces. Transfer the squares to the prepared baking sheets, staggering them slightly (they can be quite close to one another).

7. Brush the squares of dough with egg wash and dock all over with a fork. Press a 2½-inch / 6-cm round cookie cutter gently into the center of each square, not pressing all the way down, to score the dough and give you a guide for filling the dough with the bacon jam. Scoop 32 g / 1½ heaping tablespoons of the bacon jam mixture into the center of each square of dough. Transfer the pans

(CONTINUED)

to the oven and bake until the crust is deeply golden brown and the bacon jam has deepened in color, 30 to 35 minutes. Cool for at least 15 minutes before serving.

VARIATIONS //

TOMATO JAM (USED IN VARIATIONS BELOW):
To make, combine 496 g / 2½ cups chopped ripe tomatoes, 141 g / ⅔ cup light brown sugar, 30 g / 2 tablespoons balsamic vinegar, 3 g / 1 teaspoon dried oregano in a medium pot to combine. Bring to a simmer and cook, uncovered, until the tomatoes begin to soften, 5 to 6 minutes. Reduce heat to low and cook, stirring occasionally, until the mixture thickens to a jam-like consistency, 35 to 40 minutes. If desired, puree smoother with an immersion blender, or inside a food processor or blender. Season with salt and pepper to taste. Cool completely.

BLT PIES: Make a half batch of the tomato jam and cool completely. After assembling the pies, spoon 21 g / 1 tablespoon cooled tomato jam on top of the bacon jam and bake as directed. Let the pies cool completely. Toss 80 g / 4 cups arugula with 45 g / 3 tablespoons extra-virgin olive oil and 30 g / 2 tablespoons seasoned rice vinegar. Season with salt and freshly ground black pepper and toss well to combine. Top each cooled pie with 5 g / ¼ cup of the arugula mixture. Serve immediately.

TOMATO JAM PIES: Prepare the tomato jam and use it in place of the prepared bacon jam when assembling the pies.

TOMATO JAM PIES ON PARMESAN CRUST:
Substitute a full batch of the tomato jam for the bacon jam. Prepare the Golden Cheese Pie Dough with Parmesan cheese instead of cheddar. Proceed as directed.

Opposite: Bacon Jam Pies in Cheddar Golden Cheese Crust, Tomato Jam Pies in Gruyere Golden Cheese Crust, and BLT Pies in Monterey Jack Golden Cheese Crust

Make Ahead and Storage ───────────

The bacon (and/or tomato) jam can be made up to 5 days ahead and refrigerated. The pies are best eaten the same day they are made. Leftovers reheat well (see page 21).

NOTE ◇◇◇◇◇◇◇◇◇◇◇◇◇◇◇◇◇◇◇◇◇◇◇◇◇

This recipe and the variations are also great baked in mini pie plates or tart pans—just adjust the size of the dough to fit the size of the pan, and try to use shallower pans since the fillings are intense.

OTHER RECOMMENDED CRUSTS
- Other cheeses can be substituted for the cheddar—Gruyère, Manchego, pecorino, Monterey Jack, and Gouda are a few of my faves.

Tomato Jam Pies on Parmesan Crust

FRYBREAD TACO PIE

MAKES ONE 9-INCH / 23-CM PIE

DIFFICULTY: HARD

I grew up attending incredible arts festivals at Haskell Indian Nations University. After I closely inspected each and every stand of jewelry, tapestries, and gorgeous paintings on huge canvases, I'd wander the food carts. I desperately loved the frybread tacos (and frybread in general). Later, I researched the bittersweet history of frybread for an article I wrote on exactly how this food became synonymous with many American Indian tribes' cooking traditions. Now, I make this pie with a different sort of appreciation of this simple dough. It contains chemical leavener (baking powder) rather than yeast to make it fluffy and tender, then it's fried in oil until golden—lightly crisp outside, irresistibly fluffy on the inside. All the components of the frybread tacos of my youth can be found in this pie: seasoned ground beef, cheese, sour cream, salsa, and lots of green onions.

DOUGH

300 g / 2½ cups all-purpose flour

7 g / 1½ teaspoons baking powder

3 g / ¾ teaspoon fine sea salt

43 g / 3 tablespoons unsalted butter, melted

170 g / ¾ cup water

Oil for frying

FILLING

15 g / 1 tablespoon neutral oil

275 g / 1 large white onion, minced

10 g / 3 cloves garlic, minced

453 g / 1 pound 80-90% lean ground beef

30 g / 2 tablespoons tomato paste

12 g / 1 tablespoon ground chili powder

8 g / 2 teaspoons ground cumin

4 g / 1 teaspoon ground coriander

4 g / 1 teaspoon ground garlic powder

3 g / ½ teaspoon dried oregano

226 g / 8 ounces shredded cheddar cheese

Kosher salt and freshly ground black pepper, to taste

TOPPINGS

425 g / 15 ounces prepared refried beans

226 g / 8 ounces canned chopped green chiles, drained

115 g / ½ cup prepared salsa

170 g / ¾ cup sour cream

142 g / 5 ounces (about 1 bunch) scallions, trimmed and thinly sliced

1 g / ¼ packed cup cilantro leaves

1. Make the dough: In the bowl of an electric mixer fitted with the dough hook attachment, mix the flour, baking powder, and salt to combine. Add the melted butter and water and mix until a smooth dough forms, 3 to 4 minutes. Cover the bowl with plastic wrap and let the dough rest for 30 minutes to 1 hour.

2. Roll out the dough into a circle about ¼ in / 6 mm thick. It should be large enough to fully cover the outside of a 9-inch / 23-cm (at least 2 inches / 5 cm deep) silicone cake pan. Dock the dough all over with the tip of a paring knife. Place the cake pan upside down on a parchment lined baking sheet and gently transfer the dough to be draped over the surface. Bunch up a little bit of excess around the top and use a paring knife or pastry wheel to trim away any excess.

(CONTINUED)

3. Transfer the prepared crust to the freezer. Fill a large pot about two thirds full with oil (remember, the vessel needs to be at least 10 in / 25 cm wide and at least 4 in / 10 cm deep to accommodate the crust) over medium heat, until it reads 350°F / 218°C on a thermometer.

4. While the oil heats, make the filling: In a large sauté pan, heat the oil over medium heat. Add the onion and cook until translucent, 4 to 5 minutes. Add the garlic and cook until fragrant, 1 minute more.

5. Add the ground beef and cook until fully cooked, 5 to 7 minutes. Add the tomato paste and mix until well combined. Add the spices, salt, and pepper and mix to combine. Sprinkle the cheese evenly over the surface of the meat and turn the heat to low while you fry the dough.

6. When the frying oil is hot, add the frozen crust, still on the cake pan and base down, into the oil, to the pot and fry until evenly golden brown. As the crust sets, it should naturally release from the silicone cake pan—if it doesn't, don't worry, you can remove it after. Fry the crust for 3 to 4 minutes, until the dough is golden brown. Using two sets of tongs, gently lift the frybread out of the oil and flip it over to fry the other side. Fry for 3 to 4 minutes more.

7. Remove the crust and drain on absorbent paper towels (if necessary, gently remove the silicone cake pan).

8. In a small pot, heat the refried beans and green chiles over medium-low heat, stirring to combine, until fully heated through, 2 to 3 minutes.

9. To assemble, transfer the crust to a serving platter. Spoon the warm beef/cheese filling into the crust and spread into an even layer. Add the refried bean mixture and spread into an even layer. Top with an even layer of salsa, then sour cream. Garnish with scallions and cilantro. Serve immediately.

Make Ahead and Storage

The filling components can be made up to 1 day ahead and held in the refrigerator (it should be re-warmed before assembling the pie). This pie is best eaten the same day it's made. Store leftovers in the refrigerator, wrapped tightly in plastic wrap (the crust will get soggy within a few hours).

RESOURCES

Baking Steel
bakingsteel.com

Pizza Stone, Pastry Wheel, Pie Stamps, Metal Pie Plates, Rolling Mat and Accessories, Bench Knife, Scales, Silicone Crust Shield, Parchment Paper, Oven Thermometer, Fiori di Sicilia Extract, Pearl Sugar, Sparkling Sugar, Alternative Flours, Black Cocoa, Boiled Cider
shop.kingarthurflour.com

Pastry Docker, Tamper, Pastry Tips, Pastry Bags, Baking Sheets, Silicone Cake Pans and Molds, Muffin Pans, Cake Pans, Ramekins, Mini Pie Plates
bakedeco.com

Ceramic Pie and Tart Pans, Baking Dishes
pillivuytusa.com

Rose's Perfect Pie Plate
amazon.com/Beranbaums-Roses-Perfect
-Recipe-Booklet/dp/B000LHRQK

Forged Iron Pie Plates
netherton-foundry.co.uk

Cast Iron Skillets
lodgemfg.com

Rolling Pins
tomnuk.com/shop

Vanilla Beans, Paste, and Extract
heilalavanilla.com

High-Quality Chocolate, Caramelized White Chocolate (Dulcey), Crunchy Chocolate Pearls
valrhona-chocolate.com

Sprinkles, Dehydrated Marshmallows, Other Edible Décor
layercakeshop.com

High-Quality Frozen Fruit
nwwildfoods.com

The Best Marshmallows in the World
nikkidarlingconfections.com

Edible Flowers, Sprouts, and Micro Vegetables
gourmetsweetbotanicals.com

INDEX

Note: Page references in *italics* indicate photographs.

A

Agar-agar, substituting for gelatin, 247
All-Buttah Pie Dough, 48
Almond
    and Raspberry-Poached Pear Pie, 182–83, *183*
    Roll-Out Cookie Crust, 63
Animal fats, 25
Apple
    Butterscotch Pie, 274–76, *275*
    Mini, Dumplings, 149
    Pie, 145–46, *147*
    Pie, Easy-Fancy, *196*, 197
    Pie, My Own Personal Favorite, 146
    Whole-, Dumplings, *148*, 148–49
Apple Butter Pie, *144*, 146
Apricot Clafoutis Pie, 224
Arugula
    BLT Pies, *340*, 341
    BLT Quiche, 304–5, *305*
Asparagus
    Green Veggie Quiche, 304–5, *305*
Avocado Galette, *306*, 307

B

Bacon
    Beef and Mushroom Pie, 314–15, *315*
    BLT Quiche, 304–5, *305*
    Jam Mini Pies on Sharp Cheddar Crust, 339–41, *340*
    Lattice, 99, *99*
Baked Alaska Pie, "Root Beer Float," *286*, 287
Baking sheets, 18
Baking Steels/baking stones, 20
Banana
    Banulce Pie, 253, *253*
    Cream Pie, Classic, 252, *253*
    Dumplings, 149
    -Peanut Butter Cream Pie, 252–53, *253*
Banulce Pie, 253, *253*
Beach plums, 137

Beans
    Falafel Pie, 338
    Frybread Taco Pie, 342–44, *343*
Beef
    Frybread Taco Pie, 342–44, *343*
    and Mushroom Pie, 314–15, *315*
    Reuben Pie, 334–35, *335*
Beet and Herbed Cheese Skillet Pie, 328–29, *329*
Bench knife, 16
Berry(ies). *See also specific berries*
    Breakfast Pie, *276*, 277
    Cobbler Pie, Deep-Dish, 156–58, *157*
    Meringue Pie, Deep-Dish, 280, *281*
    Mixed-, Hand Pies, 159–61, *160*
    -Stone Fruit Pie, 176–78, *177*
Birthday-Cake Pie, *218*, 219–20
Biscuit Topping (Make It a Cobbler Pie), 130
Black-Bottom Base, Dark Chocolate, 110
Black-Bottom Pecan Pie, *238*, 239
Black Forest Pie, 250–51, *251*
Black Raspberry Chiffon Pie, 290–91, *291*
Blood Orange
    Brûlée Pie, *198*, 199
    Curd, 123
BLT Pies, *340*, 341
BLT Quiche, 304–5, *305*
Blueberry
    Clafoutis Pie, 224, *225*
    Lemon Meringue Pie, 280
    Lemon Pie, 179–80, *181*
    Swamp Pie, 210–11, *211*
    Whipped Cream, Sweet Corn Pie with, 256, *257*
Boysenberries, 136
Breakfast Pie, *276*, 277
Brittle, Basic, 129
Brown Butter
    Pie Dough, 53
    Press-In Cookie Crust, 64

Brown Sugar
    Chess Pie, 208, *209*
    Roll-Out Cookie Crust, 63
Buckwheat Pie Dough, 55
Butter
    All-Buttah Pie Dough, 48
    Brown, Pie Dough, 53
    Brown, Press-In Cookie Crust, 64
    for doughs, 24
Butterscotch
    Apple Pie, 274–76, *275*
    Haystack Crust, 71

C

Cake pans, 18
Caramel
    Apple Pie, *144*, 146
    -Earl Grey Custard Pie in Gingersnap Crumb Crust, 216, *217*
    Meringue Topping, 118, *119*
    Pork Pie with Chile and Scallions, 332–33, *333*
    Sauce, Salted, 126
    Sifting Sugar, 128
    -Swirled Cheesecake Pie, *102*, 237
    Truffle Pie, Triple-Chocolate, 271–73, *272*
Caramelized Pie Crust, 56
Caramelized White-Bottom Base, 110
Caraway Seed Pie Dough, 52
Cardamom
    Crème Brûlée Pie, 234, *235*
    Lemon Pie Dough, 52
Carrot(s)
    Beef and Mushroom Pie, 314–15, *315*
    Cake Custard Pie, 230, *231*
    Chicken Pot Slab Pie, 301–3, *302*
Casserole dishes, 18
Cereal-Treat Crust, 69
Chai-Caramel Custard Pie in Shortbread Crumb Crust, 216, *217*

Cheese. *See also* Cream cheese; Mascarpone
  Bacon Jam Mini Pies on Sharp Cheddar Crust, 339–41, *340*
  Cheese Lover's Quiche, 304, *305*
  Croque Monsieur Pielets, 312–13, *313*
  Frybread Taco Pie, 342–44, *343*
  Gooey, and Roasted Tomato Free-Form Pie, *316,* 317
  Green Veggie Quiche, 304–5, *305*
  Herbed, and Beet Skillet Pie, 328–29, *329*
  Peach, Shallot, and Prosciutto Pie, *324,* 325
  Pie Dough, Golden, 57
  Ratatouille Galette, 326–27, *327*
  Reuben Pie, 334–35, *335*
  Sausage and Caramelized Onion Pie with Soft Pretzel Crust, 320–22, *321*
Cheesecake Pie, 236, *237*
Cherry(ies)
  Black Forest Pie, 250–51, *251*
  Clafoutis Pie, 224, *225*
  Ginger Pie, 166–68, *167*
  Sour, Hand Pies, 161
  Sour, Pie, *167,* 168
Chess Pies
  about, 202
  Brown Sugar, 208, *209*
Chicken Pot Slab Pie, 301–3, *302*
Chiffon Pie, Black Raspberry, 290–91, *291*
Chile(s)
  Frybread Taco Pie, 342–44, *343*
  and Scallions, Caramel Pork Pie with, 332–33, *333*
  Spicy Pie Dough, 52
Chive Pie Dough, 58
Chocolate. *See also* White Chocolate
  All-Buttah Pie Dough, 48
  Black-Bottom Pecan Pie, *238,* 239
  Black Forest Pie, 250–51, *251*
  Chip Press-In Cookie Crust, 64
  Clafoutis Pie, 224, *225*
  -Covered-Raspberries Pie, 292–93, *293*
  Dark, Black-Bottom Base, 110
  Dark, Cold-Snap Topping, 127
  Dark, Drippy Glaze, 125
  German, Pie, 229, *231*
  Haystack Crust, 71
  Marshmallow Topping, 117
  Meringue Topping, 118, *119*

Milk, Black-Bottom Base, 110
Milk, Cold-Snap Topping, 127
Milk, Drippy Glaze, 125
Peanut Butter Choco-Schmallow Pie, 69
Press-In Cookie Crust, 64
Roll-Out Cookie Crust, 63
Sifting Sugar, 128
Sugar Pie, 232, *233*
-Swirled Cheesecake Pie, *102,* 236
Triple- , Caramel Truffle Pie, 271–73, *272*
Two-Bite Black-and-White Pies, *295,* 296–97
Whipped Cream, 114, *114*
Chokecherries, 136
Chow mein noodles
  Haystack Crust, 71
Cinnamon
  Pie Dough, 52
  Plum Pie, 194, *195*
  Pumpkin Spice Pie Dough, 52
  Snickerdoodle Caramelized Pie Crust, 56
  Twists, 131
Citrus. *See also specific citrus fruits*
  Eton Mess Pie, 282, *283*
  Pie, Striped, 284–85, *285*
  Roll-Out Cookie Crust, 63
  Sugar Pie, 232, *233*
  -Vanilla Caramelized Pie Crust, 56
Clafoutis Pie, Cherry, 224, *225*
Classic Banana Cream Pie, 252, *253*
Classic Custard Pie in Phyllo Crust, 206, *207*
Classic Key Lime Pie, *258,* 259
Classic Whipped Cream, 111, *114*
Clementine, Candied, Galette, 184–85, *185*
Coconut
  Cream Pie, 259, *259*
  Custard Pie, 206, *207*
  German Chocolate Pie, 229, *231*
  Haystack Crust, 71
  -Key Lime Cream Pie, 258–59, *259*
  Macaroon Crust, 70
  Press-In Cookie Crust, 64
Coffee
  Meringue Topping, 118, *119*
  Sifting Sugar, 128
Cold-set pies. *See* Cream, chiffon & cold-set pies
Cold-Snap Topping, Dark Chocolate, 127
Concord Grape
  Hand Pies, 163–64, *164*
  Meringue Pie, 280, *281*

Cookie Crust
  Press-In, 64
  Roll-Out, 62–63, *63*
Cookie cutters, 20
Corn
  Shrimp-Boil Pie, 323–24, *324*
  Sweet, Pie with Blueberry Whipped Cream, 256, *257*
Cornmeal Pie Dough, 55
Coulis, Thick Fruit, 122
Crab apples, 136
Cranberry(ies)
  -Orange Pie, 169–71, *170*
  Sugared, 171
Cream, chiffon & cold-set pies
  covering surface of, 249
  cream fillings for, 246
  garnishing, note about, 249
  gelatin-set fillings for, 247
  goopy, remedy for, 248
  list of recipes, 10–11
  meringue-based fillings for, 247
  preparing crust for, 247
  stovetop custard fillings for, 246
  troubleshooting, 247–48
  understanding "first-boil," 248–49
  understanding tempering, 248
  whipped cream–based fillings for, 246
Cream cheese
  Breakfast Pie, *276,* 277
  Cheesecake Pie, 236, *237*
  Chocolate-Covered-Raspberries Pie, 292–93, *293*
  Cranberry-Orange Pie, 169–71, *170*
  Extra-Thick and Creamy Whipped Cream, 113
  Peanut Butter Cream Pie with Raspberry Meringue, 264, *265*
  for pie crusts, 25
  Smoked Salmon Tart with "Everything" Pie Crust, 310–11, *311*
Crème Brûlée Pie, Cardamom, *234,* 235
Crimping crust edges, 80–85, *81, 83*
Croque Madame Pielets, 313, *313*
Croque Monsieur Pielets, 312–13, *313*
Crumb Crusts
  amounts for different pan sizes, 68
  Basic, 66–67
  scaling up, 68
  shrinking in pan, remedy for, 67
Crust tampers, 20

Cucumber Salad, Sesame Lamb Pie with, 336–38, *337*
Curd, Lemon, 123
Curd fillings for pies, 246
Curry Oil Press-in Crust, 65
Custard pies
  chess pies, about, 202
  classic baked, about, 202
  cooling, note about, 205
  covering imperfect edges on, 204
  defined, 202
  determining doneness, 205
  frangipane pies, about, 203
  infusing liquids for, 203
  list of recipes, 10
  preparing crusts for, 204
  storing, 205
  sugar pies, about, 202–3
  swamp pies, about, 203
  troubleshooting, 204–5
Cutouts, using, 90–91

D

Deep-dish pies, 19
Double-Crust Blueberry Swamp Pie, 211
Dough dockers, 20
Doughnuts, Pie Scrap, 108, *108*
Dulce de Leche
  Banulce Pie, 253, *253*
  Chess Pie, 208, *209*
  Tres Leches Slab Pie, 242–43, i243
Dumplings, Whole-Apple, *148*, 148–49

E

Earl Grey–Caramel Custard Pie in Gingersnap Crumb Crust, 216, *217*
Eggnog Sugar Pie, 232
Eggplant
  Ratatouille Galette, 326–27, *327*
Eggs
  Croque Madame Pielets, 313, *313*
  egg wash for crusts, 98–100
Elderberries, 136
Eton Mess Pie, 282, *283*
Extra-Large Chicken Pot Slab Pie, 303

F

Falafel Pie, 338
Fig Pie, Free-Form Honeyed, 186, *187*
Filling décor, 100–103
"First boil," understanding, 248–49

Flavored sifting sugars, 128
Flour
  for doughs, 24
  gluten-free, preparing, 49
  for work surface, 30
Frangipane Pies
  about, 203
  Fruity, 221–23, *222*
Free-form pies, about, 41
Freeze-Dried Fruity Whipped Cream, *114, 115*
Fruit. *See also* Fruit pies; *specific fruits*
  Any- , Crumb Crostata, 190, *191*
  Any- , Puff Pastry Tart, 150–51, *151*
  Any- , Tarte Tatin, 172–74, *173*
  Breakfast Pie, *276,* 277
  Coulis, Thick, 122
  Eton Mess Pie, 282, *283*
  Fresh, Whipped Cream, *114, 115*
  Fruity Frangipane Pie, 221–23, *222*
  Glaze, Thin, 122
  ripe, freezing, 135
  Stone, –Berry Pie, 176–78, *177*
  substituting, in pies, 136–37
Fruit pies
  choosing fruits for, 134
  cooling, before slicing, 139
  determining doneness, 139, 140
  determining filling preparation by ripeness, 134
  frozen fruit for, 135
  getting texture right for fillings, 141
  list of recipes, 9–10
  partially precooked fillings for, 140
  precooked fillings for, 139–40
  soggy bottom crusts, remedy for, 138
  substituting fruits in, 136–37
  uncooked fillings for, 138–39
Fruity Baked Alaska Pie, 287
Fruity Cold-Snap Topping, 127
Fruity Dripping Glaze, 124
Fruity Meringue Topping, 118, *119*
Fruity Poaching Liquid, 121
Fruity Sifting Sugar, 128
Frybread Taco Pie, 342–44, *343*

G

Galettes, about, 41
Garam Masala Pie Dough, 52
Garlic, Roasted, Pie Dough, 58
Garnishes, 105–8, 249
Gelatin-set fillings for pies, 247
German Chocolate Pie, 229, *231*
Ginger
  Cherry Pie, 166–68, *167*
  Gingerbread Pie Dough, 52

Mango Pie, 269, *269*
  Pumpkin Spice Pie Dough, 52
Glazes
  about, 104–5
  Dark Chocolate Drippy, 125
  Fruity Dripping, 124
  Thin Fruit, 122
Gluten-free flour, preparing, 49
Gluten-Free Pie Dough, 49
Goldenberries, 136
Gooseberry(ies)
  about, 136
  Vanilla Cream Pie, 171
Graham Flour Pie Dough, 54
Grapefruit
  Curd, 123
  Meringue Pie, 280, *281*
  Striped Citrus Pie, 284–85, *285*
Grapes. *See* Concord Grape
Green Veggie Quiche, 304–5, *305*

H

Ham
  Croque Monsieur Pielets, 312–13, *313*
  Peach, Shallot, and Prosciutto Pie, 324, *325*
Hand Pies
  Concord Grape, 163–64, *164*
  Lolly Pies, 162, *162*
  Mixed-Berry, 159–61, *160*
  Pie-ce Cream Sandwiches, 165, *165*
  Sour Cherry Filling for, 168
Haystack Crust, 71
Herbes de Provence Pie Dough, 52
Herby Olive Oil Press-in Crust, 65
Herby Whole Wheat Pie Dough, 54
Honey
  Free-Form Honeyed Fig Pie, 186, *187*
  Marshmallow Topping, 117
  Meringue Topping, 118, *119*
  Sifting Sugar, 128
Hot-Water Crust, 60–61
Huckleberries, 136

I

Ice Cream
  Pie-ce Cream Sandwiches, 165, *165*
  "Root Beer Float" Baked Alaska Pie, *286,* 287

J

Jam (or jelly)

Cookie Tart, *188,* 189
Jammy Whipped Cream, *114,*
    115
-Swirled Cheesecake Pie, *102,*
    236
Twists, 131
Two-Bite PB&J Pies, 294–95,
    295
Jam, Tomato, 341

K

Kale and Squash Pithiviers, Sweet-
    and-Spicy, 308–9, *309*
Key Lime
    -Coconut Cream Pie, 258–59,
        259
    Curd, 123
    Pielets, 260, *261*

L

Lamb Pie, Sesame, with Cucumber
    Salad, 336–38, *337*
Lard, 25
Lattice crusts, 92–99, *92–99*
Lemon
    Blueberry Pie, 179–80, *181*
    Cardamom Pie Dough, 52
    Curd, 123
    Custard Pie, Creamy, 240, *241*
    Meringue Pie, 280, *281*
    Meyer, Pielets, 260, *261*
Lime
    Curd, 123
    Key, -Coconut Cream Pie,
        258–59, *259*
    Key, Curd, 123
    Key, Pielets, 260, *261*
    Meringue Pie, 280
Lingonberries, 136
Loganberries, 136
Lolly Pies, 162, *162*

M

Mango Pie, Creamy, 268–69, *269*
Maple Sugar Pie, 232, *233*
Marionberries, 136
Marshmallow
    Cereal-Treat Crust, 69
    Peanut Butter Choco-
        Schmallow Pie, 69
    Sifting Sugar, 128
    Topping, 117
Mascarpone
    Beet and Herbed Cheese
        Skillet Pie, 328–29, *329*
    Peaches-and-Cream Pie, *266,*
        267
    Pie, 214, *215*
    Pumpkin Pie, 213
    Whipped Cream, 111, *114*

Matcha
    Cheesecake Pie, 237
    Sifting Sugar, 128
Mats and rolling accessories, 16
Meringue Crust, 72
Meringue fillings for pies, 247
Meringue Topper, 73, *73*
Meringue Topping, 118, *119*
Meyer Lemon Pielets, 260, *261*
Mini (Two-Bite) Crumb Crust, 67
Mini Pies. *See also* Hand Pies
    Bacon Jam, on Sharp Cheddar
        Crust, 339–41, *340*
    Croque Monsieur Pielets,
        312–13, *313*
    easy tortilla crust for, 261
    flavor pairing ideas, 262–63
    Key Lime Pielets, 260, *261*
    Two-Bite Black-and-White
        Pies, *295,* 296–97
    Two-Bite PB&J Pies, 294–95,
        295
Molasses Marshmallow Topping,
    117
Mulberries, 136
Muscadines, 136–37
Mushroom
    and Beef Pie, 314–15, *315*
    Pie, Forager's, 330–31, *331*

N

Nectarine Semifreddo Pie, 270
Nigella Seed Pie Dough, 52
Non-Fruity Poaching Liquid, 121
Nut Butter. *See also* Peanut Butter
    for pie crusts, 25
    Press-In Cookie Crust, 64
    Whipped Cream, *114,* 116
Nutmeg-Vanilla Bean Pie Dough,
    52
Nut(s)
    Almond Roll-Out Cookie
        Crust, 63
    Basic Brittle, 129
    Black-Bottom Pecan Pie, *238,*
        239
    Carrot Cake Custard Pie, 230,
        231
    Crust, Basic, 74
    crusts, amounts for different
        pan sizes, 75
    crusts, scaling up, 75
    Fruity Frangipane Pie, 221–23,
        222
    German Chocolate Pie, 229,
        231
    Pistachio Cream Pie, 278,
        279
    Raspberry-Poached Pear and
        Almond Pie, 182–83, *183*

O

Oats
    Extra-Clumpy Prebaked
        Streusel, 120
    Oatmeal Press-In Cookie Crust,
        64
    Streusel for Baking, 120
Oil, 25
Olive Oil Press-in Crust, 65
Onion
    Caramelized, and Sausage
        Pie with Soft Pretzel Crust,
        320–22, *321*
    Red, Tarte Tatin, 318–19, *319*
Orange
    Blood, Brûlée Pie, *198,* 199
    Blood, Curd, 123
    -Cranberry Pie, 169–71, *170*
    Curd, 123
    Striped Citrus Pie, 284–85, *285*
    -Vanilla Panna Cotta Pie, *254,*
        255

P

Panna Cotta Pie, Orange-Vanilla,
    254, 255
Parchment, rolling out dough on,
    36
Passionfruit
    Curd, 123
    Meringue Pie, 280, *281*
Pastry cutter, 17
Pastry wheels, 20
Pâte Brisée, 59
Paw paws, 137
Peach(es)
    -and-Cream Pie, *266,* 267
    Clafoutis Pie, 224, *225*
    donut, about, 136
    Dumplings, 149
    Pie, Rosé, *192,* 193
    Shallot, and Prosciutto Pie, *324,*
        325
Peanut Butter
    -Banana Cream Pie, 252–53,
        253
    Cereal-Treat Crust, 69
    Choco-Schmallow Pie, 69
    Cream Pie with Raspberry
        Meringue, 264, *265*
    PB&J Hand Pies, 164
    Two-Bite PB&J Pies, 294–95,
        295
Pear
    Dumplings, 149
    Raspberry-Poached, and
        Almond Pie, 182–83, *183*
Peas
    Chicken Pot Slab Pie, 301–3, *302*
    Green Veggie Quiche, 304–5,
        305

Pecan(s)
  Carrot Cake Custard Pie, 230, *231*
  German Chocolate Pie, 229, *231*
  Pie, Black-Bottom, *238, 239*
Peppermint
  Meringue Topping, 118, *119*
  -White Chocolate Pie, 226–28, *227*
Peppers
  Caramel Pork Pie with Chile and Scallions, 332–33, *333*
  Frybread Taco Pie, 342–44, *343*
  Ratatouille Galette, 326–27, *327*
Phyllo crust toppers, 77
Phyllo Dough Crust, 76
Pie-ce Cream Sandwiches, 165, *165*
Pie décor & toppings
  adding texture to top crust, 88–89
  bottom-crust techniques, 80–88
  cutting vents in top crust, 98
  egg wash for top crust, 98–100
  filling décor, 100–103
  finger crimps, 82–84, *83*
  finishing touches for top crusts, 98–100
  garnishes, 105–8
  glazes, 104–5
  lattice crusts, 92–99, *92–99*
  layering fillings, 100
  list of recipes, 8–9
  marbling two doughs for top crust, 88
  molded fillings, 103
  other finishes, *84,* 85–88, *86*
  painting the top crust, 90
  spatula finishes for fillings, 103
  swirling fillings, 100–103
  swirling toppings, 104
  top-crust techniques, 88–100
  topping décor, 103–8
  twists or braids for top crust, 98
  using cutouts, 90–91
  utensil crimps, 80–82, *81*
Pie doughs & crusts
  amount required for different pans, 40
  blind-baking, 46
  chilling, 33–34
  fixing small tears in, 42
  flaky, high temperatures for, 44
  freezing, 35
  ingredients for, 24–26
  Jam Twists, 131
  lining a pie plate with, 42
  list of recipes, 8
  making in advance, 33
  mixing dough, 27–33
  other flours for, 55
  parbaking, 43–46

parbaking double-crust pies, 47
preparing crust edges, 42–43
pressing into a pan, 61
rolling out, 34–36
spiced, ideas for, 52
transferring to pie plate, 36
troubleshooting, 32
using leftover dough scraps, 38–39, 108
Pie plates, 17–18
Pies (general information)
  baked, refreshing, 20–21
  baked, storing, 20
  covering imperfect edges, 204
  cream, chiffon & cold-set, list of, 10–11
  custard, list of, 10
  cutting into clean slices, 109
  equipment, 16–20
  freezing, 21
  fruit, list of, 9–10
  savory, list of, 11
Pie stamps, 20
Pie weights, 17
Piña Colada Pie, *258,* 259
Pineapple
  Piña Colada Pie, *258,* 259
  Roasted, Pie, *152,* 155
Piped Lattice, 99, *99*
Pistachio Cream Pie, 278, *279*
Pithiviers, Sweet-and-Spicy Kale and Squash, 308–9, *309*
Plum
  Cinnamon Pie, 194, *195*
  Clafoutis Pie, 224
Pluots, 137
Poaching Liquid, Fruity, 121
Polenta Pie Dough, 55
Poppy Seed(s)
  homemade "everything" topping, 311
  Pie Dough, 52
Pork. *See also* Bacon; Ham; Sausage
  Caramel, Pie with Chile and Scallions, 332–33, *333*
Potatoes
  Shrimp-Boil Pie, 323–24, *324*
Press-In Cookie Crust, 64
Press-in Crust, Olive Oil, 65
Pretzel Crust, Soft, Sausage and Caramelized Onion Pie with, 320–22, *321*
Prickly pears, 137
Prosciutto
  Croque Monsieur Pielets, 312–13, *313*
  Peach, and Shallot Pie, *324,* 325
Pudding-like fillings for pies, 246
Puff Pastry
  docking, 51

Rough, 50
Tart, Any-Fruit, 150–51, *151*
Pumpernickel Pie Dough, 55
Pumpkin
  Cheesecake Pie, *102, 237*
  Pie, *212,* 213
  Sugar Pie, 232, *233*
Pumpkin Spice Pie Dough, 52

Q

Quiche, Green Veggie, 304–5, *305*

R

Ramekins, 18
Ramp Pie Dough, 58
Raspberry(ies)
  Chocolate-Covered, Pie, 292–93, *293*
  -Lemon Clafoutis Pie, 224, *225*
  Meringue, Peanut Butter Cream Pie with, 264, *265*
  -Poached Pear and Almond Pie, 182–83, *183*
Ratatouille Galette, 326–27, *327*
Reuben Pie, 334–35, *335*
Rhubarb
  Clafoutis Pie, 224, *225*
  Meringue Pie, 280, *281*
  Pie, Pure, 142, *143*
Rolling pin, 16
Roll-Out Cookie Crust, 62–63, *63*
"Root Beer Float" Baked Alaska Pie, *286,* 287
Rosé Peach Pie, *192,* 193
Rough Puff Pastry, 50
Rye Pie Dough, 55

S

Saffron Compound Butter Pie Dough, 58
Salmon, Smoked, Tart with "Everything" Pie Crust, 310–11, *311*
Salmonberries, 137
Salt, 26
Salted Caramel Sauce, 126
Sand plums, 137
Saskatoon berries, 137
Sauces
  Salted Caramel, 126
  Whipped Cream, 112
Sauerkraut
  Reuben Pie, 334–35, *335*
Sausage
  and Caramelized Onion Pie with Soft Pretzel Crust, 320–22, *321*
  Shrimp-Boil Pie, 323–24, *324*
Savory pies
  doughs for, 300

fillings for, 300
list of recipes, 11
made with leftovers, 327
precooking ingredients for, 300
Scale, 16
Scallion(s)
and Chile, Caramel Pork Pie with, 332–33, *333*
Frybread Taco Pie, 342–44, *343*
Pie Dough, 58
Seeds
Basic Brittle, 129
homemade "everything" topping, 311
Sesame, Poppy, Caraway, or Nigella Seed Pie Dough, 52
Sesame Lamb Pie with Cucumber Salad, 336–38, *337*
Smoked Salmon Tart with "Everything" Pie Crust, 310–11, *311*
Semifreddo Pie, Nectarine, 270
Semolina Pie Dough, 55
Sesame Oil Press-in Crust, 65
Sesame Seed(s)
homemade "everything" topping, 311
Pie Dough, 52
Sesame Lamb Pie with Cucumber Salad, 336–38, *337*
Shallot, Peach, and Prosciutto Pie, *324*, 325
Shortening, 25
Shrimp-Boil Pie, 323–24, *324*
Sifted Lattice, 99, 99
Sifting sugars, flavored, 128
Skillets, 18
Smoked Paprika–Olive Oil Press-in Crust, 65
Smoked Salmon Tart with "Everything" Pie Crust, 310–11, *311*
Snickerdoodle Caramelized Pie Crust, 56
Soft Pretzel Crust, Sausage and Caramelized Onion Pie with, 320–22, *321*
Sour Cherry
Ginger Cherry Pie, 166–68, *167*
Hand Pies, 161
Pie, *167*, 168
Spelt Pie Dough, 55
Spiced Roll-Out Cookie Crust, 63
Spiced Sifting Sugar, 128
Spiced Sugar Pie, 232, *233*
Spicy Pie Dough, 52
Spinach
Green Veggie Quiche, 304–5, *305*

Squash. *See also* Pumpkin
and Kale Pithiviers, Sweet-and-Spicy, 308–9, *309*
Ratatouille Galette, 326–27, *327*
Stone Fruit–Berry Pie, 176–78, *177*
Strawberry(ies)
Chocolate-Covered, Pie, 292
Rhubarb Pie, 142, *143*
Roasted, Pie, *152*, 153
Roasted, Pie with Frozen Strawberries, 153
wild, about, 137
Streusel
for Baking, 120
Extra-Clumpy Prebaked, 120
Lattice, 99, 99
Striped Citrus Pie, 284–85, *285*
Sugar. *See also* Brown Sugar
flavored sifting, 128
Sugared Cranberries, 171
Sugar Pies
about, 202–3
Chocolate, 232, *233*
Swamp Pies
about, 203
Blueberry, 210–11, *211*
Swirled Whipped Cream, 112

T

Taco Pie, Frybread, 342–44, *343*
Tangerine
Curd, 123
Meringue Pie, 280, *281*
Striped Citrus Pie, 284–85, *285*
Tempering, understanding, 248
Tomato(es)
BLT Pies, *340*, 341
BLT Quiche, 304–5, *305*
Cherry, Tarte Tatin, 318, *319*
Jam, 341
Jam Pies, *340*, 341
Jam Pies on Parmesan Crust, 341, *341*
Ratatouille Galette, 326–27, *327*
Roasted, and Gooey Cheese Free-Form Pie, *316*, 317
Smoked Salmon Tart with "Everything" Pie Crust, 310–11, *311*
Sun-Dried, Pie Dough, 58
Tortillas, making mini pie crusts with, 261
Tres Leches Slab Pie, 242–43, i243
Truffle Oil Press-in Crust, 65
Turmeric Pie Dough, 52

U

Unbaked Crumb Crust, 67

V

Vanilla
Bean-Nutmeg Pie Dough, 52
-Citrus Caramelized Pie Crust, 56
-Orange Panna Cotta Pie, *254*, 255
Sifting Sugar, 128
Sugar Pie, 232, *233*
Two-Bite Black-and-White Pies, *295*, 296–97
Vegan/Dairy-Free Pie Dough, 51
Vegetables. *See also specific vegetables*
Green Veggie Quiche, 304–5, *305*
Vinegar, for pie dough, 26
Vodka, for pie dough, 26

W

Water, 26
Watermelon Pie, Fresh, 288, *289*
Whipped Cream
-based fillings for pies, 246
Chocolate, 114, *114*
Classic, 111, *114*
Eton Mess Pie, 282, *283*
Extra-Thick and Creamy, 113
Fresh Fruit, *114*, 115
Nut Butter, *114*, 116
Sauce, 112
Swirled, 112
White Chocolate
Caramelized, Drippy Glaze, 125
Caramelized Chocolate Cold-Snap Topping, 127
Caramelized White-Bottom Base, 110
Cold-Snap Topping, 127
Drippy Glaze, 125
-Peppermint Pie, 226–28, *227*
Triple-Chocolate Caramel Truffle Pie, 271–73, *272*
White-Bottom Base, 110
Whole Wheat Pie Dough, 54

Y

Yogurt
Breakfast Pie, *276*, 277
Yuzu
Curd, 123
Meringue Pie, 280, *281*

Z

Za'atar Pie Dough, 52